Parish Ecclesfield

The first book of the marriage

Baptismal and burial registers of Ecclesfield Parish Church

Parish Ecclesfield

The first book of the marriage
Baptismal and burial registers of Ecclesfield Parish Church

ISBN/EAN: 9783337262099

Printed in Europe, USA, Canada, Australia, Japan

Cover: Foto ©Lupo / pixelio.de

More available books at **www.hansebooks.com**

THE PARISH CHURCH OF ECCLESFIELD.
"THE MINSTER OF THE MOORS."

THE FIRST BOOK OF THE MARRIAGE, BAPTISMAL,
AND BURIAL

REGISTERS,

OF

Ecclesfield Parish Church, Yorkshire,

From 1558 to 1619;

ALSO THE

CHURCHWARDENS' ACCOUNTS,

From 1520 to 1546.

ANNOTATED BY

ALFRED SCOTT GATTY.

LONDON: BELL & SONS, YORK STREET, COVENT GARDEN.
SHEFFIELD: LEADER AND SONS, BANK STREET.
1878.

THIS VOLUME

IS DEDICATED

TO

JOHN SYKES, M.D.,

OF

DONCASTER,

AS A TOKEN OF AFFECTIONATE REGARD,

AND IN ACKNOWLEDGEMENT OF MANY KINDNESSES,

BY HIS GRATEFUL GENEALOGICAL PUPIL,

ALFRED SCOTT GATTY.

ECCLESFIELD,
July, 1878.

INTRODUCTION.

THE object of the following work is to preserve from destruction the contents of a record which has hitherto been confined to an unique manuscript, the loss of which would be irreparable.

The illustrative foot notes will show how valuable is the additional evidence to be drawn from wills, court rolls, and other like documents, in tracing pedigrees and the transfers of property. Moreover, in publishing early parochial registers, an authentic contribution is supplied to the history of a locality, and may assist the larger enquiry as to facts and personages, out of whom the story of a nation is formed.

It may be observed, with slighting attention, that these registers principally refer to the families of what Shakspeare calls "crestless yeomen"—which is a stock nevertheless that for centuries formed the backbone of English society, and from which also the greater part of the higher gentry have sprung. In these Registers some records occur of families who have thus advanced in social position.

The Churchwardens' Accounts, from 1520 to 1545, I have only just been in time to snatch from oblivion—they are written on paper, and are in a deplorably dilapidated state.

I have heartily to thank my father, the Rev. ALFRED GATTY, D.D., Vicar of Ecclesfield and Subdean of York, &c., for allowing me to transcribe these early Registers and Churchwardens' Accounts; also MICHAEL J. ELLISON, Esq., for giving me free access to the court rolls of the Manor of Hallamshire; also H. A. HUDSON, Esq., Deputy Registrar of the Will Office, York; Canon RAINE, of York; JOHN SYKES, Esq., M.D., of Doncaster; STEPHEN I. TUCKER, Esq., Rouge Croix, of the Heralds' College, London; CHARLES JACKSON, Esq., of Balby, Doncaster; and the Rev. J. W. DARNBROUGH, Rector of South Ottrington, Yorkshire, for their valuable assistance and information; and last, but not least, J. D. LEADER, Esq., F.S.A., for the interest he has taken, and the facilities he has afforded, in the publication of my work.

This, my first effort as an author, makes no pretensions to literary merit, but is a truthful statement of facts, offered in the most concise language, because the quantity of matter had to be condensed as much as possible, in order to keep the volume within a reasonable limit.

Although I cannot expect any general interest to be taken in the records of a country parish, in the centre of England, I am sure that it will find some local appreciation; and there will be here and there, in distant countries, an eye arrested by the sight of a name, which will remind its present owner that his family was once connected with the old Yorkshire village, and that his ancestors lie buried under the shadow of the "Minster of the Moors," as DODSWORTH named the Parish Church of Ecclesfield.

Any clerical errors that may occur I must ask my readers to be lenient with.

ALFRED SCOTT GATTY.

ECCLESFIELD,
    July, 1878.

LIST OF SUBSCRIBERS.

Sydney O. Addy, Esq., Sheffield.
John Amphlett, Esq., Clent, Stourbridge.
T. W. Badger, Esq., Rotherham.
Benjamin Bagshawe, Esq., 3, High Street, Sheffield.
John E. Bailey, Esq., F.S.A., Stretford, Manchester.
Edwin Bedford, Esq., Broomspring Lane, Sheffield.
John Bedford, Esq., Birley House, Grenoside.
Thomas Henry Bingley, Esq., Whitley Hall, Ecclesfield.
Isaac Binns, Esq., F.R.H.S., Batley, York.
Charles Booth, Esq., J.P., Brushes, Sheffield. 2 copies.
Charles E. B. Bowles, Esq., 9, Carlton Place, Clifton, Bristol.
Miss Julia Boyd, Moorhouse, Leamside, Co. Durham.
Charles Bridger, Esq., 17, Selwood Terrace, South Kensington, London.
E. Brooke, Esq., Northgate House, Honley, Huddersfield.
J. Heaton Cadman, Esq., York.
S. Camm, Esq., Beachcliffe, Rotherham.
B. E. C. Chambers, Esq., High Green House, Sheffield.
Col. Jos. Lemuel Chester, LL.D., 124, Blue Anchor Road, Bermondsey.
George E. Cockayne, Esq., M.A., F.S.A., Lancaster Herald, Heralds' College, London.
Nathaniel Creswick, Esq., Lieutnt.-Col., Handsworth Grange, Sheffield.
His Grace the Duke of Devonshire, K.G., &c.
George Davenport, Esq., Foxley, Hereford.
James Norton-Dickens, Esq., Bradford.
J. Willis Dixon, Esq., Oakfield House, Sheffield. 2 copies.
William Downing, Esq., Fern Cottage, Alcock Green, Birmingham.
Makin Durham, Esq., The Hall, Thorne.
The Right Honble. the Earl of Effingham, Tusmore House, Bicester.
George W. Elliot, Esq., M.P., Langton Hall, Northallerton.
Ecclesfield Churchwardens.
John Carr Fletcher, Esq., Glossop Road, Sheffield.
Cecil G. Savile Foljambe, Esq., Cockglode, Ollerton, Newark.
J. Foster, Esq., 21, Boundary Road, South Hampstead, London, N.W.
William Garnett, Esq., Quernmoor Park, Lancaster.
Rev. Alfred Gatty, D.D., &c., The Vicarage, Ecclesfield.
Rev. R. A. Gatty, The Rectory, Bradfield, Sheffield.

LIST OF SUBSCRIBERS.

Charles Henry Gatty, Esq., J.P., Trevalgas, Co. **Cornwall, and Felbridge** Park, East Grinstead, Sussex.
Rev. Robert Henry Gatty, the Manor House, Buckden, Huntingdon.
Stephen Herbert Gatty, Esq., Grove Cottage, Totley Dale, Sheffield.
Charles Tindal Gatty, Esq., The Museum, Liverpool.
Rev. Arthur W. Hamilton Gell, M.A., &c., 44, Eaton Square, London.
H. Sydney Grazebrook, Esq., Middleton Villa, Grove Park, Chiswick.
John Brook-Greaves, Esq., Ecclesfield. 4 *copies.*
John Guest, Esq., F.S.A., Moorgate Grange, Rotherham.
Edward Hailstone, Esq., F.S.A., Walton Hall, Wakefield.
Lady Heathcote, Hursley Park, Winchester.
James Hoole, Esq., Edgefield, Bradfield. 2 *copies.*
Robert Hovenden Heathcote, Esq., Parkhill Road, Croydon.
Thomas Hughes, Esq., F.S.A., The Groves, Chester.
Arthur Jackson, Esq., St. James' Row, Sheffield.
Charles Jackson, Esq., Balby, Doncaster.
W. F. Marsh Jackson, Esq., Smethwick, Staffordshire.
Rev. J. T. Jeffcock, M.A., F.S.A., &c., The Rectory, Wolverhampton.
John Jeffcock, Esq., J.P., Cowley Manor, Chapeltown. 2 *copies.*
T. W. Jeffcock, Esq., Shire House, Shiregreen, Sheffield.
John Kaye, Esq., Clayton West, Huddersfield.
Rev. C. Knowles, The Rectory, Winteringham, Brigg.
John Daniel Leader, **Esq., F.S.A.,** Broomhall Park, Sheffield.
Liverpool Free Library.
Library of the Corporation of the City of London, Guildhall.
George H. Machen, Esq., Parson Cross, Sheffield.
George Brown Millett, Esq., Penzance, Cornwall.
The Minster Library, York.
Rev. F. O. Morris, Nunburnholme Rectory, Hayton, **York.**
F. J. **Morrell,** Esq., Broughton Lodge, Banbury.
J. Newbould, Esq., Sharrow Bank, Sheffield.
Major Newsome, R.E., Newcastle-on-Tyne.
Miss Parker, Bodiam Vicarage, Hawkhurst, Kent.
Kenyon Parker, Esq., 13, Old Buildings, Lincolns Inn, London.
Bernard Quaritch, Esq., 15, Piccadilly, London, W. 2 *copies.*
Rev. Canon Raine, York.
J. R. Raines, Esq., Burton Pidsea, near Hull.
Samuel Rigby, Esq., Bruche Hall, Warrington.
Lieutnt.-Col. Alex. Ridgway, Sheplegh Court, Blackawton, **S. Devon.**
J. Paul Rylands, Esq., F.S.A., Highfields, Thelwall, Warrington.
Sampson, Low, Marston, Low, & Searle, 188, Fleet Street, London.
Bentley Shaw, Esq., Woodfield House, Huddersfield.
Francis P. Smith, Esq., Cliffe House, Sheffield.

LIST OF SUBSCRIBERS.

Charles Smith, Esq., Barnes Hall, Grenoside.
Alfred Harrison Smith, Esq., The Horbury, Ecclesfield.
Colin Mackenzie Smith, Esq., Barnes Hall, Grenoside.
William Smith, Esq., Barnes Hall, Grenoside.
Sheffield Free Library, Surrey Street, Sheffield.
Rev. John Stacye, Shrewsbury Hospital, Sheffield.
Mrs. Campbell-Swinton, Kimmerhame, Dunse, N.B.
John Sykes, Esq., M.D., Doncaster.
W. E. Tattershall, Esq., Sheffield.
H. Tindall, Esq., Whitley, Ecclesfield.
John Tomlinson, Esq., Doncaster.
G. W. Tomlinson, Esq., 24, Queen's Street, Huddersfield.
Wm. Townsend, Esq., Sheffield.
Sir W. C. Trevelyan, Bart., Wallington, Newcastle-on-Tyne.
Stephen I. Tucker, Esq., Rouge Croix, The Heralds' College, London.
John Robert Daniel Tyssen, Esq., F.S.A., Brighton.
Albert Vickers, Esq., 40, Inverness Terrace, Kensington Gardens, London.
Frederick Vickers, Esq., Dykes Hall, Wadsley, Sheffield.
Henry Vickers, Esq., Holmwood, Sheffield.
T. Edward Vickers, Esq., J.P., &c., Bolsover Hill, Sheffield.
Henry E. Watson, Esq., Shirecliffe Hall, Sheffield.
Right Honble. The Earl of Wharncliffe, Wortley Hall, Sheffield.
Bernard Wake, Esq., Abbeyfield, Sheffield. *2 copies.*
Captn. Edward Arthur White, F.S.A., Old Elvet, Durham.
Jos. Wilkinson, Esq., Town Clerk, York.
Charles Macro Wilson, Esq., More Hall, Bolsterstone.
Rev. Reginald W. Wilson, The Vicarage, Bolsterstone.
Sir Albert Woods, F.S.A., Garter King of Arms, The Heralds' College, London.

ERRATA.

P. 96, Note 111. "*John* Cotton" should be "*Thomas* Cotton."
P. 151, Note 221. "MCCCCXIX." should be "MCCCCCXIX."
,, "MCCCCXXXVI." should be "MCCCCCXXXVI."
,, "MCCCCXXXVI." should be "MCCCCCXXXVI."

TABLE OF CONTENTS.

	PAGE.
DEDICATION	v.
INTRODUCTION	vii.
LIST OF SUBSCRIBERS	ix—xi.
REGISTER OF MARRIAGES	1— 44.
REGISTER OF BAPTISMS	45— 78.
REGISTER OF BURIALS	79—146.
CHURCHWARDENS' ACCOUNTS	147—162.
INDEX OF PERSONS	163—183.
INDEX OF PLACES	184—186.

MARRIAGES,

1558—1621 (INCLUSIVE),

CONTAINED IN

The First Volume of the General Registers

OF

St. MARY'S, ECCLESFIELD,

In Co: YORK.

MARRIAGES.

Nuptiæ. [.1558.]

HERE FOLLOWETHE THE NAMES OF P'SONS. [PERSONS] MARYED IN ECCLESFELD.

Mense Junij. [1558.]

Nicholas Deye nupt. fuit Elizabethe Beamonde...   xiij' die.

Mense Julij.

[1] Nicholas Sampson nupt. fuit Agnes Bromelye ...   xxxj' die.

Mense Augusti.

[2] Willmo Whitmore nupt. fuit Cicilia Parker ... ... xvj' die.
henrico Symkinson nupt. fuit Elizabethe Pearson ... ... xxx' die.

Mense Septembris.

[3] Alexandro hatfeld nupta. fuit Isabell Sheirclyffe ... xj' die.
[4] Nicholas Stones nupt. fuit Alicia Brodsworthe ... ... xxv' die.

Mense Octobris.

Thome Blakburne [Blackburne] nupt. fuit Lucia Garret ... ix' die.
Willmo Johnson nupt. fuit Agnes Bedfeld ... xijth die.
Thrustin Dungworthe nupt. fuit Alicia Taylyer... xxiij' die.

Mense Novembris.

Thome Sykes nupt. fuit Alicia Byrleye ... ... xxj' die.
Petro fearuleye nupt. fuit Anna Sheirclifie ... ... xxij' die.
Johni Weynwright nupt. fuit Alicia Kyes ... ... xxvj' die.

[1] Nicholas Sampson was of Foxhill, in this parish, yeoman. Vide his Will, note 109.

[2] In the Rotherham Registers occurs this entry, "1558. Aug. 16. Mr. Wyllm Whytmore and Syselle p care." When Dodsworth made his notes on Rotherham Church there was in existence a monument with this inscription :—

        Cecily Whitmore. 1610.
"Deathe's sting away is taken quite
by Christ his payne and smart;
Death is no death but change of light
unto a righteous hart."

[3] Alexander Hatfield was eldest son of Nicholas Hatfield, of Hatfield House, Shiregreen. Isabella Shirecliffe was daughter of Alexander Shirecliffe [3rd son of Thomas Shirecliffe, "master of game."—Vide note 36.] by Isabella his wife, daughter of —— Mounteney, of Cowley, in this parish.

[4] In the Manor Court Rolls of Sheffield appears the following :—1567. Ap. 22. Robert Hurton surrenders land, &c., called Woodfield, in the soke of Southey, to the use of Alice wife of Nicholas Stones and Isabella wife of Henry Shirecliffe, the said Alice and Isabella being the daughters and coheirs of the said Robert Hurton. Here is Nicholas Stones marrying an "Alice," but the surnames differ.

Mense Januarij.

Richardo Lounde nupt. fuit Agnes Crapper	xv' die.
[5] Richardo Morton nupt. fuit Margret Twigge	xvij die.
henrico Birkinshawe nupt. fuit Alicia Bromelye...	xviij' die.
Willmo marsden **nupt. fuit** Alicia Wylkinson	xxj' die.

Mense Aprilis. [1559.]

Radulpho Rychardson nupt. fuit Elizabethe Byrleye ...	xvjto die.
henrico heilio nupt. fuit Isabell Crowshaw	xxiij' die.

Mense Maij.

[6] Johni machon nupt. fuit hellen Parker ...	xxix' die.
[7] Robto Dowke nupt. fuit Isabell Parker ...	eod. die.

Mense Junij.

[8] Willmo Scotte nupt. fuit Elizabethe Cutte vid (widow) ...	iiijto die.
Richardo hollinbriggo nupt. fuit Agnes Shooter at Shefeld ...	x' die Septembris.
[9] Richardo Adamson nupt. fuit Alicia Barbor ...	xvij' die.
Thome Watson nupt. fuit margret hinchlyffe at Wathe ...	xvij' die.
Willmo Stafford nupt. fuit Alicia Greave (Sheffeld) ...	x' die ut Sup.
Willmo Wordsworthe nupt. fuit Elizabethe Kaye **(Darton)** ...	xxiiij' die.

Mense Octobris.

Johni Brodbent nupt. fuit Alicia Jepson ...	j' die.
Johni Sheircliffe nupt. fuit Agnes Bullus ...	viij' die.
Robto Carre nupt. fuit Jana Stevenson ...	xv' die.
Nicholas Senier nupt. fuit matilda hide ...	xxij' die.
Willmo hatfeld nupt. fuit Joan Weynwright ...	xxix' die.
Richardo falleye nupt. fuit Alicia hartleye ...	eod' die.

---

[5] Was probably of Bradfield, as in these registers appears:—"1559. Ap. 27. Ellen, daughter of Richard Morton, **baptised."** Margaret Twigge was daughter of Thomas Twigge, of Ecclesfield. Vide his Will, note 107.

[6] John Machon was son and heir of John Machon, of Machon bank, in Ecclesall. Helen Parker was daughter of Thomas Parker, of Whitley Hall. Vide notes 10 and 19.

[7] **Robert Dowke was of** Herringthorpe. Isabell **Parker was daughter of Thomas Parker, of Whitley Hall. Vide note 19.**

[8] **William** Scotte was a son of Richard Scott, of Barnes Hall. Vide note 105.

[9] Richard Adamson was of Haldworth, in the chapelry of Bradfield; he was son of John, son of John, son of John, son of Richard Adamson, second son of Adam Allynson, of Haldworth, who was dead an' 1404. This is a good instance of a surname derived from a christian name. In the Court Rolls occurs this entry; "1404, July 27, John Adamson, son and heir of Adam Allynson, deceased, seeks to be admitted to 1 messuage and garden and ¼ toft in Haldworth, within the soke of Bradfield." Here we have John, son of Adam, or, John Adamson, and Adam, son of Allyn, or, Adam Allynson. Mary Adamson, daughter of Edward Adamson, baptized 28 May, 1668, married 8 August, 1687, Edward Kenyon, and had issue Rev. Adamson Kenyon, of Wickersley, and a daughter, Rachel Kenyon, born 9th October and baptized 15th October, 1702, who married Francis Parker, of Rivelin Lodge, and had issue, Kenyon Parker, attorney of Sheffield, who was ancestor of the present Arnold Parker and Kenyon Parker, solicitors of Sheffield, and Francis George Shirecliffe Parker, captain 54th regiment foot.

Mense Novembris.

Richardo Carre nupt. fuit Elizabethe hastings ... xix' die.

Mense Januarij.

Thome Smythe nupt. fuit Alicia Hoolande (Hoyland) xiiijto die.
Thome Carre nupt. fuit Jana Button ... xxviij' die.
Ambrosio Swinbanke nupt. fuit Isabell Eyre ... xxix' die.

Mense Februarij.

Robto Walshe nupt. fuit Elizabethe Whiteley ... xj' die.
[10] Thome Spenser nupt. fuit marion machon ... eod. die.

Mense Maij, [1560.]

[11] henrico Sayton nupt. fuit Elizabeth howsley ... xiiijto die.
[12] Thome howsleye nupt. fuit Alicia Scotte ... eod. die.
Thome hinchelyffe nupt. fuit Elizabethe Shawe ... xxvj' die.

Mense Junij.

Johni Lyster nupta. fuit Alicia Beighton ... xxiij' die.
Richardo Kaye nupt. fuit Elizabethe hill ... xxx' die.

Mense Julij.

jacobo morton nupt. fuit Agnes Parkin bradfeld ... vij' die.

Mense Septembris.

Richardo hill nupt. fuit Jana Crosleye ... ... viij' die.
Willmo Sheirclyffe nupt. fuit Agnes haughe ... ... xv' die.

Mense Octobris.

humfrido Bower nupt. fuit Rosam'nda Dyson ... ... vj' die.
Jacobo hattersley nupt. fuit Oliva Hunter (Wentworth) ... ... eod. die.
Richardo Slacke nupt. est Margaret Slatter ... xiij' die.
Thome Brownell nupt. fuit Margaret Gilberthorp ... eod. die.
hugoni howsley nupt. fuit Agnes Blande .... xx' die.

Mense Novembris.

Thome Barber nupt. fuit hellen Wylly ... ... xvj' die.
Christophero Wordsworth nupt. fuit Jana Swynden (Tankersley) eod. die.

[10] " Machin, of Machin banke, in the parish of Ecclesfeilde [Ecclesball?], had issue 8 daughters, one married to Mr. Spencer, of Bramley Grange, whose grandson, William Spencer, Esq., was major of a troop of horse in the civil wars in the reign of King Charles the First, and had issue —— Spencer, Esq., and a daughter married to John Wordsworth, of Swaith, gent. Another daughter of —— Machin aforesaid, was married to —— Genn, of Hullock, and had issue Annis, married to William Hetson, of Nether Holmes."—*From an old MS. in the Courthorpe Collection, Herald's College, London.*

[11] 1553. July 9. Thomas Gargrave, Miles, surrenders land in St. Mary's lane, in Ecclesfield, to Henry Sayton, 1559. May 30, Henry Sayton, surrenders the same to Thomas Shirecliffe. Elizabeth Howsley was probably daughter of Thomas Howsley, of Howsley Hall.

[12] Thomas Howsley was son and heir of Thomas Howsley, of Howsley Hall. **[Vide note 97.]** Alice Scott was daughter of Richard Scott, of Barnes Hall.

Mense Januarij.

Willmo Wilkinson nupt. fuit hellen Yates ... xxvjto die.
Jacobo Lee nupt. fuit Jana halme ... xxviij' die.

Mense Aprilis. [1561.]

[13] Robto Willye nupt. fuit Dionisia Barber ... xxvij' die.

Mense Maij.

Richardo hartleye nupt. fuit Agnes hill ... iiijto die.
Willmo Smythe nupt. fuit Catherin hotchinson... eod. die.

Mense Junij.

Thome Scargell nupt fuit Anna Parker ... xvto die.

Mense Julij.

Thome Scargell Sheffeld nupt. fuit Anna machon vjto die.

Mense Augusti.

Thome Stevenson nupt. fuit Agnes **Briggo** ... ijdo die.
Johni colleye nupt. fuit hellen Colleye ... xxiiij die.
Thome Parkin nupt. fuit Joan Chamber **apud Nowark** xxxj' die.

Mense Septembris.

Thome Bate nupt. fuit Alicia Machon (Retforthe) xxviij' die.

Mense Octobris.

Willmo marshal nupt. fuit Elizabethe Barber ... vto die.
Edwardo Spooner nupt. fuit Alicia Belfeld ... eod. die.
Richardo Ingle nupt. fuit Dorithio Blethwet (Rotherham) xiiij die.

Mense Novembris.

Johni humblocke nupt. fuit Isabell Cooper ixno die.
Johni Walshawe nupt. fuit Joan holden xvj' die.
Anthonio helys nupt. fuit Catherin Shoeter xix' die.
Nicholas Stanylande nupt. fuit Isabell Doye xxx' die.

Mense Decembris.

Johni Weynwright nupt. fuit Joan Crosleye vijmo die.
Richardo Smythe nupt. fuit Joan Wodhouse ... xiiij' die.

Mense Februarij.

Richardo Cutte nupt. fuit Elizabetho Bower iij' die.
Robto Cutte nupt. fuit Euphemia hargreave xxviij' die.

---

[13] 1558, August 20. Richard Bullus, son and heir of William Bullus, surrenders land, &c., in Ecclesfield, to Robert Willey. 1591, April 21. Robert Willey, of Toadhole, son and heir of Robert Willey, seeks to be admitted to the same.

Mense Aprilis. [1562.]

Thome Carre nupt. fuit hellen Shawe ... ... xxiij' die.

Mense Junij.

Thome Shawe nupt. fuit Elizabethe Cooper ... xiiij die.
Johni Killabecke nupt. fuit Agnes Stephenson ... xxviij' die.

Mense Julij.

Johni Gylles nupt. fuit hellen hall (Rotherham) vto die.
Thome hauslen nupt. fuit Joan Priestley ... xxviij' die.

Mense Augusti.

Robto Cooper nupta. fuit Joan Wylkinson ... ... ixno die.
Thome Phillipott nupt. fuit Margerie Byrks Sheffeld ... xxiij die.

Mense Septembris.

henrico Turneleye nupt. fuit Joan Dawre ... ... xxviij die.

Mense Novembris.

[14] Mer. Thome Cotton nupt. est Barbara Thwetes (Thwaites) ... ... xvij' die.
Thome hinchclyfe nupt. fuit Margaret Garladye ... ... xxviij' die.

Mense Februarij.

Nicholas hill nupt. fuit Agnes Grene ... ijto die.

Mense Junij. [1563.]

Willmo Goodeye nupt. fuit Jana hopkinson ... ... xxmo die.

Mense Septembris.

Thome Byrleye nupt. fuit Catherina Machon Sheffeld xij' die.

Mense Octobris.

Robto holden nupt. fuit Joan Inman ... ... iij' die.
Richardo Cooper nupt. fuit Hellen Awwodde ... ... x' die.
henrico Lastleye nupt. fuit hellen Cooper ... ... xj' die.
Georgio Copleye nupt. est Jana Gregorye ... ... xvij' die.
hugoni Shirlsbye nupt. fuit Elizabeth Wildsmith ... ... xix' die.

Mense Novembris.

Thome Beighton nupt. est Alicia machon ... xiiij' die.
Edmundo Smythe nupt. est Joan holden ... xxvij' die.
Richardo Scholes nupt. est Isabell Waller ... eod. die.
Nicholos Cooper nupt. est Isabell Swyfte ... eod. die.

---

[14] 1565. Dec. 19. Thomas Cotton, armiger, and Barbara, his wife, surrender lands in Ecclesfield, to the use of John Mounteney, gent. Barbara Thwaites was daughter of John Mounteney, of Creswick, and relict of Thomas Thwaites, Esquire.

Mense Maij. [1564.]

Radulpho Trulove nupt. fuit Isabell Crofts … xxx' die.

Mense Julij.

Thome Sayvell (Saville) nupt. fuit Maria Fletcher … xxx' die.

Mense Augusti.

Radulpho Warde nupt. fuit Alicia Brown … xiij" die.
Johni Kaye nupt. fuit Isabell Deye … xxj' die.

Mense Septembris.

Johni Sheffeld nupt. fuit Joan Adamson … iij' die.
Jacobo Bencks nupt. fuit Margeria Carre … xvij' die.
Robto Pearson nupt. fuit hellen Syddowe … xxiiij' die.

Mense Octobris.

Robto Hill nupt. fuit Alicia Ronksleye … j' die.
[15] Alexandro Hyde nupt. fuit hellen howsleye … viij' die.

Mense Novembris.

[16] Robto hurte nupt. fuit Anna Barbar … xij' die.

Mense Januarij.

Thome Bowar nupt. fuit Isabell Wyllye … xxviij' die.

Mense Februarij.

Johni Beighton nupt. fuit Alicia Clayton … xiij' die.
[17] Thome hoyland nupt. fuit Anna falleye … xviij' die.

Mense Maij. [1565.]

Richarde Collye nupt. fuit Agnes Roodes … vjto die.
Henrico Shawe nupt fuit hellen Clayton … viij' die.

---

[15] Alexr. Hyde was of Grenoside, in this parish; he had a son George, who, in 1608, surrendered his land, at Grenoside, to William Hyde. 1597. Jan. 10. Alexander Howsley and Elizabeth, his wife; Charles Croft and Phillis, his wife; and Thomas Longley and Elena, his wife, surrender land, &c., in Ecclesfield, to George and William Hyde.

[16] Robert Hert was of Haldworth, in the chapelry of Bradfield. The Hurts are a Derbyshire family, springing from a village called Alderwasley, in that county. The first notice that I have of them as of Haldworth is in 1545, when Robert Smallbeehind, alias Smallbent, surrenders land at Haldworth to Alice, his daughter and heir. 1552. Ap. 22. Walter Hurt, senior, and Alice, his wife, surrender the same, after their own deaths, to the use of Robert Hurt, their son and heir; with remainder to Walter, their second son; with remainder to Dionisie, the daughter of the said Walter the elder. Robert Hurt had issue two sons—Walter, the oldest, of Haldworth, and Nicholas, who was baptized 18th Jan., 1576-7, and settled at Woodseats, in this parish, of whom more anon. The family of Smallbeehind was settled at Haldworth as early as 1393. The Robert alluded to above was son of John, son of Thomas, son of John, son of John Smallbeehind, of Haldworth, living ano. 1393.—Court Rolls.

[17] 1508. Oct. 21. Thomas Whele surrenders 1 messuage and 2 bovats in Shire and Nether Hartley to Agnes Whele, his wife. 1525. Dec. 11. Henry Hooland or Hoyland, and Alice his wife, one of the daughters and cohelrs of Thomas Whele, seeks to be admitted to a third part of the same. 1565. Dec. 19. Thomas, son and heir of Henry Hoyland, deceased, seeks to be admitted to the same.

Henrico Barnsleye nupt. fuit Elizabeth Slatter ...   xx' die.
[18] Thome jepson nupt. fuit Margaret Bearde   ...   eod. die.
Johni Smythe nupt. fuit Elizabethe Neyler   ...   eod. die.
Thome Wagstaffe nupt. fuit Elizabethe Slatter ...   xxj' die.

Mense Julij.

Francisco Bower nupt. fuit Joan Dyson   ...   j' die.
Richardo Base nupt. fuit hellen Beale   ...   eod. die.
[19] Willmo Parker nupt. fuit Anna Eyre   ...   xvij' die.
Johni marsden nupt. fuit margaret Parker   ...   xxx' die.

Mense Augusti.

Thome Crosleye nupt. fuit Joan Kyrkbye   ...   vto die.

Mense Octobris.

Robto hurton nupt. fuit hellen haldsworthe   ...   vijmo die.
henrico Stanyforthe nupt. fuit Anna Colte   ...   xxj' die.
Willmo hall nupt. fuit Joan hoylande   ...   eod. die.
Johni Lee nupt. fuit Elizabethe Parker   ...   .

Mense Novembris.

Thome Wyldsmithe nupt. fuit jana Goodeyr   ...   xj' die.

Mense Januarij.

Edwardo Worsleye nupt. fuit Elizabethe Roodes   xx' die.
Thome Prince nupt. fuit Alicia Offrey   ...   eod. die.
[20] henrico Sheircliffe nupt. fuit Isabell hurton   ...   xxvij' die.
Willmo hepworthe nupt. fuit joan Pryest   ...   eod. die.
[21] Thome Thweytes nupt. fuit Alicia Youle (Hoole)   xxix' die.

Mense Feburarij.

Johni Cutte nupt. fuit Betriss Sydall   ...   ...   iij' die.
Johni Cooper nupt. fuit Isabell hotchinson   ...   .   x' die.

Mense Maij. [1566.]

Nicholas Grene nupt. fuit Margaret hyrst   ...   ...   xij' die.

[18] 1519. Nov. 29. Thomas Coo or Combe, surrenders **land in Ecclesfield, to the use of** Thomas Jepson. 1545. Sept. 8. Thomas Jepson seeks to be admitted as son and heir of Thomas Jepson, deceased. 1597. July 13. Thomas Jepson, of Ecclesfield, yeoman, surrenders 1 messuage 1 bovat, in Ecclesfield, to his own use for life, and after his decease to Alexander Jepson, his son and heir, and Mary his wife, daughter of Thomas Shirecliffe, late of Butterthwaite, **with** remainder to Margaret, wife of the said Thomas Jepson. The descendants of the above Alexander Jepson are still living in the village, and are publicans and coopers.

[19] William Parker, was of Whitley Hall, in this parish, **and of** Horneastle, **in co.** Lincoln. He was son of Thomas, son of John, son of Thomas, son of John Parker, **of** Norton Lees, in co. Derby. Anna Eyre was daughter of Stephen Eyre, **of co. Derby, and was second wife of the above** William Parker—they had no issue.

[20] Vide note 4.

[21] 1565. Dec. 19. Henry Hill surrenders 1 cottage and 1 acre in Ecclesfield to the use of Richard Hill and Thomas Thwaites, son and heir of Thomas Thwaites, by Johanna his wife, daughter of the aforesaid Henry Hill.

Mense Junij.

Johni Ibotson nupt. Margaret Page ... ixno die.

Mense Augusti.

Thome Gest nupt. fuit Joan hall ... ... iiijto die.
Edmundo Dernelye gen : nupt. fuit Ema. (Emmota) Scott ... xxvj' die.

Mense Octobris.

Rogero Kaye nupt. fuit Anna Atkinson ... vto die.
Johni Hublocke [Humblock] nupt. fuit Jana Feilde ... viij' die.
[22] henrico Combe nupt. fuit hellen machon ... xiij' die.
Galfrido [Godfrey] Cooke nupt. fuit maria Elando ... xv' die.
[23] Jacobo Carre nupt. fuit hellen **Goslinge** ... xxj' die.

Mense Januarij.

William Blunt nupt. est Joan Whisten ... viiijto die.
Thome Cutt nupt. fuit Margaret Sheircliffe ... ... xxj' die.
Robto Rooper nupt. fuit hellen hobson ... ... xxv' die.

Mense Aprilis.

Richardo Jephson **nupt. fuit Joan Twigge** ... **xxvj' die.**

Mense Augusti.

Johni Marsden nupt. fuit Agnes Sampson ... vto die.
Edwardo Gasken (Gascolgn ?) nupt. fuit Frances Dreaton ... xviiij' die.

Mense Septembris.

[24] Radulpho Carre nupt. fuit hellen Sampson ... ... vij' die.
Johni Roodes nupt. est Agnes Sheircliffe ... xix' die.

---

[22] Henry Combe was of Wincobank and Shiregreen in this parish, where his family had resided since ano. 1276. When Petrus de Combe paid a fine of xxd. to be admitted to 1 rood of land within the soke of Southey, 1339, William son of Henry Coo or Combe, was witness to a deed of transfer of land in this parish. 1390. Henry Combe seeks to be admitted to lands in Wincobank and Shiregreen, and had issue, John living 1443, who had issue, William dead an' 1476, who by his wife Alicia, left issue John, living 1500, who, by his wife Joanna, had issue a son Henry, who was dead an' 1536, who left issue a son Henry Combe the subject of this note.—Henry Combe had issue by his wife, Helen Machon, a son and heir, Henry Combe, who was living 1598, when he seeks to be admitted to land at Shiregreen and Wincobank on his father's death, which took place in 1597.

[23] James Carr was of Southey, in this parish where the family had held lands from an early date. The first time the name appears in the Manor Court Rolls is in 1276, when Thomas del Ker paid a fine of 20d. to be admitted to 1 rood in Wardsend. The direct ancestors of the above James, was William del Carre, who was living 1427, and married Johanna, daughter and heir of Thomas Emson; he had a son Thomas, who had a son William living 1482, who by his wife, Alice, had three sons, John, Thomas and Henry. John, the eldest son, had issue a son, William, who had issue James Carr, the subject of this note, and John Carr, a younger son. James Carr was grandfather of Sir George Carr, knt., Secretary of State in Ireland, &c., whose grandson, Charles Carr, D.D., was Bishop of Killaloe, &c. For a pedigree of this family, from James Carr down to the present time, see *Hunter's Hallamshire, Gatty's Edition*, p. 439. There was formerly an old pew in Ecclesfield Church, with this inscription upon it: " JAMES CARR AND ELLYNE HIS WYFFE OF SOWTHAR MADE THES STALLE AN NO D 1578."

[24] Ralph Carr, was of Birley, in this parish, he was son of Richard, son of William, son of John Carr, of Birley, living about 1500. In the year 1435, Joana, daughter of William Birley, of Birley, and wife of William del Ker, seeks

Mense Octobris.

Jacobo Mawre [Moore] nupt. fuit margaret Barber (Sheffeld)	vto die.
Johni Roose nupt. fuit Elizabethe machon	vjto die.

Mense Novembris.

Richardo Scoyrer [Scorer] nupt. fuit Elizabeth Combe	xvj' die.
Richardo Byrkes nupt. fuit Agnes Byrkes	xviij die.
Richardo hollinbrigge nupt. est Jana Boothe	xxix' die.
[20] Richardo Bever nupt. fuit Agnes Warde	eod die.
Martino Rooe nupt. fuit margaret Foxe	eod die.

Mense Januarij.

Willmo Waddye nupt. fuit Margaret Kyrkbye at Rotherham	xxo' die.

Mense Februarij.

Willmo Keynyon nupt. fuit Joan Cutte	xj' die.
Ric'o Tomson nupt. est margaret hoyland (Sheffeld) ...	eod die.

Mense Aprilis. [1568]

Johni Gylles nupt. fuit Agnes Crofts	xxvj' die.

Mense Maij.

Willmo Wylkinson nupt. est maria Cooke	xvj' die.
Robto Oxspringe nupt. fuit Ann Calverd	xvij' die.

Mense Julij.

Ambros Swynbanke maryed Alice Sheircliffe ...	xvij' die.

Mense Augustij.

Robert Neyler maryed Joan Jephson ...	viij die.
Thomas Oxspringe maryed Agnes Taylyer ...	xv' die.

Mense Septembris.

John Parkin maryed Agnes Rooso	xij' die.

Mense Octobris.

Wm. Button maryed johan Pudseye ...	iij' die.
John Lynthwet maryed helen Jepson ...	xxiiij' die.
[20] Thomas Unwen maryed Elizabeth Stanyforthe ...	pd die.
Richard Lee maryed margret heatou ...	xxvj' die.

to be admitted to lands, &c., in Birley, after the decease of the said William Birley. It is not improbable that by this marriage the family of Carr became settled at Birley, but I cannot fill up the gap between William, living 1435, and John, living 1500. The present representative of the family is John Carr Fletcher, of Birley and Sheffield, son of the late Rev. John Fletcher, who was of Lincoln College, Oxford, and perpetual curate of Bradfield, and died ano. 1853.

[20] In the churchwardens' accounts, ano. 1569, appears this entry "Itm. Payd to Ric. Bever and Thos. teller (Taylor) for parish business, iiijd."

[26] The name of Unwen, for several generations, has been borne by persons holding the office of sexton at Ecclesfield. The present sexton bears this name.

Mense Novembris.

Charles hill maryed margret Wroe ... ... xiiijto die.

Mense Februarij.

Robt Turnleye maried Elizabethe Roodes ... vjto die.

Mense Junij. [1569.]

Averye Tempest gent maryed Cicilye hall vjto die.
Alexandr Wodde maryed margaret Grene vij die.

Mense Septembris.

francys Bowre (Bower) maryed Katherin Walker iiijto die.
Rychard Button maryed Johan Wade ... xiiijto die.

Mense Novembris.

Rychard Tyngle maryed Bettryce Parkin ... xx' die.
John Tomson maryed Isabell Beardsell ... . xxvj' die.

Mense Januarij.

[27] Robt handleye maryed Agnes Matleye ... ... xv' die.

Mense Junij. [1570.]

Wyllm Brodheade maryed Alice Stacye ... ... iiijto die.
Wm Bearde maryed Agnes Nodder... ... ... xj' die.

Mense Augusti.

Thomas hepworthe maryed Agnes Smythe ... vto die.

Mense Octobris.

Wyllm Parkin maryed margret hartleye ... j' die.

Mense Novembris.

Robt fearnleye maryed Grace hill vto die.
Thomas Carre maryed Joan Wylkinson ... xij' die.

Mense Januarij.

Rychard Parman maryed margret Grene ... xxviiij' die.

Mense Februarij.

Thomas Clareke maryed Agnes Sharppe ... x' die.
henrye Button maryed Elizabethe Whitleye ... ccd die.

Mense Aprilis. [1571.]

Nicholas Turnleye maryed Elizabethe Carre xxix die.

---

[27] One of the parishioners chosen to examine the churchwardens' account, ano. 1571. **The family of Hanley** were for long seated in Hallam. 1386. Robertus Woodhewer surrenders land in Hallam to **Stephanus Hanley, &c.** Robert Hanley was churchwarden, ano. 1572.

Mense Maij.

Wyllm Clarcke maryed Jane Smythe	...	xiiij' die.
John Grene maryed Elizabethe Gest	...	xix' die.
Thomas Pearson maryed Jane Threnscrose	...	xxij' die.

Mense Julij.

[28] Johni Creswycke maryed Margret Creswycke ... xxx' die.

Mense Augusti.

Wyllm Tympleye maryed Elizabethe Bowre (Bower)	...	vto. die
John Briggs maryed hellen Bearde	...	xij' die.
Edward fyrthe maryed margret Walker	...	xix' die.

Mense Octobris.

John Sparcke maryed Agnes holande	...	vij' die.
Wyllm Greaves maryed Rosamunde Bower	...	xiiijto die.
John Bever maryed Johan Bromeleye	...	xxiij' die.

Mense Novembris.

henrye Parkin maryed Joan fyrthe ... ... xviij' die.

Mense Januarij.

George Gauge maryed Anne Wylkinson	...	...	xv' die.
Robt. Cooper maryed Elizabethe Turnleye	...	...	xx' die.
John Lynthwet maryed Johan Parker	...	...	xxvij' die.
Laurence Wodde maryed Em'ot Unwen	...	...	xxix' die.

Mense Aprilis. [1572.]

Roger Crofts maryed Anne fyrthe ... ... xx' die.

Mense Maij.

[29] Robt. Sheirclyffe maryed Marye Carre ... ... iiijto. die.

---

[28] John Creswick was of Burrowlee, in this parish. His will is dated 21 May, 1604. In it he mentions, Nicholas Creswick, my 3rd son, devising to him my messuage in Ecclesfield, &c., with remainder to Gilbert Creswick, my 4th son, with remainder to Roger Creswick, my 5th son, with remainder to Edward or Edmund Creswick, my 6th son. My land at Haldworth to Roger Creswick, my 5th son, John Creswick, my 2nd son, my daughters Margaret and Frances Creswick, and Ann, wife of William Ward, Thomas Creswick, my brother-in-law, &c. His eldest son was Thomas Creswick, of Burrowlee, who was baptized 8th Feb., 1575; this baptism is from the Creswick family Bible, now in the possession of the Rev. J. W. Darnborough, rector of South Otterington, near Thirsk, who is a descendant of this family. It is impossible for me, owing to my limited space, to go into the history of the family of Creswick, which is one of the most ancient and respectable in this parish; they are so to speak indigenous to the soil, springing from a hamlet called Creswick.

[29] Robert Shireeliffe was of Whitley Hall, in this parish; son of Richard Shireeliffe, of Ecclesfield. For a pedigree of this family, see Hunter's Hallamshire, Gatty's edition, pp. 446-7. It is represented by the Parkers of Sheffield, mentioned in note 9. Whitley Hall is now the seat of Thomas Henry Bingley, whose grandfather, William Bingley, of Ellerslie Lodge, in the parish of Penistone, purchased it of Mary, relict of Benjamin Hammond, who had bought it of John Parker, sometime between 1803 and 1810.

Mense Junij.

Charles Smythe maryed Agnes man	...	xv' die.
Thomas Crowder maryed Johan hopkinson	...	xxix die.

Mense Julij.

Richard Collyo married Isabell howsleye	...	viij' die.

Mense Augusti.

Thomas Shawe maryed Elizabethe Byrkes	...	iij' die.

Mense Octobris.

Godfridus Weynwright maryed johan Chadwycke		xij' die.
50 john machon maryed Elizabethe Wylkinson		xiij' die.

Mense Novembris.

john Renaldo maryed Elizabethe Bearde	...	ijdo die.
Robt Shawe maryed Agnes Shaw	... ...	ixno die.

Mense Januarij.

John Jepson maryed Margret Waddye	...	xviij' die.

Mense Aprilis. [1573.]

Charles hobson maryed Anne Smythe	...	...	xxvjto die.

Mense Maij.

31 Nicholas Sheyrclyffe maryed Isabell Roodes	...	xix' die.

Mense Junij.

32 Mr. Nicholas Wombwell maryed ms. Elizabeth mawlyverey...	xv' die.

Mense Julij.

humfrey fearnley maryed Em'ot Geslinge	...	vij' die.

Mense Augusti.

Thomas Smythe maryed Margret Crofts	...	xxiij' die.
Wm. Brooke maryed Dorythye Smythe	...	xxiiij' die.

Mense Novembris.

Rychard Sheirclyffo & margrot howle (Hoole) maryed	viij' die.

---

[30] 1550. Sept. 16. Thomas Blithe, of Hymsworth, and John Blithe, of Norton Lees, in the parish of Norton, co. Derby, surrender lands at Longley, now in the tenure of John Machon, to Thomas Wilkinson, of Crowder House. Probably son of the above John Machon.

[31] Nicolas Shirecliffe was elder brother of Robert Shirecliffe, of Whitley Hall.—Vide note 29.

[32] Mr. Nicholas Wombwell was second son of Nicholas Wombwell, of Thundercliffe Grange. He was living at Tickhill ano. 1585. Elizabeth Mauleverer was daughter of James Rolston and relict of Nicholas Mauleverer, of Letwell. The families intermarried again in the next generation; in the Rotherham registers is this entry, "1585. Nov. 9, Nicolas Molliverey and Elizth. Wombwell." Nicholas was second son of the aforesaid Elizabeth, and Elizabeth Wombwell was one of the daughters and coheirs of Thomas Wombwell, of Thundercliffe Grange, and niece of Nicolas Wombwell aforesaid.

Mense Januarij.

[33] henrye Byrlye & joan Rowleye maryed ... ... xxviij' die.
henrye jeffraye & hellen Wright maryed .... xxx' die.

Mense Februarij.

Rychard Cade & joan Bowre (Bower) maryed .. vjto die.

Mense Junij. (1574.)

Thomas Wylkinson & Alyce Osleye maryed ... ... xx' die.

Mense Julij.

[34] Alexandr howsleye & Elizabethe hyde conjugat ... vij' die.

Mense Augusti.

[35] Rychard Swyfte & Agnes Wyllye con. ... j' die.
Wyllm Barnsleye & Elizabethe Crosleye con. ... xv' die.
Thomas Parkin & margret Byrleye conjug. ... xxix' die.

Mense Octobris.

Rychard Slacke & hellen Brodheade conjug. ... x' die.
Rychard Genne & Agnes Johnson conjugat. ... xvij die.
James Sharppe & Isabell Tyngle conjug. ... xxx' die.

Mense Novembris.

john Roger & Agnes Steven conjug. ... ... xxiij' die.

Mense Maij, [1575.]

John Wodde & Joan Smythe conjug. ... ... xv' die.

Mense Junij.

Arthure Dyson & Elizabeth Brown conjug. ... xxiiij' die.

Mense Septembris.

Wm. harryson & Elizabethe conjug. ... xvj' die.

Mense Novembris.

Rychard Tylsleye & marye Broughe cojug. ... xxiiij' die.

Mense Februarij.

Raulph Stanylande & Cicelye Shawe cojug. ... viij' die.
Wm. Wylson & margret Smythe cojug. ... xij' die.
Robt. Unwen & Agnes Bullus cojug. ... xix' die.
Thomas Thorppe & joan Coward cojug. ... eod. die.

[33] Henry Byrley was probably identical with Henry Birley, of the Ewes, in the hamlet of Worrall, who was living ano. 1591, as also was his son Nicholas Byrley. Henry Birley was son of Nicholas, son of Henry, son of John, son of William de Birley living 1499.

[34] Vide Note 15.

[35] Churchwardens' Account, 1569. "Itm. paye to Rye. Swyfte for neaylls to the bell whealls, jd."

Mense Maij. [1576.]

henrye hyll & Agnes Bearde cojug....	xiij' die.
Edward Watson & Agnes Grene cojug.	xx' die.
Robt. Barlet & Elizabethe Lymer cojug.	eod. die.

Mense Junij.

Edmunde Stewardson & Elizabethe Wodde cojug.	iij' die.

Mense Novembris.

Thomas Carre & Elizabethe Charlsworthe cojug.	xxvij' die.

Mense Januarij.

Charles Clarke & Johan Crofts cojugat. ...	xxvij' die.

Mense Februarij.

Alexandr Bearde & Catherin Keyes cojugat.	vij' die.

Mense Aprilis. [1577.]

Wyllm Beale & Effam Stevenson cojugat.	xv' die.
John Stringer & Alice Parkin cojugat.	xxj' die.

Mense Maij.

Nicholas Dungworthe & hellen Wilkinson cojugat.	xj' die.
John hall & Grace Wodheade cojugat. ...	xij' die.

Mense Junij.

[36] Nicholas Sheircliffe & Barbara Wombwell cojug.	xj' die.
henrye Baylye & Cicilye Ellys cojugat. ...	xvj' die.
John Parkyn & Christine Cooper cojugat. ...	xxx' die.

Mense Julij.

Rychard holden & **Johan** Turton cojugat. ...	j' die.
Robt. Parkin & Anne Creswycke cojugat. ...	viij' die.

Mense Septembris.

james foster & Jane Watson cojugat. ...	iij' die.
Peter Kent & johan Thorppe cojugat. ...	**xxiij' die.**

Mense Novembris.

Dionis marsden & Barbara Ellys cojugat.	xviij' die.

Mense Decembris.

John Secker & Anne Roodes cojugat. ...	xvj' die.

---

[36] Nicolas Shirecliffe was of Ecclesfield Hall, gent. He was son of Nicolas, son of Alexander, third son of Thomas Shirecliffe, "master of game" to the Lords of Hallamshire, who was son of William Shirecliffe, living 1499. The name is derived from Shirecliffe, near Sheffield. The earliest record I can find of this family in the Court Rolls is 1334, Nicolas de Shirecliffe seeks to be admitted to one Rood in Shirecliffe. Barbara Wombwell was eldest daughter and co-heir of Thomas Wombwell, of Thundercliffe Grange, Esq.

Mense Januarij.

Thomas Thwaytes and margaret Roodes cojug. ... ... xxvij' die.

Mense Aprilis. [1578.]

Wyllm Bradburn & Emot Bearde cojugat. ... ... xxj' die.

Mense Maij.

Wm. Shawe & jane hill cojugat. ... ... iij' die.
John hollande & Joan Batleye cojugat. ... xxvj' die.

Mense Junij.

Robt. Pearson & hellen Watson cojugat. ... ... ij" die
Wm. Creswycke & Margret Carre cojugat. ... ... xv' die.
James Layton & Isabell Dawre cojugat. ... ... xxix' die.

Mense Julij.

Wm. Crosleye & Isabell Robinson cojugat ... xx' die.

Mense Augusti.

George Cottrell & Anne Gybson cojug. ... xxx' die.

Mense Septembris.

Wyllm Deye & Johan Lee cojugat. .. ... j' die.
Robt. Bearde & Anne Wylkinson cojugat. ... xxviij' die.

Mense Octobris.

[37] Raulphe Crofts & maude mountney cojugat. ... vjto die.

Mense Novembris.

Wm. Smythe & Agnes Lee cojugat. ... iij' die.
James Dey & margaret Walton cojugat. ... eod. die.
James Brefet & Joan Wylson cojugat. ... xxv' die.

Mense Februarij.

Rychard Saterfett & Cicilye Ryleye cojugat. ... ... x' die.
Robt. falleye & Elizabetho man cojugat. ... ... xiij' die.

Mense Junij. [1579.]

Charles Crosleye & Alice Walker cojugat. ijdo die.
[38] Thomas Bullus & Marget Sheircliffe cojugat. xxix' die.
Rychard Warde & Anne fearnleye cojugat. eod. die.

---

[37] 1543. Oct. 19. Catherine Crofts, widow, surrenders lands at Whitley to Christopher Crofts, her son and heir. 1588. April 6. Ralph Crofts surrenders the same to his own use for life, and, after his decease, to Nicholas Mounteney, of Rotherham, mercer, son of John Mounteney, of Creswick, deceased, and in default with remainder to Charles Hill, of Ecclesfield, butcher, and Thomas Hill, his son. Maude Mounteney was relict of John Mounteney, of Creswick, alluded to above.

[38] Thomas Bullus was of Birley Edge, and Margaret Shirecliffe was daughter of James Shirecliffe, of Wardsend, who was younger brother of Nicholas, of Ecclesfield. They had issue three sons, Thomas, Nicholas, and James.

Mense Julij.

Robt. Wright & Agnes hotchinson cojugat. — xx' die.
[39] Charles Croft & Phillis hyde cojugat. — xxvij die.

Mense Augusti.

Thomas Roodes & Barbara fulstone conjugat. ... — j' die.
Thomas Parkin & margret hawksworthe cojugat. — xxiij' die.
Rychard Stanyforth and margaret Bowre (Bower) cojugat. ... — eod. die.
[40] Robt. howle (Hoole) & Isabell mountneye cojugat. — xxviij die.

Mense Octobris.

[41] francis Parker & Anne hewet cojugat. ... — xij' die.
[42] Raulph Lee & Jana Parkin cojug. ... — ijdo. die Novembris.
John Plats & Alice Brodbent conjugat. ... — xxij die.

Mense Decembris.

Nicholas man & hellen fyrthe ... — j' die.

Mense Januarij.

[43] Wyllm Heye & hellen Sampson conjugat. ... ... — xxx' die.

Mense Aprilis. [1580.]

Rychard Slacke & Elizabethe Stevenson cojugat. ... — xxiiij die.

Mense Junij.

Wyllm Dynnison & Elizabethe Otes cojugat. ... — xij' die.
Thomas Lawe & john (Johana) Raworthe conjug. — xxvj' die.

Mense Julij.

Robt. Carre & Agnes Braman conjugat. — xv' die.
Wyllm Brigge & Elizabethe Ronksleye conjugat. — eod. die.
Wyllm Cooke & Marye Sayvell (Saville) cojug. — xxiiij die.

James Bullus married Mary, daughter of Thomas Eyre, of Darwent, who was son of Thomas Eyre, of Darwent, by Margaret, his wife, daughter and heir of Richard Slatter, of Dungworth, who was son of Robert, son of Robert, son of Richard, son of William, son of Thomas Slatter, of Dungworth, living 1429.—*Court Rolls.* James Bullus above, had a daughter, Mary, who married Benjamin Watts, of Barnes Hall.

[39] Vide note 15.

[40] Isabel Mountency was daughter of John Mountency, of Creswick. Robert Hoole was of Attercliffe. Vide note 149.

[41] Francis Parker was son and heir of William Parker, of Whitley Hall. [Vide note 19.] Anne Hewet was a daughter of Richard Hewet, of Killamarsh.

[42] 1553. Oct. 26. Thomas Gargrave Miles surrenders land, &c., in Ecclesfield, after the decease of Richard Cowper and William Everingham, to Ralph Lee. In 1591, Ralph Lee, son and heir of Ralph Lee, surrenders the same to his own use.

[43] Vide Will of Henry Sampson, note 200.

Mense Augusti.

Robt. Lynleye & Alice Wodheade conjugat. ...	iij' die.
Nicholas Sheyrelyffe & Agnes Staynton cojug. ...	xiiij' die.

Mense Octobris.

henrye jeffraye & johan Pegge conjugat. ...	ix' die.

Mense Novembris.

Robt. hartleye & Elizabethe Barnsleye con. ...	vjto die.
Edmunde hoole & Elizabeth hurte cojugat. ...	27' die.

Mense Januarij.

Thomas Muscrofte & johan Brefet cojugat. ...	xiiij' die.
Rychard hall & Anne hobson conjugat. ...	xxij' die.

Mense Feburarij.

Robt. Byrkes & Dyonis Dawson conjugat.	iiijto die.

Mense Aprilis. [1581.]

Christopher holmes & Alice Byrrye conjug.	ultimo die.

Mense Maij.

Robt. Shawe & Joan Carro conjug.... ...	vij' die.

Mense Junij.

Anthonye Cutte & margret Cutte cojugat. ...	xj' die.
Thomas hall & Cicilye Streete conjugat ...	xiij' die.
Thomas Gylles & Agnes Watson conjugat. ...	xxv' die.

Mense Septembris.

Robt. Bullus & Alice Unwen conjugat.	xiiijto die.
Nicholas Wodde & Isabell Grubbe conjugat.	xxiiijto die.

Mense Decembris.

Thomas Carro & Cicilye howsleye conjug. ...	x' die.

Mense Januarij.

Roger Tympleye & margret hawme conjug. ...	xiiijto die.

Mense Februarij.

Johnhaughton & marye Otes conjugat. ...	xj' die.
Thomas Osleye & margret Greve conjug. ...	xviij' die.
Thomas haughe & Cicilye Traves cojug. ...	xx' die.

Mense Aprilis. [1582.]

Thomas Bullus & helen Shawe cojugat. ...	xxij' die.

Mense Junij.

George Arther & Alice Westall cojugat.	j' die.
[44] hughe hyde & margret Wylkinson cojugat.	xxiiij' die.

Mense Julij.

henrye Bearde & margret Dawson cojugat.	j' die.

Mense Augusti.

Wyllm Sykes & Anne Dughtye conjug. ...	xxvij' die.

Mense Septembris.

[45] Rychard Waterhouse & Beatrice Tingle cojug. ...	xvj' die.
Thomas Downynge & Anne Bearde cojug. ...	ult. die.

Mense Octobris.

Edward Greaves & hellen Barber cojugat. ...	j' die.

Mense Decembris.

Thomas Tyngle & Elizabethe Shooter cojug. ...	ijdo. die.

Mense Januarij.

Robt. Neyler & Elizabethe Smythe conjugat.	xiij' die.
Raulphe hotchinson & margret Rigge cojugat.	xx' die.
Charles holden & Cicilye Gest cojug.	xxvij' die.

Mense Maij. [1583.]

Rychard Ragge & Alice Tomson conjugat. ...	xj' die.

Mense Junij.

John Brodeleye & Elizabethe Wormall cojugat.... ...	xviij' die.

Mense Augusti.

James Deye & Elizabethe Grubbe conjugat. ...	iiijto die.
Wm. Tympleye & hellen Brabmer conjug. ...	xj' die.
Robt. Shooter & Diones Wodde cojug. ...	xxvto die.
Thomas mylner & Elizabethe Bower cojug. ...	eod. die.

Mense Septembris.

Roger Gregorye & Emot. Odeson conjug.	j' die.
Nicholas hobson & Anne Ingman conjugat.	vto die.
[46] Richard Steade & Jane Grene cojug.	ix' die.

[44] Hugh Hyde was son of William Hyde, of Birley, and brother of Alexander Hyde, of Grenoside. Vide notes 15 and 171.

[45] Richard Waterhouse was probably of Onesacre, in the Chapelry of Bradfield. 1591. Oct. 12. Richard Waterhouse, of Onesacre, son and heir of Richard Waterhouse, deceased, seeks to be admitted to lands in Onesacre as proper heir of William Waterhouse, late of Onesacre, deceased, who was brother to Richard Waterhouse, the elder.—*Court Rolls*.

[46] The Steade family resided at Onesacre, in the Chapelry of Bradfield. 1379. Peter de Stede was seated there—he was one of the family of Stead, of Stead, in the parish of Wentworth. From the Court Rolls, I have the

Mense Octobris

Rychard Scholes & meryan (Marion) Townende cojugat.	vij' die.
Wyllm. martyn & Agnes Carre cojug. …	xx' die.
John Butcher & Roose Smythe conjugat. …	eod. die.
John Parkyn & johan Senyer conjugat. …	xxij' die.
hughe Wylkinson & Anne Brownell cojug. …	xxvij' die.

Mense Novembris

Wyllm. Beale & Margret Smythe cojug. … …	iij' die.
Christopher Nickson & Elizabethe hartleye cojug. ..	alt. die.

Mense Decembris

Robt. Parkin & Gartridge (Gertrude) Smylter cojug. …	x' die.
Wyllm. hodgeson & Elizabethe Cooper cojugat.... …	xij' die.

Mense Januarij

Anthonye Gest & Alice Dyckenson cojugat. …	ix' die.

Mense Februarij

[47] Gilbert Dickenson & Elizabethe howseleye cojugat. …	xvij' die.
John Lockwodde & Catherin Bower cojug. … …	xxiij' die.
Nicholas Smythe & margret Smythe cojug. … …	eod. die.

Mense Junij. [1584.]

Edward Keyes & Elizabethe Geslinge cojugat. … …	j' die.
Thomas Roodes & margret Jepson cojugat. … …	ij' die.

Mense Julij

Thomas Newton & margret Wylkinson cojugat.... …	vto. die.
Nicholas Byrleye & Agnes Sheyrclyffe cojugat. …	vij' die.
[48] Nicholas Wordsworthe & margret Wombwell cojug. …	xxij' die.

following notes :—1420. johannes de Stede surrenders 1 messuage in Southey to Robert de Stede and Matilda, his wife. 1429. Robert Stede appears in a surrender as a customary tenant. 1459. Robert de Stede surrenders 1 messuage and lands, in Onessere, to John de Stede, senior, his son. 1530. Nicholas Stede leases for 21 years all his lands, &c., in Onessere, to William Storth. 1531. Nicholas Steade surrenders 1 messuage, in Ughtibridge, to Richard Steade, his son, &c., &c. 1605. March 18. Richard Turner and Gertrude his wife, Reginald Hurt and Anna his wife seek to be admitted to lands in Oughtibridge, the said Anna and Gertrude being daughters and coheirs of Richard Stead, deceased.

[47] Gilbert Dickenson was son of William Dickenson, of Sheffield. In the court rolls appears the following:—1606. Oct. 2. William Dickenson, senior, late of Sheffield, having died about the 20th of May last, Gilbert Dickenson seeks to be admitted to lands in Chapeltown, as son and heir. 1621. Ap. 5. Gilbert Dickenson, of Howsley Hall, gent., surrenders land, &c., at Chapeltown, to the use of himself and his wife, Elizabeth. In the year 1593, he, together with William Dickenson, George Blount, Christopher Wilson, and others, were charged with felonious hunting in Wharncliffe Chase, &c. ; but they got a general pardon in 1605. Gilbert Dickenson died 1622, and was buried in Ecclesfield Church. Elizabeth Howsley was one of the daughters and co-heirs of Thomas Howsley, of Howsley Hall, gent. Vide, notes 12 and 203.

[48] Nicholas Wordsworth was of Shepherd's Castle, in the parish of Penistone; his son, Thomas Wordsworth, sold that property to the Rev. John Shaw, vicar of Rotherham. Margaret Wombwell was 3rd daughter and co-heir of Thomas Wombwell, of Thundercliffe Grange.

Mense Augusti.

Wyllm Slacke & Anne hatfeld conjug. ... iiijto die.

Mense Octobris.

⁴⁹ henrye Bannyster & Barbara Scotte cojugat. ... vjto die.
George Clarke & Catherin Jepson cojug. ... xj' die.

Mense Novembris.

Peter Kent & Agnes Swyfte cojugat. ... xxix' die.

Mense Januarij.

⁵⁰ Francis Stringer & Isabell Wombwell cojug. ... ... vjto' die.
Robt. Sheyrclyffe & jane Thwaytes conjug. cojug. ... ... ix' die.

Mense Maij. [1585.]

John Shawe & Johan Lyster cojugat. ... ... xiij' die.

Mense Augusti.

John Cooper & margret Gyldin cojugat. .. ... viij' die.
John mundye & Alice Bradley cojugat. .... ix' die.
Raulph hobson & Johan Wodde, cojug. ... ... xv' die.
Thome & hellen heye conjugat. ... ... xxij' die.

Mense Novembris.

Wyllm. Allen & Elizabeth Wroe conjugat. ... ... vij' die.

Mense Decembris.

Thomas Ellys & Alice Elmsall conjug. ... xxiij' die.

Mense Februarij.

Robt. Stones & Barbara Kaye conjug. ... ix' die.

Mense Maij. [1586.]

⁵¹ Rychard Mathyman & Elizabethe Rychardson con ... ... j' die.
henrye Yates & Johan Wylkinson conjg. ... ... viij' die.
Nicholas Watson & hellen Gylles conjug. ... ... xv' die.

Mense Junij.

⁵² Rychard Brown & margery Carre conjugat. ... vto die.

---

⁴⁹ Barbara Scott was daughter of Nicholas Scott, of Barnes Hall, gent. [Vide note 105.] Henry Bannyster had issue by her one daughter, Jane, who married William Dawson,

⁵⁰ Francis Stringer was of Whiston. Isabel Wombwell was 2nd daughter and co-heir of Thomas Wombwell, of Thundercliffe Grange.

⁵¹ Richard Mathyman was probably son of Richard Mathyman, by Margaret, his wife, daughter of Nicholas Sampson, of Foxhill. Vide note 109.

⁵² **Richard Brown was of** Cross House, in this parish. He died 1601; and his widow married secondly Ralph Richardson.

Mense Julij.

John Weynwright & Effam Cutte conjug.	...	xj' die.
John Wylkinson & margret Slatter conjug.	...	xxx' die.

Mense Septembris.

[53] Rychard Wats & Isabell Scott conjug.	...	xij' die.

Mense Octobris.

Robt. Slatter & margret hill conjug.	...	ix' die.

Mense Decembris.

John Gest & margret Raworthe conjugat.	... ...	j' die.

Mense Octobris. [1587.]

Godfreye Brooke et Gracia Coleye conjug.	... ...	xviij' die.
Robt. Sheyrcliffe & margret Bylcliffe conjug.	... ..	xxij' die.

Mense Decembris.

John Wodhouse & Anne Grubbe conjug.	...	iij' die.

Mense Januarij.

Thomas hinchlyffe & Johan Sanderson cojug.	...	xiiij' die.

Mense Februarij.

Anthonye Cutte & Elizabethe hobson conjug.	...	iiijto die.
Thomas . . . . . . & Elizabethe Chadwyeke cojug.		ood. die.
Thomas Mautham & Jane Wylde	...	. . . .
Wm. Smythe & Elizabethe hanghe cojug.		xvjto die junij'.

Mense Junij. [1588.]

Christopher West & Elizabethe Stanyforthe conjug.	...	vjto die.

Mense Augusti.

Nicholas Crofts & margaret Blowme conjug.	...	vjto die.

Mense Septembris.

Thomas Stanyforthe & johan Lawe conjug.	...	x' die.
Thomas Beale & margaret Smythe con.	...	xxijdo die.

Mense Novembris.

John Sheyrelyffe & hellen Crofts conjugat.	... ...	ijdo die.
Wyllm. Baxter & Barbara Stones conjug.	... ...	xix' die.

[53] Richard Watts was of Wortley; he was son of John Watts, of Muckleton, co. Salop, by Ann, his wife, daughter of Richard Scott, of Barnes Hall. Isabel Scott was relict of Thomas Scott, of Barnes Hall, who was grandson of the above-named Richard Scott, and daughter of Arthur Alcock, of St. Martin's Vintry, London. For a pedigree of this family, vide pp. 442-3, *Hunter's Hallamshire, Gatty's Edition.* Also see note 105.

Mense Januarij.

Thomas Cooper & marye Worsleye conjug.   xxrjto die.
Wyllm. Carre & Rose Parkin conjug.   xxij' die.

Mense Maij. [1589.]

Thomas Whiteleye . . . . conjg.   x' die.

Mense Junij.

Rychard Jepson & Johan Grubbe conjug.   ...   xxix' die.

Mense Julij.

Rychard Steede & Jane Wylson conjug.   vto die.
Thomas Crosleye & Jane Walker conjug.   j' die.

Mense Augustij.

John Greaves & margret Grene conjug.   ...   xx' die.

Mense Octobris.

Brian Ashton & Anne Tyngle conjug.   ...   ...   iij' die.
[54] Roger Scott & Anne man conjug. ...   .   xxj' die.
John hartleye & Anne Cutte conjug.   ...   ...   xxix' die.

Mense . . . .

Thomas hartleye & Elizabethe Wylkinson conjug.   ...
Wm. Jepson et Johan Waddye conjgat.   ...   ...

Mense Februarij.

John hartley & Rose Wodde conjugat.   ...   xxiij' die.

Mense Augusti. [1590.]

Wyllm. Geslinge & Anne Lyster conjugat.   ...   ...   xiiij' die.
Thomas Bowre (Bower) & Jennet Wodde conjug.   ...   xxiiij' die.
John Stigbucke & Jennet hobson conjug.   ...   ...   xvj' die.

Mense Octobris.

Nicholas Parkin & Johan Ragge conjug.   ...   vto die.
Thomas Shawe & Jane . . . . . . conjug.   ...   x' die.

Mense Decembris.

Raulphe hill & Johan Shawe conjug.   ...   x' die.
Robt. Boye & Alice Grubbe conjugat.   ...   xx' die.

Mense Januarij.

Robt. Wylkinson & Elizabethe Saursbye cojugat.   ...   ...   xxiij' die.

---

[54] Roger Scott was probably 2nd son of Richard, son of Richard Scott, of Barnes Hall. [Vide note 105.] He was a witness in the case of Dickenson and others, for felonious hunting in Wharncliffe Chase, in the year 1593, and was then aged 32 years, or thereabouts. *Vide Eastwood's History of Ecclesfield,* pp. 493—506.

Mense FEBRUARIJ.

Robt. Wyllye & jane holte congug.	vij' die.
Nicholas Slatter & margret heye conjug.	eod. die.
Rychard Saterfot & jennet Beighton conjug.	x' die.
Cotton hobson & Anne Parkin conjug.	ix' die.

Mense MAIJ. [1591.]

Francys Johnson & Barbara Chadwycke conjug.	ijdo die.
Willm. hatfeld & Dionis Nickson conjg.	xij' die.
Christopher Crofts & Elizabethe Genne conjug.	eod. die.

Mense JULIJ.

Thomas Scargell & Dorithie Sheircliffe con.	xx' die.

Mense AUGUSTI.

Robt. Rowbothom & jennet Blythman con.	x' die.
Thomas Smythe & Anne Ronksleye con.	xxix' die.

Mense SEPTEMBRIS.

John Dodworthe & Isabell hartley conjugat.	xvjto die.
James Bromheade & Isabell hartley con.	xvij' die.
Christopher haukshyrst & . . . . . . Bramald conjug.	xxj' die.
John Plats & joan Wylkinson conjugat.	xxij' die.

Mense OCTOBRIS.

Robt. Burgon & Agnes handleye cojugat.	xix' die.

Mense DECEMBRIS.

Thomas Smythe & Anne Stones cojugat.	vto die.
Wyllm. fyrthe & francys Bever cojugat.	x' die.
Christopher hunt & Elizabethe morton con.	. . . . . .

Mense JANUARIJ.

Thomas Cutler & Elizabethe Bowre (Bower) cojugat.	xx' die.
John Boye & jane foster conjugat.	xxx' die.
Richard Cutte & francys Taylyer cojug.	eod. die.

Mense MAIJ. [1592.]

John Pearson } Rychard Wodde } maryed	xx' die.

Mense AUGUSTI.

John marshe & hellen Bearde conjugat.	xx' die.

Mense SEPTEMBRIS.

Nicholas Walker & Elizabethe Boye cojug.	x' die.
John Weynwright & margret hill conju.	xvij' die.

Mense Octobris.

[55] henric Swyfte & Joan Darley con.   xxix' die.
John Taylyer & Agnes hartley cojug.   eod. die.
francs Bowre (Bower) & hellen handleye con.   xxx' die.

Mense Novembris.

Richard hobson & Agnes morton conjugat. ...   iiijto die.

Mense Decembris.

Willm. Wylkinson & Agnes Combe conjug. ...   x' die.
Laurence Saursbye & margret handley coju. ...   eod. die.

Mense Februarij.

Thomas Kaye & Dorithie Grene conjugat. ...   xviij' die.
Nicholas neyler & Alice Kent conjugat. ...   eod. die.

Mense Junij. [1593.]

Richard Carre & Catherin howle (Hoole) conjugat. ...   xij' die.
Rychard Wodde & Barbara Sheyrclyffe conjugat. ...   eod. **die.**

Mense Julij.

Edmund Senyer & Anne Tyngle conjug. ...   xvto die.

Mense Augusti.

[56] **Edward Selvester &** Anne Smythe conjug. ...   vto die.

Mense Novembris.

Alexandr. hartleye & Elizabeth Barnsleye con....   xxvto die.

Mense Decembris.

Charles Clarcke & Anne meller cejug. ...   ix' die.
John . . . . . . & Alice Smythe conjug. ...   eod. die.
John haughton & Anne haughe conjug. ...   xxj' die.

---

[55] In the churchwardens' accounts for 1584, appears the following entry:—"Itm for Henrye Swyfte his dynner when he came to vewe the bell yoke the dynners of the Churchewardens, Henrye Swyfte and his man and the Clarkes man at the amendinge of the sayd bell yoke—drincke for the ringers the same daye and wages for the sayd Henrye Swyfte and his man iiijs and iijd."

[56] Edward Silvester was of High Green, in this parish. He was churchwarden for **Grenefirth district in** the years 1594 and 1615, and ffeofee in 1616. He was married twice. By his second wife, Lucy Oxspring, whom he wedded 29 January, 1598-9 [*vide supra*] he had issue, *inter alios*, a son, Nicholas, bapt. 20 November, 1603, who married 3 November, 1623, Isabel Senior, and had issue two sons, Thomas, bapt. 9 May, 1624, and Edward Silvester. Thomas Silvester, the elder son, also married twice. By his first wife, Ellen, ... [who was buried 20 May, 1669,] he had issue John Silvester, of Birthwaite; Thomas Silvester, of the Tower of London; Edward Silvester, and Priscilla Silvester, bapt. 3 November, 1663, who married John Smith, of Ecclesfield, and was grandfather of John Silvester Smith, who was created a baronet 1783, and was ancestor of the present Sir Charles Edward Dodsworth, 5th Baronet of Newland, in the county of York, born 27 June, 1853. The following is an abstract of John Silvester, of Birthwaite's, will. It is dated 1719. He mentions Edward, son of my late brother, Edward Silvester, of the Tower of London; John Smith, son of my sister, Priscilla Smith; William, eldest **son of** my brother, Thomas Silvester, of the Tower of London, deceased; Thomas, youngest son of my brother Thomas; my niece, Sarah Senithorpe; Thomas and Hannah, younger children of my late brother Thomas; my niece, Sarah Gilbert, eldest daughter of my brother Thomas; her husband, Thomas Gilbert; my niece, Sarah Serjeantson.

Mense Januarij.

Robt. hartleye & hellen Parkin conjugat.	...	xx' die.
Wyllm. hyde & marye Cooper cojug.	...	xxx' die.

Mense Februarij.

Godfreye Byrleye & Anne Wylson conjug.	...	...	iij' die.
Thomas Carre & Rose Meller con. ...	...	...	eod. die.

Mense Junij. (1594.)

Richard Relfe (Revell) & Alice Bromheade conjugat.	...	...	xx' die.
Alexandr. Bearde & Elizabethe Shawe con.	...	...	eod. die.

Mense Julij.

Thomas Ragge & margret Crosleye conjugat. ...		vij' die.
Wm. Lockwodde & Elizabeth Senier con.	...	xx' die.

Mense Augusti.

Alexandr. Cooper & hellen Smythe conjug.	...	vjto die.
John Dobson & margret Keefe conjugat.	...	xx' die.

Mense Octobris.

Robt. Wodde & Johan Ellys con. ...	...	...	viiij' die.
Robt. Bowre (Bower) &	...	...	....
Raulphe Trulove & hellen Wylde conjug.	...	...	....
henrye foxe & johan Goodyr conjugat.	...	...	xx' die.
Josephe Lorde & Alice Rychardson conjug.	...	...	eod. die.
henry Weynwright & margret Lepton con.	...	...	eod. die.
[67] Gerard freeman & Anne howsleye con.	...	...	xxij' die maij' 1594.
George mychell & Alice Boale con. ...	...	...	xxvij' Septembris.

Mense Januarij.

Robt. Cooper & Isabell Shawe conjugat.	...	xix' die.

Mense Februarij.

Thomas Steele & margret Wylson con.	...	...	xx' die.
John Downinge & margret ...... con.	...	...	eod. die.

Mense Septembris. [1595.]

Robt. Carre & Dorithie Sheirclyffe con.	...	...	...	x' die.
henrie Rodes & Isabell Sheirclyffe conjug.	...	...	...	xix' die.

---

[67] **By this** marriage the Freemans inherited the estate of Howsley Hall. **The family died out in** the male line in 1783, when Howsley Freeman departed this life [according to Mr. Eastwood] **unmarried**. He was baptized 28 April, 1712, and I find in the registers at Wath-upon-Dearne this entry:—"1735, June 24, Mr. Howsley Freeman and Mrs. Anne Wharam, married." Anyway, he died without issue, and his three sisters succeeded to the estates. The last representative of them, Lydia Lambert, who married Rev. John Mackereth, of Wakefield, and took the name of Freeman, left by her will, proved 31 May, 1837, the Howsley Hall estate to the Right Honble. James Stuart Wortley, brother of the late Lord Wharncliffe, who has since sold it to his nephew, the present Earl of Wharncliffe.

⁵⁸ John hall & Alice Stones conjug. ... xxj' die.
John Bullus & francis Carre con. ... eod. die.
Richard Robinson & hellen Wyllye con. ... xxvj' die.

Mense Novembris.

Nicholas man & jane Shawo con. ... ... j' die.
john Parkin & Agnes Kent con. ... ... xxx' die.

Mense Junij. [1596.]

Robt. Wylkinson & An Tothill conjugat. ... ... xxviij' die.

Mense Octobris.

Robt. Cooper & francis ...... con. ... xviij' die.
Willm. Combe & Anne Carre conjug. ... ... xxx' die Januarii.

Mense Februarij.

Robt. Wyldsmithe & Rose hyne conjugat. ... ... j' die.
hughe Wolleye & jenet Sateriet con. ... ... ijdo die.
⁵⁹ Rychard Wylson & Emot Thompson con. ... ... iij' die.
Robt. haukshirst & Alice Bever con. ... ... vij die.

Mense Aprilis. [1597.]

Richard Butcher & Alice Bearde conjug. ... ... xvij' die.

⁵⁸ John Hall was of Barley Hole, in the parish of Wentworth, tanner; he was eldest son of Henry Hall, of Oughtibridge, by his first wife, Ann, daughter of Henry Morton, and was bapt. at Bradfield, 12 Feb., 1564. He had issue a son, Henry Hall, of Barley Hole and Oughtibridge, who, dying 1643, left issue, by Mary, his wife, Thomas, his eldest son, whose line ended in one Martha, who married Samuel Goodison, and George Hall, who, dying 1705, left issue by his wife Dorothy a son and heir, George Hall, who, dying 1722, left issue by his wife, Mary Hawksworth, four sons, Henry, the eldest of whom, more anon ; George Hall, a cutler; Rev. Joseph Hall, curate of Wortley; and the Rev. Benjamin Hall, of the Abbey Derwent. Henry Hall, the eldest son, married, 1719, Martha Hall, and, dying 1747, left issue Joseph Hall and others. Joseph Hall, dying 1790, left issue by Ann, his wife, an only daughter and heir, Martha Hall, who married George Grayson, of Rossington, who dying 6 December, 1838, left issue an only daughter and heir, Ann Grayson, who married John Bedford, of Ponds, in the parish of Penistone, who was father of the present John Bedford, of Birley House and Oughtibridge.

⁵⁹ Richard Wilson was of Oughtibridge Hall, son of Thomas, son of Thomas Wilson, of the same, who was 2nd son of Richard Wilson, of Broomhead. He had issue a son, Thomas Wilson, of Oughtibridge Hall, who dying in an. 1676, left issue two daughters and co-heirs, viz., Mary, who married first Thomas Shirecliffe, of Whitley Hall, and had issue, and secondly Francis Jesopp, of Braudcliffe ; and Emot Wilson, who married first Edmund Hobson, of Bradfield and Thurgoland, and secondly Leonard Reresby, of Ecclesfield, gent., 4th son of Sir George Reresby, Knt., of Thriberg. By him she had issue a son and heir, Francis Reresby, and a daughter, Mary, who married, 21 September, 1693, William Sitwell, of Sheffield, and was ancestor of the present Sir George Reresby Sitwell, Bart., of Renishaw, co. Derby. Francis Reresby, above-named, married Alice, daughter of Nicolas Herket, of Anston, and, dying ano. 1722, left issue a son, John Reresby, and a daughter, Mary, who married 18 April, 1715, George Phipps, of Wortley Hall, gent., son of George Phipps, of Highgreen House, gent. John Reresby married Hannah, daughter of ..... Johnson, of Bawtry, and settled at Caistor, in co. Lincoln. He was buried in the Reresby vault, in the nave of Ecclesfield Church, 25 September, 1732, and left issue a son, John Reresby, born 13 September, 1728, who was of Queen's College, Cambridge, and took his B.A. degree. He was living in Maryland, America, in 1777. John Reresby, of Caistor, also left issue a daughter, Ann Reresby, who lived in the town of Doncaster. She left by her will, dated 29 June, 1801, large charities to this parish ; and dying 1802, was buried in the Reresby vault, in Ecclesfield Church.

Mense Junij.

Willmo. Brownell & jennet hill con. ...	vto die.
Philippe morton & hellen Cowper conjug. ...	vjto die.
Edward Creswycke & Dionesse Crosleye con. ...	eod. die.

Mense Septembris.

Rychard Gylles & margaret Oxspringe con. ...	iiijto die.
Thomas Creswycke & Dorithie Revell con. ...	xix' die.

Mense Octobris.

[60] Thomas hoylande & Isabell Sheyrclyffe conjug....	iij' die.
henrye Spytlehouse & margret Weynwright con. ...	xvjto die.
George Byrkes & hellen Collye conjugat. ...	xxiiijto die.

Mense Novembris.

John Walker & Grace Sparke con. ...	vij' die.
Willm. Kyrkbye & Anne Burgon con. ...	xxvij' die.

Mense Maij. [1598.]

henrye hadfeld & margerye Gylles conjugat. ...	vij' die.
Richard Swynden & Lucye Aldam con. ...	xiiijto die.
Laurence Wade & Johan hill con. ...	xxx' die.

Mense Junij.

henrye foxe & jane Jopson conjug. ...	xij' die.

Mense Julij.

Nicholas Seargell & Agnes mathyman ...	ijdo. die.

Mense Septembris.

George Turner & francis Bloome conjug. ...	xxiiijto die.

Mense Octobris.

John Lockwodde & Elizabethe Shawe con. ...	xxjx' die.

Mense Decembris.

John Chappell & Elizabethe Gilberthorp conjug. ...	vto die.

Mense Januarij.

[61] Edward Selvester & Lucy Oxspringe conjugat. ...	xxix' die
Robt. Sheirclyffe & Anne Tymploye conjug. ...	xxx' die.

Mense Februarij.

willm. Parkin & margret Parkin conjug. ...	vto die.
henrye Ibotson & francys Brigge conjugat. ...	xij' die.
willm. Richardson & Isabell Grene conjug. ...	xiij' die.
Raulph Button & margret Smythe con. ...	xviij' die.

[60] Vide notes 17 and 79.

[61] Vide note 56.

Mense Aprilis. [1599.]

Thomas mylner & Elizabeth Smythe conjug. ... ... xxiij' die.

Mense Maij.

henrye Sawodde & Emot Grene con. ... j' die.
Thomas Bower & frances handleye con. ... viij' die.
Wyllm. hill & hellen Lyster con. ... ... xiij' die.

Mense Junij.

Thomas Weynwright & Elizabethe Bassette con. ... vto. die.
Johnes Ragge et Cicilia hall conjugat. ... ... xvij' die.

Mense Septembris.

henrye foxe et margret Creswycke con. ... iij' die.
Wm. Clarke & Alicia Downinge conjug. ... ix' die.
Nicholaus Sheircliffe et Jenetta Bower con. ... x' die.
Thomas Trippet et Anna Oxspringe conjug. ... xvj' die.

Mense Octobris.

Thomas Creswycke et margret Shooter con. ... ... x' die.
[62] Richardus Waterhouse & margeria Swynden conjug. ... xiiij' die.
Robt. mathyman & Jenet heye conjugat. ... xxviij' die.

Mense Novembris. [1599.]

Willus. fearnleye et Isabella hoylande cojugat. ... ... xiij' die.

Mense Decembris.

Nicholaus Sheyrclyffe et Dorithea Treeton con. ... xj' die.
Josepho Lorde et Alice Newbott con. ... xiij' die.

Mense Januarij.

John Sugden et Anne Twigge conjug. ... ... xx' die.

Mense Aprilis. [1600.]

Robto. hobson et margaret fearnleye conjugat. ... ... xiiijto die.
Alexander hill et Anne Bower con. ... ... xx' die.
John Ronksleye et Dinissa hartleye con. ... ... xxvj' die.

Mense Maij.

Johnes. Grene et Anne Seargell conjugat. ... iiij' die.
Robt. mason et margret hill con. ... eod. die.

Mense Julij.

Thomas Parkyn et margaret Neyler conjugat. ... xxij' die.

Mense Augusti.

John Wigfall & Anne Bower conjug. ... ultimo die.

[62] Vide note 45.

Mense Novembris.

Richardus Caterell et Jana Shawe con.	ixno die.
Wm. Byrkes et Catherin Keyes con.	xvjto die.

Mense Decembris.

Nicholas Caterell et Elizabetha Dyson conjug. …	primo die.

Mense Januarij.

Robto. jepson et margret Lorde conjugat. …	xxvto die.

Mense Februarij.

Petrus mylner et Anna heye conj. …	xixno die.
Thomas hartleye et margret Ragge con. …	eod. die.

Mense Aprilis. [1601.]

Leonrd. Crosse et Chirstian Dodworthe conjug. …	xixno die.

Mense Maij.

Robto. Baylye et Jane Wylde conjuga. …	ix' die.
Thomas Barnsleye et Julian Wylkinson conjugat	xxiij' die.
Richard Wygfall et jennet Butcher con. …	eod. die.

Mense Julij.

Richard Croshawe et Elizabetha Eyre conjugat.	j' die.
marke Stafforthe et jane Smythe con. …	vij' die.
Nicholas Waterall et Isabell Sheemelde con. …	xxv' die.

Mense Augusti.

Renald hutchonson & Isabell Wodde conjugat. …	iij' die.
ffrancisco hobson & hellene handleye conjugat. …	ultimo die.
Nicholaus Dyson & Isabelle Genue conjug. … …	eod. die.

Mense Septembris.

John ffyrthe & Agnes heye conjugat. … …	xxviij' die.

Mense Octobris.

Simon heye & Isabell Collye con. … …	xix' die.
John Byrrye & Jane Oxspringe con. …	xxvj' die.
Thomas Oldham & Anne Wilkinson con. …	eod. die.
henrye Page & Anne morton con. … …	eod. die.

Mense Novembris.

Rogero Throppe & margaret Twigge con.	viij' die.
Willus. Nickson & Elizabetha Clarcke con. …	xvj' die.
francis Rogers & Anne mason con. … …	xxix' die.

Mense DECEMBRIS.

Thomas haughe & Alicia Oxpringe con. ... vij' die.
[63] Thomas Sheircliffe & maria Pawson con. ... viij' die.

Mense FEBRUARIJ.

Richard Batleye & Dionysse hatfeld con. iij' die.
Nychas. Sheircliffe & Catherin Brownell con. vjto die.
Richard Breereleye & hellen Bacon con. vij' die.

Mense MAIJ. [1602.]

John Walker & Anne Gee conjugat. ... xij' die.

Mense JUNIJ.

Edwardo morton & marye Parkyn con. ... xij' die.
Laurence Place & margret Weinwright con. ... xiij' die.

Mense JULIJ.

Wm. Arsdale & Jennet Wodheade conjug. ... ... xjmo die.

Mense AUGUSTI.

francys Danyel & Alicia Parkin con. ... xxij' die.

Mense SEPTEMBRIS.

Edward Smythe & Alicia Sheircliffe con. ... ... viij' die.

Mense OCTOBRIS.

Lauretio Whitwell & margaret Smythe con. ... iij' die.
Johes. Bower & Elizabeth Bagshawe conjug. ... xvij' die.
Wyllm. Barnsleye & Dionise Byrleye conjug. xxvjto die.

Mense NOVEMBRIS.

Thomas Machon & Barbara Saterfett conjug. ... ij' die.
Thomas Bearde & frances Casson con. ... vij' die.
Thomas Byrkes & Isabell Brigge con. ... ultimo die.

Mense JANUARIJ.

Nicholas Stanyforthe & Ann Staniforthe con. ... xvij' die.

Mense MARTIJ.

Petrus Thorppe et Isabella Cutte conjug. ... vij' die.

Mense MARTIJ. [1603.]

Robts. Wilkinson & Jane Ramsden con. ... ... viij' die.
John Crosley et hellen Royse con. ... ... xxij' die.

[63] Thomas Shireeliffe was son and heir of Robert Shireeliffe, of Whitley Hall, gent. [vide note 29.] Maria Pawson was daughter of Thomas Pawson, of Windmill Hill, in this parish.

Mense Junij.

John Sparke et Elizeb. hill con.	vto die.
John hill et jenet Watson con.	code. die.
Michael Kempe et Alicia Shawe con. ...	vjto. die,
Anthonie hardye et margret Sickes (Sykes) con.	xvto die.

Mense Julij.

Nychol. foster et Bettrise Lytlewodde con. ...	x' die.
Richard holley et margr. Burton con. ...	xx' die.
Raulphe Rawlin et . . . . . Swinden con. ...	xxij' die.

Mense Octobris.

John Myrfin et francis firth con.	ij' die.

Mense Novembris.

Raulphe Basforth et hellen Gen con. ...	xiiijto die.

Mense Decembris.

Thomas Smith et Elizab. Milner con.	xj' die.
Will Relfe (Revell) et . . . . . . Bower con.	cod. die.
John Beighton et Cicill morton con.	xij' die.
Radus. Hepworth et Margret Pkin (Parkin) con. ...	xviij' die.
[64] Nycho. hurt et Jennet Broadheade con.	xixno die.
James Geslinge et hellen Ward con.	xxij' die.

Mense Aprilis. [1604.]

Thomas Gaughe et Margret Combe con. ..	xxixno die.

Mense Maij.

John hall & Anne Bower con.	j' die.

Mense Augusti.

Willm. Wodde et Elizab. . . . . . . con. ...	xij' die.
Will hartley et Bettrisse Gillot con. ...	xx' die.
Radus. Grubbe et Rose Matheman co. ...	xxvjto die.
[65] James Greene et Anne Shercliffe con. ...	xxviij' die.

[64] Nicholas Hurt was of Woodseats, in this parish, and son of Robert Hurt, of Haldworth, in the chapelry of Bradfield, where he was baptized 13 January, 1576-7 [vide note 16.] By Jennet Broadhead, who was his first wife, he had issue, *inter-alios*, a son and heir, Robert Hurt, bapt. 19 February, 1603-4, who married, 1629, Margaret, daughter and heir of Robert Warter, of Brampton-en-le-Morthen, and had issue a son, Jonathan, whose son Valentine moved from Woodseats to Hesley Farm; Valentine Hurt had issue a son, Jonathan, baptized at Rotherham, 26 November, 1691, who married, first, Frances Statham, and had issue; and, secondly, Catherine, daughter and final heir of William Sitwell, of Sheffield, by Mary Reresby, his wife [vide note 59.] By this second marriage Jonathan Hurt had issue a son and heir, Francis Hurt, who assumed, by Royal sign manual, dated 7 March, 1777, the arms and name of Sitwell, and was father of Sir Sitwell Sitwell, the first Baronet of Renishaw, and ancestor of the present Sir George Reresby Sitwell, Bart., of the same.

[65] James Green was 3rd son of Thomas Green, of Cawthorne, gent. Ann Shercliffe was daughter and co-heir of Nicholas Shercliffe, of Ecclesfield Hall, gent. [Vide note 36.] By this marriage the property of Thundercliffe Grange passed into the hands of the family of Green. For a pedigree of this family see *Hunter's Hallamshire*, *Gatty's Edition*, p. 449.

Mense SEPTEMBRIS.

henryo Wright et Anno Gillot con. ... ... iij' die.

Mense OCTOBRIS.

⁶⁶ George Burdett et Sara Browne con. xviij' die.
Eduardus Wardill et Joan Cooke con. ... xxvto die.

Mense NOVEMBRIS.

George Thorpe et Elizab Smith con. ... x' die.

Mense JANUARIJ.

John Coop (Cooper) et Joahn Swinden con. ... xiiijto die.

Mense FEBRUARIJ.

henryo Bayliffe et Margret Swath con. ... ... iij' die.
Robtus. Stepheson (Stephenson) et Bettris Marsden con. ... ixno die.

Mense APRILIS. [1605.]

Thomas Milner & Elsabethe Shawe despons. ... ... 2i' die.
Nycholas foster et Isabella Stacie despons. ... ... 28' die.

Mense MAIJ.

Carolus Crofts et Katherena Smith despons. ... ... i2' die.
Johes. hirst et Elizabethe Parkins despons. ... ... 20' die.
Thomas Parkins et Alicia Smith despons. ... ... 2i' die.
Georgius Birkinshawe et Anna Bridges despons. ... eod. die.
Renoldus Marshall et Margreta Revell despons. ... 28' die.

Mense JUNIJ.

Thomas Brooke et Alicia Warde despons. ... 4to die.
Richardus Warde & Margreta Matheman despons. ... 30' die.

Mense JULIJ.

Johes. Shoter et hellena Shoter despons. ... ... 4to die.
⁶⁷ Willus. Stonnes et Elsabel Pawson despons. ... ... 24to die.

Mense AUGUSTI.

Willms. Brownell et Janna Tayler despons. ... 4to die.
Willius. Basfordo et Alicia Lister despons. ... i0' die.
henricus Storke et Anna hill despons. ... i9' die.

---

⁶⁶ George Burdett was son and heir of Richard Burdett, of Denby Hall, gent. [*Vide Hunter's Deanery of Doncaster, vol. II., pp.* 350-1.] Sarah Browne was daughter and heir of Edward Browne, of Creswick, gent., who was son of William, son of William, son of John, son of Hugh Browne, of Creswick, living 1467.

⁶⁷ Elizabeth Pawson was a daughter of Nicholas Pawson, of Windmill Hill; by her husband, William Stones, she had issue a son, Thomas. *Hunter's Hall., Gatty's Ed.,* p. 446, *note.*

Mense Septembris.

Willm. Robts. (Roberts) et Anna hopton despons.	i5to die.
Edwardus Burie et Elizabet Smith despons. ...	22' die.

Mense Octobris.

Johes. Oxspringe et Margeria heye despons. ...	28' die.

Mense Novembris.

Johes. Mendlove et Maria milner despons. ...	i5to die.
Willius. hargrasse et Maria Secker despons. ...	22' die.

Mense Februarij.

Thomas Gilles et Anna Moorehouse despons.	i6to die.
Johes. Wilde et Maria Greeves despons.	i7' die.
[68] Radus. Richerdson et Margeria Browne despons. ...	25to die.

Mense Aprilis. [1606.]

Jacobus huscrafte et Gillia harrison despons.	24to die.

Mense Maij.

Willm. dinneson and francis Cowper conjugat. ...	ye 4 day Anno p.

June.

[69] George Spenser and dorothye brownell conjugat.	xij' die.
[70] Robert Wilkinson and Elsabell fletcher conjugat.	xxx die June.

Julij.

John Gooder and Emot Carre conjugat. ...	j die julij.
Robert Waynewright and margret Gooder conjugat	xxvj julij.

August.

Charles bullus and jennet Pickhaver conjugat. ...	iij die Augusti.

Mense September.

John clarke and Elsabethe Loxt conjugat. ..	vij die.
nicholas beane and Katteran hodskinson conjugat.	xiiij' die.

Mense October.

John basworthe and Alice fearnley conjugat.	vth of october.
Willm. Willecars (Whittaker?) and jayne bealey was married her xvij of october.	

[68] Vide note 52.

[69] George Spencer was of Newhall Grange, and 2nd son of William Spencer, of Bramley Grange. *Vide p.* 416, *Hunter's Hall., Gatty's Ed.*

[70] 1606, July 1, William Wilkinson, senior, of Crowder House, yeoman, surrenders his lands, &c., at Crowder House, to his own use for life, and after his decease to the use and behoof of Robert Wilkinson, his son and heir apparent, and Isabella, his wife, daughter of William Fletcher, of Marshburgh [Masbrough?], in co. York, yeoman. Crowder House is now the property of Bernard Wake, of Abbeyfield, near Sheffield, who purchased it a few years since from certain members of the Wilkinson family.

DECEMBER.

John Trippet and Anne Tyncker was married the vij of december.
nicholas creswicke and dinis hobson was married the viij day of december.

JANUARI.

hugh allan (Allen) and alice walker con.	xth.
John frickley and jennet barley (Byrley ?) conjugatu.	die Januarij.
[71] Humphre duckmanton and Jennet tarnell con.	xxv.

Mense FFEBRUARIJ.

Willm. crosley and Elsabethe trulove con.	primo die.
Ranlphe Stoones and Jayne Parkine con.	xth february.
Tho. flinte and Anne Jepson con.	xth februarij.
Edward Trulove and Cisselye ootes (Oates) con.	xvj februarij.
Richard Willye and Elsabethe hobson con.	xvj februarij.

Mense MAIJ. [1607.]

henry Nailor and joan Taylor congu.	decimo die.
Robert parkine and mary birst congu.	decimo die.

Mense JUNIJ.

Robert howden and Elsabethe bromhead congu.	viij' die.
James Lister and dionis Steade congu.	viiij' die.
Richard oulfeld and Elsabethe dey congu.	22.
Robert Tomlinson and Elsabeth Sparke congu.	28.
Ralphe Lee and dionis morton congu.	secundo die.

Mense JULIJ.

Willm. hall and Anne brownell congu.	28'

Mense AUGUSTI.

Thomas Wright and Elsabethe birkes conjug.	2i'

OCTOBER.

henry Turner & marget parkin congu.	i2'
Johna carr and Alice stafford conjug.	xviij'

NOVEMBER.

Robert casson & Elsabethe Tyngle con.	22'
Anthonie Rawlinson & Anne Shireliffe con.	23'

DECEMBER.

Christopher nixson and Esabell hill con.	6'

JANUARIJ.

George Birkes and marget Jepson con.	i3.

[71] Humphrey Duckmanton, or "Owmfraye Dockmantane," was fined "iijs and iiijd at the great court howlden at Sheffelde the xx day of april 1609 for breakinge of headges in the ox close."

February. [1608.]

Richard Carr and hellen Goslinge con. ... 4'

Mense Maij.

James howmes (Holmes) & dorothie Stafford con. ... j'
Thomas hall & Elsabeth Lister con. ... ... 25 die.

Mense Junij.

Robert Cawme (Combe?) and Alice Cooke conju. ... i9'
Thomas Parkin & francis Smythe con. ... ... 26'

Mense Julij.

John Shawe and Alice Lockwood conjug. ... iij'
Nicholas Twigge and mary Swallow con. ... x'
Willm. hartley and Katheran Swallowe con. ... 24'

Mense Augusti.

[72] henry hall do owghtye bridge (Oughtibridge) & dorathie fox con. ... ij'
John Bromhead and margret marshall conjuga.... ... ... iiij'
Robert Foxe and Anne hauxworthe (Hawksworth) pochim de Sheifeld conjugat. xviij'
francis Woodhouse & Elsabeth Wright conjugat. ... ... xx4'
Peter dey and Anne dale conjugat. ... ... 28'

September.

Willm. hincheclyffe and alice peycocke cong. ... j'

October.

Cotton hobson and Isabell wilkinson conju. ... 26.

November.

John morris and dorothie hartley conju. ... 6.
xxofer crofts and Anne dickonson conju. ... 13.

December.

Thomas Staniforthe and Joan carr conju. ... xj'

Januarie.

Willm. Nutt and marie Wilkinson conjugat. ... 29.

Mense Februarij.

Thomas Staniland and Barbara Jepson con. ... ... vth.

Mense Maij. [1609.]

Rychard hall ett Jann . . . . . . conjug. ... ... vijth day.
Wyllm. Baylyff ett Anne Waddie conjug. ... ... xxviijth day.

---

[72] Henry Hall, of Oughtibridge, was father of John Hall, of Barley Hole. [Vide note 58.] His first wife died ano. 1605, and he married secondly as above. He was buried at Bradfield, 20 September, 1617, and Dorothy, his wife, 5 September, 1626.

Mense Julij.

Tho. hall ett Ann Sunderland con. ... ... xvjth day.

Mense Septembris.

Tho. wryght ott Dorythye mawkin con. ... ... xxiiijth day.

Mense Octobris.

George Turner ett Ellin Jepson con. ... xvth day.

Mense Novembris.

James Tymplay ett Barbara wainwright conju. ... vjth day.
George hobson ett Elsabeth Lee con. ... xxvjth day.

Mense February.

joseph Lord ett Ann Bover con. ... ... xviijth day.
[73] James Twyvill (Twybell?) ett Ann beye con. ... xixth day.

Junius. [1610.]

Georgius Turner et Issabella Oxpringe conjugat. ... iiijto die junij.
Johannes hinchclyffe et Gertrude Stones conjug. ... xij' die junij.

Julius.

[74] Johes. Machin et Robecca Lord conjugati. ... ... viij' die Julij.

September.

Georgius hobson et Eliz. Lee conjugati tertio die Septembris.
Jacobus Tympley et Barbara Waynwright conjug. ... vjto die Sept.
Thomas Smith et Margreta Ragge conjug. ... ... xij' die Septem.
Johes. Tompson et Alicia ffoster conjugat. ... ... xxx' die Septem.

October.

Johes. hall et Margreta Genne conjugat. ... ... vij die Octobr.
Willmus. waterhouse et Anna Pearesen conjug. ... . x' die Oct.
Robertus Butcher et Dorothea Blacker conjug. ... ... xxj' die Octobr.

November.

Johes. Staniforth et jana Crashawe conjugat. ... vto die Novembr.
Robertus Carre et Dorothea Savill conjug. ... xj' die Novembris.

---

[73] In Harrison's Survey, 1637, "James Twible *alias* Cooke" is returned as holding at will a tenement, called Southall and lands, at a yearly rent of £20. He held some office in the Earl of Shrewsbury's household. He was succeeded at Southall, or Southey Hall, by three generations of James Twybells, the last of whom had a son Thomas, who succeeded on his father's death in 1750, but died in 1760. The farm then passed into the hands of William Vickers, 3rd son of Edward Vickers, or Vicars, of Ouchthorpe Lane, Wakefield, by Mary, his wife, daughter of Thomas Rawson, of Wardsend [vide *Hunter's Hall., Gatty's Ed., pp. 450-1*], who had married, 26 December, 1755, Elizabeth, daughter of the above James Twybell. For information concerning this branch of the family of Vickers, see *Eastwood's History of Ecclesfield*.

[74] John Machin was probably son of John Machin, of Longley. [Vide note 30.] Rebecca Lord was one of the daughters of Richard Lord, vicar of Ecclesfield. In her will, she directs that her body may be buried in the grave of her father. [Vide note 201.] Vicar Lord's tombstone is still in Ecclesfield churchyard, dated 1600.

JANUARIUS.

Thomas Cutler et Anna Ealand conjug.	...	xxij' die Januarij.
Johes. Beete et Margreta Gilles conjugat.	...	xxix' die Januarij.

FFEBRUARIUS.

Johes. Crosley et Katharina Bower conjug.	...	iijto die ffobruarij.

JUNE. [1611.]

John Trickett & Katherin Crosley connjugat.	...	xxth of June.

JULY.

Wyllm. machon & Ann Crofts conjugat.	...	the viijth julij.

OCTOBER.

james fosterd & cyslye hanley conjugat.	...	the xxth of october.
Robt. Broadbent & Elsabeth Cutt conjugat.	...	the xxvjth october.

DECEMBER.

Gilbart Cresswick & Elsabeth Carr conjugat.	...	ye xxth of december.

JANUARY.

henry Baylyff & Ellin clark conjugat.	...	the xvth of january.

APRILL. [1612.]

john Barnsley & mary Newell connjugat.	...	ye xxvjth.

MAIJ.

Nycholas Catterall & Elsabeth bullock con.	...	ye iiijth.

JUNE.

[75] Edward mason & Ann Phipes con...	...	ye first.
Robt. Barber & mary Shooter con. ...	...	ye xxiiijth.
Nycholas wadelove (Waddilove) & mary marsden con.	...	ye xxxth.
Wyllm. mookson & Ann morton con.	...	ye same day.

JULIJ.

Nycholas Lynfett & Ann Chatterton con.	...	...	...	ye xjth.
henry hauksworth & jane marshall con.	...	...	...	ye xijth.
[76] wyllm. hoolle & Elsabeth dickonson con.	...	...	...	ye xiiijth.

[75] Ann Phipes was probably daughter of Humphrey Flypps, of Tankersley, who in his will, dated 1 October, 1601, mentions my sons, William, Thomas, John, George, and Richard; my daughters, Anne and Frances; my wife, Jennett. Humphrey Flypps was buried at Tankersley, 6 October, 1607.

[76] William Hoole was of Crooks, in the parish of Sheffield. Elizabeth Dickenson was daughter and heir of Edward Dickenson, of Southey, by Elizabeth, his wife, daughter and co-heir of John Colley, of Southey, who was son of John, son of John, son of John Colley, of Southey, who was dead ano. 1486. The name of Colley is no doubt derived from the place Cowley, in this parish. 1414, June 8, Robertus Coop surrenders 2 Acres in Grenow (Grenoside) to Henricus Cowley and Ellena, his wife. 1420, July 6, Henricus Cowley surrenders 1 Messuage and 4 Acres in Woodeyde to Robertus del Ker. William Hoole had issue by his wife, Elizabeth, two sons, John and James, and from John is descended the Hooles, of Ravenfield and Edgefield, in the chapelry of Bradfield.

August.

Wyllm. hart & Elsabeth Curtis connjugat. ... ye ixth.

September.

Robt. Carter & Issabell mollar connjugat. ... ye xiijth.
Rogger Slatter & Elsabeth maryatt connjugat. ... yo same day.
Peter Kent & joan Sikes (Sykes) connjugat. ... ye xxth.
henry Rogger & Ellin ffalley connjugat. ... ye xxvijth.
water (Walter) hurt & mary pogmore connjugat. ... ye xxviijth.

October.

Robt. howsley & Ann hill connjugat. ye xviijth.
Wyllm. Allen & Ann Bradburne connjugat. ... xxvth.

November.

John Breffett & Elsabeth mathiman connjugat. ... ye xvth.

December.

Rychard Nedom & Ann Sharp connjugat. ... ye xxjth.

Jan.

John parkin & Ellin Broadhead connjugat. ... ye xxviijth.

ffebruary.

Tho. Walker & Issabell Breares connjugat ... ye vjth.
Nycholas Slatter & Elsabeth Crofts connjugat. ... ye ixth.

Maij. [1613.]

John Bower & Ann Rollinson connjugat. ... ye xxvth.

June.

John Crawshaw & Ann Teayler connjugat. ... ye xxviijth.

July.

Wyllm. Charlesworth & margery Catterall connjugat. ... ye iiijth.
Tho. Carr & Ann Greaves connjugat. ... ... ye vjth.

September.

John Clarke & Ann hill conjugat. ... ... the xxijth.

October.

Thomas Unwen & Ann Turnley conjugat. ... ... the ij day.

November.

John Nawte & Ann hall conjugat. ... ... the vjth.
[77] John Skyers & Martha Lord conjugat. ... the xiijth.
Rogger Cowper & Ann Wood connjugat. ... the same day.

---

[77] John Skyers was one of the Skyers of the parish of Wentworth. Martha Lord was probably one of the daughters of Richard Lord, vicar of Ecclesfield. [Vide note 201.]

DECEMBER.

Lawrence Eayre (Eyre) & Ann Stringer conjugat.	...	...	the iiijth.
Peter Pickforke & Katherin Shadforth conjugat.	...	...	yo same day.
John Peace & Elsabeth Nyckson conjugat.	...	...	the vjth.
Wyllm. Gest & Elsabeth Broadbont conjugat.	...	...	the xth.
ffebuary ffrancis Broadhead & Ann Beighton, of Sheffeld pih. conjugat.	...		the xxiiijth.
John morton & mary Chetam conjugat.	...	...	xxvijth.

MAIJ. [1614.]

Robt. Barnsley franncis Creswicko conjugat.	...	...	xxiiijth.
Tho. Swainson margret Sheppard conjugat.	...	...	xxiiijth.
John hill Elsabeth Longley conjugat.	...	...	first day of Novemb.
George Wade margrett Wilkinson conjugat.	...	...	xxx novemb.
Robt. Sheirtcliff Ann howgat conjugat.	...	...	the iiijth of dec.
Jo. Linfett Issabell Breffett conjug....	...	...	xijth.
Robt. Woodhouse Elsabeth Ashton conjug.	...	...	xixth.

ffEBURARIE.

Xxopher. Penington Joan Duckinton con.	...	...	iiijth.
henry Shaw and Als (Alice) Brooke...	...	...	vth.

APRILL. [1616.]

henry Tysdall & Anne Swallow con.	...	...	xxviijth.

MAY.

Wm. howsley & Jane hall con.	...	...	vjth.
Robt. hobson & Ellin ⁞ . . . . . con.	...	...	xvth.

AUGUST.

[78] Thomas hoyland & Issabell Shercliffe con.	...	...	iiijth.
Thomas Raggo & Margerie . . . . con.	...	...	eod. die.
Wm. Poplewell & Elsabeth . . . . . con.	...	...	eod. die.
[79] John Longlie & Ellin Marsh con.	...	...	eod. die.

SEPTEM.

Thomas Kirkbye & Ellen Senior con.	...	...	jth.
James holland & An Shooter	...	...	iijth.
Richard Broadley & An howlmes con.	...	...	xxviijth.
John Mirfin & Katherin Marsden con.	...	...	xxjx.

NOVEMBER.

Wm. Stephenson & Mary Boy con....	...	...	xth.
ffrancis Creswicke & Elsabeth hobson con.	...	...	xxjth.

[78] Thomas Hoyland, of Shiregreen, married Isabel, daughter of Nicholas Shirecliffe, of Ecclesfield Hall, gent. Vide p. 446, Hunter's Hall., Gatty's Edition. But a Thomas Hoyland married an Isabel Shiercliffe, 3 October, 1597. [Vide note 60.] Which is the right one?

[79] 1601, April 6, William Overall, gent., son of Robert Overall, by Frances his wife, and Elizabeth his wife, daughter of Edward Longley, gent., seek to be admitted to lands in Ecclesfield.

ffEBRUARIE.

Charles Smith and Mary Parkin con.	...	...	...	vth.
Nicholas hill & Elsabeth ...... con.	...	...	...	xijth.
Nicholas Cowper & Jane Carre con.	...	...	...	xviijth.
henry Sampson & Dinis Bromeheado con.	...	...	...	xxvjth.

MAY. [1617.]

Wm. Browne Elsabeth Guest	...	...	...	xjth.
francis hawksworth mary Wadilove con.	...	...	...	xxth.
[80] Wm. Yongue clerk & Als Marsten con.	...	...	...	xxiiijth.

JUNE.

Thomas Smith & Rosamand Parkin con.	...		viijth.
John Cowper & Margerie Scot con....	...		jxth.
Tho. Meller & ffrancis Rogers con.	...		xvth.
henry Wilkinson & Elsabeth howard con.	....		xxiiijth.

JULY.

Charles Howlden & Ann Relfe (Revel) con.	...	...	xiijth.

SEPTEMBER.

Richard Relfe (Revell) & Dorithie Gouldinge con.	...	...	viijth.
Thom. Smith & Margerie Dawer conjugat.	...	...	xvjth.
George Hochinson & Margrett Charlesworth con.	...	...	xxjth.

OCTOBER.

Richard hoyland Ann hill con.	...	...	xxijth.
John Meares & Joane Sharpe con. ...	...	...	xxvjth.

NOVEMBER.

James Timperley jane whitley con.	...	vth.
Brian Cooke Joanye Rawlin con. ...	...	xxiijth.
Thomas Slatter Eliza. ffrench con. ...	...	xxiiijth.

DECEMBER.

Thomas Marsden & Allis Hochkinson con.	...	vijth.
Rich. Oxpringe Eliz. Tayler con. ...	...	xvth.

JANUARIE.

Robert Greaves Ann Ibbotson con.	...	xiijth.
Thomas Osley Issabell hill con.	...	xxvth.
Rich. Ellis Ellin Croft conjugat.	...	eod. die.

FFEBRUARIE.

Edmund Waterhouse Ellin Hudson con	...	...	iij'
Thom. Hudson Eliz. Stead con. ...	...	...	ixth.

[80] William Younge, clerk, was buried 6 January, 1622.

Nicholl Hobson jenet Turner con. ...	...		xjth.
Robert Hauge Mary Mathewman con.	...		eod. die.
Willm. ffowler Margret Waringe con.	...		eod. die.
Thom. Crosley Eliz. Scott con. ...	...		xvjth.
John Beighton Eliz. Ibotson con. ...	...		eod. die.
Ric. Meller Eliz. Gillat con. ...	...		xvijth.

APRILL. [1618.]

Henric Bromehead Margret Cowdwell con.	..		xxvijth.

MAIJ.

George Ashton Eliz. Gibson con. ...	...		xvijth.
Rich. Hobson Margret Sikes con. ...	...		xxth.
Allexander Cowper Grace Nickson con.	...		xxxth.

JUNE.

Nich. Sheircliffe Ann Willson con. ...	...		ij'

AUGUST.

Rich. Woakley Eliz. Smilter con. ...	...		xth.

SEPTEMBER.

[81] Howsley ffreeman Marie Steele con.	...	...		j'
[82] Thom. Parkin Margret Askew con. ...	...	...		xiiijth.
John Buton Rose Barnsley con. ...	...	...		xvjth.
George Barnsley Ann Bacon con. ...	...	...		eod. die.
Willm. Hudson Ann Hawksworth con.	...	...		eod. die.
Henry Gray Ann Hobson con. ...	...	...		xvijth.
Henry Swift Margret Mason con. ...	...	...		xxixth.

OCTOBER.

Rich. Smith Allis Bullos con.	...	...		iiijth.
Thom. Croft Ann Webster con.	...	...		vijth.

[81] Howsley Freeman was son and heir of Gerard Freeman, of Howsley Hall. [Vide note 57.]

[82] Thomas Parkyn was of Mortomley; he was born 1563, and was eldest son of John, son of Peter, son of Robert Parkyn, of Mortomley, living temp. Henry VIII. Thomas Parkyn had issue, by Margaret Askew, his wife, three sons, of whom the youngest, Zachariah, succeeded to the Mortomley estates, &c., by the will of his eldest brother, John Parkyn, dated 18 April, 1634. He had issue by his wife, Isabel, a son and heir, John Parkyn, of Mortomley, who, dying in 1674, left issue by Sarah his wife, a son and heir, John Parkyn, of Mortomley, who, by his first wife, Elizabeth, daughter and co-heir of John Adams, of Darley Hall, had issue, inter alios, Paul Parkyn, of the Horbury, who, by his wife, Elizabeth, daughter of Francis Broadbent, of Bramley Hall, left issue on his death, in 1751, inter alios, a son and heir, Thomas Parkyn, who, succeeding to his uncle, William Parkyn's, estates, became Lord of the Manor of Darley. He married Hannah, daughter of William Wilkinson, of Crowder House, and dying 1776, left issue six daughters and one son, Thomas Parkyn, of Mortomley, who married Ann Batty, and dying 1808, left issue a son and daughter, William, born 9 October, 1807, but died a minor, and Catherine Parkyn, sole heiress, who married, 10 April, 1827, John Jeffcock, Esqre., J.P., 2nd son of John Jeffcock, of High Hazles. They had issue Parkin Jeffcock, who was killed in the Oaks Colliery explosion, when leading a body of volunteers to the rescue of those in the pit; Elizabeth Ann Jeffcock, and the Rev. John Thomas Jeffcock, M.A., of Oriel College, Oxford, and rector of the Collegiate Church of Wolverhampton, who married, 28 May, 1861, Alicia Anne, 2nd daughter of the Rev. Salisbury Everard, M.A., vicar of Swaffham, and by her has a numerous family.

Wm. Hanley Jane Burrows con.	...			xjth.
Wm. Carr Ellin Whiteley	...			xviijth.

NOVEMBER.

Gilbert Wood julian . . . . . con.	...	...	...	xxviijth.
Wm. Beale Dorithie Malin con. ...	...	...	...	xxxth.
francis Oadson Margret Mason con.	...	...	...	eod.
Henry Crawshaw Ann Nickolls con.	...	...	...	eod.

DECEMBR.

Wm. Sharp Ann Trippet con. ...	...	j'
Nich. Shercliffe Ann Greene con. ...	...	xxijth.

JANUARIE.

Thom. Ashton & Issabelle Birkinshaw con.	...	...	xxiiijth.
Hounfrey Trippet & Margret Ward con.	...	...	eod. die.
Wm. Wood & Eliz. Wood con. ...	...	...	xxvjth.
Rich. ffenton & Eliz. Hancocke con.	...	...	eod. die.
Jo. Ragge & Dorithie Robbinson con.	...	...	. . . . .

FFEBRUARIE.

Rich. Sheircliffe & Theodocia Pearsie con.	ijth.
Geo. Collie Margret Nickson con. ...	eod. die.
ffrancis Sunderland Margret Snath con.	eod. die.
Nich. Willkinson Issabell Smith con.	iij'
[83] Edward Wingfield Ann Hoyland con.	iiijto.
Wm. Shaw Elizabeth Rogers con.	. . . . .

APRILL. [1619.]

Geo. Parkin Margrett Cutt con. ...	...	xixth.
Nich. Scorer & Jenet Ibotson con. ...	...	xxxjth.

JUNE.

Nich. Hoyland marie Rawson con.	...		iij'
Gilbert Cresswicke Ellin Barnsley con.	...		xvth.
[84] **Nich.** Hurt Eliz. Cresswicke con. ...	...		xxijth.
John Gamble Issabell Woodhouse con.	...		**xxviijth.**

JULY.

John Slacke Ann Law con.	...	xjth.

---

[83] The Wingfields are of old standing in this parish, and from the subject of this note descended a family who have for some generations owned a small estate, called Butterthwaite, in this parish. The present representative is John Wingfield, of the firm of "Wade, Wingfield, and Rowbotham," cutlers, of Sheffield.

[84] Nicholas Hurt was of Woodseats, and this was his second marriage. [Vide note 64.] 1609, June 8, Nicholas Hurt, of Woodseats, surrenders 1 Messuage and ¼ bovat, in Woodseats, to his own use for life, and after his decease to Elizabeth, daughter of John Creswick, of Wadsley, whom the said Nicholas intends, God being willing, to make his wife.

AUGUST.

Peeter Brasebrigge Ellin Lockwood con.	...	j'
Thom. Dale Elvz. Bromeley con. ...	...	xxix.

SEPTEMBER.

Henry Mason & Issabell Dobson con.	...	xxjth.
Robert Wright & jane Cowldwell con.	...	eod. die.

OCTOBER.

Wm. Waynwright Margret Brownele con.	...	xith.
Ro. Mathewman Elin. Cooke con. ...	...	xviijth.
Wm. Dodwrth (Dodworth) Allis Marsden con. ...	...	xxiiijth.
Ro. Dickson julian Rogers con.	...	xxxjth.

NOVEMBER.

Godfrey Berry Issabell Buttrwrth (Butterworth) con.	...	vijth.
John Grayson Ann Bramald con. ...	...	xxvijth.
Jo. Ragge Eliz. Kaye con.	...	xxviiijth.
Robert Bacon Ellin Roggers con. ...	...	xxijth.
Edward Tingle Susan Sillito (Shilleto) con.	...	xxxth.

JANUARIE.

Thom. Ashton Eliz. Birkinshaw con.	...	xxiiijth.

FFEBRI.

Stephen Hirst Margret Barnsley con.	...	iij'
Thom. Wild Jane Crosley con.	...	xth.
John Hey Ann Browneld con.	...	xvijth.
George Wood Ann Wood con.	...	xxjth.

JUNE. [1620.]

[85] Wm. Tinley Barberie Pawson con. ...	...	xxvjth.

JULY.

Wm. Slacke Dorithie Kaye con.	...	xxiijth.

AUGUST.

Ro. Wintrbothome (Winterbottom) Margret Smith con.	...	xviijth.
Tho. Nayler Joan Wingrwrth (Wingerworth) con.	...	xxvjth.

SEPTEMBR.

John Slacke Ann Hanley con.	...	xxiiijth.

OCTOBER.

Thom. Gills Joan ffernley. con.	...	viijth.
Nich. Walker Alls hill con.	...	xvth.
Jo. ffoxe Grace Hall con.	...	xviijth.

[85] Barbara, daughter of Nicholas Pawson, of Windmill Hill, married William *Tindall*, and had issue Nicholas Tindall, &c. *P.* 446, *note, Hunter's Hallamshire, Gatty's Edition.*

NOVEMBR.

Thom. Hincliffe Ann hartly con.	...	ij'
Wm. doughtie Margret Rockly con.	...	xxvjth.

DECEMBER.

Wm. Wright Issaboll Barnsley	...	xth.

JANUARIE.

George Ibotson Dyonis Greene con.	...	xxijth.

APRILL. [1621.]

Christo. Browneld Eliz. Wood con.	...	...	xjth.
Rob. Wilkinson Eliz. Cowper con. ...	...	...	xxijth.

JUNE.

Charles hobson Marie Pashlie con.	...	...	xvijth.

JULY.

jerimie Lord Ann Smalefield con.	...	iij'

AUGUST.

ffrancis Armroyd Dorithie Houlmes con.	...	xixth.

SEPTEMBER.

Thom. Ragge Margret Carre con.	...	xvjth.

OCTOBER.

Rich. Hunter Eliz. Colleye con.	...	...	xxiiijth.

NOVEMBER.

George Gaunt & Marie Coward con.	...	...	vjth.
Edward Briggs & joan Hey con.	...	...	vijth.
Thomas Staniland & Ann Olliver con.	...	...	viijth.
Rich. Parkin & Issabell Walker con.	...	...	xjth.
John Drable & joan Button con.	...	...	xxvth.

DECEMBER.

Rich. Sutton & Rose Hotchkinson con.	...	...	ij.
Rich. Norborne & Marie Dungwrth (Dungworth) con.	...		ixth.

JANUARIE.

Robt. Gilberts & Alls Swift con. ...		...	xxiiijth.
ffebr			
.... osley conjugat.	...		vth.

[N.B. The remainder of page cut off.]

BAPTISMS

CONTAINED IN

The First Volume of the Parish Church Registers

OF

St. MARY'S, ECCLESFIELD,

In Co: YORK.

1599—1619 (INCLUSIVE).

BAPTISMS.

[.1599.]

Mense Junij.

Robt. filius Hugonis Carre de Myddletowne ... ...
Jane filia Thome Bullus de Byrlyedge ... ... bapt. xxiiijto die.
Thomas filius Thome Slatter de Hallfoylde ... ... bapt. xxjxto die.

Mense Julij.

Thomas filius Henrice Spyttlehouse de Ecclesfeld ... bapt. xv' die.
Robt. filius Robt. Butterworthe ... ... bapt. eod' die.
Willus filius Thome Hanley de Byrley Carre ... ... bapt. xxij' die.
Alexandr filius Alexandri Sadler de Wadsley ... ... bapt. eod' die.
Seth filius Nicholai Hartleye de Hesley ... ... bapt. xxjxto die.

Mense Augusti.

Anne filia Richardi Wilson de Ughtibrigge ... ... bapt. x' die.
Lucie filia Johannis Lockwood de Sowtheye ... ... bapt. xv' die.
Wyllm. fi : josephi Lord de Ecclesfeld ... ... bapt. x ......
(Spur.)

Mense Septembris.

Anne fi : Henrici Sawood de Ecclesfelde bapt. ......
Elizabeth fi : Thome Raggo de Mortomleye bapt. ......
George filius Laurantij Saursby de birley Carre bapt. ......
Anthonius filius Anthonij Lawe de Warldsende bapt. ......

Mense Octobris.

Elizabetha filia Edwardi Selvester de hyegrene ... ... bapt. ......
Robt. filius Thome Meller de Ecclesfeld ... ... bapt. ......
Roger? filius Joha .... de Mortomleye ... bapt. ......
Hellen filia Willmi. Hargreffe de Hollihouse ... bapt. ......

[N.B. The remainder of the page cut off.]

Mense Februarij.

Thomas fi : Michaelis Dughtyman de burncrosse bapt. ij die.
Anne fi : Hugonis Thomson de Potterhill bapt. x' die.
Alice fi : Wmi. fearnleye de Okes bapt. xvij' die.
Alice fi : Godfridi Byrleye de Wadsleye bapt. eod' die.
Spur : Thomas fi Robti Eyro de Shyregrene bapt. eod' die.

Mense Martij.

M'garet fi : francisci Hobson de Byrleyedge	bapt. ij' die.
M'garet fi : Alexandri Jepson de Ecclesfelde	bapt. xiij' die.
Willus. fi : Nicholai Stanylande de Ecclesfelde ...	bapt. x' die.
Anne fi : Willmi. Robts. (Roberts) de Chappell ...	bapt. xvj' die.
Anne fi : Nichi. Dungworthe de Shyregrene	bapt. xxj' die.
Spur : M'garet. fi : M'garete Cooper de Ecclesfelde spinst. ...	bapt. xxiiij' die.

Mense Martij. [1600.]

Nicholas fi : Wm. Combe de Wincowbanke	bapt. xxvj' die.
Johes. fi : Thome hartleye de hartleye brooke	bapt. xxx' die.
Elizabeth fi : Nichi. Neyler de Mortomleye	bapt. eod. die.

Mense Aprilis.

Isabell fi : Robti. Wylkinson de Neyther shyre	bapt. ij' die.
Dorithie fi : Johis. Dobson de Ecclesfelde	bapt. vj' die.
Isabell fi : Alexandri Bearde de Horberye	bapt. viij' die.
⁸⁶ Anne fi : Johis. Gest de Cooleye	bapt. eod die.
Anne fi : Rici. Hobson de Wadsleye	bapt. xv' die.
Wenefride fi : Thome Bower de Whitleye	bapt. eod. die.

Mense Maij.

Spur : joan fi : Hugonis Bower de Sheffeld & Marie Colleye (?)	bapt. xxx' die.

Mense Junij.

Henrico fi : Willmi. Brownell de Shiregreene ...	bapt. viij. die.
Spur : Elizabeth fi : Thome Scargell de Ecclesfeld	bapt. xiiij' die.
Elizabeth fi : Henrici Foxe de Wadsleye ...	bapt. xv' die.
Howsleye fi : Gerardi Freeman de Howsleye Hall	bapt. xxij' die.
Francis fi : Wm. Rychardson de Ecclesfelde ...	bapt. xxiiijto die.

Mense Julij.

Gilbertus fi : Radi Slatter de Hallfeylde ...	bapt. vjto die.
Thomas fi : Wm. Carre de greenowsyde ...	bapt. xxmo die.

⁸⁶ In the rent rolls of the Manor of Sheffield, ano. 1613, john Guest appears as tenant of Cowley Hall. In Harrison's survey, ano. 1637, "Mary Guiest, widow, holdeth at will Cowley Hall and lands by the year, &c." Gerard Guest was tenant of the same in the year 1697, and his daughter and heir, Ann Guest, married Robert Kirke, of Anston; they had issue a son, Gerard Kirke, born ano. 1691, who married, ano. 1715, Ann, daughter and final heir of George Walker, of Hunshelf, in the parish of Penistone; by her Gerard Kirke had issue, inter alios, a daughter Ann Kirke, born ano. 1719, who married Thomas Smith, of Upper House, in the parish of Cawthorne, (who was son of **William, son of Robert Smith,** of Cawthorne, living ano. 1703). They had issue, inter alios, a son, William Smith, **born ano. 1761,** who, **in the year 1823,** purchased the estate of Barnes Hall; he married Elizabeth, **daughter of** Thomas Parkyne, of Mortomley Hall, in this parish, and dying 1849, left issue, inter alios, a son and heir, **the present** William Smith, of Barnes Hall, who married Mary Ann, daughter and heir of the Rev. Alexander Mackenzie, incumbent of St. Paul's Church, Sheffield, and had issue **by her, who** died 22nd January, 1874, a numerous family.

Mense Augusti.

Willus. fi : Willi. Hinchlyffe de Ecclesfelde ...	bapt. iijtio die.
Robrt. fi : Briani Ashton de Ecclesfeld ...	bapt. xmo die.
Anne fi : johnis. Sheyrelyffe de Wyneobanke ...	bapt. eod. die.
Isabell fi : Willi. Smythe de Grenowsyde ...	bapt. xxij' die.

Mense Septembris.

Alicia fi : Nicholai Sheircliffe de Ecclesfeld	bapt. xxj' die.
Spur : Francisca fi : Nichi Dyson de Whitleye	bapt. eod. die.
Nichus fi : Robti. Sheircliffe de Ecclesfeld	bapt. xxix' die.

Mense Octobris.

Thomas fi : Edwardi Wardill de Ecclesfeldo	bapt. vto die.
Alicia fi : Johnis. Sugden de eod.	bapt. eod. die.
Thomas fi : Johnis. Grene de Ecclesfelde	bapt. xij' die.
Hellene fi : Robti. Mathyman de Hagge	bapt. eod. die.

Novembris mense.

Robt. fi : Willmi. Parkyn de Wadsleye ...	ultimo die.

Mense Decembris.

Radus. fi : Rici. Swynden de Ecclesfelde	bapt. vto die.
Radulphus fi : Rici. Carre de byrleyedge	bapt. x' die.
Elizabeth fi : Robti. Carre de Ecclesfelde	bapt. xiiij' die.
Anne fi : Georgij Turner de Ecclesfelde	bapt. xxviij' die.

Mense Januarij.

Catherin fi . Thome Dughtye de Woodseats ...	bapt. j' die.
Thomas fi : Thome Parkyn de Huddye hollens ...	bapt. iiij' die.
Richard fi : Rici. Chapman defuncti de Ecclesfelde	bapt. xj' die.
Elizabethe fi : Willi' Sampson de Ecclesfelde	bapt. eod. die.
Anne fil : Thome Bullus de byrleyedge ...	bapt. xiij' die.
Anne fi : Rici. Wodde de Warldsende ...	bapt. xviij' die.
john fi : Thome Crosleye de Chappell ...	bapt. xxvto die.

Mense Februarij.

Hugo fi : Thome Mylner de Wyncowbanke	bapt. j' die.
Nichas. fi : Alexandri Hill de Ecclesfeldo ...	bapt. eod. die.
Nichas. fi : Thome Weynwright de pkeyate. (Parkgate)	bapt. eod. die.
Mgaret. fi : Thome Barleye de Ecclesfeld ...	bapt. eod. die.
Thomas fi : Robti. Mathyman de Wadsleye	bapt. iiij' die.
Elizabeth fi : Robti. Hobson de Wadsleye	bapt. viij' die.
Willus. fi : Johis. Parkin de Sowtheye	bapt. xxiiijto die.

Mense Martij.

Robto. fi : Johis. Seargell de Wadsleye ..	bapt. primo die.

Elizabethe fi : Antonij Lawe de Warldsende ... ... bapt. xj' die.
Johes. fi : Johis. Ragge de Mortomleye ... ... bapt. xv' die.
Anne fi : Thome Hoylande de Neithershire ... ... xx' die.

Mense Aprilis. [1601.]

Wmo. fi : Hugonis Wolleye de Synecliffe grange brigge ... ... bap. vto die.
Joan fi : Willi. Hyde de grenowsyde ... ... bapt. eod. die.
Isabella fi : Edmundi Senier de Burnerosse ... ... bapt. eod. die.
Cicelye fi : Robti. Mason de Shiregrene ... ... bapt. xvij' die.
Elizabethe fi : Willmi. Fearnleye de Okes ... ... bapt. eod. die.
Nicholas fi : Johnis Burnet de Ecclesfelde ... ... bapt. xxvto die.

Mense Maij.

joan fil : Radi. Button de Grenowsyde ... bapt. xvij' die.
Anne fi : Georgij Grene de Potterhill ... bapt. xxj' die.
Thomas fi : Rici. Cutte de Mortomleye ... bapt. ultimo die.

Mense Junij.

Thomas fi : Christopheri Croftes de Whitley ... bapt. xvij' die.
Richard fi : Hugonis Carre de Myddleton grene bapt. xxiiij' die.

Mense Julij.

Willmo. fi : johnis. Ronksleye de Byrleyecarre ... bapt. xxij' die.

Mense Augusti.

Georgius fi : Thome Barnsleye de Longleye ... bapt. xxviij die.

Mense Septembris.

Elizabethe fil : Nicholai Bower de Wincowbanke bapt. xiij' die.
Isabelle fil : Nicholai Parkin de Mortomleye ... bapt. eod. die.
Elizabethe fi : Willmi. Byrkes de Doocfeilde ... bapt. xx' die.
Hellene fi : Laurentij Sawrsbye de birleycar ... bapt. eod. die.
Thomas fi : Rici. Wigfall de Mortomleye ... bapt. xxj' di.
Isabell fi : Robti. Boweman de Wodhouse ... bapt. ultimo. die.

Mense Octobris.

Thomas fi : Thome Bower de Whitley ... ... bapt. iijto die.
Barbara fi : Thome Sheffelde de Warldesende ... ... bapt. eod. die.
jenetta fi : Thome Bullus de Wincowbanke ... ... bapt. xj' die.

Mense Novembris.

Michael fi : Willi. Wilkinson de Wincowbanke ... ... bapt. xxij' die.
Edward fi : Willi. Parkin de Wadsley ... ... bapt. eod. die.
Thomas fi : Georgij Hyrst de Wincowbanke ... ... bapt. xxvij' die.

Mense Decembris.

Hellene fi : Henrici Combe de Shiregrene ... bapt. xxjmo die.

Mense JANUARIJ.

Henrico fi : Hugonis Wilkinson de Shiregreene... ... bapt. iij' die.
Spur. Hellen fi : Francisci Hobson de Wadsleybrigge ... bapt. jx' die.
John fi : Edwardi Creswycke de Wadsleye ... ... bapt. x' die.
Nicholas fi : Nichi. Hartley de Thorppe pochiæ de Rotherham ... bapt. eod. die.
Elizabethe fil : Michaelis Dughtyman de burcrosse ... bap. xviiij' die.
Maria fi : **Cottoni Hobson** de Helmeshouse ... ... bapt. ultimo die.

Mense FEBRUARIJ.

Hugo fi : Henrici Stanyforthe de Wincowbanke ... ... **bap. xxiiij' die.**
Elizabethe fi : Willi. Nickson de Huddye Hollens pochiæ de Tankersleye eod. die.

Mense MARTIJ.

Anne filia Willi. Mathiman de Wadsleye ... bapt. vij. die.

Mense MARTIJ. [1602.]

Anne fi : Willmi. Hargreave de Hollen house ... ... bapt. xxviij' die.
Thomas fi : johis. Bullus de Wincowbanko ... ... bapt. ultimo. die.

Mense APRILIS. [1602.]

Robtus fi : Robti. Hobson de Wadsleye ... ... bapt. vto die.
Anne fi : Johis. Hattersleye de Bellhouse ... ... bapt. ixno die.
Radus. fi : Petri Mathyman de Wadsleye ... ... bapt. eod. die.
Ricus. fi Francisci johnson de Parkeyate ... ... bapt. xviij' die.

Mense MAIJ.

Willus. fi : **Francisci Hobson** subter byrleyedge bapt. xvj' die.
Elizabeth fi : Johis. Lockwodde de Sowthey ... bapt. eod. die.
Anne fi : Henrici Foxe de Wadsleye ... bapt. xxj' die.
Isabelle fi : Leondi. Crosse de Mortomleye ... bapt. xxiij' die.
Richarde fi : Georgij Byrkes de Ecclesfeld ... bapt. xxviij' die.

Mense JUNIJ.

Isabell fi : Simonis Heye de Wodhouse ... ... **bapt. xiij' die.**
Nichas. fi Francisci Marshall de Worrall ... ... bapt. eod. die.
Edward fi : Francisci Barbar de Wadsleye ... ... bapt. xx' die.
Margaret fi : Nichi. Hobson de Birleycarre ... ... bapt. xxvij' die.
Johes. fi : Thome Slatter de Hallfeylde ... ... bapt. xxix' die.

Mense AUGUSTI.

Catherin fi : Thome Meller de Ecclesfelde ... bapt. jmo die.
Catherin fi : Thome Taylyer de Wodseates ... bapt. eod. die.
Frances filia Thome Ragge de Mortomley ... bapt. xvto die.
An. fi : Laurentij Place de Ecclesfelde ... bapt. xxij' die.
Elizabet. fi : Thome Sheircliffe de Sodhouse ... bapt. xxxo' die.

Mense SEPTEMBRIS.

Isabell fi : Hugonis Meller de Shyregrene		bapt. xij' die.
Edward fi : Robti. Mason de Shiregrene		bapt. xvij' die.
Elizabeth fi : Gerardi Freeman de Howsley hall		bapt. xxvjto die.
Anna fil : Robti. Ellys de Ecclesfelde		bapt. eod. die.

Mense OCTOBRIS.

Roland fi : Robti. jepson de Whitley		bapt. x' die.
Edward fi : Rici. Gylles de Chappell		bapt. xvij' die.
Petrus fi : Johnis. Sngden de Ecclesfelde		bapt. xxiiij' die.
Catherin fi : Robti. Wylkinson de Neythershire ...		bapt. ultimo die.

Mense NOVEMBRIS.

Tho. fi : Godfridi Byrley de Wadsleye bapt. apud Sheefeld ...		xxiiij' die.
Willmi. fi : Rici. Ingle de Chappell...		bapt. ultimo die.

Mense DECEMBRIS.

Georg. fi : Francisci Danyell de Mortomley		bapt. iij' die.
Hellen fi : Brian. Ashton de Ecclesfeld		bapt. vto. die.
Arthur fi : Willi. Parkin de Wadsleye		bapt. xij' die.
Johes. fi : Robti. Boll de Mortomley advene		bapt. eod. die.
Catherina fi : Rici. Raworthe de Ecclesfeld		bapt. xvij die.
An. fil : Willmi. Wodrove de Whitley advene		bapt. xxj' die.
Elizabethe fil : Thome Machon de Neithershire...		bapt. xxv' die.

Mense JANUARIJ.

Georgius fi : Johnis. Grene de Ecclesfeldo ...	bapt. xxiij' die.
Thomas fi : Rogeri Throppe de Ecclesfeld ...	bapt. xxvj' die.
An. fi : Caroli Hill de Ecclesfeld	bapt. eod. die.

Mense FEBRUARIJ.

Spur. Franciscus filius		bapt. j' die.
Willius filius Roberti Baylye de Whitley		bapt. vjto die.
Sp. Franciscus fil : Micha Marshall de Worrall		bapt. x' die.
Laurentius fil : Micha Staniforth de Wincowbanke		bapt. xj' die.
John fil : Mich. Walker de Ecclesfeld		bapt. xxiiij' die.
Dorotha fil : Alexandri Hill de Ecclesfeld		bapt. xxvij' die.

Mense MARTIJ.

Isabella filia Willi. Fernoley de Okes		bapt. vjto die.
Meria fil : Georgij Woode de Okes		bapt. xj' die.
Johes. fil : Thomæ Parkin de Huddie Hollis		bapt. xviij' die.
Thomas fil : Alex. Jepson de Ecclesfeld		bapt. xx' die.
Susa. Robec. fil : Will. Clayton de Creswicke		bapt. eod. day.

Mense Aprilis. [1603.]

Lelle filia Laurentij Eyre de Longley	bapt. j' die.
Maria fil: Will. Clarke de Eliot Lane	bapt. xviiij' die.
Jacobus fil: Will. Carre de Grenowside	bapt. xxj' die.
Radus. fil: Will. Brownhill de Shiregreene	bapt. eode. die.

Mense Maij.

Nychol. fil: Henrici Ibotson de Ecclesfeld	bapt. xxij' die.
Franciscus fil: Johis Waterall de Ecclesfeld	bapt. xxjxno die.
Margret fil: Thomæ Collye de Sowthey	bapt. die.

Mense Junij.

Agnes fil: Will. Ashton de Ecclesfeld	bapt. xij' die.

Mense Julij.

Margret fil: Robti. Sheircliffe de Ecclesfeld	bapt. xxj' die.
Richardus fil: Rich. Carre de Byrleyedge	bapt. xxij' die.

Mense Augusti.

Margeria fil: Cottoni Hobson	bapt. xiiijto die.
Thomas fil: Johis. Walker de Ecclesfeld	bapt. xixno die.
Henrie. fil: Micha Smythe de Grenowside	bapt. xx' die.
John fil: Petri Thrope de Mortomleye	bapt. eode. die.

Mense Septembris.

Gerard fil: johis. Gest de Cooley	bapt. 4to die.
Thomas fil: Johis. Shelley de Mortomley	bapt. ix' die.
Robt. fil: Nichi. Sheircliffe de Ecclesfeld	bapt. xvjto. die.
Francis filius Johis. Bower de biegreene	bapt. xviij' die.
Nich. fil: Nichi. Neyler de Mortomleye	bapt. eode. die.
Spur. Georgi. fil: Rogeri Rigge de Ecclesfeld et Isabel Byrrge	bapt. eode. die.
Thomas fi: Anthonii Hardye	bapt. xxvto die.
Maria fil: Johis. Parkin de Sowtheye	bapt. xxixno die.

Mense Octobris.

Robt. filius Joseph Lorde	bapt. xvjto die.
Lucia fili: Thomæ Haugh	bapt. eode. die.
Margret fil: Robti. Bowman de Wodhouse	bapt. xxx' die.

Mense Novembris.

Spur. Robtus. fil: Radi. Hepworth de Ecclesfeld	bapt. iiijto die.
james fil: Robti. Oxpringe de Sowthey	bapt. xiij' die.
Johis. fil: Will. Byrkes de Deefeilde	bapt. eode. die.
Isabel fil: Thomæ Hartleye de hartleye brooke	bapt. eode. die.
Isabel fil: Johis. Sheircliffe de Wincowbank	bapt. xvjto die.
Nychol. fil: Eduard Selvester	bapt. xx' die.
Anna fil: Richar. Swinden de Ecclesfeld	bapt. eod. die.

Mense DECEMBRIS.

Johes. fil: Johis. Dobson de Ecclesfelde	bapt. iiij' die.
Radus. fil: Johis. Hatersleye de Bellhouse	bapt. xj' die.
Anna fil: Robti. Hobson de Wadsleye	bapt. xxvto die.

Mense JANUARII. [1603.]

Gilbert fil: Thomæ Byrkes de doefeild	bapt. xjto die.
Nychol. fil: Thomæ Sheircliffe de Sodhouse	bapt. xvto die.
Hellen fil: Eduard Creswicke de Wadsleye	bapt. xvij' die.
james fil: Roberti Wilkinson de Ecclesfelde	bapt. xxij' die.
Nychs. fil: John Walker de Ecclesfeld	bapt. xxviij' die.

Mense FEBRUARIS.

Margret fil: Robti. Carre de Butt twaet (? Butterthwaite)	bapt. xvjto die.
Robo. fil. Nych. Hurte de Wodseate	bapt. xix' die.
Franciscus fil: Francisci Hobson de Birleye edge	bapt. eode. die.
Elizeb. fil: Rich. Hobson de Wadsleye	bapt. eod. die.
Margret fil: Georgii Wood de Okes	bapt. ultimo die.

[1603.] Mense MARTII.

Andre. fil: Edmndi. Senier de burncrosse	bapt. ij' die.
Hellen fil: Willi. Sampson de Ecclesfeld	bapt. iiijto die.
johes. fil: Thomæ Ragge de Mortomleye	bapt. xj' die.
Spur. Thomas fill: Nych. Waterall de Ecclesfelde	bapt. xiiijto die.
Francis fil: Robti. Matheman de Olerton	bapt. xvjto die.
Elizab. fil:	bapt. xxiiijto die.

Mense MARTII. [1604.]

Maria fil: Thomæ Bower de Whitley	bapt. xxvij' die.
Hellen fil: xpofer. Crofts de Whitleye	bapt. xxx' die.

Mense APRILIS.

Thomas fil: Will. Hide de Grenowside	bapt. xvto die.
Edwardus fil: Willo. Fernelye de Okes	bapt. xxij' die.
Willus. fil: Robti. Butterworth de Shiregreene	bapt. eod. die.
[87] Kather. fil: Radi. Hadfeld de Shiregreene	bapt. eod. die.
Margret. fil: Robti. Matheman de Hagge	bapt. eod. die.

---

[87] Some of the children of Ralph Hatfield were baptized at Laughton-en-le-Morthen; I have the following from those Registers:—

```
1596. August 21.  Margaret daughter of Ralph Hatfield baptized
1598. October 29. Anthony son of        ,,   ,,   ,,
1601. June 4.     Isabel daughter of    ,,   ,,   ,,
1611. Sept. 19.   Alexander son of      ,,   ,,   ,,
1614. May 25.     Barbara daughter of   ,,   ,,   ,,
1617. Nov. (?) 1. Elizabeth daughter of ,,   ,,   ,,
1621. June 7.     Gervase son of        ,,   ,,   ,,
1622. Feb. 18.    john son of           ,,   ,,   ,,
```

Mense MAIJ.

Margret. fil : Hen. Combe de Shiregreene		bapt. xx' die.
Johes. fil : Alexandri Sadler de Wadsleye		bapt. xxvij' die.
Johes. fil : Simois. Heye de Woodhouse		bapt. xxvij' die.

Mense JUNIJ.

Anna fil : Thomæ Dughtie de Whitleye ... — bapt. iij' die.
Richd. fil : Thomæ Byrley Cap. de Bradfeld ... — bapt. x' die.
Elizb. fil : Will. Meller Capre. ejusdem ... — bapt. eode. die.
Elizab. fil : Thomæ Dughtiman de Burnecrosse — bapt. eode. die.
Margret fil : Thomæ Hoylande de Nethershire ... — bapt. eode. die.
Margret fil : Thomæ Sheffeld ... — bapt. xxvij' die.
Hellen fil : cujusda paupis. advenœ... — bapt. eode. die.

Mense JULIJ.

Anna fil : Petri Matheman de Wadsley ... — bapt. xxvto die.
Hellen fil : Johis. Lockwood de Sowtheye ... — bapt. eode. die.
Anna fil : Nicho. Tayler de Ecclesfelde ... — bapt. xxixno die.

Mense AUGUSTI.

Robtus. fil : Hugois. Wilkinson de Shiregreene — bapt. vto die.
Willus. fil : Alexadri. Jepson de Ecclesfeld ... — bapt. eode. die.
Johes. fil : Johis Coop de Mortomleylane end ... — bapt. eode. die.
Johes fil : Thomæ Smith de Mortomley ... — bapt. ultimo die.

Mense SEPTEMBRIS.

Roger fil : Francisci Daniel de Mortomley ... — bapt. ij' die.
Henricus fil : Henrici Stanyforth de Wincowbanke — bapt. ixno die.
johes. fil : Johes Pkin (Parkin) de Wadsleye ... — bapt. xvjto die.
Grace fil : Johis. Sugden de Ecclesfeld ... — bapt. ultimo die.

Mense OCTOBRIS.

Anna fil : Willi. Clarke de Eliot Lane ... — bapt. xviij' die.
johes. fil : Johis Curteise de Wincowbanke ... — bapt. xxj' die.

Mense NOVEMBRIS.

Richer. fil : Henrici Wright de Toodhole ... — bapt. iiijto die.

Mense DECEMBRIS.

Robtus fil : Alexadri. Hil de Ecclesfeld — bapt. vij' die.
Willius Burnett fil : Johis ... — bapt. eode. die.

Mense JANUARIJ.

Grace fil : Jacobi Green de Synocliffe grange gen. — bapt. j' die.
Willi. fil : Will. Hartleye de Longleye — bapt. xvjto die.
Spur. Susan fil : Will. Wright de Toodhole — bapt. xxviij' die.

Mense FEBRUARIJ.

Elizabet. fil : johis Bower de Mortomley	...	bapt. iij' die.
Alicia fil : Will. Ashton de Ecclesfeld	...	bapt. vjto die.
Thomas fil : Thomæ Byrkes de Doofeld	...	bapt. viij' die.
Elizb. fil : Alexandri Hartley de Longleye	...	bapt. xvj' die.
Alicia fil : Johis. Walker de Ecclesfeld	...	bapt. eode. die.
Henricus fil : Robti. Bowman de Woodhouse	...	bapt. xxij' die.

Mense MARTIJ.

Anna filia Johis Haughton de Wadsley	... ...	bapt. et i' die.
Anna fil Francisci johnson de Parkyate	... ...	bapt. vjto die.
Isabell fil : Georgij Thorpe de Nethershire	... ...	bapt. viij' die.
Hellen fil : Will. Barnsleye de Hollihouse	... ..	bapt. xvjto die.

Mense MARTIJ. [1605.]

Thomas fil : Willi. Shawe de Nethershire	... ...	bapt. 27' die.
janna fil : Radi' Slatter de Woodhead	... ...	bapt. 28' die.
Elizab. fil : Johis. Hall de Chappell	... ...	bapt. 30' die.

Mense APRILIS.

Anna fil : Thomæ Gaughe de Bellhouse	...	...	bapt. 3' die.
Maria fil : Johis. Bullus de Wincowbanke	...	...	bapt. i9' die.
Margretta fil : Nichi. Disan de Whitley	...	...	bapt. 2i' die.
Elsab. fil : Radi. Basforth de Whitley byerley	...	...	bapt. 22' die.
Spur. Dorothea fil : ilegit Rogeri Scotte de Hattebrooke	...	..	bapt. 25to die.

Mense MAIJ.

Willius. fil : Hugois. Carr de Middleton greene...	bapt. 5to die.
Alicia fil : Cottoni Hobson de Birkhouse ...	bapt. 9no die.
Dorothea fil : Georgij Nyckson de Grangbridge...	bapt. i9no die.

Mense JUNIJ.

Willius fil : Francisci Arthur de Wadsley	...	bapt. 2' die.
Hugo fil : Hugois. Moller de oxshire	...	bapt. 9no die.
Johes. fil : Georgij Pken. (Parkin) de Mortomley	...	bapt. 23' die.

Mense JULIJ.

Robtus. fili : Radi. Buttn. de Croshouse	... ...	bapt. 7' die.
Richardus fil : Thomæ Slatter de Loershe (Lower shire)	...	bapt. i4to die.
Elizabet. fil : Thomæ Milner de Ecclesfeld	.. ...	bapt. 16to die.
Hellena fil : Henrici Storke de oxshire	... ...	bapt. 20' die.

Mense AUGUSTI.

Elizab. fil : Gadfridi Byrley de Wadsley	... ...	bapt. 4to die.
Henricus filius Thomæ Machin de Nethershire ...	...	bapt. 12' die.
Robtus. filius Radij. Grubbe de Toed hole	... ...	bapt. 16to die.

Margreta fil: Laurentij Eyre de oxshire	...	bapt. eode. die.
Anna fil: Johis. Lodge de Ecclesfeld	...	bapt. 19no die.

Mense SEPTEMBRIS.

Johes. filius Radij. Hepworth de Ecclesfeld	...	bapt. 8' die.
Katherena fil Nychol. Tayler de Ecclesfeld	...	bapt. eode. die.
Willius fil Thomæ Trippett de Wadsleye	...	bapt. 15to die.
Willius. filius Thomæ Brooke do Chappell	...	bapt. 21' die.
Matheus fil: Leonardi Crosse do mortley (Mortomley)	...	bapt. 22' die.
Thomas fil: Robti. Mason de Oxshire	...	bapt. 29' die.

Mense OCTOBRIS.

Anna fil: Wm. Stonnes de Mortoleye	...	bapt. 6to die.
Willius. fil: Willi. Brownell de oxshire	...	bapt. 9' die.
Dionis fil: Johis Shooter de Wadsleye	...	bapt. 20' die.
Nicholaus fil: Richardi Carr de Edge	...	bapt. 25to die.

Mense NOVEMBRIS.

josephus filius Rogeri Throppe de Ecclesfeld	...	bapt. 3' die.
Nychlus. fil: Nicholi Gilles et Margreta uxoris, eius et neptis eius de chappell ...	...	bapt. 10' die.
Thomas fil: Johis. Dobson de Ecclesfeld	...	bapt. 17' die.
Willius. fil: Thomæ Pkn (Parkin) de Mortomley	...	bapt. eode. die.
Elsabethe fil: Will. Matheman de Wadsley	...	bapt. eode. die.
Anna fil: Brian Ashton de Ecclesfeld	...	bapt. 30' die.

Mense DECEMBRIS.

Spur. Johes. et Katherena filii Johis. Beano illegit.	...	bapt. i' die.
Johes. fil: Edwardi Burie de Syndwell (Sinderwell)	...	bapt. i5to die.
Lucia fil: Willi. Basforde de Whitleye	...	bapt. 25to die.

Mense JANUARIJ.

Hellena fil: Roberti Hobson de Wadsley	...	bapt. i2' die.
Rogerus filius Petri Crappe de Martoley (Mortomley)	...	bapt. eode. die.
Maria fil: Jacobi Greene de Synocliffe grange (or Thundercliffe grange) gen.		bapt. i9' die.
Robertus fil: Henrici Ibutson de Ecclesfeld	...	bapt. 24to die.

Mense FFEBRUARII.

Maria fil: Johis. Ragge de Mortomleyo	...	bapt. 2' die.
Elsabet. fil: Johis. Pkin. (Parkin) de Sowetheye	...	bapt. 5to die.
Anna fil: Nychi. Nayler de Mortomleye	...	bapt. 9' die.
Henricus fil: Nychi. Foster de Ecclesfeld	...	bapt. ii' die.
Richardus fil: Eduardi Selvester de Hiegreene ...	...	bapt. i6to die.
Hugo fil: Nichi. Dungworth de oxshire	...	bapt. 2i' die.
Hellena fil: johis. Oxspringe de Shetehouse	...	bapt. 23' die.
Nathaniell fil: Richardi Robts. (Roberts) minister de Ecclesfeld	...	bapt. 28' die.

Mense Martij.

Georgius fil: Georgij Byrkes de Ecclesfeld	... ...	bapt. 5to die.
Maria fil: Roberti Elles de Ecclesfeld	... ...	bapt. 12' die.
Nycholaus fil: Willi. Fearneleye de Okes	... ...	bapt. 16to die.
Alicia fil: Thomæ Smithe de Mortomley	... ...	bapt. 23' die.

Mense Martij. [1606.]

Nichalus fil Johis. Creswicke de Wadsleye	... ...	bapt. 28' die.
Anna fil: Thomas Haghe de Eliot Lane	... ...	bapt. 30' die.

Mense Aprilis.

Raulphe fil: Roberti Carr de butterwhit	...	bapt. xxi' apr.
Anna fil: Willi. Birkes de Doofeilde	...	bapt. 6to die.
Sara fill: Johis. Burie de Southeye	...	bapt. 15to die.

John Shirtcliffe the sonne of Nicholas Shirtcliffe was baptized the xxv of Aprill

Mense Maii.

Isabell Colley the dowghter of Thomas Colley was baptized the xxv of May Anno predict
Anne the dowghter o joseph Lord was bapt. ye xj of may.
Isabell the dowghter of jo. was baptized ye xxvj of may.
Isabell Smithe dowghter of Nicholas Smithe was baptized ye xviij of may.

JUNE.

Margret Sawerbe and Dinis Sawerbe was baptized ye 2 of june.
Nicholas Croftes the sonne of Charles Crofts was baptized the sixt of June.
John Sampson was baptized the same day.

JULI.

John Thorpe the sonne of George thorpe was baptized ye vj of juli.
Marye Smithe the daughter of Willm Smithe was baptized ye xxvj of juli.

AUGUST.

Elsabeth ashton the dowghter of Willm Ashton was baptized the xvij of August.
Katheran the dowghter of John Gest was baptized ye xvij of august.
Dorothye the dowghter of Ralphe Basworthe was baptized ye same day.
Willm Shirtcliffe the sonne of Thomas shirtcliffe was baptized the xxj of August ann' p.
james hurt the sonne of Nicholas Hurt was baptized the xxiiij' of August.
Rawlphe carr the sonne of Willm carr was baptized the nyne and twentye of August.

SEPTEMBER.

Anne the dowghter of Robert Shirtcliffe was baptized the xiiijth of September.

OCTOBER.

Robert Shaw the sonne of . . . . . . Shawe was baptized ye xj' of oct.
humfrey Wilkinson the sonne of Willm Wilkinson was baptized the third day of october.

Margret the dawghter of John Shircliffe was baptized th vj day of october.
Elsabeth dowghter of Francis barber bapt. erat secundo die october.
A child of Nicholas Parkins was baptized the ix of october.
Robert Jepson ye sonne of Alexsannder Jepson baptizatus erat vth die oct.
dinis filia francisci hobson was baptized the same daye.

NOVEMBER.

Willm basworthe the sonne of John basworthe was bapt. **xxiijth**.
Robert Jepson the sonne of Alexsander Jepson the 24 day of novem. and was buried the xxxth.
Alice Tailor dowghter of thomas tayler of Wadsley was baptized the xxviij of november.

DECEMBER.

Thomas Rawlen sonne of Ralphe Rawlen was baptized the xvij day of december.
Anne Rogers dowghter of francis Rogers, was baptized the xxj of december.
Thomas hartley sonne of Thomas hartley of hartley brooke was bapt. the same day.

JANUARI.

Anne hobson the dawghter of francis hobson of hirst was baptized the 4 of jannuari.
Anne hey dowghter of **Simon** hey was baptized the ixth of januari.
Willm Grene the sonne of James Grene gentilman was baptized the xj of januarie.
base. Rawlphe the sonne of Ellen fawley was baptized the same daye base gotton.
John Wilkinson the sonne of John Wilkinson was baptized the same day.
Alice and Anne dowghters of John Grene was bapd. the xiiijth of Januari.

Menso FEBRUARIJ.

Robert yates sonne of francis yates baptized ye 8 day.
Elsabeth dyson dowghter of nicholas dyson bapt. the xth.
Elsabethe dowghter of Willm wood of Ecclesfeld bapt. 23.

MARTIJ.

Grace hobson dawghter of Cotton Hobson		baptized vj' die.
Robert Brownell sonne of Willm. Brownell baptized ...		baptized vj' die.
Francis wilde sonne of John wild of Wadsley		bapt. 15 day.
Nicholas goode sonne of John Goode		baptized the xxth day.
Mary Frickley		baptized the xxvijth day.
Anne Bowman filia Roberti Bowman		... baptized .....
Randulphus hyde filij Wilhelmi hyde		bapt. xx . . .

MARTIJ. [1607.]

George Wilkinson sonne of Roberte Wilkinson...	bapt. the xxix'

APRILIS.

Catheran Burnett dawghter of John Burnett ...	ye 8 day
Francis filia Wilhelmi Basworthe ...	bapt. xvij'
Gertride filia Nicholai Tayler	bapt. 20 d.
Ellen Hill dawghter of Alexander Hill ..	bapt. 29.

Maij.

Anne filia Lawrencij Maydon	...	bapt. primo die.
Anne Lockwod filia Johanis	...	bapt. primo die.
Alexander the sonne of Thomas brooke	...	bap. ye same day.
Alexsand. hatfeld and anne hatfeld ...	...	bap. ye 3 day.
John the sonne of Thomas Gilles	...	bap. ye xiiij' day.
henry the sonne of John Creswick	...	bap. yo same day.
Thomas Sugden sonne of John Sugden	...	baptized the xxiiijth maij.
HElline Clarke filia of Willm clarke	...	bapt. the same day.

Mense Junij.

Thomas dougmanton sonne of humphrey duckmaton		baptizatus erat viij die.
HEllinge the dowghter of Richard hobson	...	bapt. 22.
Anne the dowghter of thomas Potter	...	22.
Thomas the sonne of Richard oulfeld	...	bapt. 28.

Mense Julij.

Esabell Wagley filia Tho. Wagley	...	bapt. the xij' die.
Mary Walker filia Nicholai Walker	...	was baptized the same die.
Anne howden dawghter of Robert howden	...	was baptized the xxij.
Willm. Nutt the sonne of Robert Nutt	...	was baptized the xxv'
A child of Charles bulluses	...	bapt. yo same day.

Mense Augusti.

Hellen Bullus filia johanis bullus	...	bapt. ix'
Willm Waynwright filij Roberti Waynwright	...	bapt. ix'
Thomas Barnsley filij Willhelmi barnsley	...	bapt. ix'
Edethe Clark dawghter of John Clark	...	was baptized the xj'
Willm Curtis sonne of John Curtis	...	was baptized the xvj'
Mary daughter of William Stones	...	baptized the

September.

Jayne the dawghter of Willm Hargres	....	bapt. vij' day.
Esabell dawghter of Thomas Wright	...	bapt. xvj' die.

September.

Robert Jepson the sonne of Alexander Jepson	...	bapt. 24.
Margaret filia Richardi Warde	...	bapt. the xj'
James Nixson filij Georgij	...	bapt. xvj'

October.

Simon Wilkinson filij Roberti Wilkinson	...	bapt. the xth.
Francis Hall filij Roberti Hall	...	bapt. the xij'
Annis Trippit filia Thomæ Trippit	...	bapt. xiij'
Alice Thropp filia petri Thropp	...	bapt. xvj'
Robert mayson filij Roberti mayson	...	bapt. xx4'

November.

Thomas bower filij Johanis bower	bapt. xv'
Margret butcher filia Richardi butcher	bapt. xv'
jone filia Randulpe Rawden	bapt. xvj'
Raulphe Trulove filij Edwardi Trulowe	bap. 22'

December.

Susan Thropp filia Rogeri Thropp	bapt. vj'
Nicholas hill filij Nicholai hill	bapt. xj'
Thomas Grub filij Radulphi Grub	bapt. xxv'
Willm. Whittecars filij Wilhelmi Whittecars	bapt. 27.
Raulphe button filij Radulphi button	bapt. 28.
Thomas birkes filij Georgij birkes	bapt. 28.

Januarij.

Elsabethe Carr filia hugoni Carr	bapt. the j'
Elsabetho Ayro filia Lawrencij Ayro	bapt. the j'
George Rogers filij Francisci Rogers	bapt. the xvij'
Nicholas Genne filij margart Genne	bapt. base 22.
John filij Nicholai Gilles	bapt. 24.

Februarij.

jennet filia Thome Machine	bapt. ij'
Marke filij Johanis Cowper de mortomlay	bapt. vij'
Robertus filij Johanis basworthe	bapt. vij'
Robertus filij Thome beard de mortumley	bapt. xiiij'

Martij. [1608.]

Johan Trippit filij Johanis Trippit	bapt. ij'
Anne jesopp filia Anne jesopp base gotten	was baptized xiiij'
Anne burley filia Godfridi burley	bapt. xv'
George filij James bowmes	bapt. xxvj'
Hellen filia Jacobi Lister	bapt. xxvij.

Aprill.

A child of Robert oxspringe	bapt. xxiiij'
Anne Ashton filia brian Ashton	bapt. xxv'
. . . . . . basworthe filia Raulphe basworthe	bapt. xxv'
Elsabethe filia johanis berrey	bapt. xxv'
sonne of Edward berrey	bapt. xviij'

Maij.

Margret Slater filia Thome Slayter (Slatter)	bapt. 15.
Elsabethe filia Richardi Carr	bapt. xx'
Elizabeth filia Thome birkes	bapt. xxij'
mare filia Thome Greaves	bapt. xxij'
Willm. hill filij Johanis hill	bapt. xxix'

Junij.

Elizabethe Wilkinsone filia johanis Wilkinsone	bapt. ix' die.
Willm Lodge filij Johanis Lodge	bapt. ix'
Alice dobson filia Johanis dobson	bapt. ix'
Elizabeth filia Johanis Parkin de Wadsley ...	bapt. x'
Robert Carr filij Johanis Carr	bapt. xix'

Mense Julij.

Hellen filia Roberti Jepson	bapt. iij'
John Walker filij Johanis Walker	bapt. 24'
Margret filia Thomæ hall de Wadsley	bapt. 24'
Robert filij Nicholai Nalor	bapt. 25'
Willm filij Roberti Wilkinson	bapt. xxx'

Augusti.

Alexsande Foster filij Aliciæ Foster base gotton ...	bapt. iiij'
Thomas filij jerrat Freman	bapt. xvj'
Anne filia Jerrat Freman	bapt. xvj'
Margret filia Willm Staniforthe	bapt. 21'
Willm filij Willm barnsley	22'

September.

hellen filia Wibelmi Shawe	bapt. j'
...... fili Wilhelmi barnsley	bapt. eod. die.

October.

Anne filia Johanis Wigfall	bapt. ij'
Margret filia Wilhelmi Birkes	bapt. iij'
Elizabethe hibilson filia henrici hibisson	bapt. vij'
Anne filia Nicholai Beane	bapt. 15th.
Wm. filij Nicholai Shircliffe	bapt. 17.
Rawlphe filij hugonis Meller	bapt. 18.
Catherin filia Nicholai Catterall	bapt. xxj.
Nicholas filij Roberti Carr	bapt. 23.
Margret filia Wilhelmi hartley	bapt. 26.
Henry dyson filij nicholai dyson	bapt. xxxth.
Willm Turner filij henrici Turner	bapt. xxxth.

November.

Tho. filij nicholai hurt	bapt. j'
Wilhelmus Carr filij Wilhelmi Carr	vj'
jone filia nicholai marshall de bradfold	bapt. viij'
Tho. filij Georgij hobson	bapt. xj'
Elizabethe filia Henrici Hibitson	17'
Henricus filij francissi Woodhouse	19'
Alicia filia Tho. Trippett	25'

Elizabethe **Thomson** fili Roberti	...	...	bap. 27'
Joan filia nicholai **Parkin**	...	...	bapt. 27.
Jonæ filia Wilhelmi Brownell	...	...	bap. xxx'

DECEMBER.

Marye filia John Creswicke	...		bapt. 4'
John filij Alexsannder hartley	...		bapt. 4'
Georgij filij Johan Parkin	...		bapt. xj'
Gilbert filij Thomæ hayge	...		bapt. xj'
Anne filia Randulphus carr	...	...	bapt. xj'
Nicholas filij Wilhelmi Sampson	...	...	xj'
Margret filia John frickley	...		xj'
Elizabeth felia Jo. Shaw	...		bapt. xvj'
Ellis filij Roberti Wilkinson	...		bapt. 2j'
Alexsannder filij Wilhelmi Ashton	...		bap. 2j'

JANUARIE.

John duckmanton filij humpherdi Duckmanton...			baptized the vj'
Marie filia Richardi Wood	...		baptized viij'

FEBRUARIJ.

Anne filia Wilhelmi **Bradley**	...	...	bapt. februarie viij'
Alice filia Jo. Skargell	...	...	bapt. the ix'
Anne filia Johanis Goder	...	...	bapt. the xij'
Nicholas filij Roberti matheyman	...	...	bapt. xv.
Anne filia Jacabi Greene generos.	...	...	bapt. the xvj'
Thomas filij' Anthonij Law	...	...	bapt. the 19'

MARCIJ Anno dmi. [1609.]

Jo. filij Thomæ Parkin de hesselshonghe	...	...	bapt. x'
Henry filius Roberti mayson	...	...	bapt. xj'
Hellen filia Anthoniæ Rawlinson	...	...	bapt. xj'
Anne filia Nicholai Creswicke de Wadsley	...	...	bapt. xxiiij'
Francis Bower filij Thome Bower	...	...	bapt. xxv'
margret filia Wilhelmi Staniforthe ...	...	...	xxvj'
Nicholas filius Nicholai Tailor	...	...	bapt. xxvij'
Elizabethe filia Georgij Kirkman	...	...	bapt. 29'

APRILIS.

John filius Wilhelmi **Baswortho**	...	...	bapt. the iij'
Anne filia francisi Barber	...	...	bapt. viiij'

APRILIS.

John filij jacobi lister	...	...	bapt. xv'
Robertus filius Wilhelmi Wood	...		bapt. the xvij'

Maij.

Nycholas filij Cristopher Croft ecclesfeild ...	bap. xiiijth.
Ana filia Tho. Gills de Chappell	baptd. ye xxiijth.

Junij.

George filij Johe. Wyldo de Wadsley	bapt. ye xjth.
Frauncis filia hugh Allen	bapt. eod. die.
Issabell filia Caroli Croft de Whittley	bapt. ye xviijth.

Julij.

Elsabeth filia Francis Barbar de Wadsley ...	bapt. ye xxvth.

August.

Wylim. ffili Robt. Bowman	bapt. ye vjth.
Ann filia Tho. Shirtcliffe de hoole house (Hoyle house)	eod. die.

September.

Thomas fili ffrancis Scorer ...	bapt. the xxjxth.

October.

Hester ffilia Tho. Brooke de Chappell	bapt. ye ffirst day.
Ann filia Wyllm. Bramwith	bapt. eod. die.
Nycholas ffilij Laurence Saurbye	bapt. ye iiijth day.
Elsabeth filia Robt. Wylkinson	bapt. the viijth day.
Barbara ffilia Wyllm. Bayliffe de Whittley	bapt. ye xijth.
Tho. ffilij John Roose	bapt. the xxvijth.

November.

Leonard ffilij Tho. Parkin de his greene	primo die.
Jane ffilia Rychard hall	bapt. the xijth day.
Barbara ffilia ffrancis Johnson	bapt. the xixth day.
Ann ffilia George Thorpe	bapt. ye xxvjth day.

December.

Ann ffilia Tho. Staniland	bapt. the iij day.
Rychard ffilij Nycholas Nayler	bapt. eod. die.
Alls ffilia Robt. Tomson	bapt. the xth day.
Robt. ffilij Robt. parkin de Wadsley	bapt. eod die.
Nycholas ffilij Wyllm. Stones	bapt. the xvijth day.
Dorytye ffilia Robt. Nutt	bapt. ye xxxth day.

Januarij.

Rychard ffilij Nycholas Scoorer	bapt. primo die.
ffrauncis ffilij John Ragg	bapt. the vijth day.
Wyllm. ffilij Robt. Sheirtcliffe de ecclesfeild	bapt. ye xiiijth day.
Wyllm. filij Edward Senyer	bapt. eod. die.

Elsabeth filia Ralph Stonns	...	...	...	bapt. eod. die.
Margrett filia Ralph Rawlin	...	...	...	bapt. eod. die,
John ffilij Anthony hardy	...	...	...	bapt. the xxijth day.
Robt. ffilij Tho. Coley	...	...	...	bapt. the xxiiijth day.
Margrett filia Edward Trewlove	...	...	...	bapt. ye xxvjth day.
john ffilij Ralph Hadffeild	...	...	...	bapt. the xxviijth day.
Hugh ffilij Johe. Lockwood	...	...	...	bapt. eod. die.

FFEBRUARY.

Margrett filia ffrancis Roggers	...	...	...	bapt. the ij day.
Thomas ffilij Charles Bullus	...	...	...	bapt. ye xjth day.
Joan filia peter Thropp	...	...	...	bapt. the xvjth day.
Elsabeth filia Alexander Jepson	...	...	...	bapt. ye xxiiijth day.

MARCH Anno Dmi. [1610.]

Margrett filia Johe. Berry	...	...	...	bapt. ye ij day.
Margrett filia Tho. hobson de Wadsley	...	...	...	bapt. ye vijth day.
Nycholas ffilij Wyllm. Stanifforth	...	...	...	bapt. eod. die.
john ffilij john Bullus	...	...	...	bapt. the xxjth day.
Catherin filia Nycholas Beane	...	...	...	bapt. eod. die.

APRILL.

Barbara filia Tho. Beard	...	...	...	bapt. the iiijth day.
Ralph filij Ralph Leo	...	...	...	bapt. the xth day.
Tho. ffilij Joho. Clarke	...	...	...	bapt. the xxijth day.

MAIUS.

Willmus. filius Willmi. ffearnilie	...	...	bapt. fuit xiij' die.
Anna filia illegitima Eliz. Stockdale	...	...	bapt. fuit eode. die.

JUNIUS.

Thomas filius Thomæ Hoyland	...	...	bapt. fuit xvij' die.
Elizabetha filia Richardi Ouldfield	...	...	bapt. fuit xix' die.
Anna filia petri dey	...	...	bapt. fuit xxix' die.

JULIUS.

Willmus. filius Willmi. hargresse	...	...	bapt. fuit primo die.
Elizabetha filia Thomæ Gilles	...	...	bapt. fuit xv' die.

AUGUSTUS.

Katherina filia Willmi. Birks	...	...	bapt. fuit primo die.
Anna filia Johis. Curteise	...	...	bapt. fuit quinto die.

SEPTEMBER.

Willmus. filius Radulphi Carro	...	...	...	bapt. secundo die.
Richardus filius Radulphi Basforth	...	...	...	bapt. fuit eodem die.
Richardus filius Radulphi Button	...	...	...	bapt. fuit xxj' die.
Nicholaus filius Godfridi Birley	...	...	...	bapt. fuit xxiij' die.

Occtober.

Georgius filius johannis Gleydall baptiz. fuit septimo die Octobris.
Anna filia Thomæ Hall baptiz. fuit eodem die.
Thomas filius johannis Creswicke baptiz. fuit decimo die Octobris.

November.

Margeria filia Willmi. Hinchelyffe bapt. fuit undecimo die Novembris.
Johannes filius Willmi. Staniforth baptiz. fuit eodem die.
Anna filia johannis Wilkinson baptiz. eodem die.
Sara filia Richardi Wood bapt. fuit decimo sexto die Novembris.
Eduardus filius Willmi. Brownell bapt. xviij' die Novembris.
Robertus filius Margrete Waggaley bapt. fuit eodem die.
Eliz. filia ffrancisci Hobson baptiz. fuit xxv' Novembris.

December.

Thomas filius Thomæ Machin bapt. fuit	...	secundo die Decembris.
Margreta filia Thomæ Parkin bapt. fuit	...	quarto die Decembris.
Anna filia Eduardi Berrie bapt. fuit ...	...	... ix' die Decembris.
Issabella et Alicia gem. filiæ Thomæ Potter ...	...	xiiijto die Decembris.
Thomas filius Tho. Stanniland bapt. fuit ...	...	... xx' die Decembris.
Georgius filius Robti. Oxpringe bapt. fuit ...	...	...xxiij' die Decembris.
Willmus. filius Georgij Hobson bapt. fuit ...	...	... xxx' die Decembris.

Januarius.

Richardus filius jacobi Twibill bapt. fuit ...	...	... sexto die januarij.
Johannes filius Thomæ Birkes bapt. fuit ...	...	xiij die januarij.
Eliz. filia Willmi' Bradley bapt. fuit ...	...	eodem die.
Thomas filius Richardi Butcher bapt. fuit ..	...	xx' die januarij.
Thomas filius Willmi Barnsley bapt. ...	...	eodem die.
johannes filius Willmi. Whittakers bapt. fuit ...	...	eodem die.
Georgius filius Johis. Machin bapt. fuit ...	...	xxj' januarij.
Maria filia Willmi. Hide bapt. fuit	..	xxii' die januarij.
Helena filia illegit. Helenæ ffalley baptiz. ...	...	xxvto die januarij.
Johes. filius illegit. Aliciæ Doughtiman bapt. fuit	...	xxvj' die januarij.
Anna filia Thomæ Creswicke bapt. fuit	...	xxvij die januarij.

Ffebruarius

Alicia filia Georgij Birkes bapt. fuit ...	...	... primo die ffebruarij.
Johes. filius Johannis Basforth bapt. fuit ...	....	... quinto die ffebruarij.
Eliz. filia Tho. Crosley bapt. fuit ...	...	...decimo die ffebruarij.

Martius.

Henricus filius Johis Hall bapt. fuit ...	...	... secundo die martij.
Willmus. filius Willimi. Basforth bapt. fuit ...	...	eodem die.

Anna filia Anthonij Rollinson bapt. tertio die Martij.
Anna filia Nicholai Hill bapt. fuit. eodem die.
Nicho. filius illegit. Saræ Manton bapt. fuit eodem die.
Anna fil. Willimi. Waterhouse baptiz. fuit ... ... vto die Martij.
Katherina filia Henrici Hawksworth bapt. ... ... ix' die Martij.
Eliz. filia Roberti Wainwright bapt. fuit ... ... decimo die Martij.
Radulphus filius Xpofer. Croftes baptizat. fuit ... ... xvij' die Martij.
Lucia filia Nicholai Parkin bapt. fuit ... ... xvij' die Martij.
Emota. filia Richardi Carre bapt. fuit ... ... xxij' die Martij.
Willimus. filius johannis Slatter bapt. fuit ... ... xxiij' Martij.

Aprill. [1611.]

Robt. Sonn of Rychard Shirtcliff bapt. the ... ... xxvth.
june. Mark Sonn of John Carr bapt. yo ... ... xxth of june.

Julij.

John soun of Wyllm. Machon bapt. the ... ... xxiiijth day.

September.

Bridgett doughter of Mr. james Greene bapt. the ... ... xijth.
john Sonn of John Berry bapt. the ... ... xxixth.
Ann doughter of Tho. hartley bapt. the same day.

October.

Nycholas Sonn of james Lyster bapt the ... xxth.

November.

jane doughter of Robt. mathyman bapt. the ... ... xviijth.
Ann doughter of john Losh bapt. tho ... ... xxjth.

December.

Kathrin doughter of Wyllm. Staniforth bapt. ye ... ... viijth.
Ralph Sonn of Rychard hall bapt. the same day.
Kathrin doughter of George Birks bapt. the ... ... xvth.
Margrett doughter of Cotton hobson bapt. the ... ... xxijth.
Georg & John sonnes of Francis daniell bapt. ye ... ... xxvth.
Ann doughter of Edward Trewlove bapt. ye ... ... xxixth.

January.

Margrett doughter of John Godder bapt. yo ... ... vjth.
Robart Sonn of Robt. Carr bapt. the ... ... xijth.
Nicholas Sonn of Tho. Staniland bapt. the ... ... xxvth.
Margrett doughter of Nycholas Scoar bapt. ... ... xxvjth.
Tho. Sonn of james fosterd bapt. the ... ... xxixth.
Nycholas sonn of james Twibill bapt. the ... xxxth.

FFEBRUARYE.

George sonn of Tho. hobson bapt. the	...	ix
Ann doughter of Steven meller bapt. the	...	xxvth.
Tho. Sonn of margrett hepworth bapt. ye	...	xxvjth.
Wyllm. sonu of Ralph Lee bapt. the same day.		

MARCH.

Robt. Sonn of Robt. Bucher bapt. the	...	first day.
Wyllm. Sonn of John Creswick bapt. the	...	xiijth.
John sonn of Alexander Jepson bapt. the	...	xiiijth.
Ann doughter of henry Bayly bapt.	...	xxjth.
ffrancis sonn of Robt. more bapt. the	...	xxvijth.
Elsabeth doughter of Francis Roggers bapt.	...	xxixth.

APRILL. [1612.]

Susan doughter of Rychard wood bapt. the	...	iij daye.
Margrett doughter of John Sugden bapt. ye same day.		
Alexander sonn of John Beett bapt. ye	...	vth.
John Sonn of Robt. Bowman bapt. ye	...	xijth.
Elsabeth doughter of John Wylie bapt. ye	...	xxviijth.

MAIJ.

Nycholas Sonn of Wyllm. Clark bapt. ye	...	xvijth.
Ann doughter of John dobson bapt. ye same day.		

JUNE.

Joan doughter of Edward hartley bapt. ye	...	xxjth.

JULIJ.

Wyllm. Sonn of Tho. Smith bapt. ye	...	xijth.
Ann doughter of Tho. Trippett bapt. ye	...	xixth.
Margrett doughter of Robt. Tomson bapt. ye	...	xxjth.
Nycholas Sonn of John Basforth bapt. ye	...	xxijth.

AUGUST.

George Sonn of Robt. Jepson bapt. ye	...	vijth.
Emott doughter of John Bullas bapt. ye	...	xijth.
Tho. Sonn of Wyllm. machon bapt. ye	...	xixth.
Robt. Sonn of Robt. Howldinge bapt. ye same daye.		
Mary doughter of George hobson bapt. ye	...	xxvjth.
Anthony Sonn of Nycholas Walker bapt. ye	...	xxxth.
Mary doughter of Peter Thropp bapt. ye samo day.		
Mary doughter of Tho. crosley bapt. ye same day.		

SEPTEMBER.

Michell Sonn of Rogger dawes bapt. ye	...	ij day.

Brydgett doughter of john Burnett bapt. ye ... ... vth.
Ann doughter of John Skergell bapt. ye same day.
John Sonn of John Hall bapt. the ... ... xiijth.
Ellen doughter of Tho. Cutlar bapt. ye xxijth.
Ralphe Sonn of Ralph Carr bapt. the xxvijth.
Reneld Sonn of Tho. Eayor (Eyre) bapt. ye same day.
Ann **doughter** of Nicholas Rychardson bapt. ye... xxixth.

OCTOBER.

Alls doughter of john Stasie bapt. ye ... ... iiijth.
Margrett doughter of Tho. ganke bapt. **ye** ... ... xviijth.
Tho. Sonn of Robt. Barber bapt. ye ... ... xxjth.
Jane doughter of John Barnsley bapt. ye ... ... **xxvth.**

NOVEMBER.

Wyllm. Sonn of john ffrickley bapt. ye ... vth.
Francis Sonn of john Triggett bapt. ye ... ... viijth.
Robt. Sonn of Robt. Wilkinson bapt. ye same day.
Ann doughter of Tho. Brook bapt. ye ... ... xvth.
Tho. Sonn of Wyllm. Beaylyf bapt. ye ... ... xxijth.
Edward Sonn of Edward mason bapt. ye ... ... xxvjth.

DECEMBER.

Ellin **doughter of** Nycholas Vippan bapt. **ye** ... ... xxvjth.
Ellin **doughter of** John parkin bapt. ye ... xxvij.

JANUARYE.

Charles **Sonne of Charles hill** bapt. **ye first.**
Margrett doughter of John Carr bapt. ye ... iij day.
Elsabeth doughter of Georg Thorp bapt. **ye** ... xth.
Ann doughter of henry Roggers **bapt. ye same day.**
Tho. Sonn of peter dey bapt. ye ... ... xxxth.

FEBRUARY.

Tho. Sonn of ffrancis hobson bapt. ye xiiijth.
mary doughter of Tho. hall bapt. ye same day.
Robt. Sonn of Mr. james Greene bapt. ye ... ... xvjth.
John Sonn of Tho. Staniland bapt. ye ... ... sixth.
Ann doughter of Edward patinson bapt. ye ... ... xxjth.
Doryty doughter of Georg Turner bapt. ye ... ... xxvjth.

MARCHE.

Margrett doughter of Tho. Bower bapt. ye ... ... **vth.**
Debora doughter of John machon bapt. ye ... ... **vijth.**
Nycholas Sonn of Ralph Rawlin bapt. ye ... ... xijth.
Sara doughter of Wyllm. Byrks bapt. ye same day.

[1613.]

Georg Sonn of Rychard Nodom bapt. ye ... xxviijth.
Nycholas Sonn of Nycholas wadilove bapt. ye same day.
Isabell doughter of Robt. Coumbe bapt. ye same day.

Aprill.

Wyllm. Sonn of Nycholas Cresswick bapt. ye ... xvijth.
Wyllm. Sonn of John Lockwood bapt. ye ... xviijth.

Maij.

Ann doughter of Nicholas waterhouse bapt. ye ... ... first.
Robt. Sonn of George Nickson bapt. ye ... ... vijth.
Charles Sonn of Tho. Beard bapt. ye ... ... ixth.
Ellin doughter of Tho. parkin bapt. ye ... ... xxiijth.
Ffrancis Sonn of Edward Selvester bapt. ye ... ... xxxth.

June.

Wyllm. Sonn of Wyllm. hart bapt. ... ... iijth.
Edward Sonn of Tho. Byrks bapt. ye ... ... vth.
Wyllm. Sonn of Tho. Colly bapt. ye ... ... xxth.

Julij.

Nycholas Sonn of Nycholas Shirtcliff bapt. ... vjth.
Elsabeth doughter of Anthony Rollinson bapt. ... ... xjth.
Dorythy doughter of Nycholas Beane bapt. same day.
Issabell doughter of john Wylkinson bapt. the ... xviijth.
John Sonn of John Loshe bapt. the same day.
Elsabeth doughter of John Slatter bapt. the ... ... xxth.

August.

Rychard Sonn of Wyllm. wood bapt. the ... ... xth.
Ellin doughter of james Twibill bapt. ye ... ... xiijth.
Nycholas Sonn of Wyllm. Stones bapt. ye same day.
Anthony Sonn of . . . . . . Gamble the same day.
Nycholas Sonn of James Fosterd bapt. ye ... xvth.
Ann doughter of Robt. parkin bapt. ye same day.
John Sonn of John Cresswicke bapt. ... ... xxvijth.

September.

John Sonn of Jo. Staniforth bapt. ye ... ... iij day.
Ellin doughter of Francis Barber bapt. ye ... ... xxiiijth.

October.

Ellin doughter of Tho. Cutlar bapt. ye iiijth.

November.

Cysselye doughter of Tho. Cowper bapt. ye ... ... first day.
Tho. sonn of Tho. Walker bapt. the ... xth day.

Jo. Sonn of mary Boy basegotton bapt. ye same day.
Wyllm. Sonn of Rychard hall bapt. ye ... ... xxth.

DECEMBER.

Francis Sonn of John hall bapt. ye ... ... xvijth.
John Sonn of Alexandr. hartley bapt. ... ... xxth.

JANUARYE.

Wyllm. Sonn of John Bower bapt. ye ... ... xijth.
John Sonn of henry Roggers bapt. ye ... ... xxijth.

FFEBRUARYE.

Ralph Sonn of Ralph Basforthe bapt. ye ... ... ij day.
. Sonn of Rychard Carr bapt. ... ... vjth.
Tho. Sonn of Tho. potter bapt. ye ... ... xiijth.
jenett doughter of John Shawe bapt. ye same day.
Wyllm. Sonn of John moorhouse bapt. ye ... ... xvjth.
Willm. Sonn of Wyllm. Staniforth bapt. ... ... xixth.
Ann doughter of Mr. Dawson bapt. ye ... ... xxjth.

MARCHE.

ffrancis Sonn of Wyllm. Baylyffe bapt. ye ... ... xixth.

[1614.]

John Sonn off Robart Smithe of Bromilye bapt.... ... ... xxvijth.
Thomas Sonn of Rychard owlfeld bapt. ye same day.

APRILL.

Dorythy doughter of Georgh birks bapt. ye ... ... first day.
...... doughter of henry Ibotson bapt. ye ... ... vijth.
Nycholas Sonn of Nycholas Slatter bapt. ... ... xvjth.
Lawrence sonn of Lawrence Sawrbye bapt. ... ... xvijth.
Tho. Sonn of John Nawt bapt. ... ... xxjth.
Nycholas Sonn of James Lyster bapt. ... ... xxvjth.
Anthony Sonn of Tho. Staniland bapt. ... ... xxviijth.

MAIJ.

Issabell doughter of John Gooder bapt. the ... ... xxijth.
Jane doughter of Ralph Lee bapt. the ... ... xxvijth.
Rogger son of Roger Throp bapt. ye ... ... xxixth.

JUNIJ.

Wyllm. Sonn of Thomas machon bapt. ... ... vth.
Wyllm. Sonn of Cotton hobson bapt. ye same day.
Alls doughter of Anthonye Lawe bapt. the ... ... xixth.

JULLIJ.

Beteris doughter of John Beete bapt. ye ... ... xvijth.
Kathrin donghter of Wm. deye bapt. the ... ... xxiijth.

August.

Elsabeth dought. of Ann Falley base got bapt. ye	...	...	vijth.
Charles sonn of Elsabeth Robts. bapt. the	...	...	xvijth.
Robt. Sonn of meares base gott bapt. the	...	...	xxjth.
mary doughter of Robt. Wemwright bapt.	...	...	xxviijth.

Septemb.

Wm. Sonn of Wyllm. Shaw bapt. the	...	iiijth.
Margrett doughter of Tho. Sheirtcliffe bapt. ye ...	...	viijth.

October.

mary doughter of john Barnsley bapt. ye	...	...	ixth.
Wm. Sonn of john Stasie bapt. ye ...	...	...	xxiijth.
Alls Doughter of Nychas Scorer bapt. same day.			

November.

Wm. john & hellen sonnes & doughter of Wm. Bradley bapt. ye	...		vjth.
Elsabeth doughter of john wigfall bapt. the	...	...	xxiijth.
Gilbart Son of Rogger Slatter bapt. ye	...	...	xxvjth.
Isabell doughter of Tho. Crofte bapt. ye	...	...	xxxth.

December.

john Sonn of john Clark bapt. ye ...	...	...	...	xvjth.

Januarij.

Issabell dought. of George jobson bapt. ye	...	...	xvjth.
Elsabeth dought. of Richard Sheirtcliffe bapt. ye	...	...	xxijth.
Sonn of Nicholas Linsett bapt. ye ...	...	...	xxixth.

Febbuary.

margrett doughter of Ralph Carr bapt. ye	...	...	xth.
John & Charles sonns of Wm. Gest bapt. ye	...	...	xvjth.
Elin doughter of Wm. machin bapt. ye	...	...	xvijth.
...... Sonn of Tho. Swainson bapt. ye	...	...	xixth.

Marche. [1615.]

Issabell doughter of henry Stork bapt. ye	...	...	first day.
John Sonn of Francis barlow base gott bapt. the	...	...	xvth.
mary doughter of Nicholas dyson bapt. the	...	...	xxvjth.

Aprill.

henry Sonn of Robt. Tomson bapt. the	...	...	viijth.
Robt. Sonn of mary Boy base gott bapt. same day.			

Maij.

Ann doughter of Gilbert Creswicke bapt. ye	...	xviijth.
Ellin doughter of Francis hobson bapt. ye same day.		
jenett doughter of Nycholas Slatter bapt. same day.		

72

JUNIJ.

Elsabeth doughter of John Barnsley bapt. ye	...	...	...	xviijth.
Ann doughter of John parkin bapt. the	...	...	...	xxixth.

JULIJ.

Elsabeth doughter of Nycholas Whittakers bapt. ... xth.

AUGUST.

Anthony Sonn of Anthony hardye bapt. ... ... xxth.
. . . Sonn of Thomas Eayre bapt. the same day.

SEPTEMBER.

Issabell dowghter of Wyllm. Baylyf bapt. the	...	...	xth.
mary doughter of Robt. woodhouse bapt. the	...	...	xvijth.
Ann doughter of James Twybill bapt. the		...	xixth.
Elsabeth doughter of Thomas Walker bapt. same day.			

OCTOBER.

Ann doughter of peter deye bapt. the	...	...	viijth day.
Edward Sonn of Edward Berry bapt. the same day.			
Robt. Sonn of Rychard owlfeld bapt. the same day.			
. . Sonn of Rychard Broadbent bapt.	...	...	xxijth.
Dynes daughter of Rychard mathyman bapt.	...	...	xxvijth.
Edward Sonn of john Losh bapt. the	...	...	xxixth.
Rychard Sonn of henry Barker bapt. same day.			

NOVEMBER.

Thomas Sonn of john bapt. the	...	...	xijth.
margrett fillia Robt. howlding bapt.			eodem die.
Nycholas fillij Nycholas Walker **bapt.**		...	xxth.

JANUARIJ.

John fillij Nicholas parkin bapt.	...	...	vijth.
Francis fillij Richard hall bapt. the same day.			
Robart fillij john Hall bapt. the		...	xiiijth.
Tho. fillij Richard Gamble bapt. same day.			

FFEBRUARIJ.

John fillij Thomas Beard bapt. the	...	...	iiijth.
Alls filia Thomas Smith bapt. the same day.			
ffrancis filia Anthony Robinson bapt.	...	...	xixth.
Thomas filij mr. dawson bapt.	...	...	xxvth.
Elsabeth filia Nicholas wood bapt. same day.			
filia will hanley bapt.	...	...	**xxvjth.**

MARCH. [1616.]

Willm. filij Willm. Ashton bapt. ... ... xxviijth.

Willm. filij John Clark bapt. ... ... xxxth.

APRILL.

John filij John Carr bapt. ... ... vijth.
Elsabeth fillia Richard Raworth bapt. same day.
mary filia Willm. Carr bapt. ... ... xijth.
Ellin filia Willm. Crosley bapt. ... ... xxjth.

MAIJ.

Ellin fillia Willm. Birks bapt. ... ... xijth.

JUNIJ.

Tho. fillij Robt. Sheirtcleff bapt. ... ... iiijth.
Exvperivt fillij Willm. hart bapt.

JULLY.

Nicholas filij John Walker bapt. ... ... vijth.
Ellin filia John peace bapt. ... ... xijth.

AUGUST.

Cristian filia henry Turner bapt. ... ... xxvth.

SEPTEMBER.

Cathrin. filia Willm. hartley bapt. ... ... xviijth.

OCTOBER.

Elsabeth filia cotton hobson bapt. ... ... vjth.
mary filia John Broadbent bapt. same.
henry filij Richard Shirtcliff bapt. ... ... xiijth.
Willm. filij Willm. howsley bapt. same.
Ann & mary filiæ james foster bapt. ... ... xxv.
Robt. filij Luke yonge bapt. ... ... xxvijth.
Ann filia Georg Ashton base gott bapt. ... ... xxxth.

NOVEMBER.

Georg filij James holland bapt. ... ... xth.
Robt. filij Richard Carr bapt. ... ... xxvth.

DECEMBER.

. . . . . . filia James Lister bapt. ... ... viijth.

FFEBRUARY.

mary filia John wainwright bapt. ... ... ij day.
Elsabethe filia of . . . . . . Kellett bapt. same day.
Robt. fillij Ann Allen bapt. ... ... xvjth.

MARCH.

Elsabeth filia Tho. Kirkbye bapt. the ... ... ij day.
. . . . . . filij john Creswick bapt. the ... ... xvjth.
henry filij Francis Warter bapt. same.

[1617.]

Tho. fillij Robart parkin bapt.	xxiijth.
Willm. filij Nicholas hurt bapt.	xxx.

April.

Willm. filij John hall bapt.	iiijth.
Nycholas filij Thomas machon bapt.	vjth.
Ann filia Thomas Crosley bapt.	xijth.
. . filia John Morrhouse bapt.	xxvth.
Willm. filij Tho. Birks bapt.	xxvijth.

Junij.

John filij Nicholas Gills bapt.	8th.
John son of Thomas Parkin bapt.	24th.

July.

Robt. son of Robt. Jepson bapt.	xijth.
Anne daughter of Wm. Staniforth bapt.	eodem die.
Anne daughter of ffrancis hauksworth bapt.	xxth.

August.

Elsaboth filia john Linfet bapt.	xth.
Peter filij Thomas Staniland bapt.	xvijth.
Willm. filij Robt. Broadbent bapt.	eodem die.
Robt. filij Nicholas Shereliffe bapt.	xxiiijth.

September.

George son of Ralph Carre bapt.	vijth.
Susan daughter of Thom. Wilkinson bapt.	xiiijth.
Alexander son of Margret Bower bapt.	xxth.

October.

An filia Wiliam. Steemson bapt.	vth.
ffrancis filij Ralph Rawlin bapt.	vjth.
Mathew filij Humfrey Northoll bapt.	ixth.
Elsabeth filia John heward bapt.	xijth.
Richard son of John Beete bapt.	xxvjth.
Elsabeth daughter of james Twibell bapt. eode die.	
George filij George Birkes bapt. eodem die.	

November.

Mathew son of Robt. Coumbe bapt.	jth.
John filij henry Nayler bapt.	ijth.
Elsabeth filia Robt. Mathiman bapt.	xiiijth.
Margret filia Wm. Barnesley bapt.	xvjth.
Tho. filij Charles Smith bapt.	xxxth.

DECEMBER.

Mary filia Thomas Trippet bapt. ... ... xxjth.

JANUARY.

Elsabeth filia Wm. Carre bapt. ... ... xxviij.
Elin filia john Milner bapt. eodem die.

FFEBRUARY.

Ann filia John Barnesley bapt. ... ... j.
. . filia John Staniforth bapt. ... ... xjth.
Antho. filij Thomas Swainson bapt. ... ... xxth.

MARCH. [1618.]

Thomas son of henry Pogson bapt. ... ... jth.
Anne filia James Lister bapt. ... ... xvth.
James filij Thomas Brooke bapt. ... ... eodem die.
Margret filia Thomas Smith bapt. ... ... eodem die.
Nicholas filij John Clarke bapt. ... ... xvijth.
George son of Stephen Eller bapt. ... ... xxijth.
Edward filij Catherin Lockwod bapt. ... ... xxixth.
An filia henry Wilkinson bapt. ... ... xxxth.

APRILL.

John son of John Shaw bapt. ... ... vth.
Clemett filij ffrancis Parker bapt. ... ... xiiij.
Gilber son of Nicholas hill bapt. ... ... xix.
Mary filia Gilbert Creswicke bapt. ... ... xxij.

MAY.

Issabell filia Robt. hage bapt. ... ... j.
. . . . . . filij John hill bapt. ... ... ij.
Nicho. filij Nicholas Beane bapt. ... ... x.
Anne filia Willm. hargresse bapt. ... ... cod. die.
Elin daughter of Willm. Basforth bapt. ... ... xvij.
Mary filia Thomas hobson bapt. ... ... xxth.
James filij Charles houldinge bapt. ... ... xxiiij.
John son of Thomas Potter bapt. ... ... xxxth.

JUNE.

Nicholas filij Robt. hobson bapt. ... ... xiiijth.
Thomas filij Nicho. Richardson bapt. ... ... eode. die.
Antho. filij Thomas Ragge bapt. ... ... xx j.

JULY.

. . . . . . of John hall bapt. .. .. vij.
An filia Nicho. linfet bapt. ... ... xij.
Wm. filij Wm. heartley bapt. ... ... xxvj.

August.

Margret filia Tho. Pkin. alias Cowp. (Parkin alias Cowper) bapt.	ix.
ffrances filia Wm. Dey bapt.	xvjth.
Anne filia Robt. Shercliffe bapt.	xxxth.

September.

Elsabeth filia Thomas hoyland bapt.	ij.
Ralph filij Robt. houlden bapt.	vj.
Mary filia Bryan Cooke bapt.	eodem die.
...... filij John Wilkinson bapt.	xxj.
Thomas filij Tho. Carro bapt.	xxiiij.
Nicho. son of Robt. Jepson bapt.	xxv.
Elsabeth filia Ric. oxspringe bapt.	29.

October.

Thomas filij Jo. Twibell bapt.	xj.
Elsabeth filia Fra. hauksworth bapt. eode. die.	
Nicho. filij Jo. Losh bapt. eodem die.	
Wm. filij Ric. Shercliff bapt.	xxij.
Ani & ffrances filiis john Mias bapt.	xxv.

November.

Tho. filij Edward Berry bapt.	j.
Jo. filij Wm. Staniforth bapt.	eodem die.
Doritie filij Jo. Rivinton bapt.	eodem die.
Anne filia James holland bapt.	eodem die.
Jane filia Antho. Rollinsonne bapt....	iiij.
Rosemand filia Mr. ffrancis Nevell bapt.	xvij.
Mary filia Thomas Parkin bapt.	xxij.
George filij John Bullous bapt.	xxvij.

December.

heny filij Wm. Ashton bapt.	vj.
Mary filij Ralph Basforthe bapt.	eodm. die.
Issabell filia hen. Turner bapt.	xxvj.
John filij humfrey Northoll bapt.	xxvij.
.. of Willm. Bower bapt.	xxix.
Nicho. filij Nicho. Gill bapt.	xxx.

January.

Anthonie filij Willm. Slatter bapt.	xvij.
Thomas filij George Turner bapt.	eode. die.
Mary filia ffrancis hobson bapt.	xxj.
George filij Robert Perkin bapt.	eodem die.
John filij Cotton hobson bapt.	xxxj.
Robt. filij George Mathye bapt.	eode. die.

FFEBRUARY.

Anne filia Nicholas Wood bapt.	vij.
Mary filia John Wild bapt.	eod. die.
Charles filij Charles Smith bapt.	xiiij.

MARCH. [1619.]

Thomas filij John Clarke bapt.	vth.
Ralph filij Nicho. Perkin bapt.	vij.
Anne filia Anne Sawood bapt.	eod. die.
Robt. filij Issabell Wilkinson bapt.	xiiij.
Zakary filij Thomas Parkin bapt.	xxv.
Nary filia Georg Ashton bapt.	eodem die.
Elin filia ffrancis Watter bapt.	eode. die.

APRILL.

Nichol. filij Roger Throp bapt.	iiij.
John filij John Waynwright bapt.	eod. die.
Wm. filij Richard ffoxtone bapt.	xjth.
henr. filij henr. Wilkinsonne bapt.	xviij.
Ellis filij hen. Barbar bapt.	xxv.
Anne filia Nicho. Shercliffe bapt.	eodem die.

MAY.

jane filia Thome Kirby bapt.	ij.
Wm. filij Nicholas Shercliffe bapt.	xvj.
John filij	

. . . .

[N.B. The bottom of the page has been cut off.]

Isabell filia houmfrey Trippet bapt.	xx.
mary filia Wm. Bayliffe bapt.	xxvj.
Thomas filij Robt. Perkin bapt.	xxviij.

NOVEMBER.

Mary filia ffrancis Wilkinson bapt.	j.
Margret filia Robt. Dickonson bapt.	xix.

DECEMBER.

Elsabeth filia Ralph Carr bapt.	ij.
Willm. filij Wm. Beale bapt.	xxiv.
joan filia james Twibell bapt.	xxvij.

JANUARIE.

. . . . . . fillia John Millner bapt.	xxth.
. . . . . . fillij John Cresswicke bapt.	eod. die.
George fillij Willm. Stones bapt.	xxiijth.
Robert filij Willm. Housley bapt.	xxx'

FFEBRUARIE.

. . . . . . filia Henrio Mason bapt.	...	...	...	ij.
Anne fillia Wm. Waynwright bapt....	...	...	...	vjth.
Wm. fillij John Hall bapt.	...	...	...	...	eod. die.
Mairie filia Wm. Wood bapt.	...	...	...	...	eod. die.
Wm. fillij Willm. Birkes bapt.	...	...	...	...	xiijth.
Marie filia George Haughton bapt. ...	...	...	...	eod. die.
Ann filia Edward Wingfield bapt. ...	...	...	...	xvjth.
. . . . . . fillij Thomas Hobson bapt.	...	...	...	xxth.
John fillij John Parkin bapt.	...	...	...	...	xxvij.
Nicholas fillij Brian Cooke bapt.	...	...	...	...	eod. die.
Marie filia Geo. Collye bapt.	...	...	...	...	eod. die.

MARCH.

Thomas fillij Nich. Hoyland bapt. ...	...	...	...	xijth.
Francis fillij ffrancis Parker bapt. ...	...	...	...	eod. die.
Ellin filia John Moorhouse bapt. ...	...	...	...	xvijth.
Ellin fillia Gilbert Cresswicke bapt.	...	...	...	xxth.
Thom. fillij Thom. Willkinson bapt.	...	...	...	eod. die.
Geo. fillij Luke Yonge bapt.	...	...	...	...	xxiiijth.
Robert fillij Ralph Stones bapt.	...	...	...	...	xxvjth.
Margret filia james ffoster bapt.	...	...	...	...	eod. die.
Ellin filia Thom. Moller bapt.	...	...	...	...	eod. die.
Anthonie fillij jo. Ragge bapt.	...	...	...	...	xxvriij.
Marie filia jo. Slacke bapt.	...	...	...	...	xxix.

[N.B. The bottom of the page is cut off.]

THE END OF THE BAPTISMS CONTAINED IN THE FIRST VOLUME OF THE GENERAL REGISTER.

BURIALS

CONTAINED IN

The First Volume of the Parish Church Registers

OF

St. MARY'S, ECCLESFIELD,

In Co: YORK.

1558—Sept. 1603 (INCLUSIVE).

BURIALS.

[.1558.]

here followethe the names of psons. buryed.

Mense Marcij. [1558.]

Robt. Elvise pauper sepultus	...	...	...	...	xxvijmo die.
Isabell Scargell pauper sepulta		...	...	...	eod. die.

Mense Aprilis.

Alice Cutte pauper sepul.		...	...	...	iiijto die.
Willm. holden pauper sepult.	...	...	...	...	vij' die.
john fletcher pauper sepult.	...	...	...	...	xiij' die.
Margerie Grace & Richard machon sepult.		...	...	...	xxij' die.

Mense Maij.

Wydowe Elvise sepult.	...	...	...	...	xij' die.

Mense Augusti.

Widowe Wyldsmythe sepult.	....	...	...	...	vto die.
John Stigbucke sepult. ...	...	...	...	...	jxno die.
[86] Marye howsley sepult. ...	...	...	...	...	eod. die.
Robt. hill & puer Thome Bullus sepult.		...	...	...	x' die.
[90] Nicholas hatfeld sepult.	...	...	...	...	xj' die.

[86] Was probably wife of Thomas Howsley of Howsley Hall. [Vide note 90.]

[90] Was of Hatfield House, Shiregreen, in this parish.—He married Ann Sanderson, and was ancestor of the Hatfields of Shiregreen, Laughton en le Morthen & Hatfield.—His will is dated 2 August 1558, in it he mentions,—to be buried in Ecclesfield parish Church where my wife lyeth, "whose soul jesu pardon"—To the Church all such money as I have lent for the nesdes of the same—To Alexander Hatfield my son my farm at Shiregreen where I dwell and xxl.—To my son Nicholas Hatfield my farm in the Woodland and land at Wadsley bridge. Henry Shirecliffe and Thomas Dey to be trustees for my son john Hatfield and he to have my lands at Whitley also my right in Grubb House & Machon House and xxl.—My daughter Ann and her children xx nobles.—My daughter Elizabeth xls. and I remit and forgive her husband xl. he oweth me.—My daughter Katherine xls. & I forgive her husband xl. he oweth me.—To young Alexander Hatfield my kinsman xx nobles or cattel to that amount and the shepe he now hath.—To Francis Broke 2 Ewes & 2 Lambs—to young Nicholas Stanyforth 2 Ewes and 2 lambs—To young Robert Hoole 2 Ewes & 2 lambs and to every one of them also a heffer—Ralph Walker my servant—Widow Holden my kinswoman—Edward Hatfield's wife and Thomas Bray's wife an angell apiece—Ellen and Lawrence Hall—Robert Grubbe—Sir Richard Cowper—The children of john Brown all such money as I have of theirs in my custody—My kinsmen Robert & Alexander French—Edward Hatfield & Thomas Bray Supervisors—

Proved at York, 26 Sepl. 1558.

I think it will not be out of place to give the following will here, though I cannot say how the testator was related to the above Nicholas :—1577. Jan. 13. Nicholas Hatfield of Thriberg—To be buried in the parish Church of

[90] Thomas howsleye sepult.	...	...	...	...	xiiij' die.
Uxor jac Secker sepult.	...	...	...	...	eod. die.
Widowe Carre sepult. ...	...	...	...	...	xvjto die.
Edward Kent sepult. ...	...	...	...	...	eod. die.
Widowe Warde sepult. ...	...	...	...	...	xvij' die.
Uxor foxe pauper sepult.	...	...	...	...	eod. die.
Wyllm. Sampson sepult.	...	...	...	...	xxj' die.
Thomas Jepson sepult.	...	...	...	...	eod. die.
Margret horner sepult.	...	...	...	...	xxiij' die.
[91] Wyllm. Bromelye & Robt. Geslinge sepult.	...	...	...	xxvij' die.	
[92] Wyllm. hyde sepult. ...	...	...	...	...	xxviij' die.

Mense Septembris.

Agnes Parkin puella sepult.	...	...	iiijto die.
[93] john Machon Senior sepult.	...	..	vto die.
[94] Robt. Kent sepult.	...	...	xij' die.
Richard Wright infans sepult.	...	...	xxij' die.

Thriberg—Isabel Spencer my wife's daughter xli.—To my brethren & sisters xxvjs. & viijd. i.e.—To my sister Alice vjs. & viijd.—To my brother Edmond [or Edward] vjs. & viijd.—To my sister Margery vjs. & viijd.—To my brother William vjs. & viijd.—Robert Barker of Ashover & jane Burgon my servant, Robert Hatfield & john Spencer to every one of them one Ewe lamb at the next Spring time—Margaret Barker my wife's daughter one lamb—To Edward Camsall of Conysbro', Alice his wife and everyone of his children iiijd. apiece—jennet my wife executrix.—Oliver Robothnm, john Myrfield, john Spencer and john Waddle witnesses. Proved at York, 22 July 1579.

[90] This Thomas Howsley must have been a cadet of the House.—His will is dated 7 Dec. 1552, in it he styles himself "Thomas Howsley of Howsley Hall yeoman" to be buried in the parish church of Ecclesfield.—My goods to be divided in 3 parts, 2 parts for my son Francis Howsley and 1 part for my wife Mary Howsley.—Robert Bloome and Thomas Waterhouse supervisors.—William Young, Robert Bloome, Thomas and John Waterhouse and Edward Hanson witnesses. Proved at York, 6 Oct. 1558.

[91] 1529. Sept. 9. William Bromeley senior surrenders land in Ecclesfield to William son of John Bromeley of Whitley.—1555. June 18. William Bromeley and Joana his wife surrender the same to Nicholas Hatfield.

[92] William Hyde above was of Birley in this parish, [he was son of William, son of Hugh, son of Thomas Hyde of Birley, living 1430]. His will is dated 23 Aug. 1558: in it he mentions Ellyn my daughter to have a cottage where Lawrence Truluf dwelleth with garden and croft adjoining for her life and then to revert to my sons John Hugh and Alexander—Ralph Hyde my son to have the house where I now dwell—Agnes my wife—Margaret my daughter—the daughters of Ralph my son.—To my 3 sons John Hugh and Alexander the cottage &c. where my son John now lives.—Alexander to have my looms and all my working gear—To Richard Hawme my green jacket—" I give to the byng [buying] of ij bells vjs viijd."—My wife and 3 sons above executors Robert Cleaton, Henry Richardson, Richard Browne, Christopher Crofts and Richard Beard witnesses. Proved at York 26 Sept. 1558. On the 10 Oct., 1560, John, Hugh and Alexander Hyde seek to be admitted to lands, &c., at Birley, as sons and heirs of William Hyde, deceased.

[93] A john Machon was living at Longley in this parish ano. 1550.

[94] The family of Kent was settled at Birley in this parish at an early date. 1389 March 10 john Quenson surrenders 1 Messuago & 3 Acres in Birley to Robert Kent. 1409. July 14. john Hartley and Henry Horner surrender 1 Messuage and lands in Birley to Richard Kent. 1437. Robert Kent surrenders 1 parcel of land called Wadfield to john Shagh of Southey. 1448. Easter Leet, john son of Robert Kent junior claims to hold 1 Messuage & 11 Acres & 1 wood in Woodseats which were conceded to the said Robert Kent—At the same court joana wife of Robert Kent junior claims to hold one third of 1 Messuage & 11 Acres & 1 wood in Woodseats. 1449. john Kent son & heir of Robert Kent seeks admission to 1 Messuage & 13 Acres in Birley. 1535. Robert Kent surrenders 1 croft called jenfield to john Hurton and 1 croft on Shirecliffe Hill in Birley to john Oxspring. In the Poll tax, 2 Rich. II, appear Cecilia Kent iiijd. Robertus filius ejus iiijd. Agnes filia ejus iiijd.

L

Menso Octobris.

hellen nicolls pauper sepult.	...	ixno die.
George Cutte sepult.	...	xvj' die.
henrye Scholes puer sepult.	...	xviij' die.
[96] john Waterhouse sepult.	...	xxiij' die.
Wydowe johnson paup sepult.	...	xxviij' die.

Menso Novembris.

Emye Trippet sepult.	...	j' die.
Nicholas Turnley & George machon paup sepult.	...	xij' die.
Thomas Stevenson sepult.	...	xv' die.
humfreye hudson (pauper) sepult.	...	xvij' die.
Uxor Robti. Lee (paup) sepult.	...	xx' die.
Elizabethe Shooter (puella) sepult.	...	eod. die.

Menso Decembris.

Lawrence Parker (paup) sepult.	...	j' die.
Thomas Whittacres (paup) & John hincliffe (puer)		xx' die.

Mense Januarij.

Wydowe Whittacres (paup) sepult.	...	j' die.
[96] john jepson (clercke) sepult.	...	xiiij' die.
Wydowe Kaye & Alice Stones (infans) sepult.	...	xvj' die.
Wydow Savige (paup) sepult.	...	xviij' die.
[97] Thomas howsleye sepult.	...	xxiij' die.
Johan uxor Robti. Cooper sepult.	...	xxiiij' die.

Menso Februarij.

Widowe Elvisse (paup) sepult.	...	xv' die.
Alexandr. hudson (paup) sepult.	...	xx' die.

[96] john Waterhouse was of Wadsley in this parish; his will is dated 23 Oct. 1558.—My goods to be divided into 3 parts—1st part to myselfe; 2nd part to my children Thomas & John Waterhouse; and the 3rd part to my wife—To William my base gotten son vi. My sons John and Thomas Waterhouse my executors—Richard Waterhouse and William Waterhouse the younger supervisors—William Waterhouse senior to have the custody of my children until they be of age—Witnesses john Creswick & john Senior—Proved at York, 29 Nov. 1558.

[96] I can find no proof of his being "a clerk in Holy Orders."

[97] Thomas Howsley was of Howsley Hall—His will is dated 20 jan. 1558-9. My body to be buried in the parish church of Ecclesfield—Elsabeth, Nicholas, Cicilie and John my younger children to have my house called Barkhouse now in the tenure of my son Thomas Andrew, and another house in the tenure of William Slatter. My son Thomas Howsley to pay each of my 7 children viz. Agnes, Ellyn, Margaret, Elsabeth, Nicholas, Cicilie and john xls. apiece—To Effame my base gotten daughter "iiij shepe"—My sons Nicholas and john my executors—Thomas Parker, Thomas Waterhouse, and Elizabeth my wife supervisors. Witnesses Thomas Parker, Thomas Waterhouse, Thomas Deye and Sir Richard Beard.

Proved at York, 13 March, 1558-9.

Thomas Carr married Cicilie Howsley 10 Dec. 1581.

[98] John hill sepult.	xxij' die.
Robt. Combe (puer) & Vidua Slatter (paup) sepult.	xxv' die.
Wydowe Sampson (paup) sepult.	ultimo die.

Mense Marcij.

Alice hill (paupcula) sepult.	vij' die.
Thomas Cutte sepult.	xv' die.

[1559.]

Robt. Dawre sepult.	xxvjto die.
Nicholas Carre sepult.	xxix' die.

Mense Aprilis. [1559.]

Robt. howle (puer) sepult.	ijdo. die.
Margret Bullus (puella) sepult.	vij' die.
Robt. Genne sepult.	viij' die.
John Bullus & George Beckett sepult.	ix' die.
Willm. Sheircliffe (puer) et alt. sepult.	xij' die.
Elizabethe moore sepult.	xiij' die.
John hyde sepult.	eod. die.
[99] henrye Sheirclyffe sepult.	xv' die.
Richard Bullus sepult.	xix die.
Wydowe hyde sepult.	xx' die.
Richard Carre (puer) sepult.	xxiiijto die.

Mense Aprilis. [1559.]

Richard Collye sepult.	xxvj' die.

Mense Maij.

Thomas Sayton sepult.	ijdo die.
Nicholas Collye sepult.	iij' die.
Wydowe Shooter sepulta.	iiijto die.
Alice Parkin (puella) sepult.	vto die.
John morehouse sepult.	vij' die.
Uxor Robti. Carre sepult.	xiij' die.
Uxor henric hill sepult.	xiiijto die.

[98] His will is dated 15 Feb. 1558-9.—To my wife Elizabeth all my lands &c. during the nonage of my son john Clarkehouse—My sons Charles & john Hill my daughters Isabel, Maude, Cicilie and Margaret Hill—To Margerye Mowre a cowe on the day of her marriage—Ralph Crofts, Thomas Thwayte and Edward Colly supervisors. Henry Sayton, Richard de Shirtcliffe &c. witnesses. Proved at York, 18 Feb. 1558-9. The family of Hill are of old standing in the parish. 1541. Ap. 14. John Hill, probably identical with the above, seeks to be admitted to land, &c., in Ecclesfield, as son and heir of William Hill deceased.—This William, together with a brother Robert, were sons of john Hill, who was son of William Hill and Marion his wife, to whom Hugh Brown, on 13 June, 1464, surrendered land, &c., in Ecclesfield.

[99] 1559-60. March 7. William Shirecliffe is admitted to lands in Ecclesfield, as son & heir of Henry Shirecliffe deceased.

John Staniforthe sepult.	...	...	...	...	xv' die.
Thomas Button sepult....	...	...	...	...	eod. die.
iijes parvuli pueri sepult.	...	...	...	...	xvjto die.
Thomas haughe sepult.	...	...	...	...	xvij' die.
Thomas Sheireliffe & puer sepult.	...	...	...	...	xix' die.
Agnes hyde (puella) **sepult.**	...	...	...	...	xxij' die.
Uxor Johnis. Sheireliffe sepult.	...	...	...	...	xxiij' die.
Margerie uxor Nicholai **Cooper sepult.**	...	...	...	...	xxix' die.

Menso JUNIJ.

Thomas holden sepult....	...	...	...		ijdo' die.
Robt. Lee sepult.	...	...	...		vto die.
Henric hill et infans **Thome Parker sepult.**	...	...			xvto die.

Menso JULIJ.

[100] Raulph Wylkinson sepult.	...	...	...	...	vij' die.
Raulph hyde sepult.	...	...	...	...	ixno die.
Uxor Willmi. Smythe sepult.	...	...	...	...	xxij' die.
henric Richardson sepult.	...	...	...	...	ultimo die.

Menso AUGUSTI.

Johan. Sayton sepult.	...	...	...	ijdo die.
John foxe (paup) sepult.	...	...	...	xxj' die.
Margerie Shooter vidua sepult.	...	...	...	xxij' die.
Rychard Somersall (paup) sepult.	...	...	...	xxiiijto die.
Thomas Stones (infans) sepult.	...	...	...	xxvij' die.

Menso SEPTEMBRIS.

Dorithie Parkin **(puella) sepult.**	...	...	...	...	iij' die.
(Spur) Alice Lee **(infans spuria) sepult.**	...	...	...	...	xiiijto die.
John Wade (pauper) sepult.	...	...	...	...	xv' die.
Alice hurton (paup) sepult.	...	...	...	...	xvij' die.
Alice Weynwright **sepult.**	...	...	...	...	xxj' die.
John Tynker (puer) sepult.	...	...	...	...	xxiij' die.

Menso OCTOBRIS.

John Deye (infans) **sepult.**	...	...	...	...	vij' die.
Wyllm. Shawe (paup) sepult.	...	...	...	...	xv' die.
Alice Machon (Wydowe) sepult.	...	...	...	...	xxiiijto die.
margeryo Jepson (Wydowe) sepult....	...	...	...	xxvjto die.

Menso NOVEMBRIS.

johan holden sepult.	...	...	...	j' die.
Nicholas Robinson sepult.	...	...	...	xxijdo die.

[100] 1540. Oct. 7. Thomas Wilkinson being dead Ralph Wilkinson seeks to be admitted to lands at Birley as his son & heir. 1592. Jan. 4. Robert son & heir of Ralph Wilkinson deceased surrendered lands at Ecclesfield to Alexander Beard, of Ecclesfield.

Gilbert hieleye sepult. ...	...	...			xxvto die.
Catherin Twigge sepult.	...	...			xxviij' die.
Margret Wright sepult.	...	...			x' die Decembris.

Mense FEBRUARIJ.

james Secker sepult.	...	...	...	...	x' die.
James Gest sepult.	...	...	...	...	xiiij' die.

Mense MARCIJ.

Charles Bearde sepult. ...   .   vto die.

[1560.]

Infans Richardi Grubbe sepult.   ...   ...   xxx' die.

Mense APRILIS. [1560.]

jeffreye Thompson (infans) sepult. ...   .   xxjx' die.

Mense MAIJ.

[101] john hartleye sepult.	...	...	...	...	ijdo die.
johan. uxor Willmi Wilkinson sepult.	...	...	...	viij' die.

Mense JUNIJ.

john Beighton sepult. ...   .   xxvij' die.

Mense JULIJ.

Edward Colleye **(paup)** sepult.	...	...	...	...	xij' die.
Edward Creswycke (puer) sepult.	...	...	...	...	eod. die.
Elizabethe Shooter sepult.	...	...	...	..	xviij' die.
Rychard hawme (paup) sepult.	...	...	...	...	xxj' die.

Mense AUGUSTI.

john Bullus **(paup)** sepult.   ...   .   viij' die,

---

[101] I have the following notes of the family of Hartley from the Court Rolls :—1380 Agnes **wife of Henry** Hartley and Cecilia her sister daughters & coheirs of Richard de Ughtibridge seek to be admitted to one **Messuage in Birley. 1381.** William de Hartley seeks to be admitted to half a bovat **called** Dobfield on the surrender of William del Combe. 1409. june 14. john Hartley son & heir of Agnes Hartley and Henry Horner son & heir of Cecilia Horner the two daughters and coheirs of Richard de Ughtibridge **seek to be** admitted to one Messuage in Birley which they afterwards surrender to Richard de Kent.—1477. March 7. William Hartley, per john Scott, john Shirecliffe and William Whete customary tenants, surrenders land **&c. in** Nether Hartley to Richard Dey. 1487. May 18. john Hartley son & heir of William Hartley confirms the above surrender.—1537. Aug. 11. john Shaw & Agnes his wife surrender one croft called Stony croft to john Hartley.—1543. Sept. 21. john Hartley seeks to be admitted to one croft called Calderton in Ecclesfield on the death of john Hartley his father.—1543. Sept. 21. john Hartley seeks to be admitted to one croft called Stonecroft as son & heir of john Hartley deceased.—1565 Dec. 8. john son & heir of john Hartley seeks to be admitted to Stoneycroft and Coldwell croft on the death of john Hartley his father—1597 July 13. john Hartley has died since the last court seized of the croft called Calderton and Thomas Hartley of Hartley Brooke is his brother and proper heir and of full age. In the Poll tax, 2 Rich. II, appear Ricardus de Hertlay & Alicia ux' ejus iiijd.—Willelmus de Hertelay & Agnes ux' ejus iiijd.—Willelmus filius ejus iiijd.—johannes de Hertelay & johanna ux' ejus—Mercer—xijd.—johannes filius ejus iiijd. johannes serviens dicti johannis iiijd.

Agnes uxor henrici hinchcliffe sepult.	... ...	xviij' die.
Thomas Slatter (servus) sepult. ...	... ...	eod. die.

Mense Septembris.

Catherin Brodbent (infans) sepult. ...	...	xiij' die.

Mense Octobris.

john Cutto (infans) sepult.	... ...	xxij' die.

Mense Novembris.

[102] Wyllm. hollande sepult.	... ...	vijmo die.
John hill (infans) sepult.	... ...	xviij' die.

Mense Decembris.

Agnes Taylyer (infans) sepult.	... ...	iiijto die.
Isabell Slatter (infans) sepult.	... ...	xv' die.
Johan Osgathorpe (infans spuria) sepult.	... ...	eod. die.
Rychard Sheirclyffe (infans) sepult. ...	... ...	xxvto die.

Mense Januarij.

john Stanyfortho (puer) sepult.	... ...	vij' die.
Robt. Smythe (infans) sepult.	... ...	xxx' die.

Mense Februarij.

Elizabethe Creswycke sepult.	.. ..	iiijto die.
Raulphe Calverd sepult.	... ...	xiij' die.
Rollande Ball sepult. ...	... ...	xxiiij' die.

Mense Marcij.

john Crosloye (puer) sepult.	... ...	xv' die.
Johan Royds (uxor) sepult.	... ...	xxij' die.
Effam Ball (infans) sepult.	... ...	xxiij' die.

Mense Aprilis. [1561.]

John Thomson (infans) sepult.	... ...	vto die.
Margret Stanyfortho (puella) sepult.	... ...	vij' die.
Charles Otes (puer) sepult.	... ...	xxix' die.

[103] I have following notes of the family of Hoyland, or Holland, from the Manor court rolls:—1442. Mar. 21 john de Shaw of Bradfield surrenders 1 Messuage and 1 bovat in the Storthes, Dungworth to the use of Thomas son of Thomas de Shaw of Dungworth.—1452. Jan. 11. Thomas son of Thomas de Shaw of Dungworth surrenders the same to the use of William Hoiland. 1508, Feb. 13. Richard Hoiland of Southey in the parish of Ecclesfield surrenders the same to the use of William Hoiland.—1561 Nov.—William Hoiland surrenders the same after his decease to the use of Nicholas Hoiland with remainder to his own heirs. 1570. May 29. William Hoiland seeks to be admitted to the same as brother and heir of Nicholas Hoiland deceased.—1591. Sept. 30. William Hoiland brother and nearest heir of Nicholas Hoiland deceased has died since the last court seized of one Messuage and one bovat in Dungworth Storthes and that Elizabeth now wife of Robert Burrows & Agnes or Ann now wife of Thomas Cutt are the sisters and coheirs of the said William Hoiland deceased and seek to be admitted.

Mense Maij.

Thomas Bullus (puer) sepult.	vjto die.
John Scholes (infans) sepult.	vij' die.
Agnes Shooter sepult.	xiij' die.
Elizabethe Scholes sepult.	xviij' die.

Mense Junij.

Thomas Atkinson (spurius) sepult.	vjto die.
John Walshe (infans) sepult.	xxx' die.

Mense Julij.

Anne uxor Robti. hill sepult.	vij' die.
Elizabethe Shooter (infans) sepult.	viij' die.
Thomas Greave (infans spurius) sepult.	ix' die.

Mense Augusti.

Johan Slacke (infans) sepult.	vto. die.
Isabell Lownde (puella) sepult.	xv' die.
Robt. Thwetes (puer) sepult.	xxiij' die.

Mense Septembris.

john Bedforthe (puer) sepult.	xvij' die.

Mense Octobris.

hellen filia johnis. Brownell sepult.	xix' die.

Mense Novembris.

Elizabethe Smythe (vidua) sepult.	ixno die.
john Sheirclyffe (infans) sepult.	xx' die.

Mense Decembris.

Nicholas Sheirclyffe (infans) sepult.	xxiij' die.

Menso Februarij.

Nicholas Lownde (infans) sepult.	xx' die.

Mense Marcij.

Alice hoylande sepult.	j' die.
henrie Elande (puer) sepult.	viij' die.
Isabell Kyllabeck sepult.	xx' die.

Mense Marcij. [1562.]

Nicholas Osbonston sepult.	xxv' die.

Mense Aprilis.

Elizabethe hinchclyffe sepult.	ixno die.
Henrie hinchclyffe sepult.	xx' die.

Mense MAIJ.

ij' abortivi pueri Richardi Ingle sepult.	...	...	...	x' die.
Thomas hartleye (puer) sepult.	...	...	...	xiijto die.
Richard Denton (infans spurius) sepult.	...	...	...	xvij' die.

Mense JUNIJ.

johan Grene (infans) sepult.	...	xv' die.
John Watson (infans) sepult.	...	xix' die.

Mense JULIJ.

John Haughe (paup) sepult.	...	...	xxiiij' die.

Mense OCTOBRIS.

henrie Shawe (agabns.) sepult.	...	...	...	iijto die.
Effam Slatter sepult.	...	...	...	vij' die.
Elizabethe Beale sepult.	...	...	...	xxiij' die.

Mense DECEMBRIS.

Widowe Stringer (paup) sepult.	...	...	...	xvij' die.
Uxor johan Trulove sepult.	...	...	...	xxix' die.

Mense JANUARIJ.

Wyllm. Sheyrclyffe (infans) sepult. ...	...	iij' die.

Mense FEBRUARIJ.

Anne Parker sepult.	...	...	xvj' die.

Mense MARCIJ.

Richard Stones (infans) sepult.	...	...	...	iiijto die.

Mense APRILIS. [1563.]

Isabell Clarcke (uxor) sepult.	...	...	...	xvto die.

Mense MAIJ.

Robt. humblock sepult....	...	...	...	x' die.
[108] johan Thwetes (uxor) sepult.	...	...	...	xj' die.
John Tottington sepult.	...	...	...	xx'die.

Mense JUNIJ.

Rychard Stradlin (servus) sepult.	...	...	xviij' die.

Mense JULIJ.

Nicholas Thwetes (infans) sepult. ...	...		xixto. die.

[108] 26 Oct. 1553. Thomas Gargrave miles and Thomas Darley surrender, after the death of William Evingham and Richard Cowper chantry priests of the Church of St. Mary's Ecclesfield, one Cottage and one Acre in Ecclesfield to Henry Hill.—1565. Dec. 19. Henry Hill surrenders the same to Thomas Thwaites son of Thomas Thwaites by johanna his wife who was daughter of the said Henry Hill and Richard Hill son of the said Henry Hill —*Court Rolls*.

Mense Septembris. [1563.]

Nicholas Cooper (puer) sepult.	...	xvjto die.
Robt. Ball (puer) sepult.	...	xxiij' die.
Peter Seeker (puer) sepult.	...	xxv' die.
Willm. Carre (puer) sepult.	...	xxix' die.

Mense Octobris.

Thomas Prynce (puer) sepult.	...	vij' die.
Alice Brown sepult.	...	ix' die.
Francys Barnsleye (puer) sepult.	...	xij' die.
Elizabethe Gylles (puella) sepult.	...	xiij' die.
john Brigge (infans) sepult.	...	xxij' die.
Isabell Sheirclyffe (puella) sepult.	...	xxvjto die.
Anne Sheirclyffe (puella) sepult.	...	xxviij' die.

Mense Novembris.

Jane hill (puell.) sepult.	...	vjto die.
Francys Shawe (puer) sepult.	...	xxix' die.
Johan Byrkes sepult.	...	eod. die.

Mense Decembris.

Isabell hollande sepult.	...	xxxj' die.

Mense Januarij.

Anne Lister (infans) sepult.	...	xjx' die.
Thomas Phillipotte (infans) sepult.	...	xxiij' die.

Mense Marcij.

Richard Parkin (infans) sepult.	...	ix' die.
Uxor Richardi Swyfte sepult.	...	xx' die.

Mense Marcij. [1564.]

Rychard Turton sepult.	...	xxvjto die.
john Shooter (puer) sepult.	...	xxviij' die.

Mense Aprilis.

Margret hunter (puella) sepult.	...	xix' die.

Mense Maij.

Anne hellews (infans) sepult.	...	xxvij' die.

Mense Junij.

Anne Lownde sepult.	...	vto die.
Dionis johnson (infans) sepult.	...	ixno die.
[104] Agnes Wylson (vidua) sepult.	...	x' die.

[104] Agnes Wilson was relict of Thomas Wilson, of Oughtibridge Hall, who was second son of Richard Wilson, of Broomhead, in the Chapelry of Bradfield.—Her will is dated 28 May, 1564—To be buried in Ecclesfield Church—To Nicholas Greyve or Greyne my son one cowe and my beste brass pott, my middlinge panne and my beste pewter dubler —To Elizabeth daughter of Thomas Wilson my silver girdle—To Jane Wilson my almeburye [i.e. a cupboard] 1

Mense JULIJ.

hughe Stones (infans) sepult.	...	...	...	jmo. die.
John holden (abort) sepult.	...	...	...	xviij' die.

Mense Augusti.

[105] Nicholas Scotte sepult.... ... jmo die.

ewe and a lamb—To Richard Wilson my horse 1 ewe and a lamb—Thomas Wilson my son—Agnes Roberts—Residue of my goods to Christopher & Thomas Wilson my sons whom I also appoint my executors—witnesses Sir john Tyas vicar—Thomas Parker—Ralph Richardson and Christopher Smith—Proved at York, 20 june, 1566.

[105] Nicholas Scott was eldest son of Richard Scott, of Barnes Hall, in this parish.—In his will, dated 30 July, 1564, he describes himself as "Nicholas Scotte, of Barnes Hall," in the parish of Ecclesfield.—" And forasmuch as the houre of deathe is uncertayne to every lyvying creature, and willinglie I wold wishe that suche vile corruptible goods, and possessions, as almyghtye God hathe lent me here, in this wretched world, myght be dispossessed to the honor and glorie of hym" &c.—To be buried in the parish Church Ecclesfield—Emmota my wife—My daughter Barbara Scott—My son Thomas Scott—Westhalle, in Wentworth, which I late had of Charles Jackson, of Fyrbecks, in co. Notts, gent.—My brethren, john, William, Richard, and Edward Scott—My tenement at Thorpe, to Nicholas **Shirecliffe**. My brethren and sisters to have an old angell apiece—My brother Watts' son—To the poor of Ecclesfield xxs.—My brother William Scott to have, at the rent of xiijs. & iiijd. a year, the tenement in which he lives, during the nonage of Thomas Scott my son, he having paid a rent of xxvjs. & viijd. for the same—My brother in law Richard Fenton, Thomas Braye, john Watts, john Scott and William Scott to see my last will carried out—Codicil dated 31 july, 1564, containing legacies to john Watts—Nicholas Staniland and his wife.—Maud Grove—john Scott my brother—Richard Scott my brother—Richard Holding—Thomas Holland—Grace Smyth—Charles Stevenson—john Tyas and Ambrose Swinbanke—Witnesses Thomas Parker and Richard Cowper—Proved at York, 21 March, 1564-5.—The will of Richard Scott, father of the above, is dated 12 july, 1556; in it he describes himself as, "of Barnes Hall, yeoman."—My property to be divided among my children, except Ann, who already has had her filial portion—My sons Nicolas, john, William, Richard and Edward Scott, &c.—From the Court rolls, I get the following notes: 1521—Richard Scott seeks to be admitted to land in Shiregreen, as son and heir of john Scott, deceased.—1535, Feb. 20. Richard Scott surrenders the same to Edward Scott, his younger son; with remainder to the proper heirs of the aforesaid Richard Scott.—1604, Oct. 2. Edward Scott, having died since the last Court, Richard Scott seeks to be admitted to the same as proper heir of Richard Scott, deceased, being son & heir of Thomas Scott, deceased, who was son & heir of Nicholas Scott, deceased, who was son & heir of Richard Scott, deceased —1638, Nov. 21. Inquisition *post mortem* of Richard Scott, of Barnes Hall, miles,—that he has died seized of one Messuage or tenement and **of** two bovats in Nether Hartley, which descended to him on the death of Nicholas Scott his grandfather; and also **3 roods** in a field there lately Parker's—That the said Richard Scott died in the city of Dublin, in the realm of Ireland, about **the month** of August last past, and Barbara Banyster, relict of Henry Banyster, of the City of York, merchant, is **his** kinswoman and proper heir, being sister of his father Thomas Scott, and is aged 75 years and more.

The property of Barnes Hall came into the hands of this family by the will of Thomas Rotherham, Arch-Bishop of York, &c., dated 6 August, 1498, and the following clause, which applies to this estate, I give in full:— "*Item volo, quod johannes Scott consanguineus meus, cui est hereditas quanquam parva, in parochia de Ecclesfield successive descendens in eodem nomine et sanguine, a tempore quo non est memoria hominum, ut ipsa augeatur, me per gratiam meliorato, habeat sibi, et heredibus masculis de corpore suo legitime procreatis, manerium meum de Bernes, situatum in parochiâ predictâ, quod emi de Roberto Shatton pro cxl lib. Ac etiam manerium meum de Howesleys cum pertinen quod emi de Thoma Wortley milite pro cxx lib. Et in defectu talium heredum, volo quod frater suus Ricardus sub eâdem lege et conditione habeat prædicta maneria. Et in defectu talium heredum, volo quod prædicta maneria revertantur rectis heredibus meis. Item volo, quod sub eâdem lege et conditione prædicti johannes et Ricardus habeant tenementum meum vocatum Sugworth, in parochiâ de Bradfield, cum omnibus pertinen.*" Richard St. George, Norroy king at Arms, and others have given to this worthy prelate the patronymic of "Thomas Scott alias Rotherham," why, it is impossible to say.—It is also asserted by the above Richard St. George that john & Richard Scott, named in the Archbishop's will, both died without issue, and that George, a son of the Archbishop's brother, inherited the estates of Barnes Hall, Howsley, &c., and that he had a son john, who had a son Richard, &c., &c. Now, it is undoubted, that john Scott, father of Richard Scott, was dead ano. 1521, and the Archbishop died of the plague ano. 1500. So in 21 years the estates above alluded to must have passed through the hands of four individuals,

jane hill (vidua) sepult....	...	eod. die.
hellen Thorppe (vidu.) sepult.	...	vjto die.
hellen Shawe (uxor) sepult.	...	ix' die.
Agnes Smythe (uxor) sepult.	...	x' die.
Agnes Turnleye (vidua) sepult.	...	xvjto die.
Robt. humblocke (puer) sepult.	...	xxxj' die.

Mense Septembris.

Cotton humlocke (infans) sepult.	... ...	iij' die.
Isabell Sheircliffe (infans) sepult.	... ...	xvjto die.
Johan Beighton (uxor) sepult.	... ...	eod. die.

Mense Octobris.

[106] Heric. Hollande sepult....	... ...	vjto die.
johan Bullus (uxor) sepult.	... ...	xxj' die.

Mense Novembris.

Robt. Smythe sepult. ...	... ...	xx' die.

Mense Decembris.

Alice Bullus (vidua) sepult.	... ...	xvij' die.
Richard Linthwet sepult.	... ...	xviij' die.
Elizabethe Cooke (vidua) sepult.	... ...	xxvto die.
john motleye (infans) sepult.	... ...	eod. die.
Thomas motleye (infans) sepult.	... ...	xxviij' die.

Mense Januarij.

Hellen Croswycke (uxor) sepult.	x' die.
Alexander hill (infans) sepult.	xviij' die.
Elizabethe hurton (uxor) sepult.	xxiij' die.
Elizabethe fenton (vidua) sepult.	xxx' die.

viz., **john Scott**, his brother Richard **Scott**, George **Scott** the Archbishop's **nephew, and** john his son.—I am **not** aware that **the** plague visited Ecclesfield about this time, but certainly an epidemic **of some sort** must have taken place to prove St. George's statement.—I cannot see why john Scott, who was dead anc. **1521**, should not be identical with the john Scott mentioned in Archbishop Rotherham's will in 1498.—Other theories have been propounded with regard to the parentage and patronymic of **this** prelate, but I have not space to enter upon them even were they worthy of my doing so, the most striking point about them being their boldness of assertion and utter want of evidence. The Scotts were seated at Ecclesfield at an early date, as the Archbishop asserts in his will,—these few **notes from** Court Rolls and deeds, &c., may tend to show this.—1270, Peter Scott, of Ecclesfield, was living; 1324, William Scott was a pensioner of the convent here; 1343, Robert Scott, of Birley, was living; 1378, john Scott and john, his son; same year, john **Scott, and** Margaret his wife, arrowsmith; also john Scott, and Isabella his wife, **taylor** ; 1392, john, son of Thomas Scott, of Birley, was living; 1413—28, john Scott, of Birley, was living; 1429, **johana, wife of john** Shaw, seeks to be admitted to land at Birley, as being daughter of john Scott of the same; 1435, Robert **Scott, of Chapeltown, was living**; he had issue 3 daughters, coheirs. 1510, john Scott, of Chapeltown, was living, &c. **I have no doubt but that this** list could be much enlarged with a little research. For more on this subject see "*Notes and Queries*, 1876-7."

[106] Vide note 17.

Mense FEBRUARIJ.

francesse Crofts (infans) **sepult.**	j' die.
Thomas Crosleye sepult.	xiij' die.
john Cooper (infans) sepult.	xviij' die.
Laurence Trulove sepult.	xx' die.
Margret Pawson (vidua) sepult.	xxiiijto die.
Godfreye manton sepult.	xxvjto die.

Mense MARCIJ.

johan Parkin (infans) sepult.	vjto die.
jane hartleye sepult.	xij' die.
margret Crosley (vidua) sepult.	xiiij' die.
Emot. Weynwright (vidua) sepult.	xviij' die.

Mense MARCIJ. [1565.]

margret hollinbrigge (infans) sepult.	xxxj' die.

Mense APRILIS.

John Collye (infans) sepult.	**ijdo die.**
Elizabethe Gylles sepult.	**ixno die.**
Margret Sampson sepult.	xx' die.
Margret humblocke **sepult.**	xxiiijto die.
Rychard Cutte sepult.	xxviij' die.

Mense MAIJ.

Mres. Anne Wombwell (infans) sepult.	xj' die.
Alexander Wyllye (infans) sepult.	

Mense JUNIJ.

Elizabethe Scotte (puella) sepult.	vij' die.
Johan Waterall (infans) sepult.	xix' die.
Johan Brigge (infans) sepult.	xxj' die.

Mense JULIJ.

Dorithie hartleye (infans) **sepult.**	xv' die.
john humblocke (infans) **sepult.**	xx' die.
Isabell humblocke (uxor) **sepult.**	xxvj' die.

Mense AUGUSTI.

Gilbert Shawe **sepult.**	xiiij' die.

Mense SEPTEMBRIS.

Elizabethe Prince sepult.	xvjto die.
Thomas Whittacres (puer) sepult.	xvij' die.

Mense NOVEMBRIS.

Grace Eluar sepult.	xvjto die.

Mense Decembris.

hellen holden sepult.	j' die.
Jane Brown (vidua) sepult. ...	xxvij' die.

Mense Januarij.

james Beighton (infans) sepult.	iij' die.
Agnes Shawe sepult.	vto die.
Wyllm. Shooter sepult....	xiij' die.
jane hyde sepult.	xxj' die.
Grace Smythe (puella) sepult.	xxiij' die.
Thomas hyde (infans) sepult.	xxviij' die.

Mense Februarij.

john Brigge (servus) sepult. ...	vto die.

Mense Marcij.

John Stanylande (infans) sepult. ...	vjto die.
Isabell Bower (infans) sepult. ...	ix' die.
Wyllm. hatfeld (infans) sepult. ...	xxij' die.

Mense Aprilis. [1566.]

Rychard Sheircliffe sepult.	xj' die.

Mense Maij.

johan Combe sepult.	vto die.
Elizabethe Base sepult.... ...	viij' die.
Edward Taylyer (puer) sepult. ...	xiiij' die.

Mense Junij.

Elizabethe Shooter (puella) sepult. ...	vto die.
Elizabethe manton (vidua) sepult. ...	xvto die.
Isabell Sandboucke sepult. ...	xjx' die.
Thomas Senier (infans) sepult. ...	xxix' die.

Mense Julij.

John Ellys (infans) sepult. ...	xvj' die.

Mense Octobris.

Edmunde heaton (paup) sepult.	xxiiijto die.
Thomas hollande (paup) sepult.	xxvto die.
Et uxor eius Margret (paup) sepult. ...	xxx' die.

Mense Novembris.

henrie Stanyforthe (infans) sepult.	ijdo. die.
johan Wilkinson (vidua) sepult.	iij' die.

[107] Thomas Twigge (viduus) sepult.	... ...	x' die.
[108] Jeffrey Cooke (maritus) sepult.	... ...	xij' die.
ffrancys Parkyn sepult.	... ...	xiij' die.
[109] Nicholas Sampson sepult.	... ...	xxvj' die.
Alice hudson sepult.	... ...	xxviij' die.

Mense JANUARIJ.

John hudson sepult.	...	j' die.
John Brown sepult.	...	vjto die.
Johan Brigge sepult.	...	xxiiij' die.
Elizabethe hollinbriggo sepult.	...	xxvj' die.

Mense MARCIJ.

john Smythe sepult.	...	jmo die.
Raulphe Marshlande sepult.	...	iij' die.
Thomas marrys sepult. ...		viij' die.
Thomas Brown sepult. ...		xxij' die.

Mense MARCIJ. [1567.]

john Sheyrclyffe sepult....	... ...	xxviij' die.

Mense APRILIS.

johan Gest sepult.	... ...	vij' die.
Robt. Wyllye sepult. ...	...	xvj' die.

[107] Thomas Twigge, of Ecclesfield, will dated 20 April, 1566—My daughters johana and Elizabeth—My son john Twigge—My daughter Margaret Morton, all my other daughters to have a like portion with her which she had when she married—john Twigge my son and johana my daughter to occupy the tenement I now live in—john Roodes and Henry Shaw supervisors.—Proved at York, 10 March, **1566-7**.

[108] Jeffrey Cooke, of Ecclesfield, will dated 4 Nov., 1566.—To the most neades of the Churche ijs.—To the poore man boxe xijd.—To Robert son of William Hollande xxs.—To Thomas Holland xs.—To Isabel Hill ijs.—To Robert Hall my godson xvjd.—To Thomas johns my godson vjd.—Elizabeth Stanyforth ijs.—Jeffrey Twigg xvjd.—Robert Ealand ijs.—Nicholas Dungworth my godson ijs.—Christopher Burley my godson vs.—Elizabeth Browneld xijd.—Richard Denton xijd.—john Hoole vjs. viijd.—Isabel wife of Henry Shirecliffe xxs.—To everyone of Nicholas Stones' children ijs.—Robert Hyne iijs. & iiijd.—George Haldenworthe iijs. & iiijd.—To Richard Cooke "yf that he be alyve xxs."—To Alice Cooke sister of the said Richard "yf she also be alyve xs."—The residue of my goods to Marie Cooke my wife and to my child "yf yt fortune the saide Marie Cooke to be withe childe."—Richard Stanyforth and Henry Combe supervisors.—Proved at York, 5th Dec. 1566.

[109] **Nicholas** Sampson, of Foxhill, yeoman, will dated 6 Nov., 1566.—"I bequeathe to the most neades of the Churche xijd."—Nicholas, Henry, Elline and Margaret the children of my son Henry Sampson to everyone of them "a shoipe."—Richard, Nicholas, Peter and Agnes the children of Richard Mathyman.—To Thomas Machon "au ewe."—To William Machon "2 yeardes of corsey."—"All my smythy geare, one pare of newe wheilles & certayne iron &c." to my son Henry.—To Henry my son "my bay fille."—Charles Stephenson & Charles Cawood xijd. apiece.—Edward Hobson a jacket.—"I will that Agnes my wyfe shall take xxs. of john Machon her sonne."—My wife Agnes to have "2 pounds, a bras pot, a chawfer, a candlestick, with sex pewter dublers which I have in my keiping for hir children."—My daughters Elline and Effame to have "all the goods of Margaret Sampson which is in their custodie and keeping and xs. for one cowe of the said Margaret"—they also to have the same share as the wife of Richard Mathyman had when she married.—My farmhold where I now dwell to Henry my son and he to be my executor.—Peter fernley, Thomas Bullus and Ralphe Carre supervisors.

[110] Edward Creswycke sepult. ... xxiiij' die.
hellin Carre sepult. ... ... xxv' die.

Mense Maij.

Wyllm. Lownde sepult. ... vijmo die.
Margret Rychardson sepult. ... xvj' die.
Thomas machon sepult. ... xix' die.
humfreye Bower sepult. ... xxiij' die.

Mense Junij.

Alice hill sepult. ... ixmo die.
margret Crowder sepult. ... xxviij' die.

Mense Julij.

john Ibotson (infans) sepult. ... xiij' die.
Anne ye daughter of Robt. hartleye sepult. ... xx' die.
john Smythe sepult. ... ... xxviij' die.

Mense Augusti.

hellen hyde sepult. ... ... iij' die.
james Carre (infans) sepult. ... ... xxiiijto die.

Mense Septembris.

Wyllm. Roodes sepult. ... ... viij' die.
Thomas Sheyrclyffe sepult. ... ... xvj' die.
Catherin Kent sepult. ... ... xxvj' die.

Mense Novembris.

Alice machon sepult. ... ... vij' die.
margret Stones (vidua) sepult. ... ... xxiijto die.
Elizabethe Carre (uxor) sepult. ... ... xxvjto die.
Thomas Cooper (puer) sepult. ... ... xxx' die.

Mense Decembris.

Barbara howsleye (infans) sepult. ... ... xxj' die.

Mense Januarij.

Alice Crosleye (infans) sepult. ... ... ix' die.
margret Wilkinson (uxor) sepult. ... ... xxx' die.

Mense Februarij.

florence Grene (pauper) sepult. ... ... xj' die.
George Ibotson sepult. ... ... xxvj' die.
Vidua jackson (paup) sepult. ... ... eod. die.

Mense Marcij.

Thomas Nodder (pauper) sepult. ... ... vij' die.

---

[110] Edward Creswick was of Stannington, in this parish: his will is dated 20 March, 1566-7, and his children john and Elizabeth proved the same.

Mense Marcij. [1568.]

Agnes Tottington (puella) sepult. ... ... xxvto die.

Mense Aprilis.

Alice holden (vidua & pauper) sepult. xiij' die.

Mense Maij.

john jepson (infans) sepult. ... ... xxiij' die.
Elizabethe Goodye (pauper) sepult. ... ... xxvij' die.

Mense Junij.

Wyllm. harryson sepult. vto die.

Mense Julij.

Agnes Eyre (infans) sepult. ... ... xvj' die.

Mense Augusti.

Nicholas jepson (puer) sepult. ... ... iij' die.
Johan handleye (pauper) sepult. ... ... vij' die.

Mense Septembris.

francis Bower (infans) sepult. ... ... iij' die.
johan Bower (uxor) sepult. ... ... xiij' die.
Wyllm. helles (infans) sepult. ... ... xvj' die.
[111] Marie filia Willmi. Cotton gent. sepult. ... ... xvij' die.

Mense Octobris.

Thomas Carre (puer) sepult. ... ... ixno die.
Anne hyde (puella) sepult. ... ... eod. die.
john Smythe (infans) sepult. ... ... xxj' die.
James Morton sepult. ... ... xxvto die.

Mense Novembris.

Robt. morehouse sepult. ... iij' die.
hellen Eyre (puella) sepult. ... vjto die.
Johan Ball (puella) sepult. ... ... xxj' die.

Mense Decembris.

Thomas Crosleye (infans) sepult. ... j' die.
John Rydinge (pauper) sepult. ... xxvij' die.

Mense Januarij.

hellen Oxspringe (puella) sepult. ... ... xvij' die.

---

[111] "Mr. Wyllym Cotton, Esquire," was one of the heads of the parish ano. 1568; he must have been in some way connected with john Cotton who married Barbara Mounteney ano. 1562.

Mense FEBRUARIJ.

Wyllm. hobson (pauper) sepult.	iij' die.
Rychard Grubbe (infans) sepult.	xj' die.
[112] Robt. Cooper (senex) sepult.	xxj' die.
Rychard Barghe (pauper) sepult.	xxvto die.

Mense MARCIJ.

john Gest sepult.	j' die.
Alice Lynthwet (vidua paup) sepult.	xvto die.

Mense APRILIS. [1569.]

Isabell Cooper (puella) sepult.	xiij' die.
Margret Crookes sepult.	xxvij' die.

Mense MAIJ.

Agnes uxor hugonis howsleye paup. sepult.	vjto die.

Mense JUNIJ.

John Ellis (paup) sepult.	vjto die.
francis Turton (puer) sepult.	vij' die.

Mense JULIJ.

Thomas Aldam (infans) sepult.	vto. die.
Elizabeth haughe (infans) sepult.	xxx' die.

Mense SEPTEMBRIS.

Alice Gylberthorppe (uxor) sepult.	vto die.
[113] Rychard Brodheade sepult.	xvj' die.

Mense OCTOBRIS.

Bryan Linthwet (infans) sepult.	vij' die.
margret Boothe (uxor) sepult.	eod. die.

[112] **Robert Cowper**, of Butterthwaite, will dated 16 Feb., 1568-9.—I bequeath my soul to God almighty & my body to Christian man's burial.—To the poor man's box xijd.—To the "Churche neades" viijd.—To Sir Richard Cowper vs.—To "uxor Cowper" vs.—To my sister joan Cutt a cow.—To my wife's 3 sons John, Thomas and Nicholas Crosley "all my smithy gear except a great stethye and string balls to be dealt equally among them."—William Cowper.—To my base gotten son Nicholas xvl. in money, &c.—Nicholas Cowper my brother—Nicholas Stanilande and Thomas Shirecliffe supervisors.—Proved at York, 28 Ap., 1569.

[113] **Richard** Broadhead, of Ecclesfield, will dated 13 Sept., 1569.—To my son William a young bay mare with a white "bleaze" on the head & all my harness.—To Henry Brown xxxviijs. the rest of all his child's portion, also to the same Henry vijs. that was bequeathed to him by Thomas Brown.—To the same Henry a gray horse.—To Ralph Calvard a ewe lamb.—To Thomas Broadhead my son a black heifer and she to be kept at my house to [till] she have a calf.—To my daughter Ellen a black spelded cow.—To Ralph Hobson a ewe.—To Ellen my wife a grey mare and a side saddle and my wife to give the saddle to Ellen her daughter after her decease.—To my son Thomas two paire of Webster looms.—My son William and my wife to occupy my farmhold so long as she doth keep unmarried, if she marry my son to occupy the farmhold severally himself.—William my son and my wife to pay Thomas and herline [Ellen] my children their parts of the income of my farmhold.—My brother john Broadhead & Hugh Hyde supervisors.—To Ralph Lee, Ralph Richardson, Hugh Hyde and john Broadhead xijd.—Proved at York, 12 Ap., 1570,

john Walton (puer) sepult.	...	xvj' die.
Raulpho Peerson (infans) sepult.	...	xxiij' die.
[114] John Wombwell gent. (infans) sepult.	...	xxx' die.

Mense Novembris.

johan Cooper (uxor) sepult.	... ...	ijdo die.
francis Bradley (infans) sepult.	... ...	xxj' die.
johan Wardo (uxor) sepult.	... ...	xxvj' die.
margret Parkin (uxor) sepult.	... ...	xxix' die.

Mense Decembris.

francis Creswycko (infans) sepult. ...	...	xxv' die.
jane Tingle (infans) sepult.	... ...	xxvij' die.

Mense Januarij.

Catherin Waterall (uxor) sepult.	...	j' die.
Anne haughe (paup) sepult.	...	x' die.
Ronald Chappell sepult.	...	xiiij' die.
Alexandr. Aldam (infans) sepult.	... ...	xxv' die.
[115] Barbara filia Johnis. mounteney gent. sepult. ...		xxx' die.
Robt. hill sepult.	... ...	eod. die.

Mense Marcij. [1570.]

hellen Collye (uxor) sepult.	... ...	xxvij' die.

Mense Aprilis.

Isabell Button (uxor) sepult.		iij' die.
Rychard Lounde (pauper) sepult.		xvto die.
[116] Thomas Sheyrclyffe & johan Cooper (infans) sepult.		**xxviij' die.**

Mense Maij.

[117] Robt. Parkin sepult. ...	... ...	xj' die.
humfrey Stafforde (pauper) sepult. ...		xv' die.

---

[114] Was an infant son of Thomas Wombwell, of Thundercliffe Grange, Esqre.

[115] john Mounteney was of Creswick in this parish.

[116] Thomas Shireclifffe, of Butterthwaite, will dated 25 Sept., 1557.—My goods to be divided into 3 parts—the first to my wife—the second to my children Nicholas, Henry, Richard, Agnes, Mary and john—and the third to myself to the bringing of me forth and the rest thereof my funeral expenses and legacies paid, to be divided amongst my children.—My wife Margaret to have one third of all my lands—she and my children to be executors—Nicholas Stones and Thomas Bullus supervisors.—Witnesses Sir William Beard, &c.—Proved at York, 3 May, 1571. The above would probably be son of Henry Shirecliffe, of Butterthwaite, who was eldest son of Thomas Shirecliffe, "master of the game" to the Lords of Hallam, who was son of William Shirecliffe, of Ecclesfield, living 15 Hen. vii.

[117] Robert Parkin, of Wadsley, will dated 20 june, 1571.—Emmote my wife to be executrix.—My children William, Agnes, Margaret, Emmote, and Ellen—My son Arthur—Thomas Greaves and john Parkin supervisors.—Proved at York, 1 Sept., 1571.

Mense JULIJ.

Alice Parkin (infans) sepult.	... ...	j' die.
[118]jane Parkin (uxor) sepult.	... ...	viij' die.
John Steven (paup) sepult.	... ...	xvij' die.
margret Gest (wydowe) sepult.	... ...	xix' die.

Mense AUGUSTI.

[119]Thomas Wombwell gent. & Ambros Swinbancke sepult.		xiij' die.
Thomas Curtes sepult.	... ...	xx' die.
jane humblocke sepult.	... ...	xxvto die.
Robt. Deye (infans) sepult.	... ...	xxvij' die.
johan Basforthe (infans) sepult.	... ...	xxx' die.

Mense SEPTEMBRIS.

Thomas Savill sepult.	... ...	iij' die.
Raulphe Ingle sepult.	... ...	iiijto die.
Elizabeth Deye (infans) sepult.	... ...	x' die.
Thomas Oxspringe (infans) sepult.	... ...	xviij' die.
Alice Slatter sepult.	... ...	xxj' die.

Mense OCTOBRIS.

henrie Parkin (infans) sepult.	... ...	vij' die.

Mense NOVEMBRIS.

john Weynwright (infans) sepult.	... ...	vjto die.

Mense DECEMBRIS.

Agnes Wheatnall sepult.	... ...	xxvjto die.
Thomas Wolleye sepult.	... ...	xxvij die.
hellen Taylyer (infans) sepult.	... ...	xxviij' die.

Mense JANUARIJ.

John Base (infans) sepult.	... ...	viij' die.
Raulphe Button (infans) sepult.	... ...	xxij' die.
George Clarke (paup) sepult.	... ...	xxx' die.

Mense FEBRUARIJ.

Alice Ludge & john Tyngle sepult.	... ...	ix' die.
[120] Alice Swynbancke sepult.	... ...	xiiij' die.
John Kyllabecke sepult.	... ...	xxviij' die.

[118] In the churchwardens' Accounts ano. 1572 appears this entry "Itm owing by jhon Pkyn [Parkyn] of Mortoley [Mortomley] for the burall of his wyff iijs. & iiijd."

[119] Was probably a son of Thomas Wombwell, of Thundercliffe Grange, Esquire.

[120] Alice Swinbank, of Ecclesfield, widow, **will dated 10** feb., 1570-1.—My brother Nicholas Shirecliffe—Elizabeth Bower—Elizabeth Ryvyngton—Margery Mawre—Alice Cutt—Isabel Swinbanke—Richard Shirecliffe.—To Agnes Beard my best girdle—johane Raworth—Elizabeth daughter of john Bower—widow Mould—janne Tweates—

Mense Marcij.

Thomas Lee & Thomas hynchcliffe sepult.		ijdo die.
john Boothe sepult.		xij' die.
Nicholas hill sepult.		xvj' die.
henrie Shawe (infans) sepult.		xvij' die.

Mense Marcij. [1571.]

Robt. Turnleye sepult. ... ... xxvjto die.

Mense Aprilis.

John Sampson sepult. ... ... ixno die.
Nicholas Pearson (infans) sepult. ... ... xij' die.

Mense Maij.

Phillice handleye (singlewoma.) sepult. ...	j' die.
Spu. Thomas johnson (spurius) sepult. ...	viij' die.
Willm. Boothe (pauper) sepult.	x' die.
Willm. Eston (infans) sepult.	xiij' die.
francis Wilkinson (infans) sepult.	xv' die.
Agnes Kyllobecke (uxor) sepult.	**xviij' die.**
[121] Mr. Nicholas Wombwell (esquyre) sepult.	**xxx' die.**

Mense Junij.

Willm. Johnson **(pauper) sepult.** ... ... x' die.

Mense Julij.

Peter Lynthwet (infans) sepult. ... ... viijvo die.
Robt. Lyster (paup) sepult. .. .. xix' die.

Mense Augusti.

Thomas Carre (pauper) sepult. ... ... **vto die.**
John Boothe (infans) sepult. ... ... xxvij' die.
Elizabethe Taylyer sepult. ... ... xxviij' die.

Mense Septembris.

hellin Lynthwet sepult. ... ... xix' die.

Sir john Lee vz.—Agnes Philippo—The daughters of William Cutt.—To William Tymperley an old angel of gold.—My brothers and sisters Henry, Nicholas, Robert, Alexander and john Shirecliffe and Catherine Cutt.—Thomas Cutt my father in law and Hugh Bower executors.—Proved at York, 23 March, 1570-1. Ambrose Swinbanke married Alice Shirecliffe 17 July, 1568. Thomas Cutt married Margaret Shirecliffe 21 Jan., **1566-7.**

[121] Nicholas Wombwell was of Thundercliffe Grange [he was son of Henry of the same, who was son of Hugh, second son of Thomas Wombwell, of Wombwell.)—His wife was Isabel, daughter of Thomas Wentworth, of Wentworth Woodhouse. His will is dated 16 Sept., 1557. To be buried in the Lady quire within the parish Church of Ecclesfield—My wife Isabel.—To my son john Wombwell an annuity of v marks out of my lands at Gresbroke and Morelay.—To my youngest son Nicholas Wombwell an annuity of v marks out of my lands at Wath and Lynthwet.—Thomas Wombwell—William Wombwell & William Rookesbye Esquires to be supervisors.—My son and heir apparent **(Thomas** Wombwell) sole executor and residuary legatee.—Proved at York, 7 july, 1571.

Mense OCTOBRIS.

Elizabethe Slatter sepult.	x' die.
johan filia Johnis. Weynwright sepult. ...	xj' die.
Wyllm. Roger & Frances Stones sepult. ...	xvij' die.

Mense NOVEMBRIS.

Anne Aldam (infans) sepult.	iiijto die.

Mense DECEMBRIS.

[122] Agnes Collye (uxor) sepult.	xxiiij' die.

Mense JANUARIJ.

John heye (infans) sepult.	xix' die.
Ambros hill (infans) sepult.	xx' die.

Mense FEBRUARIJ.

John Taylyer (pauper) sepult.	vjto die.
John Stigbucke (paup) sepult. ...	xiij' die.

Mense MARCIJ.

Isabell Gylles (infans) sepult.	x' die.
Wyllm. Slatter (pauper) sepult.	xxiij' die.

Mense MARCIJ. [1572.]

Anne Kaye (infans) sepult.	xxvij' die.

Mense APRILIS.

John Sparcke (infans) sepult.	xix' die.

Mense MAIJ.

hellin malinson (paup) sepult. ...	xxiij' die.

Mense JUNIJ.

Agnes Roger (uxor) sepult. ...	xij' die.

Mense JULIJ.

margret Lounde (paup vidua) sepult. ...	xxj' die.
[123] John Creswycke sepult.	xxx' die.

Mense AUGUSTI.

Margret Smythe (uxor) sepult.	vto die.
John Roodes sepult.	xx' die.

[122] In the churchwardens' Accounts, ano. 1572, appears this entry, "Itm john Colley junior for the buriall of his mother iijs. iiijd.," and again ano. 1573 "Itm receyved for ye buriall of olde Collies wife ijs. vlijd."

[123] john Creswick was of Ecclesfield, his will was proved at York, 17 Sept., 1572, and Thomas & Robert Creswick, his sons, were the executors.

Mense Septembris.

[124] Thomas Wylkinson sepult. ... xiij' die.

Mense Octobris.

Thomas Otes sepult. ... ... xxvj' die.

Mense Novembris.

Alice Clarcke (infans) sepult.	...	...	...	...	j' die.
johan. Scott (singlewoma.) sepult.	...	...	...	...	iiijto die.
Wyllm. Buttridge (paup) sepult.	...	...	...	...	ix' die.
Wyllm. hill sepult.	...	...	...	...	xv' die.
Thomas Rydinge sepult.	...	...	...	...	xviij' die.
margret Ellys sepult.	...	...	...	...	xxij' die.
[125] Catherin Crofts (uxor) sepult.	...	...	...	...	xxiij' die.
Nicholas Grene (paup) sepult.	...	...	...	...	**xxvj**' die.
Catherin Bower (uxor) sepult.	...	...	...	...	**xxvij**' die.

Mense Decembris.

Elizabethe johns (pauper) sepult. ... ... vij' die.

Mense Januarij.

Thomas Wylkinson sepult.	...	...	...	vjto die.
Elizabethe Lyster sepult.	...	...	...	viij' die.
[126] Mr. John Mounteneye gent. sepult....	...	...		xiiij' die.
[127] james the son of John Norton sepult.	...	...		xxviij' die.

[124] **Thomas** Wilkinson, of Shiregreen, cutler, will dated 7 Sept., 1572.—To be buried in the churchyard at Ecclesfield—whereas Thomas Wilkinson my father by his will dated 12 March, 1568, granted unto me a tenement & farm in Shiregreen with the lands &c. thereto belonging with all his interest & term of years to expend, I give the same to Elizabeth my sister to pay my bastard daughter jennet Wilkinson alias Day £5—My nephew Robert Wilkinson—My brother William Wilkinson—Alice Marsden and Elizabeth Wilkinson my sisters—My brother Richard Wilkinson's son Thomas & his other children.—Proved at York, 11 jan., 1572.

[125] 1543. Oct. 19. Catherine Crofts surrenders land, &c., in Whitley, to Christopher Crofts, her son & heir.—She was daughter and coheir of **john** Woodkirke, of Whitley, by Alice, his wife, daughter & heir of William Barbott, of Whitley.—The Barbotts or Berbotts were seated at Whitley as early as ano. 1410.

[126] **Mr. john** Mounteney was of Creswick in **this** parish. His will is **dated 6 Jan., 1572.—To the poor mans** box ijs.—To the most needs of the Church—to Richard Morton's wife xijd.—To Sir john Lee ijs.—To john Brownald a freise gowne.—To Thomas Hepworth a lether doublet.—To Richard Morton my best lether doublett.—To William Adamson my best freise gowne.—To john Birrie my freise girkyn.—To Richard Houlden a pare of hose of marble coloure—My children Nicholas, Arnold, Margaret, Esabell and hellyne.—To Arnold my son my messuage called Birley Hollins &c. and james Carr & Robert Wilkinson to be his guardians.—To Nicholas my son one Messuage in Ecclesfield now in the occupation of me the said john Mounteney and other lands &c. and Nicholas Shirecliffe & Ralph Lee to be his guardians.—Also to Nicholas my son certain Messuages and lands which I bought of Mr. Thomas Wentworth.—The residue of my good to my sons Arnold & Nicholas Mounteney and my daughters Margaret Esabell and Hellyn whom I make my true and lawful Executors and I give to either of them xxs, and their charges when they travel about, &c. Witnesses john Lee clark & Ralph Lee.

In the churchwardens' Accounts ano. 1572 occurs—" Itm for the buriall of Mr. Mounteney vjs. viijd."

[127] In the churchwardens' Accounts ano. 1573 occurs—" Receyved of john Norton for ye buriall of a childe and olde debte vjs. & viijd.

Mense FEBRUARIJ.

henrie Sheircliffe (puer) sepult.	...	...	j' die.
Elizabethe Grene (infans) sepult.	....	...	xxviij' die.

Mense MARTIJ.

[128] Edward **Byrleye** sepult.	...	...	...	x' die.
John **Lee** (infans) sepult.	...	...	...	xij' die.
Edward **Hatfeld** (infans) sepult.	...	...	...	xv' die.

Mense MARTIJ. [1573.]

johan haryson (uxor) sepult.	...	...	...	xxvj' die.

Mense APRILIS.

Agnes haughe (infans) sepult.	...		vjto die.
[129] Wyllm **Cutte** sepult.	...	...	vij' die.
Elizabethe **Longge** sepult.		...	xv' die.

Mense MAIJ.

Nicholas **Clarcke** sepult.	...	...	xj' die.
Elizabethe **Brodheade** sepult.	...	...	xxiij' die.

[128] Edward Byrley, **of Wadsley**, yeoman, will dated 10 March, 1572-3.—To be buried in the Church or Church yard at Ecclesfield.—I give for my mortuary as the law hath ordained—My wife Alice Byrley—my 3 children Godfrey Margaret & Agnes—My **brother** Nicholas Byrley—Thomas Greyves, Lawrence Eyre and Ralph Richardson my brother in law to be trustees as to a messuage &c. in Wadsley lately purchased from james Parkin and Agnes his wife to bestow the profits thereof on the said Godfrey & Margaret my children.—I give to my daughter Agnes all my leases & obligations granted to me by Henry Broomhead of Colmes & Elizabeth Chappel widow.—The will of Henry Byrley my **father**—Alice Stafford my wife's daughter.—Proved at York, 26 August, 1574.—The following is an abstract of **the will of Henry Dyrley**, of the Chapelry of Bradfield, father of **the** above Edward—dated 17 July, 1551. —To be buried in the Church of St. Nicholas Bradfield—Nicholas Byrley **my son** & his children.—To Edward Byrley my son **all my purchased lands in** Wadsley & Rotherham & £10.—My daughter Elizabeth Byrley—The children of Robert Taylor my son in law.—To Thomas son of Henry Ryder xxs. and to his sister vjs. & viijd.—To William Edward & john Byrley my brethren & to Agnes Day my sister xxs. each.—Also I will that my executors dispose and **give to the poor people of the parish of Bradfield for the health of** my soul every Sunday vd. during the space of one year next ensuing my decease.—The Residue of my goods to Edward Byrley, my son in law Lawrance Eyre, my son in law Robert Taylior & my daughter Elizabeth Byrley equally and they to be my executors.— Witnesses Edmund Eyre gent.—Richard Greyve and Edward Bower.—Proved at York, 3 june, 1558.—The above Henry was son of john Dyrley, of the Ewes, Worrall—he also held lands in Birley, Longley, and Ughill. He was son of William, who was living 1499, son of john, son of William, son of john de Birlay, living ano. 1406. In the year 1541, May 17, Henry Byrley surrenders land at Longley to Edward Byrley, his son.—1559, Nov. 5, Henry Byrley, of Worrall, being dead, Nicholas Byrley seeks to be admitted to certain lands in Longley, as being his son & heir, &c., &c. Worrall is a small hamlet lying between the village of Bradfield and Wadsley. In the Poll tax, 2 RICH. II., appear johannes de Birlay senior & Isabella ux' ejus iiijd.—Simon serviens Henrici de Birlay iiijd.— Henricus de Dyrlay & Margreta ux' ejus ffrannkeleyn xl.—Agnes serviens ejus iiijd. and johannes de Birlay & Matilda ux' ejus iiijd.

[129] William Cutt, of Ecclesfield, will dated 4 Ap., 1563.—To Margaret, Isabel & jane my daughters vl. apiece, If any die before coming of age **then** their portion to be divided among the survivors.—To Effame & Elizabeth my daughters all **my goods at** Houlton in Lincolnshire.—William Cutt my son Ellen my wife & William my son to be guardians of my **daughters** Isabel & jane until they come to the age of 15 years.—Thomas Cutt my brother & William Greves supervisors.—Witnesses Thomas Thwaites, john Wainwright, Edmund Bower and john Lee.—Proved **at** York, 28 july, 1573.

Mense JUNIJ.

Margret filia Johnis. **Kaye sepult.**	xx' die.
Robt. filius Johnis. Bower sepult.	xxij' die.
Elizabethe Brownell sepult.	xxiiij' die.
Alice hill (infans) sepult.	xxviij' die.

Mense AUGUSTI.

Isabell Parkin (infans) sepult.	j' die.
[130] Sir John Lee pryest sepult.	vj' die.
jane Clareke (uxor) sepult.	xxv' die.

Mense SEPTEMBRIS.

John howle (pauper) sepult.	vij' die.
Nicholas Carre (iuvenis) sepult.	xviij' die.
Robt. Crowder sepult.	xxv' die.

Mense OCTOBRIS.

Margerie Cooper (infans) sepult.	vj' die.
Jane Cooper (infans) sepult.	xj' die.

Mense NOVEMBRIS.

Peter hartleye (infans) sepult.	xix' die.
Agnes Mathyman sepult.	xxx' die.

Mense DECEMBRIS.

Elizabeth Brigge sepult.	iiijto die.
Agnes Carre sepult.	xvj' die.
Willm. Streate sepult.	xvij' die.

Mense JANUARIJ.

Margret Collye sepult.	iij' die.
Agnes Collye sepult.	eod. die.

Mense FEBRUARIJ.

Charles hill sepult.	ijdo die.
Agnes Bedfeld sepult.	vjto die.
Margret Goodyr sepult.	eod. die.
Catherin Shepperd sepult.	**xxiiij' die.**

Mense MARTIJ.

Elizabethe hanbye sepult.	iij' die.
Elizabethe Creswycke sepult.	iiijto die.
margerye Ronksleye sepult.	**vto die.**

[130] A person of this name was chaplain of the Guild of St. Crux, Eckington, in co. Derby, ano. 1537.

Mense Maij. [1574.]

francys Roodes sepult.	viij' die.
hugho hobson sepult.	xviij' die.

Mense Junij.

john Ludge sepult.	viij' die.
Willm. Collye (infans) sepult.	xij' die.

Mense Septembris.

john Parkin sepult.	xviij' die.
john Brown sepult.	xxvj' die.

Mense Octobris.

joan Kent sepult.	ijdo die.
Agnes hill (vidua) sepult.	iij' die.
Rychard Taylyer (infans) sepult.	xix' die.

Mense Novembris.

Rychard haughe sepult.	iiijto die.
Elizabethe foxe sepult.	xj' die.
Emot. Shawe sepult.	xix' die.

Mense Decembris.

Francis hill (infans) sepult.	ix' die.
Elizabethe Cooper sepult.	ultimo die

Mense Januarij.

Margret Lyster sepult.	j' die.
James harryson sepult.	iij' die.

Mense Februarij.

Isabell Turnleye sepult.	iiijto die.
Nicholas Keyes (infans) sepult.	viij' die.

Mense Martij. [1575.]

Francys Brodheade sepult.	xxvij' die.

Mense Aprilis.

Nicholas Combe sepult.	j' die.
john the son of Willm. Sheirclyffe sepult.	iiijto die.
Joan Brownell sepult.	xxiij' die.

Mense Maij.

Rychard Cooper (infans) sepult.	ix' die.
John Collye (infans) sepult.	xxvto die.

Mense Junij.

John Oxspringe (senex) sepult.	xxiijto die.

Menso Augusti.

Thomas Wildsmythe (senex) sepult.	xj' die.
Alice Twhaytes sepult.	xviij' die.

Menso Septembris.

margret Collye sepult.	ixno die
[131] Thomas howsleye (infans) sepult.	xx' die.
Elizabethe Parkin (infans) sepult.	xxij' die.

Menso Octobris.

Thomas Carre (juvenis) sepult.	iiijto die.
Richard hollinbrigge (senex) sepult.	xiiij' die.

Mense Decembris.

Joan Smythe sepult.	j' die.
Roger Carre (juvenis) sepult.	viij' die.
Alexandr. Carre sepult.	xxj' die.
Anne johnson sepult.	xxvij die.
Wyllm. Slatter (senex) sepult.	xxjx' die.

Menso Januarij.

John Wodde (infans) sepult.	viij' die.
[132] John hill (senex) sepult.	xviij' die.

Menso Februarij.

joan Jepson (infans) sepult.	xviij' die.
hellen Carre & john her son (infans) sepult.	xxiiij' die.
Nicholas Mathyman (juvenis) sepult.	xxvto die.
Alice Cooper (vidua) sepult.	xxvj' die.
Isabell Pearson (vidua) sepult.	xxviij' die.
Thomas hartley (senex) sepult.	xxix' die.
Robt. myddleton (infans) sepult.	eod. die.
margret hill sepult.	eod. die.

Menso Martij.

Anne Tompson sepult.	vto die.
Alexander hill (infans) sepult.	vij' die.
Wm. Grene (juvenis) sepult.	xix' die.

Menso Martij. [1576.]

Robt. handley (infans) sepult.	xxviij' die.
john Button (infans) sepult.	xxix' die.

---

[131] Was infant son of Thomas Howsley, of Howsley Hall, gent.

[132] John Hill, of Ecclesfield, will dated 1 Nov., 1575.—To the poor mans box xijd.—My property to be divided into 3 parts—one part to myself—one part to Margaret Hill my wife and one part to my children.—My house to Margaret Hill my wife.—To John Hartley my godson iijs. & iiijd.—"To everie other my childrens childe ijs."—To Richard Hill my son xxs.—To Elizabeth Hill my daughter xs.—Henry, Robert and Richard Hill my sons—Elizabeth & Jone Hill my daughters.—Alexander Hatfield & Ralph Lee supervisors.—Proved at York, 2 August, 1576.

Mense Aprilis.

John Oxpringe (infans) sepult.	vjto die.
Joan myddleton sepult.	eod. die.
hellen Pearson sepult.	x' die.
johan Dawre (vidua) sepult.	xxvj' die.
Joan the daughter of john Grene (infans) sepult.	xxix' die.

Mense Maij.

Robt. Sheyrclyffe (senex) sepult.	ijdo die.
Raulphe Warde sepult.	iij' die.
John Walker (alias Slatter) sepult.	iiij' die.
Emot. Warde (infans) sepult.	xxvj' die.

Mense Junij.

francis Stones (infans) sepult.	iiijto die.
Joan Roger (infans) sepult.	xvj' die.
Robt. Smythe (juvenis) sepult.	xvij' die.
henrye Sheyrclyffe (juvenis) sepult.	xix' die.

Mense Augusti.

John Byrrye (infans) sepult.	xv' die.
John Sheffelde (infans) bapt. et sepult.	xxv' die.

Mense Septembris.

Anne Sheffeld (infans) sepult.	j' die.
Joan Sheffeld sepult.	x' die.

Mense Octobris.

[133] Isabell Stanylande sepult.	xx' die.

Mense Novembris.

Anne Turton sepult.	xxij' die.

Mense Decembris.

Phillis Brown sepult.	xv' die.
Thomas Shooter (infans) sepult.	xxviij' die.

Mense Februarij.

[134] Edward Creswycke (senex) sepult.	x' die.
Agnes Roodes (vidua) & hellen Baylye sepult.	xvij' die.
Anne harryson sepult.	xxv' die.

[133] In the churchwardens' Account ano. 1576 occurs—"Itm of Nicolas Staniland for his wifes grave iijs. & iijd."

[134] Edward Creswick, **of Wadsley**, cutler, will proved at York, 13 August, 1577.—To William Creswick my son 1 cottage & 1 Acre called Hawlyne **held of the** grant of John Creswick of Wadsley & 1 Acre 1 Rood of the grant of Henry & Thomas Shooter—Margaret **Creswick** my wife—Thomas & Edward Creswick my sons—"one hagg of Holline" of the grant of John Creswick of Ollerton to William Creswick.—Witnesses John Creswick of Ollerton Hall —John Creswick of Wadsley & Leonard Bamford.

Mense Martij.

joan Crowder sepult.	iij' die.
Jane Lee sepult.	xj' die.
Cieylye Batleye sepult.	eod. die.
John Berrye sepult.	xviij' die.
John Johnson (senex) sepult.	xxij' die.

Mense Martij. [1577.]

Isabell holden sepult.	xxv' die.

Mense Aprilis.

Wyllm. Beard (senex) sepult.	iiijto die.
John Brodbent sepult.	xij' die.

Mense Maij.

joan harryson (vidua) sepult.	vto die.
Emot. Dughtye sepult.	xiij' die.
Agnes Parkin sepult.	xxv' die.

Mense Augusti.

Wyllm. hoye (senex) sepult.	iiijto' die.
hellen grubbe (infans) sepult.	vto' die.
gem. john Jepson (infans) sepult.	xiiij' die.
Edward Greaves sepult.	eod. die.
Thomas Carre (infans) sepult.	xix' die.

Mense Novembris.

hellen Linthwet (infans) sepult.	xiij' die.

Mense Decembris.

joan the daughter of Charles myddleton bapt. et sepult.	xiiij' die.
Nicholas Wilkinson (juvenis) sepult.	xxj' die.
Rychard hill (senex) sepult.	xxiij' die.
Barbara hill (infans) sepult.	xxvij' die.
Agnes Parker (alias hall) senex. sepult.	xxix' die.

Mense Januarij.

john Pegge sepult.	xiij' die.

Mense Martij.

Agnes Sampson sepult.	vij' die.
Joan Byrdheade (infans) sepult.	xxij' die.
Joan Wylkinson (senex) sepult.	xxiij' die.

Mense Maij. [1578.]

Margret Bradburne (infans) sepult.	vto die.
John Sheffelde (senex) sepult.	vj' die.
Grace Deye sepult.	xix' die.

Mense JUNIJ.

Barbara Collye (infans) sepult.	... ...	xij' die.
Robt. Grubbe (senex) sepult.	... ...	xv' die.

Mense JULIJ.

Edward Barber (juvenis) sepult.	... ...	ijdo die.

Mense AUGUSTI.

Thomas hatfelde (infans) sepult.	... ...	vto die.
Cicilie Saterfelt (infans) sepult.	... ...	xv' die.

Mense SEPTEMBRIS.

Dionise Creswycke (infans) sepult.	... ...	ix' die.

Mense OCTOBRIS.

hellen jeffraye (alias Manton) sepult.	... ...	vij' die.
Elizabethe Lee (juvenis) sepult.	... ...	ix' die.
Joan Wodde (infans) sepult.	... ...	xviij' die.
francys jackson sepult.	... ...	xxiij' die.
Thomas hobson sepult.	... ...	xxix' die.

Mense NOVEMBRIS.

Francys hall (infans) sepult.	... ...	xvj' die.
Anne Shawe (infans) sepult.	... ...	xvij' die.

Mense DECEMBRIS.

Nicholas Banckes (juvenis) sepult.	... ...	ijdo die.
John Secker (infans) sepult.	... ...	xxiiij' die.
John Carre (infans) sepult.	... ...	eod. die.
John myddleton (infans) sepult.	... ...	xxviij' die.

Mense JANUARIJ.

[135] Margret Lee (vidua) sepult.	... ...	vjto die.

Mense FEBRUARIJ.

Rycharde Bearde (juvenis) sepult.	... ...	vto die.
Joan Wylkinson (senex) sepult.	... ...	x' die.
henrie Shawe (juvenis) sepult.	... ...	xij' die.
francys Aldam (infans) sepult.	... ...	xiij' die.
Richard Geslinge (senex) sepult.	... ...	xix' die.
james Breffet sepult.	... ...	xxvij' die.

[135] Margaret Lee, of Sinderwell, in the parish of Ecclesfield, widow, will dated 11 Oct., 1578.—To the building of Colynton Haven ijd.—Agnes Lee my daughter after my decease to have the house wherein I now live and if the said Agnes Lee die without issue then the **house to** go to Ralph Lee the younger.—Witnesses Sir William Browne—Tho. Bullus, &c.—Proved at York, 23 April, 1579.

Mense Aprilis. [1579.]

Joan Collye (adolescens) sepult.	... ...	liijto die.
[136] Rychard Collye (senex) sepult.	... ...	xij' die.
Elizabethe memot. **(paup) sepult.**	... ...	xxv' die.

Mense Maij.

[137] Raulphe Lee **(senex) sepult.**	...	xx' die.
Alice Lounde (paup) **sepult.**	...	eod. die.

Mense Junij.

[138] Thomas Parker **(senex) sepult.**	...	...	j' die.

Mense Julij.

Thomas Saterfet (infans) sepult.	... ...	...	vto' die.

Mense Augusti.

Isable Tyngle (infans) sepult.	...	...	...	xxj' die.
henrye Stevenson (paup) **sepult.**	...	...	...	xxvto die.

Mense Septembris.

Rychard Ponystone (infans) **sepult**....	...	...	8' die.

Mense Octobris.

margret Parman. (pauper) sepult.	... ...	...	xxj' die.
[139] Rychard Byrkes **(senex) sepult.**	... ...	...	xxvj' die.
Thomas Bradburn (infans) sepult.	... ...	...	eod. die.

[136] Richard Collye, of Ecclesfield, will dated 12 March, 1576.—To be buried in the churchyard at Ecclesfield.—To Isabel Collye my wife "1 bed 1 kynmell and a gret tubbe."—To Thomas Collye my son "1 standing table in the house & myne arke."—To Grace Collye my daughter "1 cubborde in the parler."—To Elizabeth Collye my daughter "1 folding bord."—My wife now great with child.—My daughter Ann Collye—John Rhodes & Thomas Howsley supervisors.—Witnesses Sir William Brown—Richard Carre & Christopher Crofts.—Proved at York, 15 Nov., 1580.

[137] Ralph Lee, of Ecclesfield, will dated 28th Feb., 1577.—To be buried in the churchyard Ecclesfield.—My goods to be divided into three parts—one to myselfe—one to Agnes Lee my wife and one to my children.—Agnes Lee my wife to have the rent of one cottage in Ecclesfield now in the tenure of Widow Moulde. Memorandum.—I have given by surrender the above cottage into the hands of Ralph Crofts & Nicholas Stauiland to the use of my son William Lee for his life and after his decease to Ralph Lee his brother.—Agnes my wife & Ralph my son to have the lease of my farm.—To Agnes my wife "one little gray Mair and her saddle."—To " Elline Dawre xxs. to bring her to her father or to keipe her one or two yeares after my decease."—To each of my sons & daughters children 1 Ewe shepe.—To Nicholas son of James Crofts of Ecclesfield ijd.—To Agnes wife of Robert Davie my daughter xls.—To William Wilde my black jackett.—Mr. Tyas & William Burroues supervisors.—Witnesses Sir William Brown, Thomas Dullus, Ralph Richardson & Hugh Hyde.—Proved at York, 5 june, 1579. Vide note 42.

[138] Thomas Parker was of Whitley Hall, 2nd son of John Parker, of Norton.—In the churchwardens' Accounts ano. 1581 occurs—" Item of William Parker for his father & Mothers graves in ye Chancell xiijs. iiijd."

[139] In the churchwardens' Accounts occurs the following—" It is covenanted & agreed betwene Richard Birkes & ye pishes (parishioners) of Eglesfold 24 die Aprilis a Dni 1575 That ye said Richard Birkes during his life shall kepe and upholde ye clocke in ye churche of Eglesfeld afforesaid with all reparacons of workemanshippe & Iron worke for ye weh he haithe receyved xxiijs. vjd. In ye presence (presence) of Willm Parker, Alexander Hadfeild, Hughe Hide, Raffe Richardson, Thomas Crosley, Nicolas Shirteliffe, Thomas Shawe, Edward Creswicke & John Bower.

+ signum manuale pdicti Richardi Birkes.

Mense Novembris.

hellen Gylles sepult.	ijdo die.
margret Slacke sepult.	xij' die.
Thurstaine Dungworth (pauper) sep.	xx' die.

Mense Decembris.

Robt. Ludge (pauper) sepult.	ijdo. die.

Mense Januarij.

Arnold Bullus (infans) sepult.	viij' die.
Nicholas Warde (pauper) sepult.	xix' die.
Alice Tympleye sepult.	xxviij' die.

Mense Februarij.

Elizabethe jeffraye (infans) sepult.	vij' die.
Francis Lee (infans) bapt. et sepult.	xxij' die.

Mense Martij.

john Dyson (infans) sepult.	vto die.
Robt. hardie (infans) sepult.	xxj' die.

Mense Martij. [1580.]

Effam Beale (pauper) sepult.	xxviij' die.
Alice Trippet (infans) sepult.	xxjx' die.

Mense Aprilis.

mychaell Roodes (infans) sepult.	xij' die.
Christine Base (infans) sepult.	xv' die.
Agnes Smythe (infans) sepult.	xx' die.

Mense Maij.

Robt. Beale (infans) sepult.	xj' die.
Catherine Grene (senex) sepult.	xij' die.
jane Gylles (infans) sepult.	xvij' die.
Grace Jeffraye (infans) sepult.	xxvj' die.
Alice Walker (alias Slatter) sepult.	xxjx' die.

Mense Junij.

[140] Elizabethe Parker (senex) sepult.	vij' die.
Wm. & Katherin Swifte (infantes) sepult.	ix' die.
[141] Isabell Clayton (senex) sepult.	xxij' die.
hellen Stigbucke (senex) sepult.	xxjx' die.

[140] Vide note 138.

[141] In the churchwardens' Accounts ano. 1580 occurs "Item received of Robert Claton and hys wife for two graves in ye church vjs. & viiijd."

Mense JULIJ.

henrie Shooter (infans) sepult.	...	...	...	xiij' die.
john hartleye (infans) sepult.	...	...	...	xxvij' die.

Mense AUGUSTI.

Elizabethe hartleye sepult.	...	...	...	vij' die.

Mense SEPTEMBRIS.

joan hyde (senex) sepult.	...	...	...	x' die.
Robt. Doghtyman (juvenis) sepult.	...	...	...	xxiij' die.
Wm. Dicksons (juvenis) sepult.	...	...	...	ultimo die.

Mense OCTOBRIS.

[142] Dns. johes. Tyas rector de Treeton et vicarius de Ecclesfield cum Bradfeld sepult. } ixno die.

Laurence morton (pauper) sepult.	xv' die.
margret Bromheade (pauper) sepult.	xvj' die.
Joan Dynison (infans) sepult. ...	xix' die.
Gylbert morewodde (senex) sepult. ...	xxvj' die.

[142] John Tyas, parson of Treeton & vicar of Ecclesfield, will dated 30 May, 1586.—To be buried in Ecclesfield churchyard . . .—"I fynde in Gods lawe & his holy worde that bona *ecclesiæ sunt bona pauperum* [Aug.] a prelate may not bequeath or give the Church goods to his cosinges or kinsfolkes, *quia Moses distribuens boves et plaustra Levitis nullum dedit filiis Caoth* [Kohath] *sibe carne propinquis* [NUM. 7]; *sed moriturus rogavit dominum idoneum ducem populo providere, nullum de stirpe sua nominavit. Josue distribuens terram Israelitis minorem partem dedit tribui suæ* [Jos. 17.] **At** *dominus noster Jesus Christus neque Jacobum majorem neque minorem, vel Joseph, Justum, Simonem aut Judam sue sibi Johannem præ ceteris dilectum promovit ad apicem et regimen suæ ecclesiæ, qui omnes consanguinei et de sua stirpe fuerunt, sed Petrum* [Joh. 21.] *Canones Apostolorum 39 et 15 docent nos clericos testamenta nostra disponere sive ordinare.*"—To Burton parish xxxs. Penistone xxs. Sheffield xxs. and one mattress coverlet blanket &c. and one alms bed for old sick sore & lame people to lie in at the Vicar's discretion.—To Glossop xs. Cawthorne xs. Wentworth xs. Tankersley xs. Rotherham xxs. Rawmarsh xs. Whiston xs. Langton xs. Aston xs. Beighton xs. Handsworth xs.—My "funeralls" and debts to be taken of my whole goods, & my debts to be given to **my** executors, then all my goods to be divided into 3 parts: the first to myself, the second to my household servants men & women boys & scholars with other poor persons such as shall be nominated in a bill [*not found*] indented subscribed with my own hand to be annexed to this will, whereof one part remaineth in the custody of my said servants & the other in the custody of my executors, and the third part thereof to the poor people of my 3 parishes. —" Item I freelye give and bequeath to the right honourable my very good Lord and maister the best yoke of oxen that God hath lente me such as his good Lordshippe shall lyke best, and I do heare most tenderly beseek his great **and** superabundant honor for the deare love of Almighty God, godly to consider the great misery & poverty of these **pore** parishes and parsons herein expressed," &c.—To every of my Godchildren xijd.—To Francis Barnby 30/.—"To my 3 parish **priests** 3 good cloaks or gownes."—To Sir Thomas Colly Mr. Ralph Roger & Sir Robert Tinmonth alias Steele 3 cloaks or cassocks.—To my 3 parish clerks 3/4 each —To Edward Pavy 20/.—To the mending of Highways in my 3 parishes 20/.—To Mr. Manleverer one velvet hat.—To Mr. Edward More of Barnborough my dagger that my Lord Darcy gave me.—To Christopher Hayford 20/.—To John Frankish 20/.—To everyone of my brethren & sisters children 3/4.—To Mr. Atkinson 20/. for his pains with George Tyas.—To the same George Tyas 20/.—To George Tyas of Barnby Hall all my books.—To William Chappell and Margaret Shaw 2 stone of wool & the price of 2 quarters of wheat or rye, all such swine or "pullayne" as are at the Vicarage & 2 kine to help them.—To my brother Jhnes [John's] wife 3 Metts of wheat.—To John Tyas wife of Thorlee a flanders bed cover with images & **my** feather bed at Ecclesfield.—To Peter Morton my coffer at Steyrehead with lock & key for his knives.—To the poor cottages of Treeton all my wood & coals within my folds.—To the poor people of Ecclesfield & Bradfield one annuity or annual rent of 28/. to be yearly for ever taken out of one messuage or one oxgang and a half of land at Thurnsco **to the use of** the poor, blind, old, lame, and impotent people of the said parishes and to none other use,

Mense NOVEMBRIS.

Robt. Clayton (senex) sepult.	... ...	ijdo die.
John Saterfett (infans) sepult.	... ...	vto die.
Edward Watson (pauper) sepult.	... ...	xiij' die.
Agnes Creswycke (juvenis) sepult.	... ...	xx' die.
Isabell Bullus (juvenis) sepult.	... ...	xxiij' die.
Agnes Brodbent (infans) sepult.	... ...	xxvj' die.
Rychard Bradburn (infans) sepult.	...	xxvij' die.

Mense DECEMBRIS.

Elizabethe Tottington (senex) sepult.	...	ijdo die.
henry Brodheade (infans) sepult.	... ...	xxiiij' die.

Mense JANUARIJ.

[143] Thomas hoylande (senex) sepult.	... ...	...	ijdo die.
Agnes Sheyrcliffe sepult.	... ...	...	eod. die.
Elizabethe Shaw (pauper) sepult.	... ...	...	ixno die.
Agnes Lee (vidua) sepult.	... ...	...	xxvj' die.
Alice Bartlemewe (pauper) sepult.	... ...	...	eod. die.

Mense FEBRUARIJ.

Elizabethe Ragge (senex) sepult.	... ...	xx' die.
[144] Robt. Wylkinson (senex) sepult.	... ...	xxj' die.
joan Walker (senex) sepult.	... ...	xxiij' die.

and the heirs, owners or occupiers of the said messuage & lands shall yearly for ever [pay?] to the Vicars, churchwardens and 4 honest men successively for their times being, that a perpetual alms & distribution of the same may be yearly for ever, on 2 Sundays yearly, the Sunday before Christmas & St. John the Baptist.—To the poor of Treeton & Treeton parish an annuity of 5/. for ever out of a cottage in Pontefract near the Castle.—To my servant Henry Lastles for his true service done all that my said messuage in Thurnscoe during his life, with remainder to his sons John & Edward jointly and to their heirs for ever, yielding yearly as above, with remainder to the right heirs of John Tyas of Thoxlee.—I make my cousin Robert Tyas, Thomas Greaves of Tickhill, Sir Thomas Cuthbert, John Tyas of Thoxlee & Ralph Croft my executors & I give each of them 20/. and all my debts on condition that they pay to Isabel Tyas daughter of my brother John Tyas £4.—I make Mr. Hudson, Dean of Doncaster, & my fellow Edward Hadfield supervisors hereof, & I give to each of them for their pains 20/. and their charges borne.—Residue of all my goods quick & dead moveable & unmoveable to the poor people of my 3 parishes to help, succour & relieve their great hunger, need & poverty—and here I most tenderly beseech my said executors for the dear love of God, the merits & death & passion of Jesus Christ that the poor little ones [Matthew 25] be never robbed, spoiled, bereft or defrauded of this my willing & free gift—for as God knoweth before whom & all the world I confess that I was never in any other thought, mind or intent "sith" I was twenty years of age & had any worldly goods but with all my heart, goodwill & mind to render & give them to the poor to whom I am double debter for the same.—This is my true & last will, and these my true honest & just servants are witnesses to record the same & hereunto have subscribed their names with the test.—Thomas Coke, Richard Steyde, George Wade, James Courtney, Richard Sheapard and Henry Taylor.—Item I give to my 2 servants Thomas Tyas & Henry Lastles all my leases of Dipkar wheat close, with one close named Cawcroft in the parish of Aston, the said Dipkar & Wheatcroft being in the parish of Rawmarsh.—Proved at York, 17 Nov., 1580.

[143] Was probably son of Henry Hoyland, of Shiregreen. Vide note 17.

[144] Robert Wilkinson, of Crowder House, in the parish of Ecclesfield, yeoman.—To be buried in the churchyard Ecclesfield.—My goods after paying funeral expenses debts &c. to be divided into 3 parts the first to myself, the second to Ann Wilkinson my wife and the third to my children.—To Edward Mathewman for his child's portion xls.—

114

Menso Martij.

[145] Roger Barber (senex) **sepult.**	...	...	...	ijdo die.
[146] Dns. Richardus Cooper (sacerdos) sepult.	...	...	...	xx' die.
francis Taylyer (infans) **sepult.**	...	...	...	xxj' die.
Robt. Dughtye (alias Waggeleye) **sepult.**	...	...	...	xxiiij' die.
Roger Bower (**senex**) sepult.	...	...	...	xxjx' die.

Menso Aprilis. [1581.]

Willm. **Carro** (infans) sepult.	...	...	...	xvij' die.
Elizabethe Renalde (paup) sepult.	...	...	...	xx' die.
Barbara Linleyo (infans) sepult.	...	...	...	xxv' die.

Menso Maij.

Elizabethe haughe (pauper) sepult.	...	...	...	xxij' die.
Isabell Bullus (paup) sepult.	...	...	...	xxv' die.

Menso Junij.

francis Creswycke (infans) sopult.	...	...	...	xxvto' die.

Menso Augusti.

john handley (infans) sepult.	...	...	...	xx' die.
John Ronald (infans) sepult.	...	...	...	xxij' die.
margret machon (senex) sepult.	...	...	...	ultimo die.

Menso Septembris.

Rychard Wylkinson (infans) **sepult.**	...	...	...	iij' die.
hellen Cony (infans) sepult.	...	...	...	x' die.
Ambrose Newbye (advena)	...	...	...	xxjx' die.

To my son Nicholas Wilkinson lilje. viijd.—To my son William Wilkinson 2 yoke, 1 plough &c. &c.—The rest of my husbandry geer to Ann my wife and John, James, Robert and George Wilkinson my sons.—The same also to have my smithy geer.—To Margaret, Ann & Katherine my daughters xxxli.—John Rawson and Alexander Hatfeld overseers.— Proved at York, 13 April, 1581.—I have the following notes from the Manor Court Rolls :—1470. feb. 20. John Wilkinson seeks to be admitted to a tenement called Crowder House in Longley in the parish of Ecclesfield as **being** the son & heir of Henry Wilkinson deceased. 1509. Dec. 4. Thomas Wilkinson seeks to be admitted to the **same** as being son & heir of John Wilkinson deceased. 1519. Nov. 10. Alice Nelson wife of William Hodgson and daughter and heir of John Nelson deceased surrenders lands in Wincobank to Thomas Wilkinson. 1537. june 15. Thomas Wilson of Crowder House surrenders lands in Longley & Wincobank to Robert Wilkinson his son & heir. 1587. jan. 3. William Wilkinson seeks to be admitted to Crowder House & lands in Longley & Wincobanke as son & heir of Robert Wilkinson deceased.—Among the title deeds of Crowder House, now in the possession of Bernard Wake, Esqre., is one dated the feast of St. Stephen the Martyr, 1402, by which Julyan, late wife of John Wilkinson, deceased, of Ecclesfield, devised, releases, &c., to Henry Wilkinson, her son, all her rights in 1 Messuage & 1 pyer of land lying in Wynkley, which is called Crowder House.—Witnesses William Hartley, John Hartley, John Collye, Henry Hartley, William Combe, & others. Vide note 70.

[145] 1550. Ap. 10. William son & heir of John Harshand surrenders 1 Messuage and ¼ a bovat in Stannington to Roger Barber of Wadsley. 1567. April 22. Roger Barber of Wadsley surrenders the same to the use of Richard Barber his younger son.—*Court Rolls.*—Roger Barber, the subject of this note, was probably father of John Barber, of Wadsley, an abstract of whose will may be found under note 151.

[146] Was a chauntrey priest.

Mense Octobris.

Edmunde Shawe (infans) sepult.	iiijto die.
Anne Creswycke (juvenis) sepult.	vij' die.
Wm. Snydall (senex advena) sepult.	xxiij' die.

Mense Novembris.

Barbara falleye (infans) sepult.	iij' die.
Effam Bearde (senex) sepult.	xxiij' die.
hellen Bullus (infans) sepult.	eod. die.
Elizabethe hartleye (juvenis) sepult.	ultimo die.

Mense Decembris.

john Dynison (infans) sepult.	xviij' die.
Robt. holden paup. sepult.	xxx' die.

Mense Januarij.

margerye machon sepult.	iij' die.
Edmund Wylkinson sepult.	xj' die.
marye Shooter (juvenis) sepult.	xv' die.
joan Carre (vidua) sepult.	xxj' die.
Barbara Cooper (infans) sepult.	xxiij' die.
margret Byrkes (vidua) sepult.	xxvj' die.

Mense Februarij.

Thomas hutton (advena) sepult.	j' die.
john Crofts (pauper) sepult.	vjto die.
Rychard Oxpringe (paup) sepult.	xiij' die.
Thomas Roodes (paup) sepult.	ultimo die.

Mense Martij.

Thomas Osseleye (infans) sepult.	ijdo die.
Spur. Francis fil. Edwardi Strale. sepult.	viij' die.
Anne francis & margret filiæ henrici hill bapt. et sepult.	ixno die.
Wm. Newton (infans) sepult.	xix' die.
francis fil. Anthonij Cutt bapt. & sepult.	xxiij' die.
[147] Thomas Greaves (senex) sepult.	xxiiij' die.

[147] Thomas Greaves, of Wadsley, in the parish of Ecclesfield, yeoman, will dated 23 March, 1581.—To be buried in the church or churchyard of Ecclesfield at the discretion of my executors.—Elizabeth Greaves my wife and Edward Hobson alias Greaves my son to have all my tenement and farm called Wadsley Hall in Wadsley during the minority of Francis Greaves my son & heir apparent.—To Mary Greaves my daughter I give xlli.—Ralfe Warde and Hellen his wife.—To Francis Greaves my son all my hereditaments leases &c. &c. in Westnall, Waldershelf and Hunshelf, and in default of issue to Edward Greaves alias Hobson my son and in default of issue to Hellen Warde and Mary Greaves my daughters.—Witnesses John Greaves, Thomas Greaves, Edward Bower and John Bower.—Proved at York, 29 Nov. 1582.—In the churchwardens' Accounts ano. 1583 occurs "Item Received for Thomas Greaves grave in ye churche iijs. & iijd."—I have the following notes of the family of Greaves from the manor court Rolls.—1276. Radus de Grove paid a fine of 24/. to be admitted to 10 Acres of land in Fulwood. 1406. Radus del Grove and Matilda his wife surrender 3 Acres and a half in West-

Mense APRILIS. [1582.]

joan filia Robti. Lynleye bapt. et sepult.	...	j' die.
john Greno (infans) sepult.	...	iij' die.
Rychard Tynglo (senex) sepult.	...	vto die.
Peter fearnleye sepult.	...	xxv' die.

Mense MAIJ.

joan filia Johnis. haughton (infans) sepult.	...	iiijto' die.
hughe Rychardson (juvenis) sepult.	...	x' die.
Catherin Grubbe (juvenis) sepult.	...	xxviij' die.

Mense JUNIJ.

Nicholas Shawe (juvenis) sepult.	...	ijdo die.
Nicholas Chamber (juvenis) sepult....	...	x' die.
Rychard Trulove (infans) sepult.	...	xvj' die.
Catherin Gylles (infans) sepult.	...	eod. die.
john Wodde (senex) sepult.	...	xix' die.

Mense JULIJ.

Wyllm. Creswicke (juvenis) sepult....	...	**xxj' die.**
john Bartlemewe (paup) sepult.	...	**xxiij' die.**

Mense AUGUSTI.

Dionis Wyllye (infans) sepult.	...	ixno die.
Isabell Cooper (paup) sepult.	...	**xij' die.**
john Greaves sepult.	...	xxix' die.

Mense SEPTEMBRIS.

[146] Wm. Scotte (senex) sepult.	...	vto die.
Margret Smythe sepult.	...	x' die.
joan Neyler pochiæ de Rotherham sepult.	...	eod. die.

monhalgh to Willielmus de Morewood. 1407. Oct. 16. John Wobbins or Wobkins surrenders 1 Messuage and 2½ Acres in Thornsetts to John de Greyfe. 1418. John son & heir of William Grove seeks admission to half a Messuage in Westmonhalgh in the soke of Bradfield. 1428. May 5. John Greve de Holdworth claims to hold 1 Messuage and 1 plot of land in Holdworth and half a messuage and one croft in Westmonhalgh *post mortem* Magot late wife of William Fernelly whose heir he is. 1428. july 17. John Greve is admitted as heir of Magot late wife of William Fernelly alias Shepherd. 1428. july 17. The same John Greve surrenders one half of a Messuage and one croft in Westmonhalgh to John Greve de Waldershelf. 1428. Aug. 8. John Greve of Holdworth surrenders 1 Messuage and 1 plot in Holdworth which he got by the surrender of the wife of Richard Hall, to the use & behoof of William Cutt. 1440. Agnes de Greve surrenders 1 Messuage and 1 bovat in Hawkesworth to John de Greve junior. 1467. Nov. 25. John Greve surrenders 1 Messuage in Westcall Bradfield to the use and behoof of William Greve his son & heir. 1513. Mar. 15. William Greve having lately died John Greve seeks to be admitted as his son & heir to 1 Messuage in Westcall Bradfield. 1528. june 9. John Greve of Waldershelf surrenders the same to the use of Thomas Greve and Thomas the son of the said Thomas Greve with remainder to Richard Greve brother of the aforesaid John Greve with remainder to Edward son of the said Richard Greve.—There was another branch of this family who held land in Fullwood and Bradfield.—In the Poll tax, 2 Ricır. ıı., appear Willelmus del Grove & Margreta ux. ejus ilijd. of Bradfield.

[146] William Scott was 3rd son of Richard Scott of Barnes Hall. In his will, dated 23 Aug., 1582, he describes himself as William Scott of Ecclesfield.—To be buried in the churchyard Ecclesfield.—To the poor of Ecclesfield iijs. & iiijd.—To each of my godchildren xijd.—To Barbery Scott my goddaughter iijli. vjs. viijd.—To my brother

Mense Octobris.

Elizabethe Crofts sepult.	iij' die.
Anne Brefet (infans) sepult.	xv' die.
Joan Crosleye (infans) sepult.	xxiij' die.

Mense Novembris.

Agnes Phillippe (senex) sepult.	xiiij' die.
margret Dungworthe (infans) sepult.	xxiij' die.

Mense Decembris.

Rychard Swifte sepult.	xiij' die.
Wyllm. Adamson (paup) sepult.	xvij' die.
Alice morewodde (senex) sepult.	xxvij' die.
hellen Cutte (senex) sepult.	xxviij' die.

Menso Januarij.

Elizabethe Barbar (senex) sepult.	vto die.
Isabell Scholes (senex) sepult.	vjto die.
Alice Lownde (paup) sepult.	viij' die.
Barbara Grubbe (infans) sepult.	xij' die.
Dorithie Adamson (pauper) sepult.	xvj' die.

Mense Februarij.

henrie Wylkinson (senex) sepult.	xiij' die.
Joan Robinson (pauper) sepult.	xiiij' die.
Richard Raworthe (senex) sepult.	xv' die.
jane Buckman (infans) sepult.	xvj' die.
Joan Grubbe (juvenis) sepult.	xix' die.
Joan Gylles (infans) sepult.	xxiiij' die.
Christine Parkin (pauper) sepult.	eod. die.

Mense Martij.

Spur. Francis fil. Robti. Wright domi bapt. et sepult.	vjto die.
Grace Gylles (infans) sepult.	vij' die.
Francis Cutte (infans) sepult.	viij' die.
John holden (infans) sepult.	xix' die.
Nicholas Ragge (infans) sepult.	xxij' die.
1583 Alexandr. Dyson (infans) sepult.	xxix' die.

Mense Aprilis. [1583.]

joan Kent (pauper) sepult.	iij' die.
margret mooke (paup) sepult.	iiij' die.
Agnes Chappell (paup) sepult.	vj' die.

Edward Scott xxs.—To my sister Alice Howsley xs.—To my sister Ann Watts xs.—To Oliver Darnelly vjs. & viijd.—To Richard Watts xs.—Elizabeth Scott my wife and Jane Scott my brother's daughter coexecutrices.—Mr. Thomas Scott and Thomas Hemeley supervisors.—Witnesses Thomas Howsley, Nicholas Stones and William Brown clericus.

[149] Raulphe Crofts sepult. ... ... vij' die.
margret Deye sepult. ... ... viij' die.
francis Grene (infans) sepult. ... ... xvj' die.
Elizabethe Weynwright sepult. ... ... xjx' die.

Menso Maij.

Thomas Weynwright (juvenis) sepult. ... xxjx' die.

Menso Junij.

Robt. Cooper (senex) sepult. ... ... xv' die.
hester Sheircliffe (infans) sepult. ... ... xx' die.
margret heye (infans) sepult. ... ... xxiij' die.

Menso Julij.

Christopher Crofts (senex) sepult. ... ... xxij' die.
Francis haughton (infans) domi bapt. et sepult. ... xxiiij' die.
henryo Bearde sepult. ... ... xxx' die.

Menso Septembris.

maude handley (paup) sepult. ... ... vij' die.
Wyllm. Creswycke (infans) sepult. ... ... xix' die.

Mense Novembris.

Isabell Bradburn (infans) sepult. ... ... xvij' die.
margerye Benekes sepult. ... ... xx' die.
Anne Bearde (senex) sepult. ... ... xxvj' die.
Robt. Lyster (juvenis) sepult. ... ... xxix' die.

Menso Decembris.

Dns. Johes hill (sacerdos) sepult. ... ... xij' die.
Robt. Swyfte (paup) sepult. ... ... xiiij' die.

Menso Januarij.

Agnes Roodes (paup) sepult. ... ... xx' die.
John Thorppe (infans) sepult. ... ... xxiiij' die.

[149] Ralph Crofts, **of Creswick**, will dated 6 April, 1580.—To be buried in the church or churchyard of Ecclesfield at the discretion of my executors.—To the poor man's box ijs.—Isabel Howle wife of Robert Howle of Attercliffe two old angels.—To Maude Sheffeld my servant xs.—To Charles son of Charles Hill of Ecclesfield viijs.—To Beatrice Slater my servant ijs.—To Isabel daughter of Robert Howle xs.—To Thomas Grub my godson xijd.—To Ralphe Carre son of James Carre my godson xijd.—The residue of my goods to Maude Crofts now my wife whom I make my executrix.—James Carre of Southey supervisor.—Witnesses James Carre, Richard Shirecliffe, Charles Hill, Robert Howle, & George Hancock, clerk.—Proved at York, 17 April, 1583.—Ralphe Crofts married ano. 1578 Maude relict of John Mounteney of Creswick [vide note 37]; and Robert Howle or Hoole of Attercliffe married ano. 1579 Isabel daughter of the above John Mounteney [vide note 40.]—I think it will not be out of place to give here the will of Robert Hoole, of Attercliffe, although he was not buried here, it is dated 15 April, 1584.—He describes himself as Robert Howle, of Attercliffe, shearsmith.—Isabel Howle my wife.—My daughters Isabel and Elizabeth.—Richard "Sheareliffe" of Ecclesfield, "Shearsmith."—My sisters Isabel and Katherine Howle.—William Howle the elder.—Elizabeth Heywood my sister.—Anne Howle my sister.—Richard Shearcliffe my brother in law.—William Howle my brother.—Nicholas Mounteney.—William Howle, the elder, of Brightside, and Richard Shearcliffe, supervisors.—Proved at York, 6 May, 1584.—Richard Shirecliffe married at Ecclesfield ano. 1573 Margaret Howle. [Vide note 37.]

Mense FEBRUARIJ.

Francis filius Robti. Neyler domi bapt. et sepult.	x' die.
Francis filius Dionisii Marsden domi bapt. et sepult.	eod. die.
Agnes Parkin sepult.	xx' die.

Mense MARTIJ.

Margret Tymploye sepult.	xix' die.
henrye Stevenson (infans) sepult.	xxiiij' die.

Mense MARTIJ. [1584.]

Nicholas Basforthe sepult.	xxvjto die.
john Collye (senex) sepult.	xxvij' die.
George Machon (pauper) sepult.	xxviij' die.
Elizabethe Stevenson (infans) sepult.	eod. die.

Mense APRILIS.

Isabell Lister (infans) sepult.	xvjto die.
[150] Thomas Cutte (senex) sepult.	xviij' die.

Mense MAIJ.

Wyllm. Bradburne (infans) sepult.	xx' die.

Mense JUNIJ.

John Norton sepult. ...	xxj' die.

Mense JULIJ.

Rychard Cooke (infans) sepult.	xix' die.

Mense AUGUSTI.

Francis fil. Christopheri Senior domi bapt. & sep. ...	xiiij' die.
Gilbert hall (infans) sepult.	xvj' die.

Mense SEPTEMBRIS.

joan fil. Gilberti Dickonson domi bapt. & sepult. ...	ix' die.

Mense OCTOBRIS.

Agnes Morton (vidua) sepult.	xiij' die.
Thomas Brodbent (juvenis) sepult.	xviij' die.
Robt. Creswycke (senex & pauper) sepult. ...	xx' die.

Mense NOVEMBRIS.

Catherin Lynthwet (infans) sepult.	j' die.

[150] Thomas Cutt of Ecclesfield, nailer, will dated **7 feb., 1583.—To** be buried in Ecclesfield churchyard.—To Agnes Cutt my sister xs.—To John son of George **Cutt** my brother deceased xs.—To Jane daughter of William Cutt my brother deceased xs.—To Robert Cutt my brother xs. and all my apparell except my cloke.—To the poor man's box ijs.—To Richard Shirecliffe of Ecclesfield iijs. & iiijd.—To "*Elexander*" Shirecliffe my son in law vii.—John Shirecliffe my son in law.—Margaret Cutt my wife.—Nicholas & Robert Shirecliffe supervisors.—Proved at York, 6 May, 1584.

Mense DECEMBRIS.

Agnes Doyo (senex) sepult.	... ...	viij' die.
Anne haughe (infans) sepult.	... ...	xij' die.
Alice Smythe (infans) sepult.	... ...	xxix' die.
John Hartleye (juvenis) sepult.	... ...	ultimo die.

Mense JANUARIJ.

Charles holmes (infans) sepult.	... ...	j' die.
Robt. Selvester (paup) sepult.	... ...	ijdo die.
Jane Carre sepult.	... ...	xxvij' die.

Mense FEBRUARIJ.

Emanuel Bullus (infans) sepult.	... ..	iij' die.
Phillippe Morton (pauper) sepult. ...	...	viij' die.
Charles Fearnleye (infans) sepult.	...	xvj' die.
Arnold Bullus (infans) sepult.	...	xviij' die.
Wyllm. Dungworthe (infans) sepult.	...	xx' die.
Anne Parker sepult. ...	...	xxvij' die.

Mense MARTIJ.

Spur. Francis fil. Thome Pearson domi bapt. et sep.	... ...	ijdo die.
Francis Parkin (infans) sepult.	... ...	xiiij' die.
Francis jesoppe (infans) sepult.	... ...	xvjto die.
Francis Haughton (infans) sepult. ...	... ...	eod. die.
Agnes Barnsley (infans) sepult.	... ...	xxj' die.
Agnes Carre (juvenis) sepult.	... ...	xxiiijto die.

Mense MARTIJ. [1585.]

[151] John Barber sepult.	... ...	xxix' die.

Mense APRILIS.

Elizabethe Bower sepult.	...	xjx' die.
Cicilye Unwen sepult.	... ...	xxiiij' die.

[151] John Barber of Wadsley, husbandman, will dated 25 March, 1585.—To be buried in the churchyard Ecclesfield.—" To Francis Barber my sonne one watter whele with a troughe and all thinges belonginge thereunto."—Item I will that the same Francis shall have " my beste panne."—To Roger Barber " my other sonne one house in Sheffeld one orcharde and one garden to the saide house belonginge against the Castle in Sheffeld aforesaid " with remainder to Francis Barber my eldest son; with remainder to Robert Barber son of Robert Barber of Coningsborough clerie; with remainder to the younger son of the said Robert Barber clerie.—To the said Robert Barber clerie " my beste coate and dublett.—Emot daughter of Richard Barber.—William Jonson, George Eyre—My son Francis to have my two houses in Bradfield with remainder, in default of issue, to Roger my second son; with remainder, in default of issue, to William son of Richard Barber of Ughill.—Ann Barber my now wife.—Roger Barber my son to have the residue of my goods.—George Brownell, John Hylley, Richard Barber, & William Marshall supervisors.—Ann Barber my wife executrix.—Witnesses Robert Hurt, John Creswick the younger, Thomas Smith & William Hartley.—Proved at York, 28th May, 1585.—Robert Barber, cleric, alluded to in this will was inducted to the living of Coningsborough, 16 August, 1571, on the presentation of John Waterhouse; he was buried there 23 July, 1590. 1571. june 17 Richard Barber married Jane Revell at Bradfield. [Vide note 145.]

Mense MAIJ.

Alice Bedforthe sepult. ...	...	ultimo die.

Mense JUNIJ.

Margret howle (pauper) sepult.	... ...	viij' die.
[152] Wyllm. Wylkinson (senex) sepult. ...	...	x' die.
John Eyrson (pauper) sepult.	... ...	xvij' die.
Isabell howle sepult.	... ...	xxij' die.

Mense AUGUSTI.

Joan Jepson (pauper) sepult.	... ...	ijdo die.
Alice Wylkinson (pauper) sepult.	... ...	xxix' die.

Mense SEPTEMBRIS.

Wm. Swift (juvenis poix. Sheffeldie) sepult.	... ...	iiijto die.
hellen Taylier (infans) sepult.	... ...	vij' die.
Francis fil. Johis. Creswycke domi bapt. et sep.	... ...	x' die.
Francis Smythe ((infans) domi bapt. & sepult. ...	... ...	xviij' die.

Mense OCTOBRIS.

Margret Sparcke (infans) sepult.	... ...	iij' die.
Roger Batleye (pauper) sepult.	... ...	xiiij' die.

Mense NOVEMBRIS.

[153] Thomas Scott gen. sepult.	... ...	ijdo' die.

[152] William Wilkinson, of Bellhouse, in the parish of Ecclesfield, yeoman.—I commend my soul to Almighty God and my body to Christian man's burial.—My debts & mortuary to be discharged and the residue to be divided into three equal parts; one part thereof to my wife, another to my natural children, viz., Robert, Thomas, William, Elizabeth, joane and Isabel equally, and the third part to myself for funeral expenses and legacies.—To the poor man's box at Ecclesfield vjd.—To my daughters Elizabeth and Isabel a cow apiece.—William Wilkinson & Robert Hartley to be supervisors.—My wife Ellen and my daughter jane to be executrices.—Dated 9 june, 1585.—Proved at York, 5 Aug., 1585.

[153] Thomas Scott, of Barnes Hall, gent., will dated 1 Nov., 1585.—To be buried in the parish church of Ecclesfield.—My goods to be divided into 3 parts—one part to Richard Scott my son—one part to Mary Scott my daughter towards her education and the third part to Isabel Scott my lovinge wife.—And concerning Barnes Hall &c. which is now in the holding and tenure of Emmott Dernelly "my dearlie beloved mother," my wife, on the death of my mother, to have one third part and my son Richard Scott the remaining two thirds.—Nicholas Scott my late father.—To Mary Scott my daughter 100 Marks.—My mother in law Elizabeth Alcock.—My sister Barbara Bannyster.—My brother Nicholas Shirecliffe gent.—Richard Watts.—Christopher Scott the eldest son of my brother Richard Scott—Henry Bannyster & Nicholas Shirecliffe to be trustees of my children who are under age.—To the poor of Ecclesfield xiijs. & iiijd.—To my brother Oliver Dernelly vjli. xiijs. iiijd.—Edward Scott my uncle.—My aunt Howsley.—My aunt Watts.—Mr. Richard Wortley.—Mr. Francis Fletcher.—My uncle Mr. Thomas Howsley, Nicholas Staniland & my uncle Edward Scott supervisors.—Proved at York, 21 Dec., 1585.—Nicholas Scott father of the above named Thomas Scott mentions in his will, dated 30 july, 1564, [vide note 105] my brother in law Richard Fenton.—Emmott Dernelley his wife mentions in her will dated 9 Oct., 1592 [vide note 180] my son Nicholas Shirecliffe ; and Thomas Scott above mentions Nicholas Shirecliffe my brother.—I have the two following abstracts of Fenton wills which point at some connection between the families of Scott, Shirecliffe, & Fenton. 1548. june 7. Robert Fenton, of Wadsley, in the parish of Ecclesfield.—My eldest son Thomas Fenton.—Richard Fenton, of Sheffield, executors.—Proved at York, 3 jan., 1548-9. 1549-50. jan. 2. Richard Fenton, of Sheffield, merchant.—

Q

Thomas Watson (senex) sepult.	... ...	xx' die.
[154] Mrs. Barbara Cotton sepult.	... ...	ultimo die.

Menso DECEMBRIS.

Joan Byrleye (senex) sepult.	...	xjx' die.
Alice Bradleye (paup vidua) sepult. ...	...	xx' die.
Margret Slatter sepult. ...	...	xxjx' die.
hellene Moulde (paup) sepult.	...	ultimo die.

Menso JANUARIJ.

Margret Kyrkbye sepult.	... ...	ijdo die.
Wm. Grene (pauper) sepult.	... ...	vto die.
henrie Stanyforthe (juvenis) sepult.	... ...	xiiij' die.

Menso FEBRUARIJ.

John Byrleye sepult. ...	... ...	ijdo' die.
[155] Nicholas Slatter sepult.	... ...	ix' die.
Laurence hobson sepult.	... ...	x' die.
[156] Thomas Taylyer sepult.	... ...	xj' die.

Menso MARTIJ.

Joan Stanyforthe sepult.	... ...	xv' die.
Alice Smythe sepult. ...	... ...	xvij' die.
Elizabethe Eyre sepult....	... .	xx' die.
Wyllm. howsleye sepult.	... ...	xxiiij' die.

Menso MARTIJ. [1586.]

Marye Slatter sepult. ...	... ...	xxvjto die.
John Shawe sepult. ...	... ...	xxviij' die.

Menso APRILIS.

hellen Wolleye sepult. ...		j' die.

My wife Agnes—my son Richard a minor my daughters by my first wife Cecily.—My daughters by my now wife.—Robert Swift of Beighton Esquire.—Hugh Smythe of North Lees.—John Browne and Nicholas Shirecliffe my sons in law.—Proved at York, 23 Ap., 1550.—From the Court Rolls I have the following: 1542. Richard Fenton is admitted to 1 Messuage and 9 Acres in Southey which were lately Thomas Swift's.

[154] Administration of the goods and effects of Barbara Cotton, of Ecclesfield, was granted to her cousin Thomas Mountency, of Creswick, Esquire. 7th Nov. 1585. She was, according to Mr. Hunter, daughter of John Mountency, of Cowley, Esquire, and married twice, first Thomas or Robert Thwaites, Esquire, and secondly, Thomas Cotton, Esquire.—In the churchwardens' Accounts ano. 1585 occurs the following entry "Item for the buryall of Mrs. Cotton vjs. & viijd."

[155] In the churchwardens' Accounts ano. 1586 occurs "Item receyved of William Slatter a legacye bequeathed by Nycholas Slatter his father the seconde daye of Apryll xijd."

[156] Thomas Tayler, of Wadsley, cowper, will dated 5 january, 1585.—To Thomas & Alexander Tayler my sons my indentures of leases of land &c. in Wadsley.—Ellin Taylor my now wife.—To Frances Oxspring my servant maid "one little coffer standinge at her bedsyde."—To the poor man's box ivd.—Christopher Tayler my brother and John Creswick the elder of Wadsley supervisors.—Proved at York, 3 june, 1587.

[157] Wyllm. Sheyrclyffe sepult.	...	...	...	...	x' die.
henrye Thorppe sepult....	...	...	...	...	xx' die.
John Pearson sepult.	...	...	...	...	xxiiij' die.
[158] Charles Hyll sepult.	...	...	...	...	xxvj' die.

Mense Maij.

Margret Stevenson sepult.	xv' die.
Isabell Sheyrcliffe sepult.	xxvj' die.
Anne Fearnleye sepult....	......

Mense Junij.

Anne Flint sepult.	...	xxiij' die.
[159] Rychard Stanyforthe sepult.	...	xxiiij' die.

Mense Augusti.

John Hyrst sepult.	...	xxiij' die.
[160] Anne Slatter sepult.	...	xxx' die.
Charles Smythe sepult....	...	xxxj' die.

[157] William **Shirecliffe**, of Ecclesfield, tanner, will dated 16 Dec., 1585.—To be buried in the churchyard Ecclesfield.—Agnes **Shirecliffe** my wife and Robert **Shirecliffe** my son to have the house I now live in and all my other lands &c. in the parish of Ecclesfield.—Alice, Isabel, Barbara and **Dorothy Shirecliffe** my daughters.—To the church for the repairs of the Highways vs.—My brothers in law Hugh Barber and Robert Haigh vjs. & viijd.—My brother Nicholas Shirecliffe.—All my children under age.—Nicholas Shirecliffe my brother, Robert Shirecliffe, Robert Fernelly and my cousin Robert Shirecliffe supervisors.—Proved at York, 3 june, 1586.—From the **Court Rolls** I have the following: **1515. Dec. 7.** John Gray & Johana his wife surrender lands in Ecclesfield to the use of John Shirecliffe. 1525. **Dec. 11.** John Shirecliffe surrenders the same to Henry Shirecliffe his cousin. 1547. **May 30.** Henry Shirecliffe surrenders the same to William Shirecliffe his son. 1558. **May 30.** Henry Shirecliffe surrenders other lands in Ecclesfield which he had by the **surrender of Thomas Gargrave** miles & Thomas Darley to Nicholas Shirecliffe his son. 1591. **Ap. 21.** William Shirecliffe being dead Robert Shirecliffe is found to be his son & heir.—In the churchwardens' Accounts occur " 1586. Item for William Sheyrclyffe his grave the xxij. of Mayo iijs. & iiijd."—" Item of Nicholas Sheyrclyffe, tanner, for a legacye bequeathed by William Sheyrcliffe to the reparon of the sayd Churche vjs. & viijd."

[158] Charles Hill, of Ecclesfield, butcher, will dated 1 Nov., 1585.—To the children of my brother John Hill all my apparel.—To the children of my sister Cecilie ijs. apiece.—To the children of my sister Mawde ijs. apiece.—To Charles Hill **my** youngest son all my furniture and **my** best featherbed.—To my sons Thomas & Charles Hill all that my indenture of lease of certain closes called the Horberie in the parish of Ecclesfield which I have of the demise of the right Honble. Lord Earl of Shrewsbury.—My wife Margaret Hill.—" I doe make my well beloved " William Parker & Richard Shirecliffe trustees and witnesses of this my last will.—Proved at York, 3 june, 1586. [Vide note 37.]

[159] Richard Stanyforth, of Wincobank, in the parish of Ecclesfield, yeoman, will dated 10 july, 1585.—My goods to be divided into three parts—one part to Agnes Stanyforth my wife—one to my children Richard Nicholas and Alexander my sons and Elizabeth Jane, Maud and Ann my daughters, and the remaining part to my self.—To the poor of Ecclesfield xijd.—To William Parkin " my best gowne."—Richard Stanyforth my nephew.—My sons Nicholas & Alexander my executors.—William Wilkinson & Thomas Bullus supervisors.—Proved at York, 21 july, 1586.—The family of Staniforth is one of the most ancient in this district: they derive their name from a small tenement called Staniforth, lying between Wincobank and Shiregreen.

[160] In the churchwardens' Accounts anno, 1586 occurs " Item of Robert Slatter a legacye bequeathed by Ann Slatter the xvth of Apryll xijd."

Mense SEPTEMBRIS.

Raulphe hobson sepult.	... ...	j' die.
Uxor Robti. Sheyrelyffe sepult.	... ...	iij' die.

Mense NOVEMBRIS.

Ryehard Grubbe sepult.	... ...	j' die.
Thomas Thweates sepult.	... ...	eod. die.
Beales childe sepult.	... ...	xx' die.
a childe of Peter Brownell sepult.	... ...	eod. die.

Mense DECEMBRIS.

Uxor henrie Swynden sepult.	... ...	xvj' die.
Uxor Winterbothome sepult.	... ...	eod. die.

Mense APRILIS. [1587.]

Elizabetho Shawe sepult.	... ...	vto die.
Uxor Wyllye sepult.	... ...	viij' die.
Thomas Stevenson sepult.	... ...	xv' die.

Mense MAIJ.

John Bromheade sepult.	... ...	xv' die.

Mense JUNIJ.

Olde Margret of the Vicaredge sepult.	... ...	xxviij' die.

Mense OCTOBRIS.

John Roodes sepult.	... ...	j' die.
[161] Willm. Brown sepult.	... ...	eod. die.
[162] Robt. Stones sepult.	... ...	vto die.

Mense NOVEMBRIS.

Uxor Anthonij Cutte sepult.	... ...	vj' die.
Vidua Calverd sepult.	... ...	xvij' die.

Mense JANUARIJ.

Thomas Waterall sepult.	... ...	j' die.
Uxor hall sepult.	... ...	ijdo die.
Uxor Nicholai Cooper sepult.	...	xxvj' die.

[161] William Brown was of Creswick in this parish.—I have the following notes of this family from the Manor Court Rolls. 1467. Ap. 13. Hugh Brown surrenders certain lands in Creswick to the use & behoof of John Brown his son & heir. 1490. March 7 (?). William Brown seeks to be admitted to the same as son & heir of John Brown deceased. 1544. September 8. William Brown seeks to be admitted to the same as son & heir of William Brown deceased. 1591. April 21. Edward Brown seeks to be admitted to the same as son & heir of William Brown deceased. In the Poll tax, 2 Rich ii., appear Johannes Browne & Agnes ux' ejus iiijd. Willelmus Browne & Cecilia ux' ejus iiijd. Willelmus Brone iiijd. Magota filia ejus iiijd. and Magota Brone iiijd. [See also Note 66.]

[162] In the churchwardens' Accounts ano. 1587 occurs "Item of Barbara Stones for her husbands buryall the fyrst daye of November iijs. & iiijd."

Mense FEBRUARIJ.

A childe of henrye Wylkinson sepult.	...	...	...	vto die.
A childe of Christopher holmes sepult.	...	...	...	viij' die.
A childe of John Lyster sepult.	...	...	...	eod' die.
[163] Marye Scotte sepult.	...	...	...	xvij' die.
Vidua Beale sepult.	...	...	...	xviij' die.

Mense MARTIJ.

Uxor boule sepult.	...	...	...	j' die.
Uxor Creswycke sepult.	...	...	...	ij' die.
[164] Uxor Morton sepult.	...	...	...	eod. die.
[165] Wm. Parker filius Francisci sepult.	...	...		viij' die.

[166] Mense MARCIJ. [1588.]

Uxor Johnis Wylkinson sepult. ... ... xxx' die.

Menso APRILIS.

Barbara filia Richardi Carre sepult.... ... iij' die.
Thomas Thweates sepult. ... ... xxvj' die.

Mense MAIJ.

Robt. Carre sepult. ... ... vto die.
Rychard Slacke sepult. ... ... x' die.
Agnes Ramsden sepult. ... ... eod. die.

Menso JULIJ.

Uxor Radulphi Stanilande sepult. ... ... ij'do die.

Mense OCTOBRIS. [1590.]

Robt. Wylkinson sepult. ... ... xix' die.

---

[163] In the churchwardens' Accounts anno. 1587 occurs "Item of Rychard Watts for ye buryall of a chylde of Mr. Scots the last daye of Marche iijs. & iiijd. She was daughter of Thomas Scott, of Barnes Hall.

[164] In the churchwardens' Accounts ano. 1588 occurs "Item off Thomas Norton for ye buryall of his mother xxixth of Marche iijs. & iiijd."

[165] Francis Parker was of Whitley Hall, son & heir of William Parker of the same. [Vide note 41.]

[166] Here occurs a gap in the registers from july 1588 to October 1590.—A few burials occur in the churchwardens' Accounts, which I give below, as also an Administration and will from York.

"1588. Item of Thomas Bullus ye same day [xx Dec.] for ye buryall of his sonne James iijs. & iiijd."
"1589. Item of Rychard Wylson for ye buryall of his father iijs. & iiijd."
"Item to Hughe Hyde for covinge (covering) of Thomas Wylson his grave."
"1590. Item of Rychard Wylson for his mothers buryall the fourth of Apryll iijs. & iiijd."

The Wilsons above were of Oughtibridge Hall.—[Vide note 59.]

Robert Slatter, of Ecclesfield, will dated 6 july, 1589.—To be buried in Ecclesfield churchyard.—Jane Slatter my wife to have half of my farm which I hold under the Earl of Shrowsbury.—To Roger Slatter "1 shepe."—To Elizabeth Hobson iiijd.—To Anne Parker iiijd.—My wife and Ralph Slatter my son executors.—Witnesses Richard Lorde and Charles Clarke.—Proved at York, 2 Oct., 1589.

Administration of the effects of John Shawe, of Whitley, granted to Jane Shawe, his widow, dated 2 Oct., 1589.

Uxor Turton sepult.		xx' die.
[167] Uxor Bullus sepult.		cod. die.

Menso Novembris.

Uxor Johnis Haughton sepult. ... ... xiiijto die.

Menso Decembris.

Uxor Dungworthe sepult.	xviij' die.
Grace hill (infans) sepult.	xx' die.

Menso Februarij.

Uxor Dyson sepult.	xiij' die.
Uxor Gregoryo sepult.	cod. die.
james Foster sepult.	xvj' die.

Menso Marcij.

[168] Uxor henryo Sheyrcliffe sepult.	j' die.
Uxor Geslinge sepult.	x' die.
Uxor Grene sepult.	xj' die.
Nicholas & John Shawe sepult.	xiij' die.
[169] Thomas Cooper sepult.	xviij' die.

Menso Maij. [1591.]

[170] Margret filia hugonis Meller sepult.	j' die.
hellen Brodheade vidua sepult.	vjto die.

[167] 1591. july 6. Johana late wife of Thomas Bullus senior and one of the daughters & coheirs of John Twigge has died since the last court seized of one fourth part of 1 Messuage, 1 bovat and a field in Stainford and Wincobank, and Thomas Bullus junior is her son & proper heir and seeks to be admitted. 1597. March 31. Thomas Bullus junior of Birley Edge and Margaret his wife surrender the same lands &c. to John Bullus of Birley Edge cutler and his heirs with remainder to the said Thomas Bullus junior of Birley Edge & his heirs, &c. *Court Rolls.*

[168] In the **churchwardens' Accounts ano. 1590 occurs** " Item of Nycholas Sheyrclyffe for the buryall of hys mother iijd. & iiijd.

[169] Thomas Parkin alias Cowper, of Hasle Clough, in the parish of Ecclesfield, Mason, will dated 15 March, 1590.—My wife Margaret to have my whole farm at Hasel Clough toward the education of my children &c.— Thomas Slack—William Hartley—James Cowper and Thomas Newell to be the guardians & tutors of **my** children Thomas Elizabeth, Richard, Mary and Ann.—To the poor of Ecclesfield vs.—To the poor of **Wortley** ijs. & viijd.—Proved at York, 2 july, 1591.

[170] Hugh Meller was churchwarden, ano. 1610, for Southey district; he was father of a Hugh Meller, who had issue a third Hugh Meller, bapt. 17 Oct., 1641, who had issue 3 sons, viz., Benjamin, Hugh, and John—the last named John Meller was bapt. 10 Nov., 1687, and married 8 Sept., 1722, Mary, daughter of Nathaniel Wilkinson, of Crowder House, & dying, ano. 1760 left issue, *inter alios*, a son Hugh Meller, bapt. 21 Aug., 1723, who bought Thundercliffe Grange from Dr. Green. On his death, without issue, ano. 1774, Nathaniel, his next brother, succeeded to his estates. Another brother of the above Hugh & Nathaniel, by name John Meller, dying 12 july, 1787, aged 55, left issue an only son, Hugh Meller, and a daughter, Elizabeth, who married William Stenton, of Hoyland. Hugh Meller married Sarah, daughter of William Booth, of Brush House, in this parish [which family is now represented by Charles Booth, Esq., J.P., & Barrister-at-Law, &c., of Brush House, who is descended from Abraham Booth, of Lounddside, in this parish, who died ano. 1671], and by her had issue, *inter alios*, 2 sons. Hugh Meller, of Sheffield, surgeon, who dying without issue, ano. 1852, was succeeded by his brother, Charles Matthias Meller, surgeon—this gentleman married his cousin, Margaret, daughter of Thomas Binns, of London, solicitor, and has issue several children.

Mense JUNIJ.

[177] hughe hyde sepult.	iij' die.
Dorithie Wygfall sepult.	iiij' die.
Thomas Bower sepult.	x' die.
[179] Rychard Burrowes sepult.	xij' die.
Rychard Carre sepult.	xiiij' die.
Thomas Clarcke sepult.	xv' die.
James Benckes sepult.	xxij' die.
Emot Fearnley sepult.	xxiiij' die.

Mense JULIJ.

Uxor Platts sepult.	iiijto die.
Elizabethe Fullylove sepult.	vto die.
Humfreye Fearnley sepult.	xx' die.
Uxor Ragge sepult.	eod. die.

Mense AUGUSTI.

Uxor Francisci Bower sepult.	j' die.
Elizabethe Seanier sepult.	xxx' die.
Margret uxor Thome Parkin sepult.	eod. die.
Agnes uxor Richardi Thorppe sepult.	eod. die.

Mense SEPTEMBRIS.

Agnes uxor henrici Stanyforthe sepult.	vto die.
Richard filius Thome Beard sepult.	xv' die.
Edward Greaves sepult.	xxv' die.
Richard Bearde filius Thome sepult.	eod. die.
john Lynthwet sepult.	xxx' die.

Mense OCTOBRIS.

Elizabethe Slatter sepult.	vjto die.
henrye filius henrici Stanyforthe sepult.	viij' die.

[177] Hugh Hyde, judging from the churchwardens' Accounts, seems to have filled the post of grave digger to the parish, for the entry "Item to Hugh Hyde for covering —— grave," is of common recurrence, and the year after his death, viz., 1592, Nicholas Man appears as "covering graves." Hugh Hyde, the subject of this note, was son of William Hyde, of Birley [vide note 92], and with a pedigree, dating back as his does in direct line from 1430, one would have thought him worthy of a higher employment than grave digging, which certainly now-a-days is not a very lofty parochial office. He was churchwarden ano. 1577.—His will is dated 31 Aug., 1591, in which he describes himself as of Grenoside, and by trade a "waller."—My goods to be divided into three parts—one to Margaret Hyde my wife—one to my children William & Alexander Hyde my sons & Margaret, Ann, & Isabel my daughters—the remaining part to myself.—To Ann Hyde my daughter "1 cowe, 1 ewe, and 2 lambes, one ribbin and one silver ringe."—To Isabel Hyde my daughter "2 ewes, 2 lambes 1 Angell of golde & 1 silver ringe."—To Alexander Hyde my son 1 pair of smith bellows.—"Ann Kendal my brother John Hyde daughter childe."—My good [God?] daughter Margaret Lee.—Ralph Richardson, Henry Sampson.—Alexander Hyde, & William Wilkinson my brethren and James Carre, William Brodhede & Ralph Lee my neighbours to be supervisors.—My brother Ralph Richardson to have the guardianship of my daughter Isabel.—Proved at York, 2 july, 1591.

[179] Richard Burrowes, of Creswick, in the parish of Ecclesfield, will dated 7 june, 1591.—To my cousin Anthony Brown my dagger "and one halfecrowne of golde."—I give all the remainder of my goods moveable or immoveable in this Realm of Gt Britain to my uncle George Brown and my aunt Effame Brown to be equally divided between them.—Francis Fearnnely and Robert Bullous supervisors.—Proved at York, 2 july, 1591.

Ann Stanyfortho sepult.	xx' die.
Infans Thomo Stanyfortho sepult.	......

Menso NOVEMBRIS.

[173] John Bower sepult.	j' die.
Margerie Carre sepult.	......
[174] Uxor Richardi Carre de Byrley edge sepult.	ijdo die.
Wm. filius Robti. Wylkinson sepult.	...
John Plats & Elizabethe filia Dionisia Marsden sepult.	iij' die.
Thomas Cooper sepult.	xxvjto die.
Charles hobson sepult.	eod. die.
Jana uxor Thomo Carre & Elizabeth Fearnley sepult.	......

Menso DECEMBRIS.

Nicholas Wodde sepult.	j' die.
Uxor Thomo Bower sepult.	vto die.
Infans Willmi. Roberts sepult.	......
Alexander Shooter sepult.	......
Richard filius Robti. Wyllye sepult.	eod. die.

[175] Menso JANUARIJ.

henrie Wyllye sepult.	viij' die.
Nicholas Shooter sepult.	xx' die.
Uxor Thome Roodes sepult.	eod. die.
Uxor Hyrst sepult.	xxvjto die.
John Gylles (senex) sepult.	eod. die.
Richard Parman sepult.	xxx' die.

Menso MARTIJ. [1592.]

[176] Robt. hartleye, **Wm.** Lyllye, et infans Radi. Slatter sep.	xxix' die.

[173] John Bower, of Wincobank, husbandman, will dated 24 Oct., 1591.—To my sons Hugh and Nicholas Bower **all** my indentures & rights in a close called Cliffe field.—To my daughter Ann 1 cow.—To my daughter Katherine a cow.—To my daughter Janet a cow.—My children conjointly to be my executors.—William Howle the elder & my neighbour Thomas Mylner supervisors.—Proved at York, 30 Nov., 1591.

[174] **She was daughter of** Ralph Greaves.

[175] The entries seem to be about this time somewhat irregular and careless, and the scribe, I think, has forgotten to enter the burial of the following parishioner, who must have died between the dates 9 Dec., 1591, and the 28 Jan., 1591-2.—Richard Carre, of Birley Edge, yeoman, will dated 9 Dec., 1591.—To Janet daughter of my late son Richard Carre deceased xls.—To Emme [Emmote?] daughter of my son Ralph Carre " 2 shepe."—To every other of the children of my son Ralph " 1 shepe."—To my brother Thomas Carre my best coat.—To Ralph Pearson my second coat.—My nephew Ralph Holden "a paire of newe hoose."—My nephew Robert Holden "my clooke."—My servant Anne Brigges.—"Item to my said sonne Raufe all my manor."—Thomas Carre my son.—My daughters Janet and Ann.—Thomas Bullus the elder and Thomas Bullus the younger being my neighbours I appoint supervisors of my will.—Proved at York, 28 Jan., 1591-2.

[176] Robert Hartley, of Mortomley, in the parish of Ecclesfield, collier, will dated 28 March, 1592.—To Richard Hartley my son all my whole lands whatsoever.—Elizabeth Hartley my wife.—Robert, John, Robert (Richard?) Thomas & Margaret my children.—To the parish of Tankersley iijs. iiijd.—To the chapelry of Wortley iijs. iiijd.—

Mense Aprilis.

[177] John hartleye sepult.	ijdo die.
Uxor Caroli Clarke sepult.	iiij' die.
Uxor Robti. Hartleye sepult.	vjto die.

Mense Januarij.

Richard filius Thome Smythe sepult.	viij' die.	1591.
Alice uxor Thome Worrall sepult.	xv' die.	1591.

Mense Februarij.

Nicholas filius Willmi. hatfeld sepult.	iij' die.	1591.
Alice mundye sepult.	vto die.	1591.
George Gest sepult.	xxvjto die.	1591.

Mense Martij.

Infans Thome Coop sepult.	xiij' die.	1591.
Infans Dorithie Parkin sepult.	xxiij' die.	1591.

Mense Maij. [1592.]

Nicholas Walker sepult.	j' die.
[178] Robt. Bearde sepult.	vto' die.
Peter Kent sepult.	viij' die.
Maria Clarke sepult.	x' die.

Mense Julij.

Dionese Marsden sepult.	xij' die.
Nicholas hoylande sepult.	xviij' die.
Joan filia Nicholai Slatter sepult.	xxviij' die.

Mense Augusti.

Margret Stanylande sepult.	xxviij' die.

Mense Septembris.

[179] Mr. Thomas Wombwell armiger sepult.	ijdo die.
Elizabeth Yates sepult.	xvj' die.

John Pawson & Thomas Parkyn the elder supervisors.—" Whereas I have two cole mynes of Mr. Wortley I do owe unto his worshipp due at Wytsontyde next for half yeares rent for the same vjl. xiijs. iiijd. his worshipp hath had of me certaine coles towards payment of the said some &c."—Proved at York, 31 May, 1592.

[177] John Hartley, of Mortomley, collier, will dated 1 April, 1592.—Ann Hartley my wife with child.—My wife executrix and my brother Richard Hartley & John Pawson supervisors.—Proved at York, 31 May, 1592.

[178] Robert Bearde, of Ecclesfield, nailer, will dated 3 April, 1592.—To Alexander Bearde my brother my great arke.—To Robert Wilkinson one other arke.—My wife sole executrix.—Alexander Bearde my brother supervisor.—Proved at York. — May, 1592.

[179] Thomas Wombwell, of Synocliffe Grange, will dated 6 March, 1592.—To be buried anywhere.—To the poor of Rotherham xxs.—To the poor of Greesbrooke xxs.—To the poor of Ecclesfield xxs.—To my wife Isabel my capital messuage in Greesbroke where Thomas Bankes lives also 3 farms 2 cottages a smithy &c. in Greesbroke aforesaid for her life with remainder to Thomas Stringer son of my late daughter Isabel wife of Francis Stringer. Also to my

R

Catherin Relfe sepult.	... ...	xx' die.
Wydowe Curtesse sepult.	... ...	xxx' die.

Mense Octobris.

Johnes filius Robti. Sheircliffe sepult.	...	iij' die.
Vidua Otes sepult.	... ...	iiij' die.
Elizabethe Shawe sepult.	... ...	xx' die.
hellen Sheirclyffe sepult.	... ...	eod. die.
Raulphe hollinbrigge sepult.	... ...	xxix' die.

Mense Novembris.

Vidua Cooper sepult.	... ...	vjto' die.
Nicholas Fyrthe sepult.	... ...	viij' die.
Alice hollinbrigge sepult.	... ...	ix' die.
John Renald sepult.	... ...	x' die.
John Pearson sepult.	... ...	xx' die.
180 Mrs. Derneley sepult.	... ...	xxix' die.

Mense Decembris.

Vidua Howet sepult.	... ...	iiijto die.
joan Jepson sepult.	... ...	xiiijto die.

Mense Januarij.

joan Crosley sepult.	... ...	iiijto die.
Margret Smythe sepult.	... ...	vjto die.
Marye Brigge sepult.	... ...	viij' die.
Peter Grene sepult.	... ...	x' die.
Wm. Gyllott sepult.	... ...	xx' die.

Mense Februarij.

Isabell hobson sepult.	... ...	xix' die.
Vidua hartley sepult.	... ...	xxviij' die.

wife my lease of lands devised to me by Richard Brown of Moxbro' gent.—Thomas Wentworth of Wentworth Woodhouse deceased my cousin.—My brother Nicholas Wombwell xx nobles which he pretended were given to him by my father's will.—To my cousin Margaret Wentworth xl nobles.—To Mr. John Williamson vjli. xiijs. ivd.—To my wife my silver cup with cover.—To Francis Poole o marks.—My daughter Julian wife of the said Francis Poole.—To Surlee Ardington & William Rockbie of Skire Hall Esq. 4 Angells each.—Residue of my goods to my sons in law Nicholas Shireeliffe & Nicholas Wordsworth equally and they to be my executors.—To Thomas son of Nicholas Shireeliffe one sheepstead in Rotherham.—Proved 8 Nov., 1592.

180 Emmott Derneley, of Barnes Hall, in the parish of Ecclesfield, widow, will dated 9 Oct., 1592.—To be buried in the parish Church of Ecclesfield.—My son in law Henry Bannyster of York.—My son Nicholas Shireeliffe.—My son Oliver Derneley xxl. " my best coveringe of arrase work, a payre of grene curtens, fyve cushinges of needle worke, my gould chyne, one rounde silver can and fyve silver spoones."—My daughter Barbara Bannyster.—To my nephew Thomas Shireeliffe " 1 gilt french bowle."—My nephew Richard Scott " my gilt silver salt."—To Barbara Bannyster " tenne poundes, my silver Kay bandes, my jewell of gould, one felt Hat lyned with velvet and all my aparell."—My nephew William Bannyster.—My niece Sara Bannyster.—My nephew William Shireeliffe.—My niece Elizabeth Shireeliffe.—My cousin Margaret Bullus.—My sister Rawson.—My sister Scott.—Roger Scott's wife.—My daughter Watts.—My cousin Ann Ward.—The wife of Thomas Shawe.—My God daughter Elizabeth Dickenson.—My sister Howsley.—My sister Watts Thomas Howsley and Nicholas Staniland supervisors.—Proved at York, 14 june, 1593.

Mense Martij.

Thomas Smythe sepult.	...	vto die.
Catherin uxor Godfridi Savige sepult.	...	x' die.
Richard Carre sepult.	...	eod. die.
Robt. Mooke sepult.	...	xiij' die.
[181] Robert Dughtyman sepult.	...	xviij' die.
Anne filia Robti. Bullus sepult.	...	eod. die.
Anne filia Radulphi sepult.	...	xij' die.
Raulfe filius Johis. Grubbe sepult.	...	xxijdo die.

Mense Martij. [1593.]

Lawrence Beardsell sepult.	...	xxviij' die.

Mense Aprilis.

John Walshawe sepult.	...	ijdo die.
Vidua Dughtyman sepult.	...	xij' die.
Rychard Shawe (infans) sepult.	...	xiij' die.
Robt. Hill (infans) sepult.	...	eod. die.

Mense Junij.

Wyllm. Man sepult.	...	iij' die.
[182] Mres. Isabell Wombwell sepult.	...	vij' die.

Mense Julij.

john Crowder sepult.	...	vto die.
jane Slatter sepult.	...	xx' die.

Mense Augusti.

Uxor Thome Cooper sepult.	...	x' die.
Vidua Ball sepult.	...	xiiij' die.

---

[181] Robert Doughtyman, of Ecclesfield, will dated 10 March, 1587.—" To my sonne Thomas Doughtyman all suche implements as appertayneth to my streng harth and also bellows stythie Tayron (?) and Tonges & yt is my will that my sonne Thomas shall have my prentice Francis Silitoo &c."—To Nicholas Butcher alias Doughtyman iijl. vjs. Hijd.—Ralph Thomas and Nicholas Doughtyman.—Alis to have the iijl. vjs. iiijd; to the bringing up of Nicholas Butcher.—Ralph, Thomas and Nicholas Doughtyman my executors.—Gilbert Dickenson supervisor.—Proved at York, 14 june, 1593.—A branch of the family of Doughtyman resided at Woodseats in this parish. 1481. August 7. William Waddislay & Johana his wife surrendered lands &c. at Woodseats to their own use for life and after their decease to the use of Robert Donghtyman & Alice his wife daughter & heir of the said William & Johana with remainder to Katherine daughter of the said Alice Doughtyman in default of male issue. 1532. june 4. Alice Doughtyman widow surrenders the same to the use of Thomas Doughtyman with remainder &c. to Robert Doughtyman with remainder &c. to John Doughtyman with remainder &c. to Katherine Doughtyman. 1590. April 8. Thomas Doughtyman son & heir of Thomas Doughtyman and Alice his wife seeks to be admitted to the same.

[182] Nuncupative will of Isabel Wombwell, widow, of Ecclesfield, in the county of York, dated 16 june [1593?].—Mr. Nicholas Wombwell to have all her goods moveable or immoveable after her Church duties and funeral expenses have been paid.—Witnesses Henry Shaw, John Smith & Richard Saterfeete.—Proved at York, 29 August, 1593.—This Lady was relict of Nicholas Wombwell, of Thundercliffe Grange, and daughter of Thomas Wentworth of Wentworth Woodhouse.—Mr. Hunter in his "*History of Hallamshire*," p. 499, *Gatty's Edition*, has fallen into a slight error as regards the **burial of this** person, as he has stated there that he supposes her to be the Isabel Wombwell who was buried at Rawmarsh 30 Nov., 1576.

Menso SEPTEMBRIS.

Henrio Stanyfortho sepult.	...	vij' die.
Uxor Waggeley sepult....	...	x' die.
Uxor Layton sepult. ...	...	xx' die.
a childe of Mr. Wyllson sepult.	...	xxvij' die.

Menso OCTOBRIS.

A childe of francis johnson sepult. ...		xvto die.
Alicia uxor Robti. Bullus sepult. ...	...	xxvij' die.

Menso DECEMBRIS.

james Croft sepult.	...	...	...	iiijto die.
Vidua Haugho sepult.	...	...	...	xxiiij' die.
Uxor Nicholai Man sepult.	...	...	...	xxvij' die janu.
Isabelle Hyde sepult.	...	...	...	xxx' die ja.

Menso MARTIJ. [1593.]

john Ashton sepult.	...	...	...	iiijto die.

Menso MAIJ. [1594.]

[153] Rychard Doyo sepult. ...	...	...	...	xvj' die.
[154] Mario uxor Robti. Sheyrcliffe sepult.	...	...		xxx' die.

Menso OCTOBRIS.

Henrie Bedfortho sepult.	...	...	xx' die.
Wydowe Seeker sepult....	...	...	xxj' die.

Menso DECEMBRIS.

[155] Thomas Carro sepult. ...	...	...	xiiijto die.

[153] **Richard Dey**, of Shiregreen, yeoman.—His will bears no date.—To be buried at Ecclesfield.—Elizabeth, William, Thomas & John children of James Dey.—My brother John Dey.—William Carr of Rotherham.—Elizabeth Dey my aunt.—James Dey my uncle to have everything after my legacies, debts and funeral expenses are paid.—James Carre of Southey and Thomas Jepson of Ecclesfield supervisors.—Proved at York, 12 April, 1595.—The Deys held land under the manor at Nether Hartley, a small Hamlet adjoining Shiregreen. 1477. March 7. William Hartley surrenders land in Nether Hartley to Richard Dey. 1496. April 26. Richard Dey being dead Richard Dey seeks to be admitted as his son & heir. 1528. Feast of St. Mary Magdalen.—Richard Dey surrenders the same to the use of himself and his wife Isabel for life & after their decease to the use of Thomas Dey their son & heir. 1591. April 21. Thomas Dey being dead Richard Dey seeks to be admitted as his next of kin & proper heir. 1596. Dec. 15. James Dey of Nether Hartley surrenders 1 Messuage & 1 bovat in Nether Hartley to the use of William son & heir apparent of James Carre of Southey.

[154] Robert Shirecliffe was second son of Richard Shirecliffe, of Ecclesfield.—He **purchased** lands at Whitley, and was father of Thomas Shirecliffe, who purchased Whitley Hall ano. 1616.—His wife was Mary Carr.

[155] Thomas Carre, of Birley Carr, cutler, will dated 12 Dec., 1594.—To Elizabeth Carre my wife "one bedde with all the furniture thereto belonginge wherein I usually lye, according to the laudable customes of Englande, and also one blacke cowe."—To Robert Holden "1 stythie & 1 paire of bellows."—To Ralph Holden "1 new fustian dublett."—Thomas Gray.—Nicholas Smith.—Henry Pearson.—To Barbara Bullus ivd.—Ralph Carr my brother.—William Winterbottom, Henry Sampson my brother.—Nicholas Gooder and Thomas Bullus the younger supervisors.—Proved at York, 16 jan., 1594-5.—Ralph Carr, brother of the above, married Helen, daughter of Nicholas Sampson, of Foxhill, and brother of Henry of the same, ano. 1567. [Vide note 24.]

Uxor Parkin sepult.		xxiiij' die.
Henrie Weynwright sepult.		xxvij' die.
Hughe Hyde filius Willmi. sepult.		xxviij' die.

Mense JANUARIJ.

Uxor Nicholai Slatter sepult. ... ...   x' die.

Mense FEBRUARIJ.

jane uxor Robti. Wyllye sepult.	vto die.
Wm. Chappell sepult.	xxvij' die.

Mense APRILIS. [1595.]

Uxor Richardi Cutte sepult.	xxiiij' die.
Hughe Spencer sepult.	xxviij' die.
Uxor Caroli Clarcke sepult.	iiijto die.
Infans Thome Ragge sepult.	xx' die.

Mense MAIJ.

John Stigbucke sepult.	xx' die.
John Grene sepult.	xxj' die.

Mense JULIJ.

186 Thomas Bullus sepult. ... ...   xxiiijto die.

Mense NOVEMBRIS.

187 Nicholas Stones sepult. ... ...   xj' die.

Mense DECEMBRIS.

188 Thomas Hobson sepult. ... ...   xiij' die.

Mense JANUARIJ.

Wm. Dyckenson (infans) sepult. ... ...   xxx' die.

Mense MARTIJ.

Agnes Dawre sepult. ... ...   vjto die.

---

186 **Thomas Bullus**, of **Birley Edge, yeoman, will dated 17 March**, 1591.—To my son Robert Bullus xl*l.*—To my son John Bullus xx*l.*—To John Lister xij*d.*—To Widow Wildsmyth xij*d.*—Thomas Bullus **my** son to be sole executor.—Nicholas Shirecliffe gent. **and Nicholas Staniland supervisors.**—Proved at York, 2 October, 1595. [Vide note 38.]

187 **From the Manor Court Rolls I** get the following:—1435. May 2. Robert Kent surrenders certain land called **Woodfield within the soke** of Southey to the use of John **de Shawe of Southey.** 1542. Robert Hurton son & heir of **John Hurton by Elizabeth his wife one** of the daughters and coheirs of John de Shawe seeks to be admitted to the same. 1567. April 22. Robert Hurton surrenders the same to his own use for life and after his decease to the use of **Alice wife** of Nicholas Stones & Isabel wife of Henry Shirecliffe the **daughters & coheirs of the said** Robert Hurton. 1568. April 14. Henry Shirecliffe & **Isabel** his wife surrender their share **to Nicholas Stones &** Alice his wife. [**Vide note 4.**]

188 Thomas Hobson, **of Ecclesfield,** will dated 10 Dec., 1595.—"I give & bequeathe to my wyfe all the Haver (?) meale in one barrell."—To "J. Towrall" (?) **my** son in law "one painter dishe."—Nicholas & Richard Hobson my sons to be my executors.—Richard Lorde, vicar.—William Broadhead and William Hyde supervisors.—Proved at York, 8 Jan., 1595-6.

Mense Martij. [1596.]

Wydowe Smythe sepult. ... ... ultimo die.

Mense Aprilis.

john Bever sepult. ... ... xx' die.

Mense Junij.

George Wyllye sepult. ... ... xxvij' die.
Wydowe Warde sepult.... ... ... xxviij' die.

Mense Octobris.

[189] Henrye Wylkinson sepult. ... ... xvj' die.
William Saterfott sepult. ... ... xvij' die.
Uxor Edwardi Silvester sepult. ... ... xxj' die.

Mense Novembris.

[190] Alexandr. Bearde sepult. ... ... xxvij' die.

Mense Decembris.

Rychard Grubbe sepult. ... ... x' die.
Wydowe hill sepult. ... ... xv' die.

[189] Henry Wilkinson, of Bellhouse, cutler, will dated 1 Oct., 1595.—To my son William Wilkinson one yonng bullock.—To my daughter Katherine Wilkinson "one younge heffer."—The residue of my goods to Ann my loving wife towards the bringing up of Henry, William & Katherine Wilkinson my children.—Thomas Scargell late of Sheffield, deceased, father of my wife and Ann widow of the said Thomas.—Nicholas Scargell of Doncaster brother of the said Thomas Scargell holds three score pounds for the use of my wife, Margaret her sister, and Robert Scargell her brother.—I give up all my claim in the said sum to William Wilkinson my son & Katherine Wilkinson my daughter.—My brother William Wilkinson & my cousin William Wilkinson to be supervisors.—Witnesses William Wilkinson of Crowder House, John Wilkinson of Shiregreen & William Wilkinson of Shiregreen.—Proved at York, 1 feb., 1596-7.—Henry Wilkinson above was son of William Wilkinson, of Longley, who was second son of Thomas Wilkinson, of Crowder House, & brother of Robert Wilkinson of the same. [Vide note 70.]—Dr. Sykes, of Doncaster, has kindly supplied me with the following notes from Scargell wills:—1575. Aug. 8. Thomas Scargell, of Sheffield, yeoman.—William Scargell my son.—Dionise my wife.—Dionise daughter of Thomas Scargell my son deceased.—Thomas son of Robert Scargell my godson.—Nicholas brother of the said Thomas Scargell.—Joana daughter of John Swyfte of White House deceased.—Ellin Scargell my daughter.—Ann Hole my wife's daughter.—Thomas & Ann children of Thomas Hall.—Elizabeth wife of Robert Scargell.—John Shemeld my uncle.—John Bullus & Nicholas Hobson my sons in law.—Proved 29 March, 1576. 1585. August 19. Nicholas Scargell, of Doncaster, alderman.—Nicholas my son.—Hugh son of Hugh Scargell of the Steel Bank, Hallam.—Thomas son of the said Hugh Scargell.—George son of the said Hugh Scargell my brother.—Robert son of Robert Scargell my brother.—Thomas son of the said Robert Scargell.—To William Tayler the lease of my shop at Rotherham.—William Snydall.—My sister Ann.—Elizabeth daughter of my brother Robert Scargell.—John Tayler my sister's son.—Edward Roebuck of Rotherham my cousin.—Elizabeth my wife.—My late brother Thomas Scargell deceased.—My brothers Anthony Ellis & Hugh Scargell supervisors.—Proved 6 Dec., 1585.

[190] I have the following notes from the Court Rolls:—1549. May 14. Thomas Greene gent. and Elizabeth his wife surrender 1 cottage and garden in Ecclesfield to the use and behoof of Thomas Bearde. 1591. April 21. Thomas Bearde being dead Alexander Bearde seeks to be admitted to the same as his son & heir, being of full age. 1596-7. March 16. Alexander Bearde having lately died Richard Bearde, clerk, vicar of Wath upon Dearn seeks to be admitted to the same as being his brother and proper heir aged 60 years and more. 1602. Nov. 8. Thomas Beard of Stubb Walden in co. York, yeoman, son & heir of William Bearde, clerk, deceased, who was brother & heir of Richard Bearde, clerk, deceased, surrenders the same to the use & behoof of Nicholas Shirecliffe of Ecclesfield, tanner. 1596-7. feb. 1. Administration of the goods of Alexander Bearde of Ecclesfield in co. York was granted to Richard and William Bearde.

Mense FEBRUARIJ.

Raulpho hill sepult.	...	...	...	...	xx' die.

Mense MARTIJ.

Uxor **Chadwycke** sepult.	...	...	...	...	vij' die.
Rychard **Chadwycke** sepult.	...	...	...	...	x' die.
[191] john **Collye** sepult.	...	...	...	...	xx' die febru.
Wydowe **Hobson** sepult.	...	...	...	...	xvjto die Martij.
Agnes **Sheyrclyffe** sepult.	..	...	...	...	eod. die.

Mense MARTIJ. [1597.]

[192] Edward **Dickenson** sepult.	...	...	...	xxviij' die.

Mense APRILIS.

Margret **Sheyrcliffe** sepult.	...	...	...	iij' die.
[193] Nicholas **Senier** sepult....	...	...	...	ix' die.
Rose **Byrkes** sepult. ...	...	...	...	xxj' die.

Mense JUNIJ.

Agnes **Norton** sepult. ...	...	...	...	...	i' die.
[194] Henric **Combe** sepult. ...	...	...	...	...	xxiiijto die.
Wydowe **Holden** sepult.	...	...	...	...	xxv' die.

Mense JULIJ.

Henric filius Henrici **Stannyforthe** de Wincowbanke sep.	...	...	xiij' die.

Mense AUGUSTI.

[195] john **Parkin** de Sowtheye (senex) sepult.	...	...	vij' die.

---

[191] 1597. june 15. Administration of the goods of John Colley, of Ecclesfield, in co. York, granted to Dorothy Colley his relict.

[192] Edward Dicconson, of Ecclesfield, in the county of York, will dated 17 March. 39 ELIZ.—My goods to be divided into 3 parts—one to Isabel **Shaw** the second to Elizabeth my wife and the third to Elizabeth my daughter.—My wife to have the tuition of my children.—Thomas Shaw, William Dicconson, Richard Birks & Robert Hartley to be overseers of this my will. [Vide note 76.]

[193] Nicholas Senier, of Mortomley, in the parish of Ecclesfield, tailor.—To my son Nicholas Senier my messuage, tenements &c. at Mortomley now in the tenure of me Nicholas Senier the father & the residue of my goods.—My daughter Emmett wife of Roger **Smilter**.—My son Edmund Senier.—My daughter Elizabeth Lockwood.—To the children of my said daughter Emmott "one blacke browne cailfe."—William Lockwood my son.—Thomas Parkin the younger & Francis Bower supervisors.—Proved at York, 13 june, 1597.

[194] 1597. August 18. Administration of the goods of Henry Combe, of Shiregreen, in the parish of Ecclesfield, yeoman, granted to Ellen Combe his relict. [Vide note 22.]

[195] 26 jan.—HEN. VIII. John Parkyn surrenders 1 Messuage and 2 Acres in Stainford near Wincobank to the use and behoof of John Parkyn his son. 3 june. 1539. John Parkyn being dead Nicholas Parkyn seeks to be admitted to the same land as being his brother and proper heir. 21 feb. 1540-1. John Parkyn son & heir of Nicholas Parkyn deceased seeks to be admitted to the same, but being under age Margaret his mother is appointed his guardian. 28 Ap. 1603. Nicholas Parkyn of Thorpe, cutler, son of John Parkyn late of Southey, cutler, deceased and Agnes wife of the said Nicholas Parkyn and John Parkyn of Southey, cutler, son & heir of the said John Parkyn deceased, surrender 1 Messuage & 2 Acres in Stanyford near Wincobank to Edward Parkyn third son of John Parkyn of Southey deceased &c.—In a later surrender mention is made of Francis Parkyn, fourth son of the said John, of Southey, deceased, and his **daughter Hellen**.

[196] Margaret uxor Thome Steele de Stanington sepult. xxiiij' die.

Mense Septembris.

Susan fil. Willmi. Sampson de Ecclesfelde sepult. j' die.
An fil. johis. Ragge paupis de Ecclesfelde sepult. iij' die.
Margaret Holmes (senex vidua) de Mortomley sep. vto die'
Marie filia Johnis. Ragge de Ecclesfelde sepult... ix' die.
Anne uxor dei. Johnis. Ragge sepult. ... xj' die.
Barbara Marsden paup vidua de Whitleye **sepult.** xiij' die.
Thomas Smythe de Mortomley lane sepult. ... xxv' **die.**
james Crofts de Ecclesfeld (senex) sepult. ... **xxvj' die.**
George fi. Rici. Cooke de Ecclesfeld **sepult.** ... **ultimo die.**

Mense Octobris.

Cat. Infans Rici, Raworth de Ecclesfeld sine baptismo sep. ... ijdo die.
Joan fi. Johis Ragge de Ecclesfeld paupis sepult. ... iij' die.
Hellen uxor Nichi. Watson de Mortomley sepult. ... vj' die.
Thomas Carre de Ecclesfeld sepult. ... ... xvij' die.

Mense Novembris.

Richard fil. Henrici Baylye de Whitleye sepult. **xxix' die.**

Mense Junij. [1598.]

Wyllm. Wylkinson de Wodseats (senex) sepult.... ... xxvij' die.

Mense Julij.

Cat. Infans Henrici Spittlehouse sine baptismo **sepu.** ... xiiij' die.

Mense Augusti.

Cat. Infans Alexandri Sadler de Wadsleye sine bapt. sep. vij' die.
Elizabeth Grubbe de Ecclesfeld senex vidua sep. xv' die.
Cat. Infans Thome Crosleye de Chappell sine bapt. sep. xxij' die.

Mense Septembris.

john Weynwright de Ecclesfeld senex sepult. ... xx' die.
Cat. Infans Nichi. Watson de Mortomley sine bap. **sep.** xxiij' die.

Mense Octobris.

jennett Dollye serva apud Wyndmil hill sepult. 4' die.
Richardus Morton de Ecclesfeld senex sepult. ... xvij' die.
Margerye Hartleye de Mortomley senex vidua **sep.** eod. die.
[197] Margret Sheyrcliffe de Butterthwet sen. vidua sep. ... ... xxij' die.

---

[196] In the churchwardens' Accounts ano. 1597 occurs "Item of Rychard Wylson for the buryall of his sister Steele iijs. & iiijd.

[197] 10 Oct. 1597. Margareta Shirecliffe, of Butterthwaite, widow, relict of Thomas Shirecliffe late of the same and daughter & coheir of John Twigge, of Winecbank, surrenders land near Jeny poole to her own use for life and then to the use of Richard Shirecliffe her fourth son with remainder to John Shirecliffe her eldest son with remainder to Henry Shirecliffe her third son.

Agnes uxor Reginald Hutchonson de Ecclesfeld sepult.   xxiiij' die.
Barbara fil. Robti. Sheircliffe de Sodhouse sep. ...   xxix' die.

Mense Novembris.

john Heye de Synoclyffe grandge sepult. ...   vij' die.
Grace uxor Johis Walker de Ecclesfeld sepult. ...   vij' die.
Hellen fil. dicti Johnis. sepult. ...   eod. die.
Elizabeth Turnley senex vidua de Ecclesfeld sepult.   ix' die.
jane Carre senex vidua de Ecclesfeld sepult. ...   xiij' die.
Isabell Brown de Croshouse senex vidua sepult.   xxj' die.
Jennet uxor Willmi. Parkin de Mortomley sep. ...   ult. die.

Mense Decembris.

Cat. Infans Rici. jepson de Ecclesfelde sine bapt. sep.   vij' die.

Mense Januarij.

Richard fil. Robti. Bowman de Longley sepult....   ijdo die.
Nicholas fi. Rici. Gylles de Chappell sep. ...   eod die.

Mense Februarij.

[196] Anthonie Brown de Creswycke sepult. ...   ix' die.
Elizabethe fi. Gerardi freman de Howsley Hall sep.   xxvj' die.

Mense Martij.

Margret fi. Oliveri Dernelye sepult....   vto die.
Elizabeth fi. Johis. Ragge de Ecclesfeld sepult....   xj' die.
john Grene de Wodseates sepult. ...   xvij' die.
Thomas Holden (alias Bradleye) sepult. ...   xx' die.
An uxor Rici. Talyor de Chappell sepult. ...   xxj' die.
Quida. advena paup apud Wadsley moriens sepult.   eod. die.

Mense Martij. [1599.]

frances uxor Robti. Mathyman de Hagge sepult. ...   xxvj' die.
[199] Maude Croftes (alias Mounteneye) de Creswicke senex generosa sepult. ...   ultimo die.

Mense Aprilis.

Agnes filia Rici Ragge de Mortomleye sepult. ...   xj' die.
Cat. Infans Nichi. Dungworth de Shiregrene sine bapt. sep. ...   xx' die.
Catherin Raworth senex vidua de Ecclesfeld sepult.   xxiij' die.
Rychard Saterfett de Neithershire adolescens sepult.   xxix' die.

---

[196] In the churchwardens' Accounts ano. 1598 occurs " Item of Mr. Brown for the buryall of his sonne Anthonye iijs. & iiijd. He was probably son of Edward Brown, of Creswick, gent.

[199] This lady was a daughter of George Wasteneys, of Headon, in co. Nottingham, she married first John Mounteney, of Creswick, who dying ano. 1573, she married secondly, 1578, Ralph son of Christopher Crofts, of Whitley, in this parish.

Mense Maij.

[200] Henrye Sampson de foxhill **senex** sepult. ...	...	**x' die.**
Cat. Infans Alexandri Coop de Chappell sine baptismo sepult.	...	xij' die.
Cat. Infans Rici. Chapman de Ecclesfelde sine baptmo. sepult.	...	xvij' **die.**
Cat. Infans Henrici foxe de Wadsleye sine baptmo. sepult. ...	...	xviij' die.
Alice uxor josephi Lorde de Ecclesfeld sepult.	...	xxj' die.
Margret uxor Radi Button de Grenalghesyde sepult. ...	...	eod die.
Jane uxor Henrici foxe de Wadsleye sepult. ...	...	xxij' die.
Elizabeth Selvester senex vidua de Hessleye **sepult.**	...	xxiiij' die.
Cat. Infans Nichi Bower de Wyncobanke sine baptmo. **sepult.**	...	**xxx' die.**

Mense Junij.

Spu. Alice filia spuria Thome Crosleye de Chappell sepu. .... xiij' die.

Mense Julij.

Isabell filia Rici. Ragge de Mortomleye sepult. ... . xxviij' **die.**

Mense Augusti.

Henrye Byrleye de Wadsleye senex paup. sepult.	...	xmo. die.
Michael Wygfall de Mortomleye senex paup sepult.	...	xiiij' die.
Dorithie uxor Johis. Wodde de Mortomleye sepult.	...	xxiij' die.
Anne uxor Robti. Oxspringe de Sowtheye sepult.	...	xxvij' die.

Mense Septembris.

Spur. Dionissa filia Thome Richardson de Grenalghsyde sep. .... iij' die.
Rychard Ragge de Mortomleye pauper sepult. .... vj' die.

Mense Octobris.

Elizabeth uxor Robti. Mathyman **do** Wadsleye sepult. .... xj' die.
Alice Crosbye de Ecclesfelde spinster sepult. .... xvij' die.
Anthonius fi. Anthonij Lawe de Warldsende sepult. .... xxv' die.
Richardus fi. Richi. Cutte de Mortomleye sepult. .... ultimo die.

Mense Novembris.

Charles Houlden de Ecclesfelde paup sepult. ... . viij' die.

Mense Decembris.

Barbara **fi. Henrici** Combe de Shiregrone sepult.	...	...	ij' die.
jenetta uxor Rici. Jepson de Ecclesfeld sepult.	...	...	vij' die.
Thomas fi. Henrici Spittlehouse de Ecclesfeld sepult.	..	...	eod. die.
Jane fi. Johis Burnet de Ecclesfelde sepult.	...	...	xij' die.
Wmus. Greaves de Thorppe senex sepult.	...	...	xxviij' die.

[200] Henry Sampson, of Foxhill, yeoman, will dated 9 May, 1599.—My land at Adwicke on Dearne purchased of Richard Brown Esquire of Mexboro' where my son Nicholas now lives.—Henry Sampson my second son.—Margerie Sampson my wife.—Hellen Hey, Margaret Baynes, Ann Cooke & Jennet Pearson my daughters.—Henry son of my son Nicholas Sampson.—William son of William Hey.—My sister Mathyman.—My sister Foores.—John son of my daughter Pearson.—Ann daughter of my son Nicholas Sampson.—Nicholas Sampson my son & Richard Hey of Finkle Street overseers.—John Cooke, William Hey, John Baynes, and Nicholas Pearson my sons-in-law.

Mense Januarij.

Robtus fi. Radi. Wilkinson de Chalton brooke sepult. — iij' die.
Margaret uxor Hugonis Ellys de Ecclesfeld sep. — vjto die.
Margaret uxor Henrici Spittlehouse de Ecclesfeld sep. — xvij' die.

Mense Februarij.

Raulph fil. Thome Dughtye (alias Waggleye) de Woodseates sep. — xxvij' die.

Mense Martij.

john Ronksleye de Byrleycarre senex sepult. — viij' die.

Mense Martij. [1600.]

Spur. Margret fi. Margret Cooper de Ecclesfeld sepult. ... — xxv' die.

Mense Aprilis.

Alice uxor Willmi. Brodeheade de Hunter House sepult. ... — vjto' die.
Emot Parkyn de Wadsleye senex vidua sepult. ... ... — xvij' die.
Robt. Mokeson de Wadsleye senex paup sep. ... ... — xx' die.
Tho. fi. Thome Creswycke de Wadsleye sepult... ... — xxviij' die.

Mense Maij.

Sara Lorde de Ecclesfelde juvenis sepult. ... ... — ij' die.
Elizabeth fi. Radi Button de Grenalghesyde sepult. ... — ix' die.
Wenefryde fi. Thome Bower de Whitleye sepult. ... — xv' die.
Wm. fi. Wmi. Hinchelyffe de Ecclesfelde sepult. ... — xxiiijto die.

Mense Junij.

Robt. fi. Hugonis Carre de Myddletongrene sepult. ... ... — ijdo die.
Anne fi. Thome Meller de Ecclesfelde sepult. ... ... — xij' die.
Spur. joan fi. Hugonis Bower de Sheffelde p Maria Grene de Whitleye sepult. — eod. die.
Robtus fi. Thome Meller de Ecclesfeld sepult. ... ... — xxviij' die.

Mense Julij.

[201] Dnus. Richardus Lorde vicarius de Ecclesfeld fuit sepult. — ixno die.
[202] Isabell uxor Nichi. Sheyrcliffe de Ecclesfeld sepult. ... — xvij die.
Alicia uxor Radi Calverd de Byrley edge sepult. ... — xxj' die.
Barbara fi. Radi Stannylande de Ecclesfeld sepult. ... — xxiiij die.
Cicilia uxor Thome Haughe de Eliot lane sepult. ... — xxvij' die.

[201] Richard Lorde, vicar of Ecclesfield, will dated 22 june, 1600.—Anne Lorde my wife to have the Gregg close for her life and after her decease to go to Jeremiah Lorde my son.—A house at Kimberworth and my lands &c. in Ecclesfield to Anne my wife for her life & after her decease to Richard Lorde my son.—My brother James Lorde.—My cousin Richard Entwysle.—Henry Demsteare and Francis Meadowcroft to be overseers of my will.—My daughters Susan, Deborah, Rebecca & Martha Lorde.—Thomas Scott and Lawrence Hardman executors of my will.—Jane my sister.—Richard Lorde was instituted to the Vicarage of Ecclesfield, 8 August, 1585, on the presentation of George, Earl of Shrewsbury.—His gravestone is still [1878] to be seen in Ecclesfield Churchyard.

[202] Nicholas Shirecliffe was eldest son of Richard Shirecliffe, of Ecclesfield, he had issue by his wife, Isabel Rhodes, one daughter, Isabel, who married Edward Saunderson, of Sheffield, who was cousin of Robert Saunderson, D.D., Bishop of Lincoln.

Ann fi. Hugonis Thomson de **Ecclesfeld** sepult. xxxo' die.
²⁰³ Thomas Howsleye de Howsleye hall senex sepult. ultimo die.

Mense Augusti.

Elizabeth fi. Willi. Dynnison de Whitleye sepult.... ... ... j' die.
Joan Holden de Whitley senex vidua sepult. ... ... xv' die.
Georgius fi. Lawrentij Sawsbye de birley carro sepult. ... ... xxj' die.
Elizabeth fi. Rici. Carro de pko yate [Parkgate] pochie **de Rotherham** sep. xxij' die.
Franciscus fi. Thome Clarke de Eliot lane defeti. sepult. ... ... xxjx' die.

Mense Septembris.

John Turton de Whitleye juvenis sepult. primo die.
Margret Harryson paup spinster de Ecclesfeld sepult. xiiij' die.
Elizabeth fi. Thome Hall de Ecclesfeld defeti. sepult. xxvj' die.

Mense Octobris.

Richardus Chapman de Ecclesfelde cutler sepult. xxvj' die.

Mense Novembris.

Francis fi. Willi. Rychardson de Ecclesfeld sepult. vto die.
Michael Scot de Chalton brooke (puer) sepult. vijmo die.
Spur. francisca fi. Nichi. Dyson de Whitleye sepult. viijvo die.

²⁰³ Thomas Howsley, of Howsley Hall, will dated 3 Nov., 33 Eliz.—To each of my servants xijd.—Alice my wife to have all my lands during her widowhood—My two daughters Elizabeth Diconson and Ann Howsley—My tonement in Chapeltown—To John Howsley & his heirs a tonement now in the tenure of Richard Haigh—My brother John Howsley.—Mr. Shirecliffe, Richard Watts, Robert Shirecliffe and Richard Lord supervisors.—Proved at York, 10 Mar., 1603.—I have these further notes of this family from Court Rolls, wills, &c., &c.—1343. Richard de Houslay was witness to a deed of transfer of property at Birley.—In the Poll tax, 2 Rich. ii., appear Johannes de Houselay & Margareta ux' ejus del Marchant de Bestos ijs.—Isabella de Houselay iiijd.—Johannes de Houselay iiijd.—and Laurencius de Hanselay & Juliana ux' ejus iiijd. 1400. John Howsley surrenders land in Chapel Green & 2 buildings to John Howsley his son & heir. 1409. John Howsley the son surrenders half of the same to John Howsley his father.— 1415. John son & heir **of** John Howsley seeks to be admitted to 1 toft and 1 bovat in "Le Chappell." 1416. John Howsley junior seeks **to** be admitted to 1 parcel of land in Chapel Green, which is 40 feet square and other lands, &c. 1436. feb. 21. Robert Normanton, vicar of Ecclesfield; Richard Pigbirn, of Scausby; John Skyres, of Wath; Thomas Greff, of Sturch hill; and John Wilson, of Wadsley, granted to John Howsley and Joan his wife, for their lives, all the lands &c. which they had of the gift or feoffment of the said John Howsley, within the bounds of Chapell, in the parish of Ecclesfield, to hold &c., to the said John and Joan his wife; with remainder to William son of John, with remainder to John brother of William.—The will of John Howsley, of Ecclesfield, dated 15 Nov., **1463.** My soul to the blessed Mary and all the saints & my body to be buried in the Church or Churchyard of Ecclesfield.—To the High Altar iijs. & iiijd.—To the Church vjs.—To Dmn. Robert Kyrkby vijs.—To Alice wife of Thomas Hawksworth v marks.—To Agnes wife of Adam Kaye iv marks.—To Johane wife of Pencaill Thrist (?) iv marks. —My daughters.—To Robert son of John Parkyn of Tickhill xxd.—Thomas Wood ijd.—Agnes my servant vjs. & viijd. —Elizabeth my servant vjs. & viijd.—Eufemie Modilton vjs. & viijd.—John Barcroft—Richard Kirkby—Isabella Dawson—To the wife of Christopher Oxley iijs. & iiijd.—The Residue of my goods to Johans my wife whom I ordain my executrix.—Thomas Wortley to be supervisor.—Proved 6 May, 1484.—The will of John Howsley, of Ecclesfield, dated 26 March, 1509.—To be buried in the parish church of Ecclesfield.—To the same church iijs. & iiijd.—To Thomas Hotchinson xs.—To William Walker xxxs.—To William Howsley xls.—To Thomas Parker iiijd.—To John Witkinson vs.—To John Woodkirke iiijs. & viiijd.—The residue to Agnes & "Maerlee" my daughters.—Johana my wife and Thomas Howsley my son executors.—Thomas Clarke vicar & William Hedon witnesses.—Proved 26 April, 1509. Thomas Howsley claims to hold in Chapel one parcel of land being 40 feet square and another of the same size.—He was admitted at the Easter Leet ano. 1510.

[204] Margeria Sampson de foxhill senex vidua sepult.   xvto die.
Thomas fi. johnis. Grene de Ecclesfeld sepult.   xxjmo die.

Mense Decembris.

[205] Margaret uxor johis. Creswicke de Burrowlee sep.   primo die.
Robt. fi. Willmi. Parkyn de Wadsleye sepult.   vto die.
Cat. Infans Georgij foster de Wodseates sepult.   vij' die.
Maria uxor Georgij foster de Wodseates sepult.   xij' die.
Thomas infans Edri Wardill de Ecclesfeld sepult.   xiiij' die.

Mense Januarij.

[206] Agnes uxor Radi Carre de Byrley edge sepult.   iiijto die
joan Cooke senex et paup vidua de Creswycke sepult.   xvto die
francisco fi. johis Kyrshawe de Whitleye sepult.   xix' die

Mense Februarij.

Agnes uxor johis. Sparke de Ecclesfeld sepult.   iiijto' die.
Radus fi. Rici. Swynden de Ecclesfelde sepult.   ix' die.

Mense Martij.

Elizabeth Haughe de Ecclesfelde senex vidua sepult. ...   iij' die.
Hugo Bower mutus juvenis de Wincowbanke sepu. ...   iiijto die.

Mense Aprilis. [1601.]

Anne uxor Wmi. Roberts de Chappell sepult. ... ...   vij' die.

[204] Margerie Sampson, of Foxhill, in the parish of Ecclesfield, widow, will dated 9 Nov., 1600.—I commend my soule to Almyghtie God my creator & Redeemer trustinge faythfullye throughe the effusion of his most precious bloude to be saved & by none other wayes nor meanes &c.—My body to Christyan man's buryall &c.—My debts to be paid &c.—To my son Henry Sampson six & twentye shyllinges eightpence.—To William Hey one cow.—To William son of the said William Hey one ewe sheep.—To Margerye Hey one ewe sheep.—To John Forman one ewe sheep.—To my servant Edward Yates twelve pence.—To everyone of my godchildren iiijd.—The Residue of my goods to Nicholas Sampson my son & William Heye, John Boanes, John Cooke and Nicholas Pearson my sons in law & they to be my executors.—Ralph Carre, Ralph Richardson, Nicholas Goodyre & Robert Ballus supervisors.

[205] Her gravestone is still in existence, on the west side of the churchyard; it bears this inscription :

MARGARET
WIFE OF IOHN
CRESWIC OF
BOROLY AND
BVRIED THE
FIRST DAY OF
DECEMBER
1600.

[206] She was a daughter of Richard Broomhead, of Thornseats, in the Chapelry of Bradfield.—I have the following notes of the family of Broomhead from the Court Rolls :—1443. November 30. Thomas Rawson surrenders one half bovat to Addam Broomhead. 1443. february 22. Richardus de Locksley surrenders one Messuage and one bovat in Bradfield to Willielmus Broomhead senior. 1507. Richard Broomhead leases of George Earl of Shrewsbury 1 Messuage & 1 bovat in Thornseats and ½ bovat in Bradfield for 40 years. 1526. John Birks surrenders ¼ Messuage and the half of all his lands in Bradfield to Henry Broomhead.—In the Poll tax of Bradfield, 2 Rich. II., appear Willelmus Bromhead & Isabella ux' ejus iiijd.

[207] Alice uxor johis Hall de Barleyhoole sepult. ix' die.
Margret uxor Willmi. Parkyn de Mortomleye sepult. xiiij' die.
Hellen uxor Francisci Hobson de Byrleyedge sepult. xxj' die.
Cat. Infans ejusdem francisci sine baptismo sepult. eod. die.

Mense Maij.

Margeria Creswycke de Burrowlee spinster sep. ... ... xiiij' die.
Elizabethe Button de Grenowsyde senex vidua sepult. ... eod. die.
Cat. Infans Georgij Byrkes de Doofeylde sine baptismo sep. ... xv' die.
[208] Richardus Mathyman de Hagge senex sepult. ... xviij' die.
Richard Chapman infans de Ecclesfeld sepult. ... xix' die.
Cat. Infans Thome Taylyer de Wadsleye sine baptismo sep. ... **xxviij' die.**
[209] Richard Brown de Crosschouse sepult. **xxix' die.**

Mense Junij.

Hellen Howsleye de Grenowside spinster sepult. xj' die.
Margret Chapman de Ecclesfelde vidua sepult. ... ... xviij' die.

Mense Julij.

Isabell uxor Willi. Crosleye de Sowedyche sepult. vij' die.

Mense Augusti.

Dorithie uxor **Rici. Thorpe** de Ecclesfeld sepult. **vto die.**
Anno fi. Nicholaij Dungworthe de Shiregreen sepult. ultimo die.

[207] Vide note 58.

[208] Richard Mathyman, of the Hagge, in the parish of Ecclesfield, will dated 9 january, 1660.—My body to Christian man's burial.—My debts to be paid, and my mortuary as the Statute directs.—The residue of my goods to be divided into three equal parts—one part to Jennet my loving wife—another part to my children, Richard, Robert, Peter, & William Mathyman my sons; Hellen Hutchinson and Agnes Scargell my daughters to be equally divided among them.—The third part to pay my legacies.—To my son Robert all my tools belonging to my occupation, with all my teams & harrows.—To Ann daughter of my said son Robert my youngest heifer.—To everyone of my childrens' children xijd.—To my sister Isabel Sherneld xs. which she oweth me.—To my brother Ralph Mathyman vjs. & viijd. & my best coat or jacket.—Residue of my goods to my sons Richard, Peter, Robert and William Mathyman and my sons in law Edward Hutchinson & Nicholas Scargell.—James Carr and Ralph Carr supervisors.—Witnesses Ralph Carr & William Wilkinson.—Proved at York, 4 August, 1661.—I have the following notes from the Court Rolls:—28 Hen. viii. April 5. Robert Kent surrenders one Acre above Milnefield in Ecclesfield to William Mathyman. 33 Hen. viii. November 15. John Mathyman son & heir of William Mathyman seeks to be admitted to the same. 6 Eliz. October 5. John Matthyman surrenders the same after his decease to Edward Mathyman his son. 1593. june 5. Edward Mathyman, son & heir of John Mathyman, and Alice his wife, surrender the same to Richard and Robert Mathyman.

[209] The following notes are from the Court Rolls:—1594. feb. 16. Richard Browne of Cross House surrenders certain land in Ecclesfield to the use of Agnes Shireeliffe for 21 years. 1601. Oct. 5. Margeria Browne, widow, late wife of Richard Browne, deceased, surrenders her share of land in Ecclesfield to Agnes Shireeliffe, widow. 1605. May 17. Richard Browne, corviser, son & heir of Richard Browne, nailer, son & heir of Richard Browne, nailer, died about three years since and Ellen Browne seek to be admitted to lands in Ecclesfield as his sister and heir aged 12 years at the time of her brother's death. 1607. Sept. 24. Elena Browne, sister & heir of Richard Browne, deceased, having lately died, Ralph Browne of Coal Aston, Webster, seeks to be admitted to lands in Ecclesfield as proper heir of the said Elena being her uncle and aged 40 years. 1607. Sept. 24. Ralph Browne of Cold Aston in co. Derby, leynen Webster, and Ann his wife; and Ralph Richardson of Cross House, and Margery his wife, late relict of Richard Browne of Cross House, deceased, surrender lands in Ecclesfield to the use of Thomas Browne of Rotherham, mercer, cousin of the said Ralph Browne, and son of Henry Browne of Rotherham, mercer, deceased.

Mense SEPTEMBRIS.

Margaret Lytlewodde de Whitley senex vidua sepult.   xxj' die.

Mense OCTOBRIS.

Robt. Ryton juvenis de Wodseats sepult.	ijdo die.
Isabell fi. Johis. Cooper de Sowdyche sepult.	vij' die.
Thomas Cooper de Sowdyche senex sepult.	ix' die.
[210] Willus. Hatfeld de Ecclesfeld senex sepult.	xvij' die.
Johan Shooter de Wadsley senex vidua sepult.	xxjx' die.

Mense NOVEMBRIS.

Catherina uxor Johnis. Smythe de Potter hill sepult.	viij' die.
Isabell uxor Nicholai Goodyre de birley carre sepult.	xv' die.
Thomas Bearde de Horberye senex sepult.	eod. die.
Lucie fi. johnis Lockewodde de Longleye sepult.	xvj' die.
Cat. Infans Nichi. Dyson de Whitleye sine bapt. sepult.	xix' die.
Cat. Infans Thome Smythe de Potter hill sine bapt. sep.	eod. die.
Robt. Bower de Chappell sepult.	xxvj' die.
Anne Hoylande de neythershyre senex vidua sepult.	xxviij' die.

Mense DECEMBRIS.

Elizabeth fi. Nicholai Bower de Wincowbanke sep.	vjto' die.
john Smythe de Potter hill senex sepult.	viij' die.
Alicia Brown de Crosshouse spinster sepult.	ixno die.
Edwardus fi. Willmi. Parkin de Wadsley sepult.	xxiiij' die.
[211] Alexander Hatfelde de Shyregreen senex sepult.	xxx' die.
[212] Richard Carre de Butterthwet senex sepult.	eod. die.

[210] William Hatfield, of Ecclesfeld, tanner, will dated 8 Aug., 1601.—To my son John Hatfield iijli.—My loving wife Dionise—My son Henry Hatfield—Margaret Shaw, Alice Hearnige and Anne Wade my daughters.—Nicholas Shirecliffe, my landlord, and Robert Fernell supervisors.—Proved at York, 14 Dec., 1601.

[211] Alexander Hatfield was son of Nicholas Hatfield, of Shyregreen. [Vide note 89.]—I cannot find either his will or administration at York.—He left issue by his wife Isabel, daughter of Alexander Shirecliffe, 3 sons & 2 daughters.—Ralph Hatfield, the eldest son, married Margaret, daughter of Robert Mirfield, of Thurcroft, in the parish of Laughton-en-le-Morthen, and was ancestor of the Hatfields of that place.—For a pedigree of this family, see "Hunter's Deanery of Doncaster," vol. 1, p. 291.

[212] Richard Carr, of Butterthwaite, yeoman, will dated 20 Dec., 1601.—Elizabeth Carr my wife to have one Messuage or tenement in Rotherham purchased of —— Robinson.—To Robert Carr my youngest son the same Messuage on the death of my wife, and he is to pay out of it £20 to Elizabeth daughter of my son William Carr.—To my wife one shop in Rotherham for her life and after her decease to Richard son of my son Nicholas Carr.—To my wife one Messuage with two shops in Rotherham near the shambles in the occupation of Edward Benson & Robert Carr my son.—Of my messuage at Butterthwaite I leave one half to my wife and the other half to Robert Carr my son.—To William Creswick my son in law £8.—To Robert Saunderson my son in law 3s. & 4d.—To Nicholas Sannderson my son in law 3s. & 4d.—To William Combe my son in law one milk cow.—To William, Richard & Robert Carr my sons 3s. & 4d.—To Ann daughter of my son in law Robert Shirecliffe 20s.—Robert Sanderson & Robert Shirecliffe my sons in law to be supervisors.—Proved at York, 22 April, 1602.

Elizabeth Carr, daughter of the above, married Robert Saunderson, of Sheffield, Gilthwaite & Blith, gent., whose second son, Robert Saunderson, afterwards became Bishop of Lincoln.

Richard Carr is supposed to be the author of certain old sayings & prophecies which after his death were published; a copy of these may be found on p. 545 of "Eastwood's History of Ecclesfield."

Menso JANUARIJ.

Richard Thorppe de Ecclesfeld pauper sepult. ...	ij' die.
john Lockewodde de Smythye Carre paup sepult.	v' die.
Nicholas Man de Ecclesfelde pauper sepult.	ixno die.
Agnes Smalebent de Wadsley brigge senex spinster sepult.	xix' die.
Marye Grene de Whitley spinster sepult.	xxiij' die.

Menso FEBRUARIJ.

Elizabeth fil. Nichi. Man de Ecclesfeld sepult.	iiij' die.
Nichas. Watson de Mortomleye claudus pauper sepult.	v' die.
[213] Alicia Howsleye de Howsleye hall senex vidua sepult.	ultimo die.

Menso MARTIJ. [1602.]

Richard Cutto de Mortomley paup sepult. ...	xxviij' die.

Menso APRILIS.

Hugo Ellys de Ecclesfeld senex paup sepult. ...	**ij' die.**
Dorithie fi. Rici. Thorppe de Ecclesfeld defcti. sepult. ...	**iiij' die.**
Cat. Infans Nichi. Sampson de foxhill sine baptismo sept. ...	**ix' die.**
Ricus fi. Petri Mathyman de Wadsley sepult. ...	**xviij' die.**
[214] Thomas Parkyn de Mortomleye senex sepult. ...	**xxiij' die.**

Menso MAIJ.

johes. Baylye de Whitley puer sepult. ...	viij' die.
Elizabeth uxor Robti. oxspring de **Southey** sepult.	xxij' die.
johna. Mathyman de Hagge **senex vidua** sepult.	xxviij' die.

Menso JUNIJ.

Isabell uxor Nichi. Dyson de Whitleye sepult. ...	vto die.

Menso JULIJ.

[215] **Radulphus Carre de Birleyedge senex sepult.** ...	xiiijto die.
Elizabeth uxor Willi. Dinnison de Whitley paup sep.	xviij' die.
jana Man pauper vidua de Ecclesfeld sepult. ...	xxiiij' die.

Menso AUGUSTI.

john. Brownell **de** Whitley senex paup. sepult.	xviij' die.
Henricus Ibotson **de** Ecclesfeld senex pauper sepult.	xxxmo die.

---

[213] Alice Howsley was relict of Thomas Howaley, of Howsley Hall, & daughter of Richard Scott, of Barnes Hall.

[214] Vide note 82.

[215] Ralph Carr, of Birley Edge, will dated july 11, 1602.—My estate to be divided into two equal parts, one part to my children, Ralph Carr, Elizabeth Hall, Ellen Mathyman, Margerie Brown, Frances Bullas, and Emmott Carr, to be divided equally among them.—Peter Mathyman my son in law—Thomas Creswick—Richard Carr my son & heir apparent—My lands in Wadsley.—To my uncle Thomas Carr one old jacket.—To Ralph Carr son of my son Richard Carr " one byble book."—Thomas Creswick, of Ollerton Hall.

Mense Octobris.

Anne fi. johis. Hattersleye de Bellhouso sepult....	xiij' die.
Cat. Infans Robti. Butterwortho de overshyre sine baptismo sepult.	xx' die.

Mense Novembris.

Thomas Stannyforthe senex advena & sepult.	vij' die.
Am fi. infans Laurentij Place de **Ecclesfeld** sep.	eod. die.
Spur. Infans Caroli Hill de Ecclesfeld (natus **mortuus**) sepu.	xvj' die.
Ricus. Basforthe de Whitleye senex sepult.	xxvto die.
[25] Edward **Scotte** de Shiregrene senex sepult.	xxix' die.

Mense Decembris.

Elizabetha fi. **Gerardi ffreeman** de Howseley Hall sepu.	viij' die.
Elizas uxor Robti. ffalley de Smythyearr sepult.	xiiijto die.

Mense Januarij.

Arthur fi. Willi. Parkin de Wadsleye sepult.	xvjto die.
An. fi. Willi. Wodrove de Whitley sepult.	xxiiijto die.
Spu. Thomas Bramall (als. Harryson) de Whitley sep.	xxvto die.
An uxor Robti. Wilkinson de Ecclesfeld sepult.	xxvjto die.
Barbara uxor Rici. Wodde de Wardlsende sep. ...	eod. die.
Petrus Morton de Whitley sepult.	xxx' die.
Radulphus Truelove de Chappell senex sep.	ultimo die.

Mense Februarij.

Alicia uxor **Richardi Relfe** de **Ecclesfeldo** sepult.	vij' die.
Cat. Infans johis. Burie de Sowthey sine bapt. sep.	x' die.
Isabell uxor johis. Brefet do **Ecclesfeld** sep.	xj' die.
Nycholas Greene de Potter hill senex sep.	xij' die.
Richardus Gylles de **Chappell** sep.	xiij' die.
Georgius fil. francisci **Daniell** de Mortomleye sepult.	xvto die.
Richus. fil. Richi. Gylles de Chappell defuncti sep.	xvjto die.
Frances filia **Thome** Ragge de Mortomley sep.	ultimo die.

Mense Martij.

Maria fil. Gregorij **Wodde** de **Okes** sep.	xxij' die.
Isabella fil. Willi. fearnelly de **Okes** sep.	xxiij' die.

[115] Edward Scott, of Shiregreen, yeoman, will dated 25 Nov., 1602.—To be buried in the Church at Ecclesfield.— My nephew Richard Watts of Wortley, yeoman—One Messuage and tenement &c. at Skinnerthorpe in the parish of Sheffield called Barker House.—To the poor of Ecclesfield vjs. & viijd. per annum.—To my sister Watts xxs.—To my nieces Elizabeth Diconson and Ann Freeman xxvs. apiece.—My nephews Christopher and Roger Scott iijli. apiece.— My nieces Ann Goodyson & Elizabeth Rodes her sister xls.—My niece Jane Thompson xs.—My Godson Edward Hartley xs.—My three Goddaughters Cecilie Mason Susan Bullus & Margaret Brownell iiis. & ivd. apiece &c. [Vide note 105.]

Menso Martij. [1603.]

jennetta Swinden de Wadsleye senex vidua sep.	...	ultimo die.
Thomas fil. Alexandri jepson de Ecclesfeld sep.	...	eod. die.

Menso Aprilis.

Alicia Stones de Morttomleye senex vidua sep.	...	...	ij' die.
johes. Eyre de Wadsley senex sep.	...	...	iij' die.
Alicia Sugworth de Morttoleye senex vidua sep....	...	...	vto die.
johes. Hadfeld de Shiregreene juvenis sep.	...	...	vij' die.
Nichus. Dungworth **de** Mortomleye juvenis sep...	...	...	xj' die.
johana uxor Hugois. Thwetes de Ecclesfeld sep.	...	...	xvij' die.
Cycelye uxor Henrici Baylye de Whitleye sep.	...	...	xviij' die.
Willus. Bays de Ecclesfeld senex sep.	...	...	xixno die.
Anne Ragge de Morttomley paup spinster sep.	...	...	xxij' die.
Radus. fil. Willi. Brownhill de Shirgreene sep.	. .	...	eod. die.
jenetta uxor Willi. Brownhill de Shiregreene sep.	...	...	xiiijto die.
Hellen Eyre de Shiregreene senex **vidua** sep.	...	...	xxixno die.

Menso Maij.

Margeria **uxor Rici Ingle de** Chappell sep.	...	...	**j' die.**
Elizb. Hill de Longley juvenis spinster sep.	...	...	iij' die.
Elizab. uxor Nycholai Tayler subter Byrleyedge sep.	...	...	viij' die.
Grace Brownhill de Shiregreene senex vidua sep.	...	...	ixno die.
Dorot filia Robti. Bell de Mortomley sep.	...	...	xvto die.
. . . . ell Wormall de Eland juvenis occisus in **Grenowe 23 die** . . . Sep.			xxiiij' die.
Anne fil. Willi. Hargreave de Hollinhouse sep.	...	...	xxvjto die.

Menso Julij.

Richus. Browne de Crossehouse juvenis **sep.**	...	...	iiijto die.
Richus. Byrkes de Crowder house juvenis **sep.**	...	...	xvjto die.
Henricus Alinson de Longley paup. sep.	...	...	xxj' die.
Anna uxor Willi. Whitteeres **sep.**	...	...	xxx' die.

Menso Augusti.

Anna fi. Willi. **Roberts** de Chappell sep.	...	...	xviij' die.
Thomas Wilkinson de Ecclesfeld juvenis sep.	...	...	ultimo die.

Menso Septembris.

Hugo Thwaites de Ecclesfeld paup. senex sep.	...	...	xixno die.
[217] jenetta Swinden **de** Potterhill senex vidua sep. **extra** cæmeterium quia exca. fuit	...	...	xxiij' die.

[217] This means that Jenetta Swinden, of Potter hill, **widow, having been excommunicated, was buried outside** the churchyard.

CHURCH WARDENS' ACCOUNTS.

1520—1545 (INCLUSIVE).

CHURCH WARDENS' ACCOUNTS.

Ano. Mlmo. CCCCCmo. vicessimo.

It. **In pmys** Willm. Schyrtclyffe ys in debeth   xvs. & vjd.

[218] It. Alexander Schytclyffe ys in debeth for ye same   xviijs.

    Also yt ys agreyd yt ye sayd Alexand. shall well and truly pay to ye church of Ecklysfeld yerly xvs. dewryng thre yers foloyng usuall yt to tymys of ye yeyr and ye sayd Alexand. schall bayr all chardgs of ye hows and wheyll.

[218] The following will explain this entry:—Thomas Shircoliffe, of Ecclesfield, will dated 12 December, 1516.—To be buried in the Church at Ecclesfield.—I bequeath my little House with the croft called the March House and the water wheel for the buying and towards a suit of vestments and the making of the Rood loft for the term of seven years.—John Wilkinson and John Woodkirk to be trustees.—John Wilkinson, Richard Dey & John Shircliffe my feoffees to see all my lands sold, except my wife's feoffment, to pay my debts; after they are paid my feoffeers to make an estate first for my son William Shircliffe &c.—Also my son William to have the house that John Fitzwilliam dwells in.—Alexander Shircliffe my son.—Agnes my wife.—Isabella daughter of Henry Shircliffe.—To Robert Shircliffe, son of John Shircliffe, the take of Wolley Hall for the term of xij years next ensuing and if he die to Agnes & Isabel his sisters and Jennetta his mother.—To young Thomas Dey my counter in Ecclesfield Hall.—Item I bequeath to John Eyre "a littyl newe fedder bedd, a payre of lynnyn sheit, a payre of blankets, ij coverlets, ij pillows & xxxiijs. & ivd. in moneye."—To Alexander my son and Laurance Smythe my take and farmhold in Sheffield.—To young Ralph Smythe "my littyl meser [measure?] of silver and gilte."—Isabel Dey & Agnes Smythe to have a pair of corrall beeds betwixt them.—William Shircliffe my son & Alexander Shircliffe my son to be my executors.—Mr. Mounteney of Cowley Esquire, John Wilkinson of Ecclesfield, John Shircliffe of the same and Lawrence Smythe of Sheffield overseers.—Proved at York, 20 March, 1516-17.—The above Thomas Shircliffe was "Master of Game" to the Lords of Hallamshire.—Dodsworth gives the following epitaph as being in the "South quyer" of Ecclesfield Church:—

> "Here lyeth Thomas Shercliffe
> In Hallamshire Mr of Game
> Who for justice, truth, love, and bounty,
> Had alwaies the fame
> Alexander his son and heire
> Lies here hard by.
> Who languished in sorrow
> By his Mris cruelty.
> No Goddess she was
> But of like nomination
> As prudence to the Goddesses
> Made application.
> Progeny that reads this
> Eschew like Fate. Jehoba say Amen.
> Continue your posterity on earth
> And I rest in Heaven. Anis."

I have the following from the Court Rolls:—15 Hen. vii., Oct. 24. Thomas Shircliffe son & heir of William Shircliffe deceased seeks to be admitted to 1 Messuage & garden adjoining and 1 garden called Iveyard and half a **bovat in** Ecclesfield lately in the tenure of William Kiddars 1 bovat in Creswick lately in the tenure of Henry

[219] It. owyng of ye beqwest of Willm. **Wheyte**   xxs.
[220] It. owyng of ye beqwest of **Thoms. Parker**   xxs.
It. owyng of **john Clarke**   ...   vis. & viijd.

Kiddars and a close abutting on **the** land of William Browne and another close adjoining.—1 Messuage & half a bovat in Ecclesfield lately in the tenure of Thomas Wood.—Also 1 Messuage, 1 toft & 1 croft abutting upon William Hill & William Crosleigh **& 3½** Acres **in** Ecclesfield lately in the tenure of Nicholas Casse and 1 Acre and 1½ **Acres** lying between the land of John Wilkinson and William Hill, and 1 Acre between John Wilkinson and John Colley.— Also **to 1 Messuage** and garden in Ecclesfield lately in the tenure of Thomas Penereth of Aston.—Also to 2 **Acres** in Ecclesfield lying between Copping land and Lawcockfield.—In the Poll tax, 2 Rich. ii., appear the following:—Johannes de Shirclyf & Johanna ux' ejus iiijd.—Robertus de Shirclyf iiijd.—Robertus Shirclyf & Johanna ux' ejus iiijd.— Thomas Shirclyf & Isabella ux' ejus iiijd.

[219] William Whete, of Ecclesfield, will dated 4 March, 1506.—To be buried in the South " quere " in the parish Church of Ecclesfield before the altar of " Saynt John Baptiste."—**I bequeath to my** mortuary my best beast.—To the altar of St. John the Baptist vjs. & **viijd.—I request a stone of Roche stone** be procured and my name graven thereon.—To the Roodloft xxs.—To William Fulston the **elder ijs.** & iiijd.—To John Hill, nailer, ijs.—To William Fulston the younger iijs. & iiijd.—To Margery Hill and John her son xijd.—To John Hill " futterler " xijd.—William Cowper's **wife of** Rotherham.—Christopher Tor.—John & William Hunt.—Katherine Whete my wife.—" I, William Whete hath becqwested & sett all my lands & as followeth to Johana my daughter that is be name expressed her." Robert Whete of Cowley, Richard Hill of Ecclesfield, Henry Holland, William Fulstone & John Shaw of Sheffield trustees.—" If **ought come** to Johanie my daughter then Katheren **my wife to** inherit," &c.—Proved **at** York, 30 june, 1517.

[220] Thomas Parker, of Whitley, will dated 20 August, 1510.—To be buried within my parish church of Ecclesfeld.—To the making of the rode lofte & stalls in the said chirch xls.—To the reparying of Seint Mychel's chapell within the said parish lijs. iiijd.—To Ellyn Parker my doghter xl marks to her marriage, if it may be born.—I will that Thomas Shircliff of Ecclesfield, John Wilkynson, of the same, and John Grubbe, of Nether Hertley, surrender into the hands of my lorde of Shrewsbury all such meses, lands, &c., as I have in Whitley purchased of William Whete, in Wodsettes, purchased of Wm. Houlle, holden of my seid lord by copy of Court rolle, to the use of John Parker my sonne, and the heires of his body; remainder to Richard Parker his broder; remainder to the right heires of me the forseid Thomas Parker. Same persons to surrender into the hands of the prior and convent of Coventre Charter house all such meses, lands, &c., as I have in Nether Hertley, late purchased of Thomas Barnley, holden of the seid prior and convent by copie of Court rolle as of their lordeship of Ecclesfield, to the use of Richard Parker my sonne remainder to John Parker his broder &c.—Same persons to surrender to the prior and convent of the Charter house of Coventry a mese, lands, &c., in Nether Hertley, to Richard Parker my sonne, with like remainder.—The said Richard Parker to make to Agnes Parker my doghter a surrender of a yearly rent of xxs. out of all the landes &c. in Nether Hertley: if, as God forbede, hit happen that the seid Agnes be decrepyd, or in such case that she may not stere herselff, or come to a grete necessite, then seid Richard Parker to pay above the seid xxs., vjs. viijd.—I will that Richard Parker my sonne have the takke of my water wheles after my decesse; also a mese in Broke house in par: Laghton; also an annual rent of ixs. lying in Dennaby; my right in ij closes with a meadow called Horbury, a close called Longlands, and a croft callyd Ryfarecrofte; also, at Neder Hertley a fournes, a fourme lede, a woort stoon, a kneding trough, a mulding borde, a stopefatt, ij grete arkes, ij chayres, a mete borde, a folding borde, a chymney, ij bedds, an arke, a long chist, a saing borde, ij bedds in the new chambre, oon in the parlor and an awmery in the new parlor at Whitley; also ij stythes, ij bare bales, all oder smythy gere &c.—I will that John Parker my sonne have at Whitley ij stones troughes called Coltroughs, a stythy, and a pair of bellows &c.—Out of the meses in Dalton, yerely, xlijs. vjd. to find a preist at Ecclesfield to sing yerely lx messes, that is, ij tymes Seint Gregory trentall with servyce therto belonging: liijd. to the vicar of the same chirche to pray for the soules of me, **my ij wifis,** my fader and moder, and all myn auncestors and childer soules, on the Sunday in the chirch; for an obyt for Thomas Parker, Elsabeth and Agnes, his wiffs, his fader and moders soules, vd.; To the clere for v mynnyngs, vd.; The residue of the mese, i.e., ijs. iiijd. my childer jd. and the residue to poore folkes having most nede. St. Mychell Warke shall **have vjs. viijd.; prior and covent** of Charter house vjs. viijd. Overseers, Mr. Henry Everingham, esquier, xxs. **Thomas Everingham sonne of the** seid Henry, xs. Sir Thomas Thorley, parson of Thorley, xxs., Robert Parker my sonne, **Robert Gilberthorp,** William Crofte, to the two latter vjs. viijd.—Residue, my wiff hir thirde parte; the second parte to **be spendyd at my** buriall and afterwarde **for** the well of my soule; the thirde part to

[221] It. owyng of Mr. R. **Mounteney** xviijs. & viijd.
It. owyng of Ric. Ecar ... xiijs.
It. owyng of john Ecar and hys wyff iijs. & iiijd.
It. owyng of jenett Ecar xijd.
It. owyng for ye berrall of Elsabeth Coplay vjs. & viijd.
It. for ye berrall of ij chyld of Herre Womwell ... xiijs. & iiijd.
It. for ye berrall of a child of Thoms. Serylbe ... vjs. & viijd.

Richard Parker my sonne.—Robert Parker, my sonne, to pay to Agnes my wiff yerely during her liff xiijs. iiijd.—John Parker, my sonne, to pay to same Agnes, his moder, xxvjs. viijd. of hir dowery; Richard Parker, my sonne, to pay to same Agnes, his moder, xxvjs. viijd. for hir dowery.—Agnes Parker, my wiff, John Parker and Richard Parker my sonnes, executors.—Witnesses, Sir Thomas Clerc, vicar of Ecclesfield, Thomas Shireclif, John Wilkinson, Robert Grubbe.—Proved at York, ano. 1510.—[*The above will was kindly supplied to me by Mr. Charles Jackson, of Balby.*]—The following notes are from the Court Rolls:—1435. Johana, wife of Robert Scott; Alice, wife of John Roades; and Agnes, wife of William Hill, daughters and coheirs of John de Lound, seek to be admitted to one Messuage and half a bovat in Chappell, and one Messuage and two crofts in Whitley *post mortem* of the said John de Lound. 1447. John Wade de Makesburgh [Mexborough?] surrenders 1 Messuage & a third part of half a bovat in Chapple and a third part of a toft and a croft lately in the tenure of John de Lound and a third of one toft & 4 crofts in Whaley to Robert Scott. 1484. May 13. John Shirecliffe and Agnes his wife; Margerie Holand; and Richard Hawkhirst son & heir of Johana Hawkhirst the three daughters and coheirs of Robert Scott, deceased, seek to be admitted to lands in Ecclesfield, Whitley, &c. 1494. Oct. 24. Thomas Barnby surrenders certain lands at Hartley in the parish of **Ecclesfield to** Thomas Parker of Whitley. 1499. jan. 7. William Hull surrenders 1 croft & a third part of 2 **cottages & a parcel of** land called Brerefields in Wodsettes to Thomas Parker. 1512. Nov. 10. Thomas Shirecliffe and others come to the court and say that they hold certain lands in Hartley for Richard Parker a young child of Thomas Parker of Whitley deceased, with remainder to John Parker brother of the said Richard Parker. 1527. Sept. 11. Elizabeth Parker, Alicia Gryffyn, Isola Ellys & Johana Cawthorne, daughters and coheirs of Margerie Swyft, lately deceased, who was daughter and coheir of Robert Scott deceased, seek to be admitted to lands in Ecclesfield. 1527. Sept. 11. Robert Gryffyn & Alicia his wife surrender their share in the same to John Parker of Ecclesfield. 1538. july 9. John Parker of Whitley surrenders lands at Hartley to the use of Thomas Parker his son & heir. 1538. Aug. 20. John Cawthorne surrenders his share in lands at Ecclesfield lately in the tenure of Margerie Swyfte to John Hawkhirst. 1542. April 14. John Hawkhirst surrenders the same to John & Richard sons of John Parker. 1542. April 14. John Parker and Elizabeth his wife surrender lands in Ecclesfield to the use of Richard Parker their son. 1545. Sept. 8. William Ellys & Isola his wife one of the daughters and coheirs of Margerie Swyfte, deceased, surrender their share in her lands to John Parker of Ecclesfield. 1573. june 16. Richard Parker of Brampton Bierlow surrenders certain lands in Ecclesfield to the use of his three daughters & coheirs, viz.: Agnes, wife of Thomas Skyers gent.; Katherine, wife of Richard Sympson, and their son Richard Sympson; and Ann, wife of Thomas Bloome of Middlewood in the parish of Darfield, gent. 1591. April 24. Thomas Parker of Whitley being dead, William Parker of Horncastle, in the county of Lincoln, gent., seeks to be admitted to lands **in Ecclesfield,** Whitley &c. as his son & heir. 1592. March 22. William Parker of Horncastle, **in the** county of Lincoln, gent., surrenders lands in Hartley to the use of himself and his wife Margret for life, **and after their decease** to the use of Francis Parker their son & heir.—Mr. Charles Jackson has also supplied me with the following:—1581. july 3. *Caveat*, against administration to Francis Parker of Whitley, in par. Ecclesfield, and proof of his will if he made one before the 17th of that instant july, except Robert Parker, his brother, be called and made privy thereto. 1584. April 11. *Caveat* against administration to the same Francis Parker to anyone before Pentecost next, unless Robert Parker of Medda Hall, his brother, be warned.—This Francis Parker was 4th son of Thomas Parker, of Whitley Hall.—For a pedigree of this family see "*Hunter's Hallamshire, Gatty's Edition,*" p. 445.

[221] Such evidences as I have been able to collect concerning the Mounteneys are of a rather conflicting nature; but still they may be useful to those who are interested in that family.

1499. june 6. Nicholas Mounteney, *armiger*.—To be buried in Ecclesfield in front of the Imago of the Blessed Virgin Mary.—"*Fabricæ eccl. de Ecclesfield ij seme of gren.*"—My son and heir Robert Mounteney.—My sons Thomas, Alexander and Nicholas Mounteney.—My daughter Joan.—"*Robertus, filius meus, habeat hayre-loomes* [heir looms] *viz., ij salt selaria arg., j peciam arg. de aur. cum coopertoris, j pouder box arg. & j blak nutt, j calicem*

It. for ye bereall of Thoms. Schyrtclyffe	...	vjs. & viijd.
It. for ye bereall of Willm. Wheyt ...	...	vjs. & viijd.
It. for Mr. Mountenay bereall ...	...	vjs. & viijd.
It. for ye beqwest of john Wilkynson	...	vjs. & viijd.

arg., 1 **Messe-boke**, *j Primarium cum armis intus pictis et ornamentis capellæ*, etc.—*Isabella uxor Roberti filii mei habeat j zonam cerecam quæ fuit usitata per Eliz. uxorem* **meam**. *Margt. Bravyson quam Nich. filius meus ducit in uxorem.*" My three younger sons my executors, and my eldest to be supervisor.—Proved 12 july, 1499. [*Reg. Rotherham*, 369 *a.*]

Robert Mounteney, of Cowley, in the parish of Ecclesfield, Esquire, will dated 3 August, 1519.—To be buried in the "quere" of St. John the Baptist in Ecclesfield Church.—Elizabeth and Dorothy daughters of my son Robert Mounteney.—Anthony son of my son Robert Mounteney.—Thomas Mounteney my brother.—Nicholas Mounteney my brother.—Katherine Mounteney my wife &c.—Proved 10 March, 1519-20.

Chancery Inq. P.M. ano. 12 HEN. VIII.—No. 10.—Taken at Rotherham, Saturday after the Feast of St. Luke the Evangelist ano. 12 HEN. VIII. after the death of Robert Mounteney Esquire.—He was seised of the Manors of Cowley and Shirecliffe in the county of York, also of lands &c. in Cowley, Shirecliffe, &c.; and, being so seised, by his deed granted to Robert Mounteney his son and to Anne wife of the same Robert [one of the daughters of Sir John Draycotes Knt.] the manor of Hesteley [Hesley] with appurtenances being a parcel of the manor of Cowley aforesaid &c. to hold to them & their heirs lawfully begotten with remainder to the right heirs of Robert Mounteney the father of Robert. Recites his will, dated 3 August 1519.—My brother Thomas Mounteney and Nicholas Mounteney.—Anthony son of Robert Mounteney my son.—The jurors say he died 5 August, ano. 11 HEN. VIII., and that John Mounteney is "*consanguineus*" of Robert Mounteney, viz., son of Robert Mounteney, and is aged eleven years and more.

1539. july 31. Thomas Mounteney.—My bodie to be buried in the churchyard of Sandall, if I die there.—The Residue of my goods to Ralph Denman whom I appoint my executor.—In witness whereof I put my seal, these being witnesses—Christopher Calverley, John Skott, Thomas Grenewode, and Richard Thornton.—Item, certayne articles & bequestes the which I, Thomas Mounteney, gentleman, will & desier myne executor to performe &c. I bequeath vjli. to be gyvyn to power men & power women in xij parishes, viz., Sandall, Wakefield, Kirkthorpe, Normanton, Wragbie, Felkirke, Roiston, Wolley, Wath, Darfield, Ecclesfield, Tankersley, &c.—To my [blank] Nicholas Mounteney a silver spoone and a booke called "*Legendia Aurea,*" and another booke called "*The booke of goode manners.*"—My nephie Denman of Retforthe iij bookes, that is to say the booke called "*Ball*" and the booke "*Mandevell,*" and the booke "*Scala celi.*"—To John Mounteney, my brother Nicholas' son, my jackett of damask, gowded with velvett, and iij bookes, one called "*The exposicion of the vij Psalms,*" another called, "*Shepherde's booke,*" and the thirde called "*Dicta Philosopha.*"—To Edward Mounteney, my brother's son, iij bookes &c.—The iij bookes haith Edward Mounteney wrytten in the first side &c.—The glass at Burton Abbey with the Mounteney Arms on to Mr. Thomas Wentworth of Woddes Hall, also my beste prymer and if of my beste drinking glasses.—To my cousin William Wentworth dwellinge at Newall Grange, in Wathe parish, a sylver spoone.—To my cousin Drax dwellinge at Woddall Hall in Darfeld my cloake &c., &c.—Proved 12 April, 1543.

Nicholas Mounteney, of Ecclesfield, Esquire, will dated 22 April, 1543.—To be buried in Ecclesfield Church.—Edward Mounteney my son to have all my bargain & take of the Mill at Ecclesfield & the closes at Lee Chapel.—To John Wombwell my servant, "one gowne, excepte the velvett therupon."—Richard Jeffray.—Richard Rawode.—John Jephson.—To Sir William Hall, St. John's Priest viijs. iiijd.—John and Edward Mounteney my sons, to be executors.—Witnesses Sir Robert Cobcroft, priest, William Broadbent, Henry Shirecliffe, John Rhodes, and John Jephson.—Proved 7 May, 1543.

According to Dodsworth, the following inscriptions were on two ancient tombstones in the South quire in Ecclesfield Church, but little of them is now remaining:—

"*Orate pro anima Roberti Mowntney de Cowley, armigeri, qui obiit tertio die mensis Augusti, A'. M'.CCCC.xix', Cujus animæ propitietur Deus.*"

"*Orate pro anima johis Mowntney de Cowley, armigeri, qui obiit secundo die mensis Augusti, A.' Dni. M'.CCCC.'xxx'vi'. Cujus animæ propitietur Deus. Amen.*"

There is still in existence [1878] in Ecclesfield Church, under the East window of the South quire, a pew, along the top of which is carved in relief, the following inscription :—

"*Orate pro animabus Robarti Mowntney et Anne uxoris eius. ac pro bono statu johannis Mowntney et johanne uxoris eius, qui hoc oratorium fieri fecerunt xxiiij die mensis iulii, anno dni M.CCCC.xxx.vi.*"

It. for the berrall of Annes Schyrtclyffe	...	...	...	vjs. & viijd.
It. for yᵉ bereall of Thomas Sotton...	...	...	...	vjs. & viijd.
and for hys beqwest to yᵉ Rodloft	...	...	...	vjs. & viijd.
It. Mayst john Talbott hays gyffyn to yᵉ church wark	...	...	...	xxxs.
It. for yᵉ beqwest of Annes Schyrtclyffo to yᵉ Rodo	...	...	...	xxd.
It. for yᵉ beqwest of Sr. Thoms. drewro	...	...	...	vjs. & viijd.
It. owyng of Robert Wilkynson for yᵉ beqwest Robt. broksells	...	...	...	. . . .

From the Court Rolls I have the following notes:—1379. Thomas Page surrenders that land in Skinnerthorpe, which was formerly in the tenure of Henry Page, to the use & behoof of John Mounteney. 1380. August 2. John son of John Mounteney seeks to be admitted to the lands his father held, viz.: one acre of Mattock land between Ollerton bridge and Stonebridge. 1406. May 11. John Mounteney surrenders half a Bovat containing 10 Acres near Shirecliffe Park to Thomas Reson. 1441. April 18. John del More, senior, surrenders 1 Messuage, 1 cottage & 1 Bovat in Ecclesfield to Richard del More his son. 1441. October 4. Thomas Hartley surrenders 2 Messuages, 2 Bovats, and 1 field in Creswick to John Mounteney, miles. 1480. April 22. Richard del More surrenders 1 Messuage, 1 cottage & 1 Bovat in Ecclesfield to Nicholas Mounteney. 1480. April 22. Thomas Hill surrenders 1 Messuage, 1 Toft, and 2 Bovats in Creswick to Nicholas Mounteney, Armiger. 1499. Easter Leet, Nicholas Mounteney, Armiger, surrenders 1 Messuage & certain land called Birley Hollins and 3 Acres in Birley called Andrew Carr, in tayle. 1499. September 12. Robert Mounteney son & heir of John Mounteney [?] miles seeks to be admitted to land at Creswick. 1543. September 21. John son & heir of Nicholas Mounteney seeks to be admitted to lands in Creswick. 1543. Sept. 21. John son & heir of Nicholas Mounteney, armiger seeks to be admitted to lands in Ecclesfield. 1565. December 19. Thomas Cotton, arm., and Barbara his **wife** surrender 1 Messuage 1 cottage & 1 Bovat now in the holding of Henry Shaw and Robert Haldham to John Mounteney, gen. 1568. April 6. Ralph Croft surrenders all his customary tenements &c. within the parish of Ecclesfield to his own use for life and after his decease to the use & behoof of Nicolae Mounteney of Rotherham, younger son of John Mounteney, late of Creswick, deceased, with remainder to Charles Hill, of Ecclesfield, butcher ; with remainder to Thomas Hill, son of Charles Hill aforesaid. 1597. january 11. At a court held at Sheffield, it is found that John Mounteney, armiger, has lately died seized of 2 Messuages, & 2 Bovats in Creswick, and that Thomas Mounteney is his son & heir, and of full age.—At the same court it is also shown that the same John Mounteney, armiger, deceased, did surrender by the hands of Ralph Leo & Nicholas Shirecliffe, 1 Messuage, 1 cottage & 1 Bovat in Ecclesfield, which he had by the surrender of Thomas Cotton and Barbara his wife, to the use & behoof of Nicholas Mounteney his son, who seeks to be admitted to the same.

The points in the Mountney pedigree on which genealogists seem most to differ are :—1. Who was Robert Mountney, of Cowley, living ano. 1499, the son of ? 2. Was John Mountney, who succeeded him, his son, or a relative not so closely allied ?—In Brocks' MSS. The College of Arms [i, I.C.B., fol. 246] Robert is made to be the son of Nicholas Mountney (second son of Sir John Mountney, Knt.], by Isabel, his wife, daughter of Robert Drax, of Woodhall, and that he had a brother Nicholas and a sister Isabel, who married Mr. John Denman.—Robert Mountney **is made to marry Isabel, daughter of** Nicholas Wortley, of Wortley, and relict of John Bosvile, of Ardsley, by whom he had issue a daughter Beatrix, wife of Robert Thwaites, of Marston. Again [93, I.C.B., fol. 30], Robert is made to be the son of Thomas Mountency (eldest son of Sir John Mountney, Knt.], by Maud, his wife, daughter of John Fitzwilliam, of Woodhall.—Robert Mountney is here made to marry Ann, daughter of Nicholas Wortley, of Wortley, and to have issue a son John Mountney, who, by his wife Joan, was father of Barbara Mountney, wife of Robert Thwaites, of Marston.—In Dugdale's visitation, ano. 1665, Robert Mountney is made to be son of Sir John Mountney, Knt., and to have issue a daughter Barbara, wife of Robert Thwaites, of Marston.—Mr. Hunter, in the pedigree of this family in his "History of Hallamshire," makes Robert Mountney to be son of Nicholas, and to have issue John, who was father of Barbara, wife of Robert Thwaites, of Marston.—Perhaps the reader, by using the evidences contained in this note, may be able to clear up these two much disputed points.

1476. Jan. 19. Perceval Creasacre, of Darnborough, mentions in his will that he wishes to be buried near to the tomb of Alice, his wife, who was daughter of Thomas Mountney. 1489. April 21. Dispensation for Robert Mountney and Isabel Boswell to marry ; related twice in the 4th degree—Issued by Julian, Cardinal Bishop of Ostia. 22 Dec., 5 INNOCENT, VIII. [Test. Ebor., vol. iii., fol. 354]. Robert and Anthony Mountney were members of the Guild of Corpus Christi, in the City of York. [Surtees Soc., vol. 57, folio 174.]

It. john Cowmbe	vjs. & viijd.
Sm xjli. vijs. vjd.	
Willm. Browne senior & Henrwy Howland	. . . . .
And ye first ye said Willm. & herre owyth of ye Rent of martmes as last past as it Apeyrs by a byll unto them delivd the said day.	
Also remayns in the hands of ye tenands of our lady the same day ye witsonday rente last past ye sm...	iiijli. iiijs. . . .

1521.

Md. that Mayst Mountenay hath delivd into ye graves hand of such money yt he haith ressayvyd of Sr. Thoms twisbe by hym gewyne unto ye church of Eckylisfelde toward the byyng a Sewytt of westemet the secnd day of july anno vicessimo pmo ...	xxvjs. viijd.

1522.

. . . . . . (beq ?) west of Thoms Wilkynson ...	iijs. iiijd.
[222] These Ayre the Namys of the churmastis	
Robert Hyll Willm. Ssoons'.	
Artur greves & Thoms. Schole	

1524.

Md. that Saynt johns greyffs haith maid Reckenyng the xxjti day of july (in) ye yeir of our Lord an. CCCCC and xxiiijti and thai ar cleyrly dischargyd.	
Md. Reckenyd wt Sant Machaell greyffs in ye same yeir & day afore wrytyne and yai have in their hands ...	vjs. viijd.
It. john Ecar of ye towne owys of Sant johns rent ...	xxs.
It. john Parker haith paid to lawrence Ayston of yar byerley ...	iiijli. xxs.
It. john Clerke haith paid to lawrenc Ayston for yar byerley ...	xxs.
Md. yt our lady greyffs haith maid their acowns In ye day & yeir afoyrs wrytyn and thai ar cleyrly dischargyd sayffyng the Detts owyng ungethered.	
It. ye fyrst of maist Mountency ...	xijs.
It. of Thomas Stevynson ...	vjs.
It. of john hyll ...	iiijs.
It. of Willm Turnley ...	xijd.
John Growb ...	xvd.
It. of Thomas homblocke ...	vjs.
Md. yt yr remaynyth of ye lyght money of ye town byerley In ye hauds of John Schryclyff ...	viijs.
Md. yt yr remaynyth in ye hands of John Clerke of ye lyght money of ye Shyre byerley ...	ixs.

[222] i.e. "These are the names of the Churchwardens."

Md. that Rawff Lee haith receyvid of **our lady lyght** of ye Weitley byerley & paid hit agayn In ye yeir of owr **Lord** M.CCCC.xxiiij afore Maist holmes & Mast' Nicolas & other moo of ye pychyng[228] to ye church use... ... ...   **xiijs. xd.**

Md. that yr remaynyth In ye HANDS of Thos. Bullus of ye lyght Detts owyng to ye Church of Eglissfeld A.' dni M.'D.'xxiiij.' In p'ms Alexandr Schyrclyff p'messys and g'unts (*promises & grants*) a foyre maist holme ye vicar of Eglisfeld mist Nicolas Mountney and ye Church maistys wt other moo of ye pychyng to pay afore ye fest of Saynt Marten in Wyntr. ... ...   **viijs.**

Also ye said Alexandr. g'unts to pay at ye fest of the exaltacion of ye Croyse In ye yeir of owr lord A thousand foyf hondyth feyff twenty towerds a seutie of vestiments. ... ...   **xlvs.**

St. John Clerke g'unts to pay at ye fest of Saynt Michaell ye archangell   **xld.**

It. Ric Ecar g'unts to pay at ye fest of Sant Michaell & at ye fest of ye **nativite of** our lord by evyn portions ...   **ixs. viijd.**

It. Maist Nicolas Denniot gent. g'unts to pay at ye fest of Saynt Marten in Wyntr. and **at** ye fest of pentecost next folowyng by evyn portions...   **xs. vd.**

It. Maist' Nicolas Mountney for ye beriall of Maisty's Mountney **bys wyff** g'unts to pay at ye fest of Saynt Michaell ye archangell ...   **vjs. viiijd.**

It. john p'ker (*Parker*) grants to pay at **ye fest** of **Sant** Michaell & ye nativite of owr lord god by evyn portions ...   **xiijs. iiijd.**

Itm. Ric Rawson g'unts to pay at ye fest of ye nativite of owr lord ...   **xld.**

It. Willm. Browne of Creswek g'unts to pay at Michael messe ...   **xviijd.**

Md. that ther ys remayng of angell halpens And other yll money ...   **vjs. viijd.**

It. Ric Rawson ... ...   **ijs.**

Med. that Willm Browne and **herre** howland hays payd to Sr. Richard Cowp' (*Cowper*) & Sr. Willm Ev'yngham of our ladys money   **xs.**

Mr. Nicolas Mountenay   **xvs.**

1529—1530.

Md. that the Kyrkmaisters haith made theyr Recknyngs on New yers day ye xx' yer of ye reyn of Kyng Herre ye eight and they ayre in debet lykwys owr lady grayves the same day haith made theyr recknyng and they **ayr in** debet   **iiijli. xjs. & ijd.**

And of thys the sayd owr lady grayves haith paid to Sr. Ric. Cowper And to Sr Willm ev'yngham   **xxviijs.**

To Sr. john Stauefurthe for a qters (*quarter's*) wags paiabill at Candelmas after next.   **xxvjs. viijd.**

It. to Sr. john Stauefurthe paiabill at Sant Hellin day ...   **xxvjs. viijd.**

It. paid to Sr. Richard Cowp' & to Sr. Willm. Ev'yngham ... ...   **xlviijs. iiijd.**

of ye wich sm was takyne of owt of ye beqwest of Sr. Thoms Clark delived by ye hand of Sr. Thoms Twisbe ...   **xxvjs. viijd.**

[228] "Parishioners."

And of our lady **rents** ...	xxs. xxd.
It. for wesching of the **weylls & too Awbs (Albs)**	iijd.
It. payd **for braggs** ...	jd.
It. paid **to James Ford** same for medyng of a ball collor ...	jd.

[N.B. *The following also probably belong to the years 1529-1530.*—ED.]

Towarde a sewite of westemets.

It. the bequest of Mr. Thoms Rokbe xli to be askyd of Mr. provest of rotherm.	
It. for ye bereall of Mr. Rokkeby ...	vjs. & viijd.
It. for ye bereall of Thomas **Shyrtclyff** ...	vjs. & viijd.
It. owyng for ye beqweste of ye same **Willm** toward ye yemags (images)	xs.
It. for hys taxe to ye rod loft ...	xs.
It. for ye bereall of John **Wylkynson** ...	iijs. & iiijd.
It. of Robert Brownele ...	vjs. & viijd.
It. **of George Cutt wyff** ...	iijs. & iiijd.
[224] It. owyng **for ye beqwest of john Stanefurth of wadeslay**. ...	iijs.
[225] It. for the bereall of Mr. Nicholas Ev'yngm ...	xjs. & viijd.
It. for **the beryall of** Thoms Schyrtclyff ...	vjs. & viijd.
[226] It. **for the beryall of** Willm Schyyrtclyff ...	vjs. & viijd.

[224] 1521. Will of John Stanfurth, of Wadislay, **in the parish of Ecclesfield.**—To be buried in the Churchyard at Ecclesfield.—To a suit of vestments iijs. & iiijd.—Robert and Nicolas Stanfurth my sons **executors.**—Witnesses Sir John Stanfurth, priest; Thomas Creswick and John Parkyn.—Proved 20 Nov., 1522.

[225] 1437. Johannes Jepson surrenders 1 Bovat in Westmonhalgh near Oughtibridge to **Willielmus de Dows.** 1463. july 9. **Roger** Dower surrenders land &c. in **Westnall** near Oughtibridge to Thomas Dower. 1483. **june 1.** Thomas Dower surrenders the same to John **Dower his son** & heir. 1494. John Dower was tried for felony, murder, and robbery of a poor fiddler, and was sentenced by the court "*per collu pendere usque mortum esset.*" 1495. Dec. 1. Thomas Dore seeks to be admitted as son & heir of John Dore deceased. 1510. Dec. 10. Thomas Dore son & heir of **John** Dore surrenders land &c. called Haslehough to Henry Everingham, *armiger*. 1516. Thomas Everingham *Armiger*, seeks **to be admitted as** son & heir of Henry Everingham. 1517 (?). April 8. Henry Everingham seeks to be **admitted as son & heir of Thomas** Everingham. 1536. April 5. Henry Everingham, *armiger*, surrenders the same to Alice Hobson for life, and after her decease to the right heirs of the said Henry. 1549. March 19. Henry Everingham, senior, *armiger*, surrenders **the same to** the use & behoof of Henry Hall. [*Court Rolls.*]

Dr. Sykes, of Doncaster, has kindly supplied me with the following notes from wills and administrations at York :—1475. Oct. 10. Administration of the goods of Thomas Everingham of Silkstone granted to Ann his widow and Richard his son. 1482. **Sept. 7.** Agnes Everingham of Darthington [*i.e.*, Darrington] widow.—To be buried in the church of Egglesfield.—Dmn. Thomas Clarke and Dmn. Thomas Everingham executors.—Thomas Everingham Esquire and Thomas Vavasor supervisors.—Proved 8 October, 1482. 1482. Aug. 31. Richard Everingham of Darthington.—My brother Richard (*sic*.)—Edmund & John Everingham my sons.—My brother Robert Everingham, executor, **Dmn.** Thomas Clarke, vicar of Ecclesfield, and my brother Henry Everingham, supervisors.—Proved 8 October, **1482.** 1553. May 5. Christopher Everingham, of Egglesfield.—My brother John Everingham.—My brother Richard Everingham.—Catherine Keye.—Joane daughter of Thomas Robinson, Nicholas and Richard sons of Thomas Robinson, my brother in law.—My brother Sir William Everingham.—My father William Everingham.—Thomas Robinson and Agnes my sister.—Proved **30 March,** 1554. **1556.** july 16. Sir William Everingham, priest, at Ecclesfeld.—To the buying of **a fourth bell vjs. & viijd.**—Richard, Nicolas, John, Agnes, Isabel and Alice.—**Catherine Eyes** (?) **widow.—Proved 17 Nov.,** 1556.

[226] 1526. **October 5.** William Shirecliffe, of Ecclesfield.—" To the hye altar iijs. iiijd."—To Henry Shirecliffe "my sworde and my buttler."—To Alexander Shirecliffe, my brother, my take of Ecclesfield Kirke during my years. —The half of my goods to my wife.—To Richard Whitehed a jacket.—To Robert Ridlay a jacket.—To George Clerk,

It. john Parker debet	... ...	vijs. & vd.
It. Sr. Ri. Rawson debet	... ...	iiijs. & vd.
It. of the beqwest of jenet Schyrtclyff towards a **sewyte of westmet**		xxs.
It. for the beqwest of Rawff Wilkynson	... ...	ijs. & iiijd.

1535—1536.

Med. that Robert Wille haith mad hys Acouns the xijth day of may the **yere and the Regn** of Kyng Henry ye viijth. xxvijth. ffor all such **chyrch** guds as he haith recevyd into his hands sawyng ye said **Robt. is** in debet to ye chyrch ... ... xxs. & jd.

It. ther is in the hands of Petur Pkyne of Sant **Antony moneye** xjs. & ijd.
It. ther is in the hands of Willm. browne of Sant loy money xviijs.
Md. that Willm. browne haith mad hys Acounes ye same day and ye yeer a bouff writtyn of owre lady fynes and he is in debeth to ye same xjs. & xd.

Md. that thies ayre ye detts oyng to the church duodecimo die maij Anno Regni regis Henrici octavi vicesimo septimo.

ffirst in the hands of Sr. Robert Cobcroft towards a crosse, of ye beqwest of Richard Colle ... ... xxs.
It. of the bequest of Elezabet Wodkyrk ... ... xijd.
It. of the bequest of Johane Carllyll ... ... xvjd.
It. of the bequest of Ellyne Wille ... ... xiiijs.
It. of the bequest of Willm Mathema(n) lyyng **in hys hands of ye said Willm.** ... ... vjs. & xd.
It. of the bequest of johane Wille ... ... vjs. & viijd.
It. of the bequest of xptoferor Tore... ... ... iijs. & iiijd.
It. of the bequest of John Colle ynger ... ... xxs.
It. of the beqwest of Alexand. Schireliff ... ... xs.
[227] It. of the bequest of Willm. Colle ... ... **xxd.**
It. in ye hand of Thomas Wylkynson ... ... lijs. & iiijd.
It. Sr. **john** Stynyforth Wylls & grawnts to be takyn & payd as ys **A bove** wrytyn ... ... xs. ut supa. pt. [patet].
It. yer ys in Sr. **Robert** Cobcrofts hands for Mr. john Mownt. (**Mounteney**) as ys **A** bove wrytyn ... ... xxd. ut supa. pt.
It. yer remayngs in Herry Holand hands ... ... xxd. ut supa. pat.

Thes Ayr the detts owyng unto our lady of Ecclesfeld the xxi day **of** Novebr ye xxvijth **yer of rg** of Kyng Herre ye viijth.

It. for waxe ... ... ijs.
It. receyvyd **for wod** ... iijs. iiijd.

my work day suit and vjs. viijd.—Sir John Stancforth.—James Fordsame.—The residue of my goods to Lawrence Smith, whom I do appoint my true & lawful executor.—Witnesses Maister Holmes—Sir Edward Richardson, John Stanfurth, John Parker & Richard Whitebed.—Proved 23 Dec., 1526.

[227] 1532. March 20. William Collye, of Ecclesfield.—To be buried in the Churchyard at Ecclesfield.—To Ecclesfield Church xxd.—To Sir Robert Cobcroft xvjd.—To Richard Hull xvjd.—To Thomas Wilkinson xvjd.—To John Jepson viijd.—To Thomas Collye my son xls.—To Margaret Bullus xls., "a mantill and my beste coverlett."—To

It. receyvyd of john Pker & john Morhows for wod	...	iijs. xd.
It. john Rodds ows to our lady	...	iij iij
It. woying of john Hertlay for ye cunstabilship	...	......
It. woying of Bertilmew Cowp' of worall ...	...	viijd.
It. woying of Willm. Tornlay for on yer rent ...	...	ijs.

Md. off ye Rentall betakyn & delyvyd to ye nowe grevys Thoms Day and Herry Shryrclyff iijli. xjs. xd. ut postea pat. and lant to Thome senieri jefson de pecuniis bte Marie p Willm bec'.

It. off ye beqwest off Rawyff Lye to ye crosse ... .

1537.

...... Ecclesie de Ecclesfeld an'. dni 1537.

...... Artur Greyve Robt Hyll Thoms Shawe & Wyllelm Stonys Receptiones p'dictor &c. a pmo die jan. . . usq ad anu fut . . . .

In pmis receyvyd off John Parkar off or ladys money	... ...	xs.
It. off Robert Wylly off ye church money ...	... ...	xvijs. ixd.
It. off Thoms Dey off ye lyght money ...	... ...	ijs. iiijd.
It. off Peter Parkyn	... ..	iiijs. iiijd.
It. off Thoms Wylkynson	... ...	xld.
It. off Bartylmewo Cowper	... ...	vijs. vjd.
It. Boroyd off or lady grevys to ye bell castying	... ...	xxs.
It. off ye same grevys to ye organs	... ...	vjs. viijd.

P. Sepulturis.

It. off Mr. Nycolas Mawntney for hs wyff beryall	... ...	xld.
It. off Robert Wylly for both hys wyvys ye half...	... ...	vjs. viijd.
[228] It. for Rauff Lye	... ...	vjs. viijd.
It. off Mr. Rokeby p puero	... ...	xld.
It. off john Parker	... ...	xld.
It. off Wyllm bromeley for osgothorpe wyff	... ...	xxd.
It. off Edmund Wyter (winter) bothem wyff	... ...	xld.
Md. yat we had at ye church Ale declare	... ...	xviijs. ijd.

Sma. total recept vli. xviijs. vjd.

Soluta a pdict'talio libro.]

It. payd to Thoms Twigge for bleddyg (blending) lyme & sand	...	iiijd.
It. to ye clerke wyffe for washyng	... ...	vjd.
It. to Wyllm. Hyll for ye bellys & feyng (fixing) tymber	... ...	ijd.

John Collye my son ij oxen.—To Richard Collye my son i ox & i cow.—To John Raywood i cow.—Raulph Cawood.—To Katherine Collye "my best cow."—George Bownes wife.—Alice daughter of Richard Collye and Johanna daughter of William Bullos.—Thomas and Margaret children of Richard Collye.—Proved 13 November, 1533.

[228] 1537. May 3. Ralphe Lee, of Ecclesfield.—To be buried in the Church at Ecclesfield.—To the Church vjs. & viijd.—My daughters, Elizabeth, Alice and Anne.—To Nicholas son of Thomas Lee xls.—My sons Robert, Richard and James Lee.—Agnes Clarke.—To the children of Thomas Bullus xlijs. & iiijd.—Johanna my wife, Ralph and John my sons my executors.—John Parker, John Bulloke, John Berryne, Richard Wilkinson, Thomas Wilkinson, and Edmund Philipe, overseers.—Proved 3 Oct., 1537.

[229] It. for An Amys ... ... vij*d*.
It. gyvyn to ye bell fonder for **hys dynar** ... iiij*d*.
It. for a cord to ye vayle ... ... j*d*.
It. gyvyn to john Carre for goyng to ye **bell fowndr** ij*d*.
It. for a lant hord (*lantern ?*) ... .. vij*d*.
It. for fat dryng & carryng A carbyll rope ... iiij*d*.
for spens (*expences ?*) to ye bell ffownder & hys hors iiij*d*.
Rychard Brydge for ye bellys iiij*d*.
[230] Recept A ppot Eccles. Ano. di 1538.
A pmo die januarij Ad ann futuru
In pmis recept off john Parkar off or ladys money ... xj*s*.
It. off Pet pkyn ... ... iiij*s*.
It. off Rychard Hyll ... ... xv*s*. ij*d*.
It. off Thoms Wylkynson **off longly** ... ... xj*s*. v*d*.
It. off **Bartylmewe Cowper** ... ... vij*s*.
It. off john pker (*parker*) & Wyllm browne for ij sergys ... vj*d*.
It. for ye beryall off Thoms Stonys... ... ... xl*d*.
   Sma. recept ... ... liij*s*. j*d*.
   Coputat ad Ann soqucte
Recept pposit An'. Di 1539. Apmo die januarij Annu futuru.
In pmis receyvyd by ye bequeste off Rye Hobson ... ... vj*s*. viij*d*.
It. by ye bequest off Thoms Stonys ... ... iij*s*. iiij*d*.
and both yes bequests was patt ito (*into*) ye hands off Sr Rob **Cob** (*croft*)
It. gatheryd in ye Church for lyght ... ... iiij*s*. ij*d*.
It. off Wyllm bromely for hs wyff beryall ... ... iij*s*. iiij*d*.
It. Md. yt john pkar receyvyd & had off Wyllm **Stonys for ye bell** . . . . .
It. gatheryd i (*in*) yo chyrch on Passyon Sondey ... iij*s*. iiij*d*.
   Recept ppt An'. Dni 1540 a pmo die januarij.
It. pmis receyvyd off yo lyght money for ye towne byreley ... iiij*s*.
It. off ye Sowghawe (*Southey*) byrelawe ... vj*s*. ij*d*.
It. off Mortoley (*Mortomley*) byrelawe ... vj*s*.
It. for ye beryall of Mr. Rokeby Chyld
It. for ye beryall off Mr. Wubewell Chyld
It. for ye beryall off St. Rychard Cobecroft pst (*priest*)
It. for ye beryall off Thome Shyrelyff
It. off Wyllm Bromely for Osgothorpe wyff
It. off Herry Holand for hys son beryall
It. gatheryd in Sawthawe byrle to ye bybyll
   Sm. xxix*s*. iiij*d*.
   Recept a pposit Ano. Dni. 1541.
In pmis A wedder shepe of Rye Browne ye pryc ij*s*. ij*d*.

---

[229] An amice was a square linen cloth worn by priests.

[230] This means "the receipts of those placed over the Church," or, in other words, "the Churchwardens' receipts."

It. gatheryd i Sawthawe byrloy to ye lyght	vs. ijd.
It. gatheryd i Sawthawe byrele to ye bybyll	iijs. viijd.
It. gatheryd in ye towne byreley ye on syde to ye bybyll	xviijd.
It. gatheryd i ye towne byreloy ye nether syde for lyghts	iijs. ijd.
It. gatheryd by Wyllm Browne & Wyllm Ward to lyghts	xxjd.
It. gatheryd i Mortoley byrlowe to ye bybyll	ixs.
It. to ye lyghts i Mortoley byrloy	vijs. xd.
In the hands of Pet Pken & Remenyng	xjs. vjd.
of that he hath payd	vjs.

Sma. xxxiiijs. iijd. comput ad ann sequo.

1542.

Md. that Sr. John Stanyforth wylls & grants yt yer shall be takyn vs. off john Royds off ye chappell wych he lent to hym & yat ys iijs. for john Stanyforth off Waddysley & ijs. for hymselff to a sewte off vestments ... ...

. . . . postea vult & concedit ijs. ad altare bte Marie . . . . . . iijs. dat ad suum altare . . . . . . pd de Wadsley test Dno Ricardo Cowp' et (Nichol) ao Stanyford.

Postea locand &c.

Md. hec oia (omnia) computata et Sumata fuisse p Edwardu hadfeld clericu et comits Solopie Receptore Ano. dni. 1542 iiijto. die mensis Aprilis et smd. totalis solut eode anno ac p die fuit xiijli. xxix. et remanebat eode tepore in manibus ppositoru vs. et Dn Robert Cobecroft habuit xs. (ut alias patet) quo p vestiment solvit apd Roche &c.

Recept a pposit Ano. Dni 1542.

a primo die januariij ad Ann futuru.

In pmis gatheryd i Sauthawe byrley to ye lyghts ...	. . . . . .
It. gatheryd i ye towneno byreley ye nethersyde for lyghts ...	. . . . . .
It. gatheryd by Robert Hyll & Wyllm Ward to ye lyghts ...	ijs.
It. in Mortoley byreley to ye lyghts...	vijs. vjd.

Sma; xxs. vd.

Md. that on the xxvij day off Auguste in ye yere off or lord M.CCCC.xlij the pyshenars was callyd before Mr. Wombewell and Maystr. Mowntney to see for or lady rents & for a howse that john Parker had boght off john Royds off ye chapell where in ther was gyvyn to or lady sues (services) xijd. And then yt was agreyd that john Parkar shuld be clerely aquytyd in hys howse & john Royds & hys wyff to gyff ye seyd xijd. uppe the nexte cowrte day in a nother howse by at ye Kyrke stele and to pforme that truly wt. hys wyffe where he was behynd for rererages vs. he peyd xxd. and they forgaff him ye xld. and other xld. boreyd off or lady money & condycyonally to pforme thgs & wytnes Mr. Wombewell herry Shyrclyff Thomas Deye wt. many moo.

Md. that yo sayd day and yere John Parkar gaff uppe by a Straur . . . . .
Wyllm browne herry Shyrclyff and Thome day **ye shoppe yat he**
buyldyd in ye churche yarde syde and grawntyd to gyff hyt frely to
or. lady sues (*services*) after his discese and they to take yt uppe in
the courte by fyne and they to have hys copy delyvyd & to pey **yo**
Kyngs fyne vj*d*. &c. It. he grawntyd to pay peceably ye xvj*d*.
gyvyn by Thom. Barneby in too closys at hartley wt all arerages
. . . . . .

Md. (**ut supra**) yat john Royds senior & hys wyff dyd not come **as he**
pmysyd to ye coyrte & hys son john sayd he shuld nott nor hys
wyff wold not bot hys son & hys wyff payd to or. lady greves xl*d*.
& **he hath ye copy that tells** wher ye xij*d*. shuld **be** takyn &c. and
. . . . **xl***d***. to** ye hye Alter &c. It. ther was pdonyd &
forgyvyn then so codycyonally all arrerages &c.

1543.

Mod. that Robert Wille haith paid to **the** church nedeyes **of ye money**
that he haith receyvyd of ye Kyrke Ayll . . . . **marhs and**
vs. xj*d*.

Payd to Robert Wille toward ye ymage (*imago*) gilldyng		
It. for the beqwest of Willm. Stanefurth		ijs.
It. for the beqwest of Herr Sha wiff		xx*d*.
It. of Thoms Slatter wiff		vj*d*.
It. payd for a surples to ye clarke		ijs. iij*d*.
It. for ye makyng of it		vj*d*.
It. paid for bred		vj*d*.
It. paid to perlynton for a bell streyn & for mendyng of another ...		xiiij*d*.
It. paid to James Hodsone for makyng of iiij bellcollers ...		xiiij*d*.
It. paid to Robert Dawyre medyng (*mending*) a bell wheyll ...		iij*d*.
It. paid to plynton for a weyk (*week*)		iij*d*.
[281] It. paid to ye clerke for whessyng of ye cloyss		ij*d*.
It. paid for a bellstreng to ye sanctus **bell**		viij*d*.
It. paid to Robert Dawyr for a day wark & for tymbyr to **ye bells** ...		viij*d*.
It. paid for naylls		ij*d*.
It. paid to james Hodsone for me(n)dyng of ye bell collers ...		ij*d*.
And at the fawrth (*fourth*) Kyrk Aill ye said Robert dyd receyvd ...		xxijs. vj*d*.
And at ye fifth Kyrk ayll ye said Robert haith receyvyd xxijs. vj*d*.	**Recept**	

Ano. Dni. 1543 A primo die januarij usq ad Ann. futur

In primis gatheryd in ye towne byrelay		vjs.
It. in Mortomlay bryelawe ...		vjs. ix*d*.
It. in Sawthawe ...		vjs. **xd**.
It. for ye beryall off jamys Morley		. . . . . .

[281] Item, paid to the clerk for washing of the clothes.

It. for ye beryall off Petr. P'kyn (*Parkin*) wyffe ... ...
It. for ye beryall of Mayst. Nicolas Mountney ... ...
It. for the bequest off xpor. Torre (ut infra pat.) payd by Shawe ... iijs. iiijd.
It. p. sepultura ij pueror Ricardi Everyngam ... ...

Recepta A primo die januarij usq. Ad Ann futur. Anno Dmni 1544.

It. primis Receyvyd off Richard Hyll for ye towne byrelowe ... vj. ijd.
It. off Pet. P'ken & Thome Howseley for Mortomley byrelowe to the lyghts ... ... iiijs. & viijd.
It. for Sowthawe byreley ... ... vijs.
It. off Thome Dey to ye lyghts ... ... xjd.
It. off Robert P'kyn & Wyllm berde ... ... ixd.
It. gatheryd in ye church ... ... iijs. iiijd.
It. gatheryd in ye churche for bok me(n)dyng ... ... vs. viiijd.
[232] It. Receyvyd off john Parker to go to Yorke ... ... iijs.
It. off Thome Prestley ... ... xijd.
It. off Herry Rychardson ... ... iiijd.
Thome Shawe ... ... xviijd.
It. off Robert Hyll for ye same use... ... ... iijs.

Sm. xxxvs. & xd.

[232] Mr. **Charles Jackson**, of Balby, has kindly supplied me with an abstract of the will of John Parker, which I here give :—1552, 6 Edw. vi., feb. 26.—John Parker, of Egglesfeld, co. York.—My body to be buried by my wife's in the Church of our blessed Lady in Egglesfeld.—To Thomas Parker, my son, a clock, a chime, a missall, a chalice, a super altare and vestments, and one altar cloth, as heirlooms.—To the said Thomas Parker my tenement I hold of the grant of Francis, Earl of Shrewsbury, with **a water-wheel and watercourse, at** Wadsley Bridge, during the term that I have.—To Thomas Parker and Richard **Parker, my sons, my tenement or ferm** of Wadsley Smithies and Treeton Smithies, with Treeton Mill during my lord's pleasure, **with all the iron** &c.—To Richard Parker, my son, my smythye at Whitley, my take of **my wheel under Egglesfeld, with a stithe** &c. and my sithe-mark, if he be aminded to occupy the occupation.—To **Thomas Parker and Richard** Parker, Thomas Howsley, and George Mawer, all raiment unbequeathed, to be equally **divided.—To the wife of the said** Thomas Parker the best belt that was my second wife's.—To the wife of the said Richard Parker a pair **of the best beeds** that were my said wife's.—To Cielie Parker, my wife, all the silver and gold of mine that she hath in **her custody, one iron-bound chest, and all the** silver and gold therein, as it standeth at Henry Savin's.—To Frances Parker my daughter.—And also, whereas there are eight keys belonging to the said chest, I will that Cicily my wife have the keeping of two of them, Nicholas Grace other two, Thomas Parker other two, and Thomas Howsley other two.—Nicholas Grace, **son of Thomas** Parker ; Thomas Howsley and Elizabeth his wife, and their children ; George Mawer, Agnes his wife, and their children.—My Granddaughter Margaret **Parker, daughter of** Thomas Parker—Effame Howsley.—Forty of the poorest people in Egglesfeld **to** have a peck of **rye, or sixpence** in money. **Cicily Parker**, my wife, Frances Parker, my daughter, Thomas Howsley, my **son-in-law, and George** Mawer, my son-in-law, to be executors.—Robert Swift, of Beighton, Esq. ; Robert Blunt, gentleman ; **Thomas Parker**, and Nicholas **Grace, supervisors.—Witnesses** Sir Edmund Robinson, chaplain, Robert Blunt, gent., Humphrey Staniforth, and Edward Bower.—I have bought of Richard Parker, my son, a messuage &c. in Egglesfeld, and other lands &c.—To the church of Egglesfeld **xxs. towards the** buying of two **bells**, to be paid at such times as the parishioners shall fortune to buy and pay for the said bells, and not else.—Cicily, my wife, to keep and find Frances, my daughter, meat, drink, and clothing till she comes to lawful age, and for the profits of her lands.—Proved at York, 27 April, 1555.

1514. Nov. 21. George More surrenders 1 close **in Warder de Shirecliffe called Elliott field to his own use** and the use of Ann his wife.—*Court Rolls*.

Cicily wife of John **Parker above is probably identical with Cicilia Parker, who married William Whitmore** ano. 1558. [Vide note 2.]

1545.

Recepta A primo die januarij Ano. Dni 1545. usq. Ad Ann. ffuturum &c.

ffor lyghts. In primis Reyceyvyd off Wyllm Warde & Rye Hyll for ye towne byrelowe ...	vjs. xjd.
It. off Nycolas Hadfeld & Thome Wylkynson for Sawythowe ...	vijs. ijd.
It. off Thome Dey for Butterworth ...	xjd.
It. off Radulph Lye for lyghts ...	iiijs.
It. off Robert Parkyn ...	xxjd.
It. Receyvyd for ij gauge off feloys ...	iiijs. vjd.
It. for A nother gauge ...	xvjd.
It. for vj feyloys ...	viijd.
It. for ye browyse off ye tree ...	xviijd.
It. Receyvyd off Rychard Hyll to go to Yorke ...	xs.
It. off Thomas Shawe ...	xviijd.
It. off Wyllm Ward for A gaugge of feloys ...	xxjd.
It. gatheryd in ye churche ...	ijs. vjd.
It. by ye bequest off Wyllm Berdsell ...	ijs.

Sm Totalis xviijli. xvijs.

N.B. Here occurs a gap in the Churchwardens' Accounts until the year 1568.—EDITOR.

INDEX OF PERSONS.

INSTRUCTIONS.

All numbers refer to the pages alone ; N. after a number means that the name occurs in a note on that page ; N., *bis*, &c., means that the name occurs in two notes on the same page ; the number of times the same name occurs in the same note is not indicated ; a plain number, with *bis*, *ter*, &c., after it, means that the name occurs twice or thrice, &c., **on the same page.**

N.B. The different modes of spelling both Christian and Surnames are not given in full in this index, but rather I have tried to bring all under as few headings as possible.

EDITOR.

ADAMS,
   Eliz., 41 N.
   John, 41 N.
ADAMSON,
   Dorothy, 117.
   Edward, 2 N.
   Joan, 6.
   John, 2 N.
   Mary, 2 N.
   Richard, 2, 2 N.
   William, 102, 117.
ALCOCK,
   Arthur, 21 N.
   Elizabeth, 121 N.
   Isabel, 21 N.
ALDAM,
   Alexander, 98.
   Ann, 101.
   Francis, 109.
   Lucy, 27.
   Thomas, 97.
ALLEN,
   Ann, 73.
   Frances, 63.
   Hugh, 34, 63.
   Robert, 73.
   William, 20, 38.
ALLINSON, or ALLYNSON,
   Adam, 2 N.
   Henry, 146.
ANDREW,
   Thomas, **82 N.**
ARLINGTON,
   Surlee, 130 N.
ARMROYD,
   Francis, 44.
ARSDALE,
   William, 30.
ARTHUR,
   Francis, 55.
   George, 18.
   William, 55.
ASHTON,
   Agnes, 52.
   Alexander, 62.
   Alice, 55.
   Ann, 56, 60, 73.
   Brian, 22, 48, 51, 56, **60.**
   Elizabeth, 39, 57.
   George, 41, 73, 77.
   Helen, 51.

ASHTON (*continued*),
   Henry, 76.
   John, 132.
   Mary, 77.
   Robert, 48.
   Thomas, 42, 43.
   William, 52, 55, 57, **62**, 72 *bis*, 76.
ASKEW,
   Margaret, 41, **41** N.
ATKINSON,
   Ann, 8.
   Mr., 112.
   Thomas, 87.
AWWOOD,
   Helen, 5.
AYSTON,
   Lawrence, 153 *bis*.
BACON,
   Ann, 41.
   Helen, 30.
   Robert, 43.
BAGSHAWE,
   Elizabeth, 30.
BALL,
   Effame, 86.
   Johanna, 96.
   Robert, 89.
   Roland, 86.
   Widow, 131.
BAMFORD,
   Leonard, 107 N.
BANKES,
   James, 6, 127.
   Margery, 118.
   Nicholas, 109.
   Thomas, 129 N.
BANYSTER,
   Barbara, 90 N., 121 N., 130 N.
   Henry, 20, 20 N., 90 N., 121 N., 130 N.
   Jane, 20 N.
   Sarah, 130 N.
   William, 130 N.
BARBER,
   Alice, 2, 62.
   Ann, 6, 120 N.
   Dionis, 4.
   Edward, 50, 109.
   Elizabeth, 4, 58, 63, **117.**
   Ellis, 77.
   Emote, 120 N.

BARBER (*continued*),
   Francis, 50, 58, 62, 63, 69, 120 N.
   Helen, 18, 69.
   Henry, 77.
   Hugh, 123 N.
   John, 114 N., **120**, 120 N.
   Margaret, 9.
   Richard, 114 N., 120 N.
   Robert, 37, 68, 120 N.
   Roger, 114, 114 N., 120 N.
   Thomas, 3, 68.
   William, 120 N.
BARBOTT,
   William, **102** N.
BARCROFT,
   John, 140 N.
BARGHE,
   Richard, 97.
BARKER,
   Henry, 72.
   Margaret, **81 N.**
   Richard, 72.
   Robert, 81 N.
BARLET,
   Robert, 14.
BARLEY,
   Jennet, 34.
   Margaret, 48.
   Thomas, 48.
BARLOW,
   Francis, **71.**
   John, 71.
BARNBY,
   Francis, 112 N.
   Thomas, 149 N., 150 N., 160.
BARNSLEY,
   Agnes, 120.
   Ann, 75.
   Elizabeth, 17, 24, 72.
   Ellen, 42, 55.
   Francis, 89.
   George, 41, 49.
   Henry, 7.
   Isabel, 44.
   Jane, 68.
   John, 37, 68, **71, 72, 75.**
   Margaret, 43.
   Mary, 71, 74.
   Robert, 39.
   Rose, 41.
   Thomas, 29, **49, 59, 65.**

INDEX.

BARNSLEY (continued),
  William, 13, 30, 55, 59, 61 ter, 65, 74.
BARTLEMEW,
  Alice, 113.
  John, 116.
BASE,
  Christine, 111.
  Elizabeth, 23.
  John, 99.
  Richard, 7.
BASFORTH, or BASFORD, &c.,
  Dorothy, 57.
  Elizabeth, 55.
  Ellen, 75.
  Francis, 58.
  Johanna, 99.
  John, 33, 58, 60, 62, 65 bis, 67.
  Lucy, 56.
  Mary, 76.
  Nicholas, 67, 119.
  Ralph, 31, 55, 57, 60, 64, 70 bis, 76.
  Richard, 64, 145.
  Robert, 60.
  William, 32, 56, 58 bis, 62, 65 bis, 75.
BASSET,
  Elizabeth, 38.
BASWORTH, see BASFORTH.
BATE,
  Thomas, 4.
BATLEY,
  Cecily, 108.
  Joan, 15.
  Richard, 30.
  Roger, 121.
BATTY,
  Ann, 41 N.
BAXTER,
  William, 21.
BAYLEY,
  Ann, 67.
  Cecily, 146.
  Helen, 107.
  Henry, 14, 67, 136, 146.
  John, 144.
  Richard, 136.
  Robert, 29, 51.
  William, 51.
BAYLIFFE,
  Barbara, 63.
  Francis, 70.
  Henry, 32, 37.
  Isabel, 72.
  Mary, 77.
  Thomas, 68.
  William, 35, 63, 68, **70, 72, 77**.
BAYNES,
  John, 138 N.
  Margaret, 138 N.
BAYS,
  William, 146.
BEALE,
  Effame, 111.
  Elizabeth, 58.
  Helen, 7.
  Robert, 111.
  Thomas, 21.
  Widow, 125.
  William, 14, 19, 42, 77 bis.
BEALEY,
  Jane, 32.
BEAMONDE,
  Elizabeth, 1.
BEANE,
  Ann, 61.
  Catherine, 56, 64.
  Dorothy, 69.
  John, 56 bis, 141 N.
  Nicholas, 33, 61, 64, 69, 75 bis.
BEARDE,
  Agnes, 14, 99 N.

BEARDE (continued),
  Alexander, 14, 25, 47, 84 N., 129 N., 134, 134 N.
  Alice, 26.
  Ann, 18, 118.
  Barbara, 64.
  Charles, 69, 85.
  Effame, 115.
  Elizabeth, 12.
  Emote, 15.
  Helen, 11, 23.
  Henry, 18, 118.
  Isabel, 47.
  John, 72.
  Margaret, 7.
  Richard, 81 N., 109, 127 bis, 134 N.
  Sir Richard, 82 N.
  Robert, 15, 65, 129, 129 N.
  Thomas, 30, 60, 64, 69, 72, 127 bis, 134 N., 143.
  William, 10, 108, 134 N., 161.
  Sir William, 98 N.
BEARDSELL,
  Isabel, 10.
  Lawrence, 131.
  William, 162.
BEATE,
  Alexander, 67.
  Beatrice, 70.
  John, 37, 67, 70, 74.
  Richard, 74.
BECKET,
  George 83.
BEDFELD,
  Agnes, 1, 104.
  Alice, 4.
BEDFORD, or BEDFORTH,
  Alice, 121.
  Henry, 132.
  John, 26 N., 87.
BEIGHTON,
  Alice, 3.
  Ann, 39.
  James, 93.
  Jennet, 23.
  Johanna, 91.
  John, 6, 31, 41, 85.
  Thomas, 5.
  ———, 122 N.
BELL,
  Dorothy, 146.
  John, 51.
  Robert, 51, 146.
BENSON,
  Edward, 143 N.
BERRY,
  Alice, 17.
  Ann, 65.
  Edward, 33, 56, 60, 65, 72 bis, 76.
  Elizabeth, 60.
  Godfrey, 43.
  Isabel, 52.
  John, 29, 56, 57, 60, 64, 65 bis, 102 N., 107, 108, 145.
  Margaret, 64.
  Sarah, 57.
  Thomas, 76.
BERRYNE,
  John, 157 N.
BEVER,
  Alice, 26.
  Ann, 36.
  Frances, 23.
  John, 11, 134.
  Richard, 9, 9 N.
BINGLEY,
  Thomas Henry, 11 N.
  William, 11 N.
BINNS,
  Margaret, 126 N.

BINNS (continued),
  Thomas, 126 N.
BIRKINSHAW,
  Elizabeth, 43.
  George, 32.
  Henry, 2.
  Isabel, 42.
BIRKS,
  Agnes, 9.
  Alice, 65.
  Ann, 57.
  Catherine, 64, 66.
  Dorothy, 70.
  Edward, 69.
  Elizabeth, 12, 34, 49, 60.
  Ellen, 73.
  George, 27, 34, 50, 57 bis, 60, 65, 66, 70, 74 bis, 142.
  Gilbert, 53.
  Johanna, 89.
  John, 52, 65, 141 N.
  Margaret, 61, 115.
  Margery, 5.
  Richard, 9, 50, 110, 110 N., 146.
  Robert, 17.
  Rose, 135.
  Sarah, 68.
  Thomas, 30, 53, 55 bis, 60 bis, 65, 69, 74.
  William, 29, 49, 52, 57, 61, 64, 68, 73, 74, 78 bis.
BIRLEY, or BURLEY,
  Agnes, 103 N.
  Alice, 1, 46, 103 N.
  Ann, 60.
  Christopher, 94 N.
  Dionis, 30.
  Edward, 103, 103 N.
  Elizabeth, 2, 56, 103 N.
  Godfrey, 25, 46, 51, 55, 60, 64, 103N.
  Henricus de, 103 N.
  Henry, 13, 13 N., 103 N., 133.
  Isabella de, 103 N.
  Joana, 8 N., 122.
  Johannes de, 103 N.
  John, 13 N., 103 N., 122.
  Margaret, 13, 103 N.
  Margreta de, 103 N.
  Matilda de, 103 N.
  Nicholas, 13 N., 19, 64, 103 N.
  Richard, 54.
  Thomas, 5, 51, 54.
  William, 8 N., 9 N., 103 N.
  William de, 13 N.
BLACKBURN,
  Thomas 1.
BLACKER,
  Dorothy, 36.
BLAND,
  Agnes, 3.
BLETHWET,
  Dorothy, 4.
BLITHE,
  John, 12 N.
  Thomas, 12 N.
BLOOME, or BLOWME,
  Ann, 150 N.
  Frances, 27.
  Margaret, 21.
  Robert, 81 N.
  Thomas, 150 N.
BLUNT, or BLOUNT,
  George, 19 N.
  Robert, 161 N.
  William, 8.
BLYTHMAN,
  Jennet, 23.
BOALE,
  Alice, 25.

INDEX.

BOOTH,
  Abraham, 126 N.
  Charles, 126 N.
  Jane, 9.
  John, 100 bis.
  Margaret, 97.
  Sarah, 126 N.
  William, 100, 126 N.
BOSVILE, or BOSWELL,
  Isabel, 152 N.
  John, 152 N.
BOWEMAN,
  Ann, 58.
  Henry, 55.
  Isabel, 49.
  John, 67.
  Margaret, 52.
  Richard, 137.
  Robert, 49, 52, 55, 58, 63, 67, 137.
  William, 63.
BOWER, or BOWRE,
  Alexander, 74.
  Ann, 28 bis, 31, 128 N.
  Catherine, 19, 37, 102, 128 N.
  Edmund, 103 N.
  Edward, 103 N., 115 N., 161 N.
  Elizabeth, 4, 11, 18, 23, 49, 55, 99 N., 120, 143.
  Francis, 7, 10, 24, 52, 62, 96, 127, 135 N.
  Hugh, 47, 100 N., 128 N., 139, 141.
  Humphrey, 3, 95.
  Isabel, 93.
  Jennet, 28, 128 N.
  Joan, 13, 139.
  Johanna, 96.
  John, 30, 38, 52, 55, 60, 70, 99 N., 104, 110 N., 115 N., 128 N.
  Margaret, 16, 68, 74.
  Maria, 53.
  Nicholas, 49, 128 N., 138, 143.
  Robert, 25, 104, 143.
  Roger, 114.
  Rosamund, 11.
  Thomas, 6, 22, 28, 47, 49 bis, 53, 60, 62, 68, 127, 128, 139.
  William, 70, 76.
  Winifred, 47, 139.
  . . . . . . , 31.
BOWNES,
  George, 137 N.
BOYE,
  Elizabeth, 23.
  John, 23, 70.
  Mary, 39, 70, 71.
  Robert, 22, 71.
BRABMER,
  Helen, 18.
BRADBURN,
  Ann, 38.
  Isabel, 118.
  Margaret, 108.
  Richard, 113.
  Thomas, 110.
  William, 15, 119.
BRADLEY, see also BROADLEY,
  Alice, 20, 122.
  Ann, 62.
  Elizabeth, 65.
  Francis, 98.
  Hellen, 71.
  John, 71.
  William, 62, 65, 71.
BRADLEY, alias HOLDEN,
  Thomas, 137.
BRAMALD,
  Ann, 43.
  . . . . , 23.
BRAMALL, alias HARRISON,
  Thomas, 145.

BRAMAN,
  Agnes, 16.
BRAMWITH,
  Ann, 63.
  William, 63.
BRASEBRIDGE,
  Peter, 43.
BRAVYSON,
  Margaret, 151 N.
BRAY,
  Thomas, 80 N., 90 N.
BREARES,
  Isabel, 38.
BREFET,
  Ann, 117.
  Isabel, 39, 145.
  James, 15, 109.
  Johanna, 17.
  John, 38, 145.
BRERELEY,
  Richard, 30.
BRIDGES,
  Ann, 32.
  Richard, 158.
BRIGG, or BRIGGS,
  Agnes, 4, 128 N.
  Edward, 44.
  Elizabeth, 104.
  Frances, 27.
  Isabel, 30.
  Johanna, 92, 94.
  John, 11, 89, 93.
  Mary, 130.
  William, 16.
BROADBENT,
  Agnes, 113.
  Alice, 16.
  Catherine, 86.
  Elizabeth, 39, 41 N.
  Francis, 41 N.
  John, 2, 73, 108.
  Mary, 73.
  Richard, 72.
  Robert, 37, 74.
  Thomas, 119.
  William, 74, 151 N.
BROADHEAD,
  Alice, 139.
  Elizabeth, 103.
  Francis, 39, 105.
  Helen, or Ellen, 13, 38, 97 N., 126.
  Henry, 113.
  Jennet, 31, 31 N.
  John, 97 N.
  Richard, 97, 97 N.
  Thomas, 97 N.
BROADLEY, or BRODELEY,
  John, 18.
  Richard, 39.
BRODSWORTH,
  Alice, 1.
BROKSELLS,
  Robert, 152.
BROMELEY,
  Agnes, 1.
  Alice, 2.
  Elizabeth, 43.
  Johanna, 11, 82 N.
  John, 81 N.
  William, 81, 81 N., 157, 158 bis.
BROOKE,
  Alexander, 59.
  Alice, 39.
  Ann, 68.
  Francis, 80 N.
  Godfrey, 21.
  Hester, 63.
  James, 75.
  Thomas, 32, 56, 59, 63, 68, 75.
  William, 12, 56.

BROOMHEAD,
  Adam, 141 N.
  Alice, 25.
  Dionis, 40.
  Elizabeth, 34.
  Henry, 41, 103 N., 141 N.
  Isabel, 141 N.
  James, 23.
  John, 35, 124.
  Margaret, 112.
  Richard, 141 N.
  William, 141 N.
BROWNE,
  Agnes, 124 N.
  Alice, 6, 89, 143.
  Ann, 142 N.
  Anthony, 127 N., 137, 137 N.
  Cecilia, 124 N.
  Edward, 32 N., 124 N., 137 N.
  Effame, 127 N.
  Elizabeth, 13.
  Ellen, 142 N.
  George, 127 N.
  Henry, 97 N., 142 N.
  Hugh, 32 N., 83 N., 124 N.
  Isabel, 137.
  Jane, 93.
  John, 32 N., 80 N., 94, 105, 122 N., 124 N.
  Margery, 33, 142 N., 144 N.
  Magota, 124 N.
  Mr., 137 N.
  Philis, 107.
  Ralph, 142 N.
  Richard, 20, 20 N., 81 N., 130 N., 138 N., 142, 142 N., 146, 158.
  Sarah, 32, 32 N.
  Thomas, 94, 97 N., 142 N.
  William, 32 N., 40, 117 N., 124, 124 N., 149 N., 153, 154 bis, 156 bis, 158, 159, 160.
  Sir William, 109 N., 110 N. bis.
BROWNELL, BROWNELD, or BROWNHILL, &c.,
  Ann, 19, 34, 43.
  Catherine, 30.
  Christopher, 44.
  Dorothy, 33.
  Edward, 65.
  Elizabeth, 94 N., 104.
  George, 120 N.
  Grace, 146.
  Helen, 87.
  Henry, 47.
  Joan, 62, 105.
  John, 87, 102 N., 144.
  Margaret, 43, 145 N.
  Peter, 124.
  Ralph, 52, 146.
  Robert, 58, 155.
  Thomas, 3.
  William, 27, 32, 47, 52, 56 bis, 58, 62, 65, 146.
BROUGHE,
  Mary, 13.
BUCKMAN,
  Jane, 117.
BULLOCK,
  Elizabeth, 37.
  John, 157 N.
BULLUS,
  Agnes, 2, 13.
  Alice, 41, 91, 132.
  Ann, 48, 131.
  Arnold, 111, 120.
  Barbara, 132 N.
  Charles, 33, 59, 64.
  Emmanuel, 120.
  Emote, 67.
  Frances, 144 N.

BULLUS (continued),
George, 76.
Helen, 59, 115.
Isabel, 113, 114.
James, 15 N., 16 N., 125 N.
Jane, 46.
Jennet, 49.
Johanna, 91, 126 N., 157 N.
John, 26, 50, 55, 59, 64 bis, 67, **76**, 83, 85, 126 N., 133 N., 134 N.
Margaret, 83, 126 N., 130 N., 156 N.
Maria, 55.
Mary, 16 N.
Nicholas, 15 N.
Richard, 4 N., 83.
Robert, 17, 127 N., 131, 132, 133 N., 141 N.
Susan, 145 N.
Thomas, 15, 15 N., 17, 46, 48, 49, 50, 64, 80, 87, 94 N., 98 N., 109 N., 110 N., 123 N., 125 N., 126 N., 128 N., 132 N., 133 N., 154, 157 N.
Uxor, 126.
William, 4 N., 157 N.
BURDETT,
George, 32, 32 N.
Richard, 32 N.
BURGON,
Ann, 27.
Jane, 31, N.
Robert, 23.
BURNETT,
Bridget, 65.
Catherine, 58.
Jane, 138.
John, 49, 54, 58, 68, **138**.
Nicholas, 49.
William, 54.
BURROWES,
Elizabeth, 86 N.
Jane, 42.
Richard, 127, 127 **N.**
Robert, 86 N.
William, 110 N.
BURTON,
Margaret, 31.
BUTCHER,
Jennet, 29.
John, 19.
Margaret, 60.
Nicholas, 131 N.
Richard, 26, 60, 65.
Robert, 36, 67 bis.
Thomas, 65.
BUTCHER, alias DOUGHTYMAN,
Nicholas, 131 N.
BUTTERWORTH,
Isabel, 43.
Robert, 46 bis, 53, 145.
William, 53.
. . . . 162.
BUTTON,
Elizabeth, 139, 142.
Henry, 10.
Isabel, 98.
Jane, 3.
Joan, 44, 49.
John, 41, 106.
Margaret, 138.
Ralph, 27, 49, 55, 60 bis, 64, 99, 138, 139.
Richard, 10, **64**.
Robert, 55.
Thomas, 84.
William, 9.
BUTTRIDGE,
William, 102.
BYLCLIFFE,
Margaret, 21.

BYRDHEADE,
Joan, **108**.

CADE,
Richard, 13.
CALVERD,
Alice, 139.
Ann, 9.
Ralph, 86, 97 N., 139.
Widow, 124.
CALVERLEY,
Christopher, 151 N.
CAMSALL,
Alice, 81 N.
Edward, 81 **N.**
CARLLYLL,
Johanna, 156.
CARR, or KERR,
Agnes, 19, 104, 120, 141.
Alexander, 106.
Alice, 8 N.
Ann, 26, 62.
Barbara, 125.
Charles, 8 N.
Elizabeth, 10, 37, 48, 60 bis, 75, 77, 95, 132 N., 140, 143 N.
Ellen, 8 N., 95, 106.
Emote, 33, 66, 128 N., 144 N.
Frances, 26.
George, 74.
Sir George, 8 N.
Henry, 8 N.
Hugh, 46, 49, 55, 60, 139.
James, 3, 8 N., 52, 95, 102 N., 118 N., 127 N., 132 N., 142 N.
Jane, 40, 120, 128, 137.
Janet, 128 N.
Joan, 17, 35, 115.
Joanna del, 8 N.
John 8 N. bis, 9 N., 34, 61, 66, 68, 73 bis, 106, 109, 158.
Margaret, 15, 44, 53, 68, 71.
Margery, 6, 20, 128.
Mark, 66.
Mary 11, 73, 132 N.
Nicholas, 56, 61, 83, 104, 143 N.
Ralph, 8, 8 N., 48, 57 bis, 62, 64, 68 bis, 71, 74, 77, 94 N., 118 N., 128 N., 132 N., 141, 141 N., 142 N., 144, 144 N.
Richard, 3, 8 N. 24, 35, 48, 49, 52 bis, 56, 60, 66, 70, 73, 83, 110 N., 125, 127, 128, 128 N., 131, 140, 143, 143 N., 144 N.
Robert, 2, 16, 25, 36, 46, 48, 53, 57, 61 bis, 66 bis, 73, 83, 125, 139, 143 N.
Robertus del, 37 N.
Roger, 106.
Thomas, 3, 5, 8 N., 9 N., 14, 17, 25, 38, 47, 76 bis, 82 N., 96, 100, 106, 108, 128, 128 N., 132, 132 N., 136, 144 N.
Thomas del, 8 N.
Widow, 81.
William, 8 N. bis, 9 N., 22, 42, 47, 52, 55, 57, 61 bis, 64, 73, 75, 89, 114, 132 N., 143 N.
William del, 8 N.
CARTER,
Robert, 38.
CASSE,
Nicholas, 149 N.
CASSON,
Frances, 30.
Robert, 34.
CATTERALL,
Catherine, 61.
Margery, 38.
Nicholas, 29, 37, 61.

CATTERALL (continued),
Richard, 29.
CAWOOD, Charles, 94 N.
Ralph, 157 N.
CAWTHORN,
Johanna, 150 N.
John, 150 N.
CHADWICK,
Barbara, 23.
Elizabeth, 21.
Johanna, 12.
Richard, 135.
Uxor, 135.
CHAMBERS,
Joan, 4.
Nicholas, 116.
CHAPMAN,
Margaret, 142.
Richard, 48 bis, 138, 140, 142.
CHAPPELL,
Agnes, 117.
Elizabeth, 103 N.
John, 27.
Ronald, 98.
William, 112 N., 133.
CHARLES I., KING, 3 N.
CHARLESWORTH,
Elizabeth, 14.
Margaret, 40.
William, 38.
CHATTERTON,
Ann, 37.
CHETAM,
Mary, 39.
CLARKE,
Alice, 102.
Ann, 54.
Charles, 14, 24, 125 N., 129, 133.
Edith, 59.
Elizabeth, 29.
Ellen, or Helen, 37, 59.
Francis, 140.
George, 20, 99, 155 N.
Isabel, 88.
Jane, 104.
John, 33, 38, 59, 64, 71 bis, 73, 75, 77, 149, 153 bis.
Sir John, 154.
Maria, 52, 129.
Nicholas, 67, 75, 103.
Thomas, 10, 64, 77, 127, 140, 140 N.
Sir Thomas, 150 N., 154, 155 N.
William, 11, 28, 52, 54, 59, 67, 73.
CLARKHOUSE,
John, 83.
CLAYTON, or CLEATON.
Alice, 6.
Helen, 6.
Isabel, 111.
Rebecca, 51.
Robert, 81 N., 111 N., 213.
William, 51.
COBCROFT,
Sir Robert, 151 N., 156 bis, 156 N., 158 bis, 159.
COLLEY, see also COWLEY,
Agnes, 101, 104.
Alice, 157 N.
Ann, 110 N.
Barbara, 109.
Dorothy, 135 N.
Edward, 83 N., 85.
Elizabeth, 37 N., 44, 110 N.
George, 42, 78.
Grace, 21, 110 N.
Helen, 4, 27, 98.
Isabel, 29, 57, 110 N.
Joan, 110.
John, 4, 37 N., 92, 101 N., 105, 114, 119, 135, 135 N. 149 N., 156, 157 N.

INDEX.   167

COLLEY (continued),
　Katherine, 157 N.
　Margaret, 52, 104, 106, 157 N.
　Mary, 47, 78.
　Nicholas, 83.
　Richard, 6, 12, **83, 110, 110 N., 156,** 157.
　Robert, 64.
　Thomas, 52, 57, 64, 69, 110 N., 156 N. 157.
　Sir Thomas, 110 N.
　William, 69, 105, 156, 156 **N.**
COLTE,
　Ann, 7.
COMBE, or COO,
　Agnes, 24.
　Alice, 8 N.
　Barbara, 138.
　Elizabeth, 9.
　Helen, or Ellen, 49, 135 N.
　Henry, 8, 8 N., 49, 54, 94 N., 135, 135 N., 138.
　Isabel, 69.
　Johanna, 8 N., 93.
　John, 8 N., 153.
　Margaret, 31, 54.
　Mathew, 74.
　Nicholas, 47, 105.
　Petrus de, 8 N.
　Robert, 35, 69, 74, 83.
　Thomas, 7 N.
　William, 8 N., 26, **47, 114, 143 N.**
　William del, 85 N.
CONY,
　Helen, **114.**
COOKE,
　Alice, 35, 94 N.
　Ann, 138 N.
　Brian, 40, 76, **78.**
　Elizabeth, 91.
　Ellen, 43.
　George, 136.
　Godfrey, 8.
　Jeffrey, 94, 94 N.
　Joan, 32, 141.
　John, 138 N., 141 N.
　Maria, 9.
　Mary, 76, 94N.
　Nicholas, 78.
　Richard, 94 N., 119, 136.
　Thomas, 113 N.
　William, 16.
COOKE, alias TWYBELL,
　James, 36 N.
COOP, see also COOPER,
　Alexander, 138.
　John, 54 bis.
　Robertus, 37 N.
　Thomas, 129.
COOPER, or COWPER,
　Alexander, 25, 41.
　Alice, 106.
　Barbara, 115.
　Bartholomew, 157 bis, 158.
　Christine, 14.
　Cicily, 69.
　Elizabeth, 5, 19, 44, 105.
　Frances, 33.
　Helen, 5, 27.
　Isabel, 4, 97, 116, **143.**
　James, 126 N.
　Jane, 104.
　Johanna, 82, 98 bis.
　John, 7, 20, 32, 40, 60, 92, 143.
　Margaret, 47, 139.
　Margery, 54, 104.
　Mark, 60.
　Mary, 25.
　Nicholas, **5, 40, 84, 89, 97 N.,** 124.

COOPER (continued),
　Richard, 5, 16 N., 82, **88** N., 90 N., 105, 114, 114 N.
　Sir Richard, 80 N., 97 N., **154** bis, 159.
　Robert, 5, 11, 26, 97, 97 N., **118.**
　Roger, 38.
　Thomas, 22, 69, 95, **126 N., 128, 131,** 143.
　Uxor, 97 N.
　Widow, 130.
　William, 97 N., 149 N.
COOPER, alias PARKIN,
　Ann, 126 N.
　Elizabeth, 126 N.
　Margaret, 76, 126 N.
　Mary, 126 N.
　Richard, 126 N.
　Thomas, 76, 126 N.
COPLEY,
　Elizabeth, 150.
　George, 5.
COTTON,
　Barbara, **5 N., 122, 122** N., **152 N.**
　John, 96 N.
　Mary, 96.
　Mrs., 122 N.
　Thomas, 5, 5 N., 122 N., **152** N.
　William, 96, 96 N.
COTTRELL, see also CATTERALL,
　George, 15.
COURTNEY,
　James, 113 N.
COWARD,
　Joan, 13.
　Mary, 44.
COWLDWELL,
　Jane, 43.
　Margaret, 41.
COWLEY, see also **COLLEY,**
　Ellena, 37 N.
　Henricus, 37 N.
CRAPPE, or CRAPPER,
　Agnes, 2.
　Peter, 56.
　Roger, 56.
CRAWSHAWE,
　Henry, 42.
　Isabel, 2.
　Jane, 36.
　John, 38.
　Richard, 29.
CRESACRE,
　Alice, 152 N.
　Percival, 152 N.
CRESWICK,
　Agnes, 113.
　Ann, 14, 62, 65, **71, 115.**
　Dionis, 109.
　Edmund, 11 N.
　Edward, 11 N., 27, 50, 53, 85, **95,** 95 N., 107, 107 N., 110 N.
　Elizabeth, 42, 42 N., 86, **95** N., 104.
　Frances, 11 N., 39.
　Francis, 39, 98, 114, 121.
　Gilbert, 11 N., 37, 42, 71, 75, **78.**
　Helen, or Ellen, 53, 78, 91.
　Henry, 59.
　John, 11, 11 N., 42 N., 50, 57, 59, 62, 65, 67, 69 bis, 73, 77, 82 N., 95 N., 101, 101 N., 107 N., 120 N., 121, 121 N., 141, 141 N.
　Margaret, 11, 11 N., 28, 107 **N., 141,** 141 N.
　Margery, 142.
　Mary, 62, 75.
　Nicholas, 11 N., 34, **57, 62, 69.**
　Robert, 101 N., 119.
　Roger, 11 N.

CRESWICK (continued),
　Thomas, 11 N., 27, 28, 65 bis, 101 N., 107 N., 139, 144 N., 155 N.
　Uxor, 125.
　William, 15, **67, 69, 107 N., 116,** 118, 143 N.
CROFT, or CROFTS,
　Agnes, 9.
　Ann, 37.
　Catherine, 15 N., 102, 102 N.
　Charles, 6 N., 16, 32, 57, 63.
　Christopher, 15 N., 23, 35, 49, 53, 63, 66, 81 N., 102 N., 110 N., 118, 137 N.
　Elizabeth, 38, 117.
　Frances, 92.
　Helen, or Ellen, 21, 40, 53.
　Isabel, 6, 63, 71.
　James, 110 N., 132, 136.
　Johanna, 14.
　John, 115.
　Margaret, 12.
　Maud, 118 N.
　Nicholas, 21, **57, 63, 110** N.
　Phillis, 6 N.
　Ralph, 15, 15 N., 66, 83 N., 110 N., 113 N., 118, 118 N., 137 N., 152 N.
　Roger, 11.
　Thomas, 41, 49, 71.
　William, 149 N.
CROFTS, alias MOUNTENEY,
　Maud, 137.
CROOKES,
　Margaret, 97.
CROSBYE,
　Alice, 138.
CROSS,
　Isabel, 50.
　Leonard, 29, 50, 56.
　Mathew, 56.
CROSSLEY, or CROSSLEIGH, &c.,
　Alice, 95, 138.
　Ann, 74.
　Charles, 15.
　Dionis, 27.
　Elizabeth, 13, 65.
　Ellen, 73.
　Isabel, 142.
　Jane, 3, 43.
　Joan, 4, 117, 130.
　John, 30, 37, 48, **86, 97 N.**
　Katherine, 37.
　Margaret, 25, 92.
　Mary, 67.
　Nicholas, 97 N.
　Thomas, 7, 22, 41, 48, 65, 67, 74, 92, 96, 97 N., 110 N., 136, 138.
　William, 15, 34, 73, 142, 149 N.
CROWDER,
　Joan, 108.
　John, 131.
　Margaret, 95.
　Robert, 104.
　Thomas, 12.
CURTIS, or CURTESSE, &c.,
　Ann, 64.
　Elizabeth, 38.
　John, 54 bis, 59, 64.
　Thomas, 99.
　Widow, 130.
　William, 59.
CUTHBERT,
　Sir Thomas, 113 N.
CUTLER,
　Ellen, 68, 69.
　Thomas, 23, 37, 68, 69.
CUTT, or CUTTS,
　Agnes, 86 N., 119 N.
　Alice, 80, 99 N.
　Ann, 22, 86 N.

INDEX.

CUTT (continued),
  Anthony, 17, 21, 115, 124.
  Catherine, 106 N.
  Effamie, 21, 103 N.
  Elizabeth, 2, 37, 103 N.
  Ellen, or Helen, 103 N., 117.
  Francis, 115, 117.
  George, 82, 119 N., 155.
  Isabel, 30, 103 N.
  Jane, 103 N., 119 N.
  Joan, 9, 97 N.
  John, 7, 86, 119 N.
  Margaret, 17, 42, 103 N., 119 N.
  Richard, 4, 23, 49, 92, 133, 138, 144.
  Robert, 4, 119 N.
  Thomas, 8, 49, 83, 86 N., 100 N., 103 N., 119, 119 N.
  William, 100 N., 103, 103 N., 116 N., 119 N.

DALE,
  Ann, 35.
  Thomas, **43**.
DANYEL,
  Francis, 30, 51, 54, 66, **145**.
  George, 51, 66, 145.
  John, 66.
  Roger, 54.
DARCY,
  Lord, 112 N.
DARLEY,
  Joan, 24.
  Thomas, 84 N., **123 N.**
DARNBOROUGH,
  Rev. J. W., 11 N.
DAVIE,
  Agnes, 110 N.
  Robert, 110 N.
DAWRE,
  Agnes, 133.
  Ellen, 110 N.
  Isabel, 15.
  Joan, 5.
  Johanna, 107.
  Margery, 40.
  Michael, 67.
  Robert, 83, 160 bis.
  Roger, 67.
DAWSON,
  Ann, 70.
  Dionis, 17.
  Isabel, 140 N.
  Margaret, 18.
  Mr., 70, 72.
  Thomas, 72.
  William, 20 N.
DEMSTEARE,
  Henry, 139 N.
DENMAN,
  Isabel, 152 **N.**
  John, 152 N.
  Ralph, 151 **N.**
DENNIOT,
  Nicholas, 154.
DENTON,
  Richard, 88, 94 N.
DERNELY,
  Edmund, 8.
  Emote, 121 N., 130 N.
  Margaret, 137.
  Mrs., 130.
  Oliver, 117 **N.**, **121 N.**, **130 N.**, **137**.
DEY,
  Agnes, 103 N., 120.
  Ann, 64, 72.
  Elizabeth, 34, 99, 132 N.
  Frances, 76.
  Grace, 108.
  Isabel, 4, 6, 132 N., 148 N.
  James, 15, 18, 132 N.

DEY (continued),
  John, 84, 132 N.
  Katherine, 70.
  Margaret, 118.
  Nicholas, 1.
  Peter, 35, 64, 68, 72.
  Richard, 85 N., 132, 132 N., 148 N.
  Robert, 99.
  Thomas, 68, 80 N., 82 N., 132 N., 148 N., 157 bis, 159, 160, 161, 162.
  William, 15, 70, 76, 132 N.
DEY, alias WILKINSON,
  Jennet, 102 N.
DICKENSON, or DICONSON,
  Alice, 19.
  Ann, 35.
  Edward, 37 N., 135, 135 N.
  Elizabeth, 19 N., 37, 37 N., **130 N.**, 135 N., 140 N., 145.
  Gilbert, 19, 19 N., 119, **131 N,**
  Joan, 119.
  Mary, 77.
  Robert, 77.
  William, 19 N., 133, 135 N.
DICKSON,
  Ro., 43.
  William, 112.
DOBSON,
  Alice, 61.
  Ann, 67.
  Dorothy, 47.
  Isabel, 43.
  John, 25, 47, 53 bis, 56, 61, 67.
  Thomas, 56.
DODWORTH,
  Christian, 29.
  John, 23.
  William, 43.
DODSWORTH,
  Sir Charles Edward, Bart., 24 N.
  [The Antiquary,] 1 N., 148 N., 151 N.
DOLLY,
  Jennet, 136.
DONCASTER,
  Dean of, 113 N.
DOUGHTY,
  Ann, 18, **54**.
  Catherine, 48.
  Emote, 108.
  Thomas, 48, 54.
  William, 44.
DOUGHTY, alias **WAGGALEY**,
  Ralph, 139.
  Robert, 114.
  Thomas, 139.
DOUGHTYMAN,
  Alice, 65, 131 N.
  Elizabeth, 50, 54.
  John, 65, 131 N.
  Katherine, 131 N.
  Michael, 46, 50.
  Nicholas, 131 N.
  Ralph, 131 N.
  Robert, 112, 131, 131 N.
  Thomas, 46, 54, 131 N.
  Widow, 131.
DOUGTYMAN, alias BUTCHER,
  Nicholas, 131 N.
DOWER, see also DAWRE,
  John, 155 N.
  Roger, 155 N.
  Thomas, 155 N.
  William do, 155 N.
DOWKE,
  Robert, **2, 2 N.**
DOWNING,
  Alice, 28.
  John, 25.
  Thomas, 18.

DRABLE,
  John, 44.
DRAX,
  Isabel, 152 N.
  Robert, 152 N.
  ———, 151 N.
DRAYCOTES,
  Ann, 151 N.
  Sir John, 151 **N.**
DREATON,
  Frances, 3.
DREWRE,
  Sir Thomas, **152**.
DUCKINGTON,
  Joan, 39.
DUCKMANTON,
  Humphrey, **34, 34 N., 59, 62.**
  John, 62.
  Thomas, 59.
DUNGWORTH,
  Ann, 47, 142.
  Hugh, 56.
  Margaret, 117.
  Mary, 44.
  Nicholas, 14, 47, 56, 94 N., 137, 142, 146.
  Thurstaine, 1, 111.
  Uxor, 126.
  William, 120.
DYNNISON,
  Elizabeth, **140, 144.**
  Joan, 142 N.
  John, 115.
  William, 16, 23, 140, **144.**
DYSON,
  Alexander, 117.
  Arthur, 13.
  Elizabeth, 29, 58.
  Frances, 48, 140.
  Henry, 61.
  Isabel, 144.
  Joan, 7.
  John, 111.
  Margaret, 55.
  Mary, 71.
  Nicholas, **29, 48, 55, 58, 61, 71, 140,** 143, 144.
  Rosamond, 3.
  Uxor, 126.

EASTWOOD,
  Mr. [The Historian], 25 N.
ECARR, see also CARR,
  Janet, 150.
  John, 150, 153.
  Richard, 150, 154.
ECCLESFIELD,
  Vicar of, 36 N., 38 N., 139, 139 N., 140 N., 150 N., 154, 155 N.
ELAND, or EALAND,
  Ann, 47.
  Henry, 87.
  Maria, 8.
  Robert, 94 N.
ELLER,
  George, 75.
  Stephen, 75.
ELLIS,
  Ann, 51.
  Anthony, 134 N.
  Barbara, 14.
  Cecily, 14.
  Hugh, 139, 144.
  Isola, 150 N.
  Johanna, 25.
  John, 93, 97.
  Margaret, 102, 139.
  Maria, 57.
  Richard, 40.
  Robert, 51, 57.

INDEX.

ELLIS (continued),
  Thomas, 20.
  William, 150 N.
ELMSALL,
  Alice, 20.
ELUAR,
  Grace, **92.**
ELVISE,
  Robert, **80.**
  Widow, **80, 82.**
EMSON,
  Johanna, 3 N.
  Thomas, 3 N.
ENTWYSLE,
  Richard, 139 N.
ESTON,
  William, **100.**
EVERARD
  Alicia Ann, 41 N.
  Rev. Salisbury, 41 N.
EVERINGHAM,
  Agnes, 155 N.
  Ann, 155 N.
  Christopher, 155 N.
  Edmund, 155 N.
  Henry, 149 N., 155 **N.**
  John, 155 N.
  Nicholas, 155, 155 N.
  Richard, 155 N., 161.
  Robert. 155 N.
  Thomas, 149 N., 155 N.
  William, 16 N., 88 N., 155 N.
  Sir William, 154 *bis*, 155 N.
EYRE,
  Agnes, 96.
  Ann, 7, 7 N.
  Edmund, 103 N.
  Elizabeth, 29, 60, **122.**
  George, 120 N.
  Helen, 96, 146.
  Isabel, 3.
  John, 146, **148 N.**
  Lawrence, **39, 52, 56, 60, 103** N.
  Lelle, 52.
  Margaret, 16 **N., 56.**
  Mary, 16 N.
  Renald, 68.
  Robert, 46.
  Stephen, 7 N.
  Thomas, 16 N., 46, 68, 72.
EYRESON,
  John, 121.

FALLEY, or FAWLEY,
  Ann, 6, 71.
  Barbara, 115.
  Elizabeth, 71, 145.
  Ellen, 38, 58, 65 *bis*.
  Ralph, 58.
  Richard, 2.
  Robert, 15, 145.
FEARNELEY,
  Alice, 11, 46.
  Ann, 15, 123.
  Charles, 120.
  Edward, 53.
  Elizabeth, 49, 128.
  Emote, 127.
  Francis, 127 N.
  Humphrey, 12, 127.
  Isabel, 51, 145.
  Joan, 43.
  Magot, 116N.
  Margaret, 28.
  Nicholas, 57.
  Peter, 1, 94N., 116.
  Robert, 10, 123N.
  William, 28, 46, 49, 51, 53, 57, 64 *bis*, 116, 145.

FEARNELEY, *alias* **SHEPHERD,**
  Magot, 116N.
  William, 116N.
FENTON,
  Agnes, 122N.
  Cecily, 122N.
  Elizabeth, 91.
  Richard, 42, 90N., 121N., **122N.**
  Robert, 121N.
  Thomas, 121N.
FERNELL,
  Robert, 143N.
FIELD,
  Jane, 8.
FIRTH, or FYRTH,
  Ann, 11.
  Edward, 11.
  Frances, 31.
  Helen, 16.
  Joan, 11.
  John, 29.
  Nicholas, 130.
  William, 23.
FITZWILLIAM,
  John, 148N., 152N.
  Maud, 152N.
FLETCHER,
  Francis, 121N.
  Isabel, 33, 33N.
  John, 80.
  Rev. John, 9N.
  John Carr, 9N.
  Maria, 6.
  William, 33N.
FLINT,
  Ann, 123.
  Thomas, 34.
FOORES,
  . . . . **138**N.
FORD,
  James, 154.
FORDSAME,
  James, 156N.
FORMAN,
  John, 141N.
FOSTER,
  Alexander, 61.
  Alice, 36, 61.
  Ann, 73.
  George, 141.
  Henry, 56.
  James, 14, 37, **66, 69, 73, 78, 126.**
  Jane, 23.
  Margaret, 78.
  Mary, 73.
  Nicholas, 31, 32, **56, 69.**
  Thomas, 66.
FOX,
  Ann, 50.
  Dorothy, 35, 35N.
  Elizabeth, 47, 105.
  Henry, 25, 27, 28, 47, **50, 138** *bis*.
  Jane, 138.
  John, 43, 84.
  Margaret, 9.
  Robert, 35.
  Uxor, 81.
FOXTON,
  Richard, 77.
  William, 77.
FOWLER,
  William, 41.
FRANKISH,
  John, 112N.
FREEMAN,
  Ann, 61, 145N.
  Elizabeth, 51, 137, 145.
  Gerard, 25, 41N, 47, 51, 61 *bis*, 137, 145.
  Howsley, 25N., **41, 41**N., **47.**

FREEMAN (*continued*),
  Thomas, 61.
FRENCH,
  Alexander, 80N.
  Eliza, 40.
  Robert, 80N.
FRICKLEY,
  John, 34, 62, 68.
  Mary, 58, 62.
  William, 68.
FULLYLOVE,
  Elizabeth, 127.
FULSTONE,
  Barbara, 16.
  William, 149N.
FYPPS, see PHIPPS.

GAMBLE,
  Anthony, 69.
  John, 42.
  Richard, 72.
  Thomas, 72.
GARGRAVE,
  Thomas, 3N., 16N., 88N., 123N.
GARLADY,
  Margaret, 5.
GARRET,
  Lucy, 1.
GASKEN, or GASCOIGN,
  Edward, 8.
GAUGH,
  Ann, 55.
  George, 11.
  Thomas, 31, 55.
GAUKE,
  Margaret, 68.
  Thomas, 68.
GAUNT,
  George, 44.
GEE,
  Ann, 30.
GENN,
  Annis, 3N.
  Elizabeth, **23.**
  Helen, 31.
  Isabel, 29.
  Margaret, 36, 60.
  Nicholas, 60.
  Richard, 13.
  Robert, 83.
  . . . . 3 N.
GESLING, or GOSLING,
  Elizabeth, 19.
  Emote, 12.
  Helen, 8, 35.
  James, 31.
  Richard, 109.
  Robert, 81.
  Uxor, 126.
  William, 22.
GIBSON,
  Ann, 15.
  Elizabeth, 41.
GILBERT,
  Robert, 44.
  Sarah, 24 N.
  Thomas, 24 N.
GILBERTHORPE,
  Alice, 97.
  Elizabeth, 27.
  Margaret, 3.
  Robert, 149, N.
GILLES, or GYLLES, &c.,
  Ann, 63.
  Catherine, 116.
  Edward, 51.
  Elizabeth, 64, 89, **92.**
  Grace, 117.
  Helen, 20, 111.
  Isabel, 101.

Y

INDEX

GILLES (continued),
  Jane, 111.
  Joan, 117.
  John, 5, 9, 59, 60, **74, 128.**
  Margaret, 37, 56.
  Margery, 27.
  Nicholas, 56 bis, 60, 74, 76 bis, 137.
  Richard, 27, 51, 137, 145 ter.
  Thomas, 17, 33, 43, 59, 63, 64.
GILLOT,
  Ann, 32.
  Beatrice, 31.
  Elizabeth, 41.
  William, 130.
GLEYDALE,
  George, 65.
  John, 65.
GOODE,
  John, 58.
  Nicholas, 58.
GOODEY,
  Elizabeth, 96.
  William, 5.
GOODEYRE, or GOODER,
  Ann, 62.
  Isabel, 70, 143.
  Jane, 7.
  Johanna, 25.
  John, 33, 62, 66, 70.
  Margaret, 33, 66, 104.
  Nicholas, 132 N., 141 N., 143.
GOODISON,
  Ann, 145 N.
  Samuel, 26 N.
GOSLING, see GESLING.
GOULDING,
  Dorothy, 40.
GRACE,
  Margery, 80.
  Nicholas, 151 N.
GRAY,
  Henry, 41.
  Johanna, 123 N.
  John, 123 N.
  Thomas, 132 N.
GRAYSON,
  Ann, 26 N.
  George, 26 N.
  John, 43.
GREAVES, GREVE, or GREFF, &c.,
  Alice, 2.
  Ann, 38.
  Arthur, 153, 157.
  Catherine, 111.
  Edward, 18, 108, 116 N., 127.
  Elizabeth, 115 N.
  Francis, 115 N.
  John, 22, 115 N., 116, 116 N.
  John de, 116 N.
  Margaret, 17.
  Maria, 33.
  Mary, 60, 115 N.
  Matilda del, 115 N.
  Maude, 90.
  Nicholas, 89.
  Radus del, 115 N.
  Ralph, 128 N.
  Richard, 103 N., 116 N.
  Robert, 40.
  Thomas, 60, 87, 98 N., 103 N., 113 N., 115, 115 N., 116 N., 140 N.
  William, 11, 103 N., 116 N., 138.
GREAVES, alias HOBSON,
  Edward, 115 N.
GREEN,
  Agnes, 5, 14.
  Alice, 58.
  Ann, 42, 49, 58, 62.
  Bridget, 66.
  Dionis, 44.

GREEN (continued),
  Dorothy, 24.
  Dr., 126 N.
  Elizabeth, 103, 134 N.
  Emote, 28.
  Florence, 95.
  Francis, 118.
  George, 49, 51.
  Grace, 54.
  Isabel, 27.
  James, 31, 31 N., 54, 56, 58, 62, 66, 68.
  Jane, 18.
  Joan, 107.
  Johanna, 88.
  John, 11, 28, 48, **51, 58, 107, 133,** 137, 141.
  Margaret, 10 bis, 22.
  Maria, 56, 139.
  Mary, 144.
  Nicholas, 7, 89, 102, 145.
  Peter, 130.
  Robert, 68.
  Thomas, 31 N., 48, 134 N., 141.
  Uxor, 126.
  William, 58, 106, 122.
GREENWOOD,
  Thomas, 151 N.
GREGORY,
  Jane, 5.
  Roger, 18.
  Uxor, 126.
GROVE,
  Margareta del, 116 N.
  Willelmus del, 116 N.
GRUBB,
  Alice, 22.
  Ann, 21.
  Barbara, 117.
  Catherine, 116.
  Elizabeth, 18, 136.
  Helen, 108.
  Isabel, 17.
  Joan, 117.
  Johanna, 22.
  John, 131, 149 N., 153.
  Ralph, 31, 55, 60, 131.
  Richard, 85, 97, 124, 134.
  Robert, 55, 80 N., 109, 150 N.
  Thomas, 60, 118 N.
GRYFFYN,
  Alice, 150 N.
  Robert, 150 N.
GUEST, or GEST,
  Ann, 47, 47 N.
  Anthony, 19.
  Cecily, 18.
  Charles, 71.
  Elizabeth, 11, 40.
  George, 129.
  Gerard, 47 N., 52.
  James, 85.
  Johanna, 94.
  John, 21, 47, 47 N., 52, 57, 71, 97.
  Katherine, 57.
  Margaret, 99.
  Mary, 47 N.
  Thomas, 8.
  William, 39, **71.**
GYLDIN,
  Margaret, **20.**

HACKET,
  Alice, 26 N.
  Nicholas, 26 N.
HAIGH, HAGUE, or HAUGH, &c.,
  Agnes, 3, 103.
  Ann, 24, 57, 98, 120.
  Cecily, 139.
  Elizabeth, 21, 97, 114, 141.

HAIGH (continued),
  Gilbert, 62.
  Isabel, 65.
  John, 88.
  Lacy, 52.
  Richard, 105, 140 S.
  Robert, 41, 75, 123 N.
  Thomas, 17, 30, 52, 57, 62, 84, 139.
  Widow, 132.
HALDHAM,
  Robert, 152 N.
HALDSWORTH,
  George, 94 N.
  Helen, 7.
HALL,
  Alice, 142.
  Ann, 26 N., 33, 65, 134 N.
  Rev. Benjamin, 26 N.
  Cecily, 16, 28.
  Dorothy, 26 N.
  Elizabeth, 55, 140, 144 N.
  Francis, 59, 70, 72, 109.
  George, 26 N.
  Gilbert, 119.
  Grace, 43.
  Helen, 5, 80 N.
  Henry, 26 N., 35, 35 N., 65, 155 N.
  Jane, 39, 63.
  Joan, 8.
  John, 14, 26, 26 N., 31, 35 N., 36, 55, 65, 68 bis, 70, 72, 74, 75, 78, 142.
  Joseph, 26 N.
  Rev. Joseph, 26 N.
  Lawrence, 80 N.
  Margaret, 61.
  Martha, 26 N.
  Mary, 26 N., 68.
  Ralph, 66.
  Richard, 17, 35, 63, 66, 70, 72, 116 N.
  Robert, 59, 72, 94 N.
  Thomas, 17, 26 N., 35, 36, 61, 65, 68, 134 N., 140.
  Uxor, 124.
  William, 7, 34, 70, 74, 78.
  Sir William, 151 N.
HALL, alias PARKER,
  Agnes, 108.
HALLAMSHIRE,
  Lord of, 14 N., 98 N., 148 N.
HAMMOND,
  Benjamin, 11 N.
  Mary, 11 N.
HANBY,
  Elizabeth, 104.
HANCOCK,
  Elizabeth, 42.
  George, 118 N.
HANDLEY or HANLEY,
  Agnes, 23.
  Ann, 43.
  Cecily, 37.
  Frances, 23.
  Helen, 24, 29.
  Johanna, 96.
  John, 114.
  Margaret, 24.
  Maude, 118.
  Phillice, 100.
  Robert, 10, 10 N., 106.
  Stephanus, 10 N.
  Thomas, 46.
  William, 42, 46, 72, 73 bis.
HANSON,
  Edward, 81 N.
HARDMAN,
  Lawrence, 139, N.
HARDY,
  Anthony, 31, 52, 64, 72 bis.
  John, 64.

INDEX.

HARDY (continued),
  Robert, 111.
  Thomas, 52.
HARGREAVE or HARGRESS, &c.,
  Ann, 50, 75, 146.
  Euphemia, 4.
  Helen, 46.
  Jane, 59.
  William, 33, 46, 50, 59, 64 bis, 75, 146.
HARRISON,
  Ann, 107.
  Gillis, 33.
  James, 105.
  Jean, 108.
  Johanna, 103.
  Margaret, 140.
  William, 13, 96.
HARRISON, alias BRAMALL,
  Thomas, 145.
HARSHAND,
  John, 114 N.
  William, 114 N.
HART,
  Experint, 73.
  William, 33, 69 bis, 73.
HARTLEY,
  Agnes, 24, 85 N.
  Agnes de 85 N.
  Alexander, 24, 55, 62, 70.
  Alice, 2.
  Alicia de, 85 N.
  Ann, 44, 66, 95, 129 N.
  Catherine, 73.
  Dionis, 28.
  Dorothy, 35, 92.
  Edward, 67, 145 N.
  Elizabeth, 19, 55, 112, 115, 128 N.
  Henry, 85 N., 114 N.
  Isabel, 23 bis, 52.
  Jane, 92.
  Jean, 67
  Johanna de, 85 N.
  Johannes de, 85 N.
  John, 22 bis, 47, 62, 70, 81 N., 85, 85 N., 106 N., 112, 114 N., 120, 128 N., 129, 129 N., 157.
  Margaret, 10, 61, 128 N.
  Margery, 136.
  Nicholas, 46, 50 bis.
  Peter, 104.
  Ricardus de, 85 N.
  Richard, 4, 128 N., 129 N.
  Robert, 17, 25, 95, 121 N., 128, 128 N., 129, 135 N.
  Seth, 46.
  Thomas, 22, 29, 47, 52, 58 bis, 66, 85 N., 88, 106, 128 N., 152, N.
  Widow, 130.
  Willielmus de, 85 N.
  William, 31, 35, 54 bis, 61, 73, 75 bis, 85 N., 114 N., 120 N., 126 N., 132 N.
HASTINGS,
  Elizabeth, 3.
HATFIELD, or HADFIELD,
  Alexander, 1, 1 N., 53 N., 59, 80 N., 106 N., 110 N., 114 N., 143, 143 N.,
  Alice, 81 N.
  Ann, 20, 80 N.
  Anthony, 53 N.
  Barbara, 53 N.
  Catherine, 53, 80 N.
  Dionis, 30, 143 N.
  Edmund, 81 N.
  Edward, 80 N., 81 N., 103, 113 N., 159.
  Elizabeth, 53 N., 80 N.
  Ellen, 59.
  Gervase, 53 N.
  Henry, 27, 143 N.

HATFIELD (continued),
  Isabel, 53 N., 143 N.
  Jennet, 81 N.
  John, 53 N., 64, 80 N., 143 N., 146.
  Margaret, 53 N., 81 N.
  Nicholas, 1 N., 80, 80 N., 81 N., 129, 143 N., 162.
  Ralph, 53, 53 N., 64, 143 N.
  Robert, 81 N.
  Thomas, 109.
  William, 2, 23, 81 N., 93, 129, 143, 143 N.
HATTERSLEY,
  Ann, 50, 145.
  James, 3.
  John, 50, 53, 145.
  Ralph, 53.
HAUGHTON,
  Ann, 55.
  Francis, 113, 120.
  George, 73.
  Joan, 116.
  John, 17, 24, 55, 116, 126.
  Mary, 75.
HAUSLEN,
  Thomas, 5.
HAWKESWORTH,
  Alice, 140 N.
  Ann, 35, 41, 74.
  Elizabeth, 76.
  Francis, 40, 74, 76.
  Henry, 37, 66.
  Katherine, 66.
  Margaret, 16.
  Mary, 26 N.
  Thomas, 140 N.
HAWKHIRST,
  Christopher, 150.
  Johanna, 150 N.
  John, 150 N.
  Richard, 150 N.
  Robert, 26.
HAWME,
  Richard, 85.
  Robert, 81 N.
HAYFORD,
  Christopher, 112 N.
HEARNIGE,
  Alice, 143 N.
HEATON,
  Edmund, 93.
  Margaret, 9.
HEDON,
  William, 140 N.
HEILIE,
  Gilbert, 85.
  Henry, 2.
HELLEWS,
  Ann, 89.
HELYS, or HELLES, see also ELLIS,
  Anthony, 4.
  William, 96.
HEMELEY,
  Thomas, 117 N.
HEPWORTH,
  John, 56.
  Margaret, 67.
  Ralph, 31, 52, 56.
  Robert, 52.
  Thomas, 10, 67, 102 N.
  William, 7.
HEWARD,
  Elizabeth, 74.
  John, 74.
HEWET,
  Ann, 16, 16 N.
  Richard, 16 N.
  Widow, 130.
HEY,
  Agnes, 29.

HEY (continued),
  Ann, 29, 36, 58.
  Helen, 20, 138 N.
  Isabel, 50.
  Jennet, 28.
  Joan, 44.
  John, 43, 54, 101, 137.
  Margaret, 23, 118.
  Margery, 33, 141 N.
  Richard, 138 N.
  Simon, 29, 50, 54, 58.
  William, 16, 108, 138 N., 141 N.
HEYWOOD,
  Elizabeth, 118 N.
HIBITSON, see also IBOTSON,
  Elizabeth, 61 bis.
  Henry, 61 bis.
HILL,
  Agnes, 4, 87, 105, 150 N.
  Alexander, 28, 48, 51, 54, 58, 91, 105.
  Alice, 43, 83, 95, 104.
  Ambrose, 101.
  Ann, 32, 38 bis, 40, 51, 66, 115.
  Barbara, 108.
  Cecily, 83 N., 123 N.
  Charles, 10, 15 N., 51, 68 bis, 83 N., 104, 118 N., 123, 123 N., 145, 152 N.
  Dorothy, 51.
  Elizabeth, 3, 31, 83 N., 106 N., 146.
  Ellen, 58.
  Frances, 115.
  Francis, 105.
  Gilbert, 75.
  Grace, 10, 126.
  Henry, 7 N., 14, 83, 84, 88 N., 106 N., 115.
  Isabel, 34, 40, 83 N., 94 N.
  Jane, 15, 89, 91.
  Jennet, 27.
  Joan, 106 N.
  Johanna, 27, 88 N.
  John, 31, 39, 60, 75, 83, 83 N., 86, 106, 106 N., 118, 123 N., 149, 153.
  Margaret, 21, 23, 28, 83 N., 106, 106 N., 115, 123 N.
  Margery, 149 N.
  Marion, 83 N.
  Maud, 83 N., 123 N.
  Nicholas, 5, 40, 48, 60 bis, 66, 75, 100.
  Ralph, 22, 135.
  Richard, 3, 7 N., 88 N., 106 N., 108, 149 N., 158, 161, 162 bis.
  Robert, 6, 54, 80, 83 N., 87, 98, 106 N., 131, 153, 157, 159, 161.
  Thomas, 15 N., 123 N., 152 N.
  Widow, 134.
  William, 28, 60, 83 N., 102, 149 N., 150 N., 157.
HINCHCLIFFE,
  Agnes, 86.
  Elizabeth, 87.
  Henry, 86, 87.
  John, 36, 82.
  Margaret, 2.
  Margery, 65.
  Thomas, 3, 5, 21, 44, 100.
  William, 35, 48 bis, 65, 139.
HIRST,
  George, 49.
  John, 32, 123.
  Margaret, 7.
  Mary, 34.
  Robert, 120 N.
  Stephen, 43.
  Thomas, 49.
  Uxor, 128.
HOBSON,
  Alice, 55, 155 N.

INDEX.

HOBSON (continued),
  Charles, 12, 44, 128.
  Cotton, 23, 35, 50, 52, 55, 58, 66, 70, 73, 76.
  Dionis, 34, 58.
  Edmund, 26 N.
  Edward, 94, N.
  Elizabeth, 21, 34, 39, 48, 53, 65, 73, 125 N.
  Francis, 29, 47, 50 bis, 53 bis, 58 bis, 65, 68, 71, 76, 142 bis.
  George, 36 bis, 61, 65, 67 bis.
  Grace, 58.
  Helen, 8, 50, 56, 59, 71, 142.
  Hugh, 105.
  Isabel, 130.
  Jennet, 22.
  John, 76.
  Lawrence, 122.
  Margaret, 47, 50, 64, 66.
  Margery, 52.
  Mary, 50, 67, 75, 76.
  Nicholas, 18, 41, 50, 75, 133 N., 134 N.
  Ralph, 20, 97 N., 124.
  Richard, 24, 41, 47, 53, 59, 133 N., 158.
  Robert, 28, 39, 48, 50 bis, 53, 56, 75.
  Thomas, 61, 64, 67, 68, 75, 78, 109, 133, 133 N.
  Widow, 135.
  William, 3 N., 50, 65, 70, 97.
HOBSON, alias GREAVES,
  Edward, 115 N.
HOCKINSON,
  Alice, 40.
HODGSON,
  James, 160 bis.
  William, 19, 114 N.
HODSKINSON,
  Katherine, 33.
HOLDEN, HOLDING, or HOWLDEN,
  Alice, 96.
  Charles, 18, 49, 75, 138.
  Helen, 93.
  Isabel, 108.
  James, 75.
  Jean, 4, 5.
  Johanna, 84.
  John, 90, 117, 160.
  Margaret, 72.
  Ralph, 76, 128 N., 132 N.
  Richard, 14, 90 N., 102 N.
  Robert, 5, 67 bis, 72, 76, 115, 128 N., 132 N.
  Thomas, 84.
  Widow, 80 N., 135.
  William, 80.
HOLDEN, alias BRADLEY,
  Thomas, 137.
HOLLAND, see HOYLAND.
HOLLEY,
  Richard, 31.
HOLLINGHRIGGE,
  Alice, 130.
  Elizabeth, 94.
  Margaret, 92.
  Ralph, 130.
  Richard, 2, 9, 106.
HOLMES, HOLME, or HALME,
  Ann, 39.
  Charles, 120.
  Christopher, 17, 125.
  Dorothy, 44.
  George, 60.
  James, 35, 60.
  Jane, 4.
  Margaret, 17, 136.
  Mr. 154, 156 N.
HOLTE,
  Jane, **23.**

HOOLE, or HOWLE,
  Alice, 7.
  Ann, 118 N., 134 N.
  Catherine, 24, 118 N.
  Edmund, 17.
  Elizabeth, 118 N.
  Isabel, 118 N., 121.
  James, 37 N.
  John, 37 N., 94 N., 104.
  Margaret, 12, 118 N., 121.
  Robert, 16, 16 N., 80 N., 83, 118 N.
  Uxor, 125.
  William, 37, 37 N., 118 N., 128 N.
HOPKINSON,
  Jane, 5.
  Johanna, 12.
HOPTON,
  Ann, 33.
HORNER,
  Cecilia, 85 N.
  Henry, 81 N., 85 N.
  Margaret, 81.
HOULLE, see also HULL.
  William, 149 N.
HOWARD,
  Elizabeth, 40.
HOWDEN,
  Ann, 59.
  Robert, 34, 59.
HOWGAT,
  Ann, 39.
HOWSLEY,
  Agnes, 82 N., 97, 140 N.
  Alexander, 6 N., 13.
  Alice, 117 N., 140 N., 144, 144 N.
  Ann, 25, 140 N.
  Barbara, 95.
  Cecily, 17, 82 N.
  Effame, 82 N., 161 N.
  Elizabeth, 3, 3 N., 6 N., 19, 19 N., 82 N., 161 N.
  Francis, 81 N.
  Helen, 6, 82 N., 142.
  Hugh, 3, 97.
  Isabel, 12.
  Isabella de, 140 N.,
  Jean, 140 N.,
  Johannes de, 140 N.
  John, 82 N., 140 N.
  Laurencius de, 140 N.
  Maerlec, 140 N.
  Margaret, 82 N.
  Margareta de, 140 N.
  Mary, 80, 81 N.
  Nicholas, 82 N.
  Ricardus de, 140 N.
  Robert, 38, 77.
  Thomas, 3, 3 N. bis, 19 N., 80 N., 81, 81 N., 82, 82 N., 106, 106 N., 110 N., 117 N., 121 N., 130 N., 140, 140 N., 144 N., 161, 161 N.
  William, 39, 77, 122, 140 N.
  ———— 121 N., 130 N.
HOYLAND, or HOLLAND,
  Agnes, 11, 86 N.
  Alice, 3, 6 N., 87.
  Ann, 42, 49, 76, 86 N., 143.
  Elizabeth, 76, 86 N.,
  George, 73.
  Henry, 6 N., 91, 113 N., 149 N., 153, 156, 158.
  Isabel, 28, 80.
  James, 39, 73, 76.
  Joan, 7.
  John, 15.
  Margaret, 9, 54, 95.
  Margery, 150 N.
  Nicholas, 42, 75, 86 **N., 129.**
  Richard, 40, 86 N.
  Robert, 94 N.

HOYLAND (continued),
  Thomas, 6, 6 N., 27, 39, 39 N., 40, 54, 64 bis, 76, 78, 90 N., 93, 94 N., 113.
  William, 85, 86 N., 94 N.
HUDSON,
  Alexander, 82.
  Alice, 94.
  Ellen, 40.
  Humphrey, 82.
  John, 94.
  Mr. 113 N.
  Thomas, 40.
  William, 41.
HULL, see also HOULLE.
  Richard, 156 N.
  William, 150 N.
HUMBLOCK,
  Cotton, 91.
  Isabel, 92.
  Jane, 90.
  John, 4, 8, 92.
  Margaret, 92.
  Robert, 88, 91.
  Thomas, 153.
HUNT,
  Christopher, 23.
  John, 149 N.
  William, 149 N.
HUNTER,
  Margaret, 39.
  Mr. (the Historian), 122 N., 131 N., 152 N.
  Oliva, 3.
  Richard, 44.
HURT,
  Alice, 6 N.
  Ann, 19 N.
  Dionis, 6 N.
  Elizabeth, 17.
  Francis, 31 N.
  James, 57.
  Jonathan, 31 N.
  Nicholas, 6 N., 31, 31 N., 42, 42 N., 55, 57, 61, 74.
  Reginald, 19 N.
  Robert, 6, 6 N., 31 N., 53.
  Thomas, 61.
  Valentine, 31 N.
  Walter, 6 N., 33.
  William, 74.
HURTON,
  Alice, 1 N., 84.
  Elizabeth, 91, 133 N.
  Isabel, 1 N., 7.
  John, 81 N., 133 N.
  Robert, 1 N., 7, 133 N.
HUSCROFT,
  James, 33.
HUTCHINSON,
  Agnes, 16, 137.
  Catherine, 4.
  Edward, 142 N.
  George, 40.
  Helen, 142 N.
  Isabel, 7.
  Ralph, 18.
  Reginald, 137.
  Rewald, 29.
  Rosa, 44.
  Thomas, 140 N.
HUTTON,
  Thomas, 115.
HYDE,
  Agnes, 81 N., 84.
  Alexander, 6, 6 N., 13 **N., 81 N.,** 127 N.
  Ann, 96, 127 N.
  Elizabeth, 13.
  Ellen, 31 N., 95.

INDEX.

HYDE (continued),
 Ann, 17, 41, 47, 53, 58.
 George, 6 N.
 Hugh, 18, 18 N., 81 N., 97 N.,
  110 N. bis, 125 N., 127, 127 N., 133.
 Isabel, 127 N., 132.
 Jane, 93.
 Joan, 49, 112.
 John, 81 N., 83, 127 N.
 Margaret, 81 N., 127 N.
 Mary, 65.
 Matilda, 2.
 Phillis, 16.
 Ralph, 58, 81 N., 84.
 Thomas, 53, 81 N., 93.
 Widow, 83.
 William, 6 N., 18 N., 25, 49, 53, 58,
  65, 81, 81 N., 127 N., 133, 133 N.
HYNE,
 Robert, 94 N.
 Rose, 26.

IBOTSON, see also HIBITSON,
 Ann, 40.
 Elizabeth, 41.
 George, 44, 95.
 Henry, 27, 52, 56, 70, 144.
 Jennet, 42.
 John, 8, 95.
 Nicholas, 52.
 Robert, 56.
INGLE,
 Margery, 146.
 Ralph, 99.
 Richard, 4, 51, 88, 146.
 William, 51.
INMAN,
 Ann, 18.
 Joan, 5.

JACKSON,
 Charles, 90 N., 150 N., 161 N.
 Francis, 109.
 Widow, 95.
JEFFCOCK,
 Elizabeth Ann, 41 N.
 John, 41 N.
 Rev. John Thomas, 41 N.
 Parkyn, 41 N.
JEFFRAY,
 Elizabeth, 111.
 Grace, 111.
 Henry, 13, 17.
 Richard, 151 N.
JEFFRAY, alias MANTON,
 Helen, 109.
JEPSON,
 Alexander, 7 N., 47, 51, 54, 58 bis,
  59, 64, 67, 146.
 Alice, 2.
 Ann, 34.
 Barbara, 35.
 Catherine, 20.
 Elizabeth, 64.
 George, 67.
 Helen or Ellen, 9, 36, 61.
 Jane, 27.
 Jenetta, 138.
 Joan, 9, 106, 121, 130.
 John, 12, 67, 82, 96, 108, 151 N.,
  154 N., 156 N.
 Margaret, 7 N., 19, 34, 47.
 Margery, 84.
 Mary, 7 N.
 Nicholas, 76, 96.
 Richard, 8, 22, 137, 138.
 Robert, 29, 51, 58 bis, 59, 61, 67,
  74 bis, 76.
 Roland, 51.
 Thomas, 7, 7 N., 51, 81, 132 N., 146, 157.

JEPSON (continued),
 William, 22, 54.
JESSOP,
 Ann, 60 bis.
 Francis, 26 N., 120.
JOBSON,
 George, 71.
 Isabel, 71.
JOHNS,
 Elizabeth, 102.
 Thomas, 94 N.
JOHNSON,
 Agnes, 13.
 Ann, 55, 106.
 Barbara, 53.
 Dionis, 89.
 Francis, 23, 50, 55, 63, 132.
 Hannah, 26 N.
 John, 108.
 Richard, 50.
 Thomas, 100.
 Widow, 82.
 William, 1, 100, 120 N.
JULIAN,
 Cardinal, Bishop of Ostia, 152 N.

KAY,
 Adam, 140 N.
 Agnes, 140 N.
 Ann, 101.
 Barbara, 20.
 Dorothy, 43.
 Elizabeth, 2, 43.
 John, 6, 104.
 Margaret, 104.
 Richard, 3.
 Roger, 8.
 Thomas, 24.
 Widow, 82.
KEEFE,
 Margaret, 25.
KELLET,
 Elizabeth, 73.
KEMPE,
 Michael, 31.
KENDALL,
 Ann, 127 N.
KENT,
 Agnes, 26.
 Alice, 24.
 Catherine, 95.
 Cecilia, 81 N.
 Edward, 81.
 Joana, 81 N., 105, 117.
 John, 81 N.
 Peter, 14, 20, 38, 129.
 Richard, 81 N.
 Richard de, 85 N.
 Robert, 81, 81 N., 133 N., 142 N.
KENYON,
 Adamson, 2 N.
 Edward, 2 N.
 Rachel, 2 N.
 William, 9.
KERR, see CARR.
KEYES,
 Alice, 1.
 Catherine, 14, 29, 155 N.
 Edward, 19.
 Nicholas, 105.
KIDDARS,
 Henry, 148 N., 149 N.
 William, 148 N.
KILLABECK,
 Agnes, 100.
 Isabel, 87.
 John, 5, 99.
KILLALOE,
 Bishop of, 8 N.

KIRKBY,
 Elizabeth, 73.
 Jane, 77.
 Joan, 7.
 Margaret, 9, 122.
 Richard, 140 N.
 Robert, 140 N.
 Thomas, 39, 73, 77.
 William, 27.
KIRKE,
 Ann, 47 N.
 Gerard, 47 N.
 Robert, 47 N.
KIRKMAN,
 Elizabeth, 62.
 George, 62.
KIRSHAW,
 Francis, 141.
 John, 141.
LAMBERT,
 Lydia, 25 N.
LASTLES,
 Edward, 113 N.
 Henry, 113 N.
 John, 113 N.
LASTLEYE,
 Henry, 5.
LAWE,
 Alice, 70.
 Ann, 42.
 Anthony, 46 bis, 49, 62, 70, 138.
 Elizabeth, 49.
 Johanna, 21.
 Thomas, 16, 62.
LAYTON,
 James, 15.
 Uxor, 132.
LEE,
 Agnes, 15, 109 N., 110 N., 113.
 Alice, 84, 157 N.
 Ann, 157 N.
 Elizabeth, 36 bis, 109, 157 N.
 Francis, 111.
 James, 4, 157 N.
 Jane, 70, 108.
 Johanna, 15, 157 N.
 John, 7, 103, 103 N., 157 N.
 Sir John, 100 N., 102 N., 104.
 Margaret, 109, 109 N., 127 N.
 Nicholas, 157 N.
 Ralph, 15, 16 N., 34, 64 bis, 67, 70,
  97 N., 102 N., 106 N., 109 N., 110,
  110 N., 127 N., 152 N., 154, 157 bis,
  157 N., 162.
 Richard, 9, 157 N.
 Robert, 82, 84, 157 N.
 Thomas, 100, 157 N.
 William, 67, 110 N.
LEPTON,
 Margaret, 25.
LINCOLN,
 Bishop of, 139 N., 143 N.
LINLEY,
 Barbara, 114.
 Joan, 116.
 Robert, 17, 116.
LINSETT, see LYNTHWET.
LISTER,
 Alice, 32.
 Ann, 22, 75, 89.
 Elizabeth, 35, 102.
 Helen, 28.
 Hester, 60.
 Isabel, 119.
 James, 34, 60, 62, 66, 70, 73, 75.
 Johanna, 20.
 John, 3, 62, 125, 133 N.
 Margaret, 105.
 Nicholas, 66, 70.

INDEX.

LISTER (continued),
　Robert, 100, 118.
LITTLEWOOD,
　Beatrice, 31.
　Margaret, 143.
LOCKSLEY,
　Ricardus de, 141 N.
LOCKWOOD,
　Alice, 35.
　Ann, 59.
　Catherine, 75.
　Edward, 75.
　Elizabeth, 50, 135 N.
　Ellen, 43, 54.
　Hugh, 64.
　John, 19, 27, 46, 50, 54, 59, 64, 69, 143, 144.
　Lucy, 46, 143.
　William, 25, 69, 135 N.
LODGE,
　Ann, 56.
　John, 56, 61.
　William, 61.
LONG,
　Elizabeth, 103.
LONGLEY,
　Edward, 39 N.
　Elena, 6 N.
　Elizabeth, 39, 39 N.
　John, 39.
　Thomas, 6 N.
LORD,
　Alice, 138.
　Ann, 57, 139 N.
　Deborah, 139 N.
　James, 139 N.
　Jane, 139 N.
　Jeremiah, 44, 139 N.
　Joseph, 25, 28, 36, 46, 52, 57, 138.
　Margaret, 29.
　Martha, 38, 38 N., 139 N.
　Rebecca, 36, 36 N., 139 N.
　Richard, 36 N., 38, 125 N., 133 N., 139, 139 N., 140 N.
　Robert, 52.
　Sarah, 139.
　Susan, 139 N.
　William, 46.
LOSH,
　Ann, 66.
　Edward, 72.
　John, 66, 69 bis, 72, 76.
　Nicholas, 76.
LOUND, or LOWNDE,
　Alice, 110, 117.
　Ann, 89.
　Isabel, 87.
　John de, 150 N.
　Margaret, 101.
　Nicholas, 87.
　Richard, 2, 98.
　William, 95.
LOXT,
　Elizabeth, **33**.
LUDGE,
　John, 105.
　Robert, 111.
LYLLEY,
　William, 128.
LYMER,
　Elizabeth, 14.
LYNTHWET, LYNFETT, or LINSETT, &c.,
　Alice, 97.
　Ann, 75.
　Brian, 97.
　Catherine, 119.
　Elizabeth, 74.
　Helen, 100, 108.
　John, 9, 11, 39, 74, 127.

LYNTHWET (continued)
　Nicholas, 37, 71, 75.
　Peter, 100.
　Richard, 91.

MACHON,
　Alice, 4, 5, 84, 95.
　Ann, 4.
　Catherine, 5.
　Deborah, 68.
　Elizabeth, 9, 51.
　George, 65, 82, 119.
　Helen, 8, 8 N., 71.
　Henry, 55.
　Jennet, 60.
　John, 2, 2 N., 12, 12 N., 36, 36 N., 65, 66, 68, 81, 81 N., 94 N.
　Margaret, 114.
　Margery, 115.
　Marion, 3.
　Nicholas, 74.
　Richard, 80.
　Thomas, 30, 51, 55, 60, 65 bis, 67, 70, 74, 94 N., 95.
　William, 37, 66, 67, 70, 72, 94 N.
　——— 3 N.
MACKENZIE,
　Rev. Alexander, 47 N.
　Mary Ann, 47 N.
MACKERETH,
　Rev. John, 25 N.
MALIN,
　Dorothy, 42.
MALINSON,
　Helen, 101.
MAN,
　Agnes, 12.
　Ann, 22.
　Elizabeth, 15, 144.
　Jane, 144.
　Nicholas, 16, 26, 127 N., 132, 144 bis.
　William, 131.
MANTON,
　Elizabeth, 93.
　Godfrey, 92.
　Nicholas, 66.
　Sarah, 66.
MANTON, alias JEFFRAY,
　Helen, 109.
MARRIOT,
　Elizabeth, 38.
MARRIS,
　Thomas, 94.
MARSDEN, or MARSTEN,
　Alice, 40, 43, 102 N.
　Barbara, 136.
　Beatrice, 32.
　Dionis, 14, 119, 128, 129.
　Elizabeth, 128.
　Francis, 119.
　John, 7, 8.
　Katherine, 39.
　Mary, 37.
　Thomas, 40.
　William, 2.
MARSH,
　Ellen, 39.
　John, 23.
MARSHALL,
　Francis, 50, 51, 53.
　Jane, 37.
　Joane, 61.
　Margaret, 35.
　Michael, 51.
　Nicholas, 50, 61.
　Ronald, 50.
　William, 4, 120 N.
MARSHLAND,
　Ralph, 94.

MARTIN,
　William, 19.
MASON,
　Ann, 29.
　Cecily, 49, 145 N.
　Edward, 37, 51, 68 bis.
　Henry, 43, 62, 78.
　Margaret, 41, 42.
　Robert, 28, 49, 51, 56, 59 bis, 62.
　Thomas, 56.
MATHY,
　George, 76.
　Robert, 76.
MATHYMAN, or MATHEWMAN,
　Agnes, 27, 94 N., 104.
　Alice, 142 N.
　Ann, 50, 54, 142 N.
　Dionis, 72.
　Edward, 113 N., 142 N.
　Elizabeth, 38, 56, 74, 138.
　Frances, 137.
　Helen, 48, 144.
　Jane, 66.
　Jennet, 142 N.
　Johanna, 144 N.
　John, 142 N.
　Margaret, 20 N., 32, 53.
　Mary, 41.
　Nicholas, 62, 94 N., 106.
　Peter, 50, 54, 94 N., 142 N., 144, 144 N.
　Ralph, 50, 142 N.
　Richard, 20, 20 N., 72, 94 N., 142, 142 N., 144.
　Robert, 28, 48 bis, 53 bis, 62, 66, 74, 137, 138, 142 N.
　Roger, 43.
　Rose, 31.
　Thomas, 48.
　William, 50, 56, 142 N., 156.
　——— 138 N.
MATLEY, or MOTLEY,
　Agnes, 10.
　John, 91.
　Thomas, 91.
MAULEVERER,
　Elizabeth, 12, 12 N.
　Mr., 112 N.
　Nicholas, 12 N.
MAUTHAM,
　Thomas, 21.
MAWKIN,
　Dorothy, 46.
MAWRE, see MOORE.
MAYDEN,
　Ann, 59.
　Lawrence, 59.
MEADOWCROFT,
　Francis, 139 N.
MEARES, see also MIAS,
　John, 40.
　Robert, 71.
MELLER, see also MILNER,
　Ann, 24, 67, 139.
　Benjamin, 126 N.
　Catherine, 50.
　Charles Mathias, 126 N.
　Elizabeth, 54, 126 N.
　Ellen, 78.
　Hugh, 51, 55 bis, 61, 126, 126 N.
　Isabel, 38, 51.
　John, 126 N.
　Margaret, 126.
　Ralph, 61.
　Richard, 41.
　Robert, 46, 139.
　Rose, 25.
　Stephen, 67.
　Thomas, 40, 46, 50, 78, 139 bis.
　William, 54.

INDEX. 175

MEMOT,
  Elizabeth, **110**.
MENDLOVE,
  John, 33.
MIAS, see also MEARES,
  Ann, 76.
  Frances, **76**.
  John, 76.
MICHELL,
  George, 25.
MIDDLETON,
  Charles, 108.
  Euphemia, 140 N.
  Joan, 107, 108.
  John, 109.
  Robert, 106.
MILNER, see also MELLER,
  Elizabeth, 31, 55.
  Ellen, 75.
  Hugh, 48.
  John, 75, 77.
  Maria, 33.
  Peter, 29.
  Thomas, 18, 23, 32, 48, 55, 128 N.
MIRFIELD,
  John, 81.
  Margaret, 143 N.
  Robert, 143 N.
MIRFIN,
  John, **31, 39**.
MOOKE,
  Margaret, 117.
  Robert, 131.
MOOKSON,
  Robert, 139.
  William, 37.
MOORE, or MAWRE,
  Agnes, 161 N.
  Ann, 161 N.
  Edward, 112 N.
  Elizabeth, 83.
  Francis, 67.
  George, 161 **N**.
  James, 9.
  John del, 152 N.
  Margery, 83 N., 99 N., 110 N.
  Richard del, 152 N.
  Robert, 67.
MOORHOUSE,
  Ann, 33.
  Ellen, 78.
  John, 70, 74, 78, 83, 157.
  Robert, 96.
  William, 70.
MOREWOOD,
  Alice, 117.
  Gilbert, 112.
  Willielmus de, **116 N**.
MORLEY,
  James, 160.
MORRIS,
  John, 25.
MORTON,
  Agnes, 24, 119.
  Ann, 26 N., 29, 37.
  Cecily, 31.
  Dionis, 34.
  Edward, 30.
  Elizabeth, 23.
  Ellen, 2 **N**.
  Henry, 26 **N**.
  James, 3, **96**.
  John, 39.
  Lawrence, 112.
  Margaret, 94 N.
  Peter, 112 N., 145.
  Philip, 27, 120.
  Richard, 2, 2 N., 102 N., 136.
  Uxor, 125.

MOULD,
  Helen, 122.
  Widow, 99 N.
MOUNTENEY,
  Alexander, 150 N.
  Alice, 152 N.
  Ann, 151 N., 152 N.
  Anthony, 151 N., 152 N.
  Arnold, 102 N.
  Barbara, 96 N., 98, 152 N.
  Beatrice, 152 N.
  Dorothy, 151 N.
  Edward, 151 N.
  Elizabeth, 151 N.
  Helen, 102 N.
  Isabel, 1 N., 16, 16 N., 102 N., 118 N., 151 N., 152 N.
  Joan, 150 N., 152 N.
  John, 5 N., 15 N., 16 N., 98, 98 N., 102, 102 N., 118 N., 122 N., 137 N., 151 N., 152 N., 156.
  Sir John, 152 N.
  Katherine, 151 N.
  Margaret, 102 N.
  Maud, 15, 15 N., 118 N., 152 N.
  Mr., 148 N., 151, 153 bis, 154, 159.
  Nicholas, 15 N., 102 N., 118 N., 150 N., 151 N., 152 N., 154 ter, 157, 161.
  R., 150, 150 N.
  Robert, 150 N., 151 N., 152 N.
  Thomas, 122 N., 150 N., 151 N., 152 N.
MOUNTENEY, *alias* **CROFTS**,
  Maud, 137.
MUNDY,
  Alice, 129.
  John, 29.
MUSCROFT,
  Thomas 17.

NAWT,
  John, 38, 70.
  Thomas, 70.
NEDOM,
  George, 69.
  Richard, 38, 69.
NELSON,
  Alice, **114 N**.
  John, **114 N**.
NEVELL,
  Francis, 76.
  Rosamond, **76**.
NEWBOTT,
  Alice, 28.
NEWBY,
  Ambrose, 114.
NEWELL,
  Mary, 37.
  Thomas, 126 N.
NEWTON,
  Thomas, 19.
  William, 115.
NEYLER, or NAILOR, &c.
  Ann, 56.
  Elizabeth, 7.
  Francis, 119.
  Henry, 34, 74.
  Joan, 116.
  John, 74.
  Margaret, 28.
  Nicholas, 24, 47, 52 bis, 56, 61, 63.
  Richard, 63.
  Robert, 9, 18, **61, 119**.
  Thomas, 43.
NICHOLLS,
  Ann, 42.
  Helen, 82.
NICKSON,
  Christopher, 19, 34.

NICKSON (*continued*),
  Dionis, 23.
  Dorothy, 55.
  Elizabeth, 39, 47, 50.
  George, 55, 59, 69.
  Grace, 41.
  James, 59.
  Margaret, 42.
  Robert, 69.
  William, 29, 50.
NODDER,
  Agnes, 10.
  Thomas, 95.
NORBORNE,
  Richard, 44.
NORMANTON,
  Robert, 140 N.
NORTHOLL,
  Humphrey, **74, 76**.
  John, 76.
  Mathew, 74.
NORTON,
  Agnes, 135.
  James, 102.
  John, 102, 102 N., 119.
  Thomas, 125 N.
NUTT,
  Dorothy, 63.
  Robert, 59, 63.
  William, 34, 59.
ODESON,
  Emote, 18.
  Francis, 42.
OFFREY,
  Alice, 7.
OLDHAM,
  Thomas, 29.
OLLIVER,
  Ann, 44.
OSBONSTON,
  Nicholas, 87.
OSGATHORPE,
  Johanna, 86.
  ———, 157, 158.
OSLEY,
  Alice, 13.
  Thomas, 17, 40, 115.
OSTIA,
  Julian, Cardinal, Bishop of, 152 N.,
OTES, or OATES,
  Cecily, 34.
  Charles, 36.
  Elizabeth, 16.
  Mary, 17.
  Thomas, 102.
  Widow, 130.
OULFIELD, or OULFELD,
  Elizabeth, 64.
  Richard, 34, 59, 64, **70, 72**.
  Robert, 72.
  Thomas, 59, **70**.
OVERALL,
  Frances, 39 **N**.
  Robert, 39 N.
  William, 39 N.
OXLEY,
  Christopher, 140 N.
OXSPRING,
  Alice, 30.
  Ann, 28, 138.
  Elizabeth, 76, 144.
  Frances, 122 N.
  George, 65.
  Helen, 56, 96.
  Isabel, 36.
  James, 52.
  Jane, 29.
  John, 33, 56, 81 N., 105, 107.
  Lucy, 24 N., 27.

INDEX.

OXSPRING (continued),
  Margaret, 27.
  Richard, 40, 76, 115.
  Robert, 9, 52, 60, 65, **138, 144.**
  Thomas, 9, 99.

PAGE,
  Henry, 29, 152 N.
  Margaret, 8.
  Thomas, 152 N.
PARKER,
  Agnes, 149 N., 150 N.
  Ann, 4, 88, 120, 125 N.
  Arnold, 2 N.
  Cecily, 1, 1 N., 161 N.
  Clement, 75.
  Elizabeth, 7, 111, 149 N., 150 N.
  Frances, 161 N.
  Francis, 2 N., 16 N., 75, 78 bis, 125, 125 N., 150 N.
  Francis George Shircliffe, 2 N.
  Helen, 2, 2 N., 149 N.
  Isabel, 2, 2N.
  Johanna, 11.
  John, 7 N., 11 N., 110 N., 149 N., 150 N., 153, 154, 156, 156 N., 157 ter, 157 N., 158 ter, 159, 160, 161, 161 N.
  Kenyon, 2 N.
  Lawrence, 82.
  Margaret, 7, 150 N., 161 N.
  Nicholas, 161 N.
  Richard, 149 N., 150 N., 161 N.
  Robert, 149 N., 150 N.
  Thomas, 2 N. bis, 7 N. 82 N., 84, 90 N. bis, 110, 140 N., 149, 149 N., 150 N., 161 N.
  William, 7, 7 N., 16 N., 110 N. bis, 123 N., 125, 125 N., 150 N.
  ———, 90 N.
PARKER, alias HALL,
  Agnes, 108.
PARKIN, or PARKYN,
  Agnes, 3, 81, 98 N., 103 N., 108, 119, 135 N.
  Alice, 14, 30, 83, 99.
  Ann, 23, 65, 72.
  Arthur, 51, 98 N., 145.
  Beatrice, 10.
  Catherine, 41 N.
  Christine, 117.
  Dorothy, 84, 129.
  Edward, 49, 135 N., 143.
  Elizabeth, 32, 47 N., 56, 61, 106.
  Emote, 98 N., 139.
  Francis, 91, 120, 135 N.
  George, 42, 55, 62, 76.
  Helen, 25, 68, 69, 98 N., 135 N.
  Henry, 11, 99.
  Isabel, 41 N., 49, 104.
  James, 103 N.
  Jane, 16, 34, 99.
  Jennet, 137.
  Joan, 62.
  Johanna, 92.
  John, 9, 14, 19, 26, 38, 41 N., 48, 51, 52, 54 bis, 55, 56, 61, 62 bis, 68, 72 bis, 74, 78 bis, 98 N., 99 N., 105, 135, 135 N., 140 N., 154 N.
  Leonard, 63.
  Lucy, 66.
  Margaret, 27, 31, 34, 65, 98, 98 N., 127, 135 N., 142.
  Maria, 52, 76.
  Mary, 30, 40.
  Nicholas, 22, 49, 58, 62, 66, 72, 77, 135 N.
  Paul, 41 N.
  Peter, 41 N., 156, 157, 158, 159, 161 bis.

PARKIN (continued),
  Ralph, 77.
  Richard, 44, 89.
  Robert, 14, 19, 34, 41 N., 48, 63 bis, 69, 74, 76, 77, 98 N., 140 N., 141, 161, 162.
  Rosamond, 40.
  Rose, 22.
  Sarah, 41 N.
  Thomas, 4, 13, 16, 28, 32, 35, 41, 41 N., 47 N., 48 bis, 51, 56, 62, 63, 65, 69, 74 bis, 76, 77, 127, 129 N., 135 N., 144.
  Uxor, 133.
  William, 10, 27, 41 N., 48 bis, 49, 51, 56, 98 N., 123 N., 137, 141, 142, 143, 145.
  Zachariah, 41 N., 77.
PARKIN, alias COOPER,
  Ann, 126 N.
  Elizabeth, 126 N.
  Margaret, 76, 126 N.
  Mary, 126 N.
  Richard, 126 N.
  Thomas, 76, 126 N.
PARMAN,
  Margaret, 110.
  Richard, 10, 128.
PASHLIE,
  Mary, 44.
PATINSON,
  Ann, 68.
  Edward, 68.
PAVY,
  Edward, 112 N.
PAWSON,
  Barbara, 43, 43 N.
  Elizabeth, 32 N.
  Isabel, 32.
  John, 129 N. bis.
  Margaret, 92.
  Maria, 30, 30 N.
  Nicholas, 32 N., 43 N.
  Thomas, 30 N.
PEACOCK,
  Alice, 35.
PEACE,
  Ellen, 73.
  John, 39, 73.
PEARSIE,
  Theodocia, 42.
PEARSON,
  Ann, 36.
  Elizabeth, 1.
  Francis, 120.
  Helen, 107.
  Henry, 132 N.
  Isabel, 106.
  Jennet, 138 N.
  John, 23, 123, 130, 138 N.
  Nicholas, 100, 138 N., 141 N.
  Ralph, 98, 128 N.
  Robert, 6, 15.
  Thomas, 11, 120.
PEGGE,
  Johanna, 17.
  John, 108.
PENERETH,
  Thomas, 149 N.
PENISTONE,
  Richard, 110.
PENNINGTON,
  Christopher, 39.
PERLYNGTON,
  ———, 160 bis.
PHILIPPE,
  Agnes, 100 N., 117.
  Edmund, 157 N.
PHILLIPOT,
  Thomas, 5, 89.

PHIPPS, or FYPPS,
  Ann, 37, 37 N.
  Frances, 37 N.
  George, 26 N., 37 N.
  Humphrey, 37 N.
  Jennett, 37 N.
  John, 37 N.
  Richard, 37 N.
  Thomas, 37 N.
  William, 37 N.
PICKFORD,
  Peter, 39.
PICKHAVER,
  Jennet, 33.
PIGBURN,
  Richard, 140 N.
PLACE,
  Ann, 50, 145.
  Lawrence, 30, 50, 145.
PLATTS,
  John, 16, 23, 128.
  Uxor, 127.
POGMORE,
  Mary, 38.
POGSON,
  Henry, 75.
  Thomas, 75.
POOLE,
  Francis, 130 N.
  Julian, 130 N.
POPPLEWELL,
  William, 39.
POTTER,
  Alice, 65.
  Ann, 59.
  Isabel, 65.
  John, 75.
  Thomas, 59, 65, 70 bis, 75.
PRINCE,
  Elizabeth, 92.
  Thomas, 7, 89.
PRIESTLEY,
  Joan, 51.
  John, 161.
PRYEST,
  Joan, 7.
PUDSEY,
  Johanna, 9.

QUENSON,
  John, 81 N.

RAGGE,
  Agnes, 137.
  Ann, 136 bis, 146.
  Anthony, 75, 78.
  Elizabeth, 46, 113, 137.
  Frances, 50, 145.
  Francis, 63.
  Isabel, 138.
  Joan, 136.
  Johanna, 22.
  John, 28, 42, 43, 49 bis, 53, 56, 63, 75, 136 quater, 137.
  Margaret, 29, 36.
  Maria, 56.
  Mary, 136.
  Nicholas, 117.
  Richard, 15, 137, 138 bis.
  Thomas, 25, 39, 44, 46, 50, 53, 75, 133, 145.
  Uxor, 127.
RAMSDEN,
  Agnes, 125.
  Jane, 30.
RAWDEN,
  Joan, 60.
  Ralph, 60.
RAWLIN,
  Francis, 74.

INDEX.

RAWLIN (*continued*),
  Joanye, 40.
  Margaret, 64.
  Nicholas, 68.
  Ralph, 31, 58, **64, 68, 74.**
  Thomas, 58.
RAWLINSON, or ROLLINSON,
  Ann, 38, 66.
  Anthony, 34, 62, 66, 69, 76.
  Elizabeth, 69.
  Helen, 62.
  Jane, 76.
RAWOOD,
  John, 157 N.
  Richard, 151 N.
RAWORTH,
  Elizabeth, 73.
  Johanna, 16, 99 N.
  Katherine, 51, 137.
  Margaret, 21.
  Richard, 51, 73, 117, 136.
RAWSON,
  John, 114 N.
  Mary, 36 N., 42.
  Richard, 154 *bis.*
  Sir Richard, 156.
  Thomas, 36 N., 141 N.
  ———, 130 N.
RENALD,
  Elizabeth, 114.
  John, 12, 114, 130.
RERESBY,
  Ann, 26 N.
  Francis, 26 N.
  Sir George, 26 N.
  John, 26 N.
  Leonard, 26 N.
  Mary, 26 N., 31 N.
RESON,
  Thomas, 152 N.
REVELL, or RELFE,
  Alice, 145.
  Ann, 40.
  Catherine, 130.
  Dorothy, 27.
  Jane, 120 N.
  Margaret, 32.
  Richard, 25, 40, 145.
  William, 31.
RICHARDSON,
  Alice, 35.
  Ann, 68.
  Dionisia, 138.
  Sir Edward, 156 N.,
  Elizabeth, 20.
  Francis, 47, 140.
  Henry, 81 N., 84, 161.
  Hugh, 115.
  Margaret, 95.
  Margery, 142 N.
  Nicholas, 68, 75.
  Ralph, 2, 20 N., 23, 90 N., 97 N., 103 N., 110 N. *bis*, 127 N., 141 N., 142 N.,
  Thomas, 75, 138.
  William, 27, 47, 140.
RIDLEY,
  Robert, **155 N.**
RIGGE,
  Margaret, **18.**
  Roger, 52.
RIVINGTON,
  Dorothy, **76.**
  Elizabeth, **99 N.**
  John, 76.
ROBERTS,
  Agnes, 90 N.
  Ann, 47, 141, 147.
  Charles, 71.
  Elizabeth, 71.

ROBERTS (*continued*),
  Nathaniel, 56.
  Richard, 56.
  William, 33, **47, 128, 141, 147.**
ROBINSON,
  Anthony, 72.
  Dorothy, 42.
  Sir Edmund, 161 N.
  Francis, 72.
  Isabel, 15.
  Joan, 117, 155 N.
  Nicholas, 84, 155 N.
  Richard, 26, 155 N.
  Thomas, 155 N.
  ———, 143 N.
ROCKLEY,
  Margaret, 44.
ROEBUCK,
  Edward, 134 N.
ROGER, or ROGERS,
  Agnes, 101.
  Ann, 58, 68.
  Elizabeth, 42, 67.
  Ellen, 43.
  Francis, 29, **40, 58, 60, 64,** 67.
  George, 60.
  Henry, 38, 68, **70.**
  Joan, 107.
  John, 13, 70.
  Julian, 43.
  Margaret, 64.
  Ralph, 112 N.
  William, 101.
ROLLINSON, see RAWLINSON,
ROLSTON,
  James, 12 N.
RONKSLEY,
  Alice, 6.
  Ann, 23.
  Elizabeth, 16.
  John, 28, 49, 139.
  Margery, 104.
  William, 49.
ROODES, or RHODES,
  Agnes, 6, 107, 118.
  Alice, 150 N.
  Ann, 14.
  Elizabeth, 7, 10, 145 N.
  Francis, 105.
  Henry, 25.
  Isabel, 12, 139 N.
  John, 8, 94 N., 101, 110, 124, **150 N.,** 151 N., 157.
  Margaret, 15.
  Michael, 111.
  Thomas, 16, 19, 115, 128.
  William, 95.
ROOE, see also WROE,
  Martin, 9.
ROOKBY,
  Mr., 155, 157, **158.**
  Thomas, 155.
  William, 100 N., 130 N,
ROOPER,
  Robert, 8.
ROOSE,
  Agnes, 9.
  John, 9, 63.
  Thomas, 63.
ROTHERHAM,
  Archbishop, 91 N.
  Thomas, 90 N.
ROTHERHAM, *alias* **SCOTT,**
  Thomas, 90 N.
ROWBOTHAM,
  Oliver, 81 N.
  Robert 23.
ROWLEYE,
  Joan, 13.

ROYSE,
  Helen, 30.
RYDER,
  Henry, 103 N.
  Thomas, 103 N.
RYDING,
  John, 96.
  Thomas, 102.
RYLEYE,
  Cecily, 15.
RYTON,
  Robert, 143.

SADLER,
  Alexander, 46 *bis*, 54, 136.
  John, 54.
ST. GEORGE,
  Richard, 90 N., 91 N.
SAMPSON,
  Agnes, 8, 94 N., **108.**
  Ann, 138 N.
  Effame, 94 N.
  Elizabeth, 48.
  Helen, 8, 16, 53, 94 N., 132 N.
  Henry, 16 N., 40, 94 N., 127 N., 132 N., 138, 138 N., 141 N.
  John, 57, 100.
  Margaret, 92, 94 N.
  Margery, 138 N., 141, 141 N.
  Nicholas, 1, 1 N., 20 N., 62, 94, 94 N., 132 N., 138 N., 141 N., 144.
  Susan, 136.
  Widow, 83.
  William, 48, **53, 62, 81, 136.**
SANBOUKE,
  Isabel, 93.
SATERFETT,
  Barbara, 30.
  Cecily, 109.
  Jennet, 26.
  John, 113.
  Richard, 15, 23, 131 N., **137.**
  Thomas, 110.
  William, 134.
SAUNDERSON,
  Ann, 80 N.
  Edward, 139 N.
  Isabel, 139 N.
  Johanna, 21.
  Nicholas, 143 N.
  Robert, 139 N., 143 N.
SAURSBY,
  Dionis, 57.
  Elizabeth, 22.
  George, 46, 140.
  Helen, 49.
  Lawrence, 24, 46, 49, 63, 70 *bis*, 140.
  Margaret, 57.
  Nicholas, 63.
SAVIDGE,
  Catherine, 131.
  Godfrey, 131.
  Widow, 82.
SAVILE,
  Dorothy, 36.
  Mary, 16.
  Thomas, 6, 99.
SAVIN,
  Henry, 161 N.
SAWOOD,
  Ann, 46, 77 *bis.*
  Henry, 28, 46.
SAYTON,
  Henry, 3, 3 N., 83 N.
  Johanna, 84.
  Thomas, 83.
SCARGELL,
  Agnes, 142 N.
  Alice, 62.
  Ann, 28, 68, 134 N.

z

SCARGELL (continued),
  Dionis, 134 N.
  Elizabeth, 47, 134 N.
  Ellen, 134 N.
  George, 134 N.
  Hugh, 134 N.
  Isabel, 80.
  John, 48, 62, 68.
  Margaret, 134 N.
  Nicholas, 27, 134 N., 142 N.
  Robert, 48, 134 N.
  Thomas, 6 bis, 23, 47, 134 N.
  William, 134 N.
SCHOLES,
  Elizabeth, 87.
  Henry, 82.
  Isabel, 117.
  John, 87.
  Richard, 5, 19.
  Thomas, 153.
SCORER, SCOYRER, or **SCOAR**, &c.,
  Alice, 71.
  Francis, 63.
  Margaret, 66.
  Nicholas, 42, 63, 66, 71.
  Richard, 9, 63.
  Thomas, 63.
SCOTT,
  Alice, 3, 3 N.
  Ann, 21 N.
  Barbara, 20 N., 90 N., 116 N.
  Christopher, 121 N., 145 N.
  Dorothy, 55.
  Edward, 90 N., 117 N., 121 N., 145, 145 N.
  Elizabeth, 41, 92, 117 N.
  Emote, 8, 90 N.
  George, 90 N., 91 N.
  Isabel, 21, 21 N., 91 N., 121 N.
  Jane, 117 N.
  Johanna, 91 N., 102, 150 N.
  John, 85 N., 90 N., 91 N., 151 N.
  Margaret, 91 N.
  Margery, 40.
  Mary, 121 N., 125.
  Michael, 140.
  Mr. 125 N.
  Nicholas, 20 N., 90, 90 N., 121 N.
  Peter, 91 N.
  Richard, 2 N., 3 N., 21 N., 22 N., 90 N., 91 N., 116 N., 130 N., 144 N.
  Sir Richard, 90 N.
  Robert, 91 N., 150 N.
  Roger, 22, 22 N., 55, 130 N., 145 N.
  Thomas, 21 N., 90 N., 91 N., 117 N., 121, 121 N., 125 N., 139 N.
  William, 2, 2 N., 90 N., 91 N., 116, 116 N.
  ———, 130 N.
SCOTT, alias ROTHERHAM,
  Thomas, 90 N.
SCULTHORPE,
  Sarah, 24 N.
SECKER,
  James, 81, 85.
  John, 14, 100.
  Maria, 33.
  Peter, 89.
  Widow, 132.
SENIOR, or SENIER,
  Andrew, 53.
  Christopher, 119.
  Edmund, 24, 49, 53, 135 N.
  Edward, 63.
  Elizabeth, 25, 127.
  Ellen, 39.
  Francis, 119.
  Isabel, 24 N., 49.
  Johanna, 19.

SENIOR (continued),
  John, 82 N.
  Nicholas 2, 135, 135 N.
  Thomas, 93.
  William, 63.
SERJEANTSON,
  Sarah, 24 N.
SERYLBY,
  Thomas, 150.
SHADFORD,
  Katherine, 39.
SHARP,
  Agnes, 10.
  Ann, 38.
  James, 13.
  Joan, 40.
  William, 42.
SHATTON,
  Robert, 90 N.
SHAW,
  Agnes, 12, 85 N., 93.
  Alice, 31.
  Ann, 109.
  Cecily, 13.
  Edmund, 115.
  Elizabeth, 3, 25, 27, 32, 62, 113, 124, 130.
  Emote, 105.
  Francis, 59.
  Gilbert, 92.
  Helen, 5, 17, 61, 91.
  Henry, 6, 39, 88, 94 N., 100, 109, 131 N., 132 N., 160.
  Isabel, 25, 135 N.
  Jane, 26, 29, 125 N.
  Jennet, 70.
  Johanna, 22, 91 N.
  John, 20, 35, 62, 75 bis, 81 N., 85 N., 91 N., 122, 125 N., 126, 149 N.
  Rev. John, 19 N.
  John de, 86 N., 133 N.
  Margaret, 112 N., 143 N.
  Nicholas, 116, 126.
  Richard, 131.
  Robert, 12, 17, 57.
  Thomas, 5, 12, 22, 55, 110 N., 130 N., 135 N., 157, 161, 162.
  Thomas de, 86 N.
  William, 15, 42, 55, 61, 71 bis, 84.
  ———, 161.
SHEFFIELD,
  Ann, 107.
  Barbara, 49.
  Joan, 107.
  John, 107, 108.
  Margaret, 54.
  Maud, 118 N.
  Thomas, 6, 49, 54.
SHELLEY,
  John, 52.
  Thomas, 52.
SHEMELD,
  Isabel, 29, 142 N.
  John, 134 N.
SHEPHERD,
  Catherine, 104.
  Margaret, 39.
  Richard, 113 N.
SHEPHERD, alias FEARNELEY,
  Magot, 116 N.
  William, 116 N.
SHIRECLIFFE,
  Agnes, 8, 19, 98 N., 113, 123 N., 135, 142 N., 148 N., 150 N.
  Alexander, 1 N., 14 N., 100 N., 119 N., 143 N., 148, 148 N., 154, 156 N., 156.
  Alice, 9, 30, 48, 100 N., 123 N.
  Ann, 1, 31, 31 N., 34, 48, 57, 63, 76, 77, 89, 143 N., 152.

SHIRECLIFFE (continued),
  Barbara, 24, 123 N., 137.
  Dorothy, 23, 25, 123 N.
  Elizabeth, 50, 71, 130 N.
  Helen, 130.
  Henry, 1 N., 7, 73, 80 N., 83, 83 N., 94 N., 98 N., 100 N., 103, 107, 123 N., 126, 133 N., 136 N., 148 N., 151 N., 155 N., 157, 159, 160.
  Hester, 118.
  Isabel, 1, 1 N., 25, 27, 39, 39 N., 52, 89, 91, 94 N., 123, 123 N., 133 N., 139, 139 N., 143 N., 148 N., 149 N.
  James, 15 N.
  Jennet, 148 N., 156.
  Johanna de, 149 N.
  Johannes de, 149 N.
  John, 2, 21, 48, 52, 57, 95, 84, 85, 87, 94, 98 N., 100 N., 105, 119 N., 123 N., 130, 136 N., 148 N., 150 N., 153.
  Margaret, 8, 15, 15 N., 52, 58, 71, 98 N., 100 N., 135, 136, 136 N.
  Mary, 98 N., 132.
  Mr. 140 N.
  Nicholas, 12, 12 N., 14, 14 N., 15 N., 17, 28 bis, 30, 31 N., 39 N., 41, 42, 48 bis, 52, 53, 57, 61, 69 bis, 74, 77 bis, 87, 90 N., 98 N., 99 N., 100 N., 102 N., 110 N., 119 N., 121 N., 122 N., 123 N., 125 N., 130 N. bis, 133 N., 134 N., 139, 139 N., 143 N., 152 N.
  Nicholas de, 14 N.
  Richard, 11 N., 12, 42, 66, 71, 73, 76, 86, 93, 98 N., 99 N., 118 N., 119 N., 123 N., 132 N., 136 N., 139 N.
  Richard de, 83 N.
  Robert, 11, 11 N., 12 N., 20, 21, 27, 30 N., 39, 48, 52 bis, 57, 63, 66, 73, 74, 76, 100 N., 107, 119 N., 123 N., 124, 130, 132, 132 N., 137, 140 N., 143 N., 148 N.
  Robertus de, 149 N.
  Thomas, 1 N., 3 N., 7 N., 14 N., 25 N., 30, 30 N., 50, 53, 57, 63, 71, 73, 84, 95, 97 N., 98, 98 N., 130 bis, 132 N., 136 N., 148 N., 149 N., 150 N., 151, 155 bis, 158.
SHIRECLIFFE,
  William, 3, 14 N., 57, 61, 63, 76, 77, 83, 83 N., 88, 98 N., 105, 123, 123 N., 130 N., 148, 148 N., 155, 155 N.
SHIRLSBYE,
  Hugh, 5.
SHOOTER,
  Agnes, 2, 87.
  Alexander, 128.
  Ann, 39.
  Catherine, 4.
  Dionis, 56.
  Elizabeth, 18, 82, 85, 87, 93.
  Helen, 32.
  Henry, 107 N., 112.
  Johanna, 143.
  John, 32, 56, 89.
  Margaret, 28.
  Margery, 84.
  Mary, 37, 115.
  Robert, 18.
  Thomas, 107, 107 N.
  Widow, 83.
  William, 93.
SHREWSBURY,
  Earl of, 36 N., 123 N., 135 N., 139 N., 141 N., 149 N., 161 N.
SILLITOO,
  Francis, 131 N.
  Susan, 43.

INDEX. 179

SILVESTER,
    Edward, 24, 24 N, 27, 46, 52, 56, 69, 154.
    Elizabeth, 46, 138.
    Ellen, 24 N.
    Francis, **69.**
    Hannah, **24 N.**
    John, 24 N.
    Nicholas, 24 N., **52.**
    Priscilla, 24 N.
    Richard, 56.
    Robert, 120.
    Thomas, 24 N.
    William, 24 N.
SIMPSON,
    Katherine, 150 N.
    Richard, 150 N.
SITWELL,
    Catherine, 31 N.
    Sir George Reresby, 26 N., 31 N.
    Sir Sitwell, 31 N.
    William, 26 N., 31 N.
SKYERS,
    Agnes, 150 N.
    John, 38, 38 N., 140 N.
    Thomas, 150 N.
SLACK,
    Johanna, 87.
    John, 42, 43, 78.
    Margaret, 111.
    Mary, 78.
    Richard, 13, 16, 125.
    Robert, 3.
    Thomas, 126 N.
    William, 20, 43.
SLATTER,
    Alice, 99.
    Ann, 123, 123 N.
    Anthony, 76.
    Beatrice, 118 N.
    Effame, 88.
    Elizabeth, 7 bis, **69, 101, 127.**
    Gilbert, 47, 71.
    Isabel, 86.
    Jane, 55, 125 N., **131.**
    Jennet, 71.
    Joan, 129.
    John, 50, 66, 69.
    Margaret, 3, 16 N., 21, 60, 122.
    Nicholas, 23, 38, 70 bis, 71, 122, 122 N, 129, 133.
    Ralph, 47, 55, 125 N., 123.
    Richard, 16 N., 55.
    Robert, 16 N., 21, 123 N., 125 N.
    Roger, 38, 71, 125 N.
    Thomas, 16 N., 40, 46 bis, **50,** 55, 60, 86, 160.
    Widow, 83.
    William, 16 N., **66, 76, 82 N.,** 101, 106, 122 N.
SLATTER, alias **WALKER,**
    Alice, 111.
    John, 107.
SMALLBEEHIND, or SMALLBENT,
    Agnes, 144.
    Alice, 6 N.
    John, 6 N.
    Robert, **6 N.**
    Thomas, 6 N.
SMALLFIELD,
    Ann, 44.
SMILTER,
    Elizabeth, 41.
    Emote, 135 N.
    Gertrude, 19.
    Roger, 135 N.
SMITH, or **SMYTH,**
    Agnes, 10, 91, 111, 148 N.
    Alice, 24, 32, 72, 120, 122.
    Ann, 12, 24.

SMITH (continued),
    Charles, 12, 40, 74, 77 bis, 123.
    Christopher, 90 N.
    Dorothy, 12.
    Edmund, 5.
    Edward, 30.
    Elizabeth, 18, 28, 32, 33, 87.
    Frances, 35.
    Francis, 121.
    Grace, 90 N., **93.**
    Helen, 25.
    Henry, 52.
    Hugh, 122 N.
    Isabel, 42, 48, **57.**
    Jane, 11, 29.
    Joan, 13, 106.
    John, 7, 24 N., 54, 70, 94, 95, 96, 131 N., 143 bis.
    John Silvester, 24 N.
    Katherine, 32, 143.
    Lawrence, 148 N., 156 N.
    Margaret, 13, 19 bis, 21, 27, 30, 43, 101, 116, 130.
    Mary, 57, 75.
    Michael, 52.
    Nicholas, 19, 57, 132 N.
    Ralph, 148 N.
    Richard, 4, 41, 129.
    Robert, 47 N., 70, 86, 91, **107.**
    Rose, 19.
    Thomas, 3, 12, 23 bis, 31, 36, 40 bis, 47 N., 54, 67, 72, 74, 75, 120 N., 129, 131, 136, 143.
    Widow, 134.
    William, **4,** 15, 21, 47 N., 48, 57, 67, 84.
SNATH,
    Margaret, 42.
SNYDALL,
    William, 115, 134 N.
SOMERSALL,
    Richard, 84.
SPARK,
    Agnes, 141.
    Elizabeth, 34.
    Grace, 27.
    John, 11, 31, 101, 141.
    Margaret, 121.
SPENCER,
    George, 33, 33 N.
    Hugh, 133.
    Isabel, 81 N.
    John, 81 N.
    Mr., 3 N.
    Thomas, 3.
    William, 3 N, **33 N.**
    ——— 3 N.
SPITTLEHOUSE,
    Henry, 27, 46, 136, 138, 139.
    Margaret, 139.
    Thomas, 46, 138.
SPOONER,
    Edward, **4.**
S'SOONS,
    William, **153.**
STACEY,
    Alice, 10, **68.**
    Isabel, 32.
    John, 68, **71.**
    William, **71.**
STAFFORD,
    Alice, 34, 103 N.
    Dorothy, 35.
    Humphrey, 98.
    Mark, 29.
    William, **2.**
STANYFORTH,
    Agnes, 123 N., 127.
    Alexander, 123 N.
    Ann, 30, 74, 123 N., 128.
    Catherine, 66.

STANYFORTH (continued),
    Elizabeth, 9, 21, 94 N., 123 N.
    Henry, 7, 50, 54 bis, 93, 122, 127 ter, 132, 135.
    Hugh, 50.
    Humphrey, **161 N.**
    Jane, 123 N.
    Joan, 122.
    John, 36, 65, 69 bis, **75, 76, 84, 86,** 155, 155 N, 159.
    Sir John, 154, 155 N., **156, 156 N.,** 159.
    Lawrence, **51.**
    Margaret, **61, 62, 86.**
    Maud, 123 N.
    Michael, 51.
    Nicholas, 30, **64, 80 N., 123 N.,** 155 N., 159.
    Richard, 16, 94 N., **123, 123 N.**
    Robert, 155 N.
    Thomas, 21, 35, 128, 145.
    William, 61, 62, 64, 65, 66, **70 bis,** 74, 76, 160.
STANYLAND,
    Ann, 63.
    Anthony, 70.
    Barbara, 139.
    Isabel, 107.
    John, 68, 93.
    Margaret, 129.
    Nicholas, 4, 47, 66, 90, 97 N., **107 N.,** 110 N., 121 N., 130 N., 133 N.
    Peter, 74.
    Ralph, 13, 125, **139.**
    Thomas, 35, 44, **63, 65 bis, 66, 68,** 70, 74.
    William, **47.**
STATHAM,
    Frances, 31 N.
STAYNTON,
    Agnes, 17.
STEAD, or STEDE,
    Ann, 19 N.
    Dionis, 34.
    Elizabeth, **40.**
    Gertrude, 19 N.
    Johannes de, 19 N.
    Matilda de, 19 N.
    Nicholas, 19 N.
    Peter de, 18 N.
    Richard, 18, 19 N., **22, 113 N.**
    Robert, 19 N.
    Robertus de, **19 N.**
STEELE,
    Margaret, 136.
    Mary, 41.
    Thomas, 25, 136.
STEELE, alias TINMOUTH,
    Sir Robert, 112 N.
STEEMSON,
    Ann, 74.
    William, **74.**
STENTON,
    William, **126 N.**
STEVEN,
    Agnes, **13.**
    John, 99.
STEVENSON,
    Agnes, 5.
    Charles, 90 N, **94 N.**
    Effame, 14.
    Elizabeth, 16, 119.
    Henry, 110, 119.
    Jane, 2.
    Margaret, 123.
    Robert, 32.
    Thomas, 4, 82, **124, 153.**
    William, 39.
STEWARDSON,
    Edmund, 14.

STIGBUCK,
  Helen, 111.
  John, 22, 50, 101, 133.
STOCKDALE,
  Ann, 64.
  Elizabeth, 64.
STONES,
  Alice, 1 N., 26, 82, 133 N., 146.
  Ann, 23, 56.
  Barbara, 21, 124 N.
  Elizabeth, 64.
  Frances, 101.
  Francis, 107.
  George, 77.
  Hugh, 90.
  Margaret, 35.
  Mary, 99.
  Nicholas, 1, 1 N., 63, 69, 94 N., 98 N., 117 N., 133, 133 N.
  Ralph, 34, 64, 78.
  Richard, 88.
  Robert, 20, 78, 124.
  Thomas, 32 N., 84, 158 bis.
  William, 32, 32 N., 56, 59, 63, 69, 77, 157, 158.
STORKE,
  Helen, 55.
  Henry, 32 N., 55, 71.
  Isabel, 71.
STORTH,
  Thomas, 86 N.
  William, 19 N.
STRADLIN,
  Richard, 88.
STREET,
  Cecily, 17.
  William, 104.
STRINGER,
  Ann, 39.
  Francis, 20, 20 N., 129 N.
  Isabel, 129 N.
  John, 14.
  Thomas, 129 N.
  Widow, 83.
STRULE,
  Edward, 115.
  Francis, 115.
SUGDEN,
  Alice, 48.
  Grace, 54.
  John, 28, 48, 51, 54, 59, 67.
  Margaret, 67.
  Peter, 51.
  Thomas, 59.
SUGWORTH,
  Alice, 146.
SUNDERLAND,
  Ann, 36.
  Francis, 42.
SUTTON,
  Richard, 44.
  Thomas, 152.
SWAINSON,
  Anthony, 75.
  Thomas, 39, **71, 75**.
SWALLOW,
  Ann, 39.
  Katherine, 35.
  Mary, 35.
SWATH,
  Margaret, 32.
SWIFT,
  Agnes, 20.
  Alice, 44.
  Henry, 24, 24 **N., 41**.
  Isabel, 5.
  Joana, 134 N.
  John, 134 N.
  Katherine, 111.
  Margery, 150 N.

SWIFT (continued),
  Richard, 13, 13 N., 89, 117.
  Robert, 118, 122 N., 161 N.
  Thomas, 122 N.
  William, 111, 121.
SWINBANK,
  Alice, 99, 99 N.
  Ambrose, 3, 9, 90 N., 99, 100 N.
  Isabel, 99 N.
SWINDEN,
  Ann, 52.
  Henry, 121.
  Jane, 3.
  Jenetta, 146 bis, 146 N.
  Johanna, 32.
  Margery, 28.
  Ralph, 48, 141.
  Richard, 27, 48, 52, 141.
  ———, 31.
SYDALL,
  Beatrice, 7.
SYDDOWE,
  Helen, 6.
SYKES,
  Dr., 134 N., 155 N.
  Joan, 38.
  Margaret, 31, 41.
  Thomas, 1.
  William, 18.
SYMKINSON,
  Henry, 1.

TALBOT,
  John, 152.
TARNELL,
  Jennet, 34.
TAYLER,
  Agnes, 9, 36.
  Alexander, 122 N.
  Alice, 1, 58.
  Ann, 38, 54, 137.
  Catherine, 50, 56.
  Christopher, 122 N.
  Edward, 93.
  Elizabeth, 40, 100, 146.
  Frances, 23.
  Francis, 114.
  Gertrude, 58.
  Helen, 99, 121, 122 N.
  Henry, 113 N.
  Jane, 32.
  Joan, 34.
  John, 24, 101, 134 N.
  Nicholas, 54, 56, 58, 62 bis, 146.
  Richard, 105, 137.
  Robert, 103 N.
  Thomas, 9 N., 50, 58, 122, 122 N., 142.
  William, 134 N.
TEMPEST,
  Avery, 10.
THOMPSON, or TOMSON,
  Alice, 18, 63, 140.
  Ann, 46, 106.
  Elizabeth, 62.
  Ernote, 26.
  Henry, 71.
  Hugh, 46, 140.
  Jane, 145 N.
  Jeffrey, 85.
  John, 10, 36, 86.
  Margaret, 67.
  Richard, 9.
  Robert, 62, 63, 67, 71.
THORLEY,
  Sir Thomas, 149 N.
  Vicar of, 149 N.
THORNTON,
  Richard, 151 N.
THORP, or THROPP,
  Agnes, 127.

THORP (continued),
  Alice, 59.
  Ann, 63.
  Dorothy, 142, 144.
  Elizabeth, 68.
  George, 32, 55, 57, 63, 68.
  Helen, 91.
  Henry, 123.
  Isabel, 55.
  Johanna, 14.
  John, 52, 57, 64, 118.
  Joseph, 56.
  Mary, 67.
  Nicholas, 77.
  Peter, 30, 52, 59, 64, 67.
  Richard, 127, 142, 144 bis.
  Roger, 29, 51, 56, 60, 70 bis, 77.
  Susan, 60.
  Thomas, 13, 51.
THRENCROSSE,
  Jane, 11.
THRIST,
  Johanna, 140 N.
  Pencalli, 140 N.
THROPP, see THORP.
THWAITES or THWETES,
  Alice, 106.
  Barbara, 5, 5 N., 152 N.
  Beatrice, 152 N.
  Hugh, 146 bis.
  Jane, 20, 99 N.
  Johanna, 7 N., 88, 88 N., 146.
  Nicholas, 88.
  Robert, 87, 122 N., 152 N.
  Thomas, 5 N., 7, 7 N., 15, 83 N., 88 N., 103 N., 122 N., 124, 125.
TIMPERLEY, or TYMPLEY,
  Alice, 111.
  Ann, 27.
  James, 36 bis, 40.
  Margaret, 119.
  Roger, 17.
  William, 11, 18, 100 N.
TINDALL,
  Nicholas, 43 N.
  William, 43 N.
TINGLE,
  Ann, 22.
  Beatrice, 18.
  Edward, 43.
  Elizabeth, 43.
  Isabel, 13, 110.
  Jane, 96.
  John, 99.
  Richard, 10, 116.
  Thomas, 18.
TINKER,
  Ann, 34.
  John, 34.
TINLEY,
  William, 43.
TINMOUTH, alias STEELE,
  Sir Robert, 112 N.
TOMLINSON,
  Robert, 34.
TORR,
  Christopher, 149 N., 161.
TOTHILL,
  Ann, 26.
TOTTINGTON,
  Agnes, 96.
  Elizabeth, 113.
  John, 83.
TOWNEND,
  Marion, 19.
TOWRALL,
  J., 133 N.
TRAVES,
  Cecily, 17.

INDEX.

TREETON,
  Dorothy, 28.
TRICKET, or TRIGGETT,
  Francis, **68.**
  John, 37, **68.**
TRIPPET,
  Alice, 61, 111.
  Ann, 42, 59, 67.
  Emye, 52.
  Humphrey, 42, 77.
  Isabel, 77.
  John, 34, 60 bis.
  Mary, 75.
  Thomas, **28, 56, 59, 61, 67,** 75.
  William, 56.
TRUELOVE,
  Ann, 66.
  Edward, 34, 60, 64, 66.
  Elizabeth, 34.
  Johanna, 88.
  Lawrence, 81 N., 92.
  Margaret, 64.
  Ralph, 6, 25, 60, 145.
  Richard, 116.
TURNER,
  Ann, 43.
  Christine, 73.
  Dorothy, 68.
  George, 27, 36 bis, 48, 68, 76.
  Gertrude, 19 N.
  Henry, 34, 61, 73, 76.
  Isabel, 76.
  Jennet, 41.
  Richard, 19 N.
  Thomas, 76.
  William, 61.
TURNLEY,
  Agnes, 91.
  Ann, 38.
  Elizabeth, **11, 137.**
  Henry, 5.
  Isabel, 105.
  Nicholas, 10, 82.
  Robert, 10, 100.
  William, 153, 157.
TURTON,
  Ann, 107.
  Francis, 97.
  Johanna, 14.
  John, 140.
  Richard, 89.
  Uxor, 126.
TWIGGE,
  Ann, 28.
  Catherine, 85.
  Elizabeth, 94 N.
  Jeffrey, 94 N.
  Joan, 8.
  Johanna, 94 N.
  John, 94 N., 126 N., 136 N.
  Margaret, 2, 2 N., 29.
  Nicholas, 35.
  Thomas, 2 N., **94, 94 N., 157.**
TWISBY,
  Sir Thomas, 153, **154.**
TWYBELL,
  Ann, 72.
  Elizabeth, 36 N., 74.
  Ellen, 69.
  James, 36, 36 N., 65, 66, 69, **72, 74,** 77.
  Joan, 77.
  John, 76.
  Nicholas, 66.
  Richard, 65.
  Thomas, 36 N., 76.
TYAS,
  George, 112 N.
  Isabel, 113 N.

TYAS (continued),
  John, 90 N., 112, 112 N., 113 N.
  Sir John, 90 N.
  Mr., 110 N.
  Robert, 113 N.
  Thomas, 113 N.
TYLSLEY,
  Richard, 13.
TYMPLEY, see TIMPERLEY.
TYSDALL,
  Henry, **39.**

UGHTIBRIDGE, or **OUGHTIBRIDGE**
  Agnes de, 85 N.
  Cecilia de, 85 N.
  Ricardus de, 85 N.
UNWEN,
  Alice, 17.
  Cecily, 120.
  Emote, 11.
  Robert, 13.
  Thomas, 9, 38.

VAVASOUR,
  Thomas, 155 N.
VICKERS,
  Edward, 36 N.
  William, 36 N.
VIPPAN,
  Ellen, 68.
  Nicholas, 68.

WADDILOVE,
  Mary, 40.
  Nicholas, 37, 69 bis.
WADDISLAY,
  Johanna, 131 N.
  William, 131 N.
WADDY, or WADDIE,
  Ann, 35.
  Johanna, 22.
  John, 81 N.
  Margaret, 12.
  William, 9.
WADE,
  Ann, 143 N.
  George, 39, 113 N.
  Johanna, 10.
  John, 84, 150 N.
  Lawrence, 27.
WAGGALEY, or WAGLEY,
  Isabel, 59.
  Margaret, 65.
  Robert, 65.
  Thomas, 59.
  Uxor, 132.
WAGGALEY, alias **DOUGHTY,**
  Robert, 114.
WAGSTAFFE,
  Thomas, 7.
WAINWRIGHT, see **WEYNWRIGHT.**
WAKE,
  Bernard, **33 N., 114 N.**
WALKER,
  Alice, 15, 34, 55.
  Ann, 47 N.
  Anthony, 67.
  Elizabeth, 72.
  George, 47 N.
  Grace, 137.
  Helen, 137.
  Isabel, 44.
  Jane, 22.
  Joan, 113.
  John, 27, 30, 51, **52, 53, 55, 61 bis,** 75, 76, 137 bis.
  Katherine, 10.
  Margaret, 11.
  Mary, 59.

WALKER (continued),
  Michael, 51.
  Nicholas, 23, **43, 53, 59, 67, 72** bis, 73, 129.
  Ralph, 80 N.
  Thomas, 38, **52, 69** bis, **72, 74, 78** bis.
  William, 140 N.
WALKER, alias SLATTER,
  Alice, 111.
  John, 107.
WALLER,
  Isabel, 5.
WALSHAWE,
  John, 4, 131.
WALSHE,
  John, 87.
  Robert, 3.
WALTON,
  John, 98.
  Margaret, 15.
WARDE,
  Agnes, 9.
  Alice, 32.
  Ann, 11 N., 130 N.
  Emote, 107.
  Helen, 31, 115 N.
  Johanna, 98.
  Margaret, 42, 59.
  Nicholas, 111.
  Ralph, 6, 107, 115 N.
  Richard, 15, 32, 59.
  Widow, 81, 134.
  William, 11 N., 159 bis, **162** bis.
WARDILL,
  Edward, **32, 48, 141.**
  Thomas, **48, 141.**
WARING,
  Margaret, 41.
WARTER, or WATTER,
  Ellen, 77.
  Francis, 73, **77.**
  Henry, 73.
  Margaret, 31 N.
  Robert, 31 N.
WASTENEYS,
  George, 137 N.
WATERALL,
  Catherine, 98.
  Francis, 52.
  Johanna, 92.
  John, 52.
  Nicholas, 29, 53.
  Thomas, 53, 124.
WATERHOUSE,
  Ann, 66, 69.
  Edmund, 40.
  John, 81 N., 82, 82 N., 120 N.
  Nicholas, 69.
  Richard, 18, 18 N., 28, 82 N.
  Thomas, 81 N., 82 N.
  William, 18 N., 36, 66, 82 N.
WATSON,
  Agnes, 17.
  Edward, 14, 113.
  Helen, 15, 136.
  Jane, 14.
  Jennet, 31.
  John, 85.
  Nicholas, 20, 136 bis, 144.
  Thomas, 2, 122.
WATTS,
  Ann, 21 N., 117 N.
  Benjamin, 16 N.
  John, 21 N., 90 N.
  Richard, 21, 21 N., **117 N., 121 N.,** 125 N., 140 N., 145 N.
  — 121 N., 130 N., 145 N.
WEBSTER,
  Ann, 41.

INDEX.

WENTWORTH,
  Isabel, 100 N.
  Margaret, 130 N.
  Thomas, 100 N., 102 N., 130 N., 131 N., 151 N.
  William, 151 N.
WEST,
  Christopher, 21.
WESTALL,
  Alice, 18.
WEYNWRIGHT, or WAINWRIGHT,
  Alice, 84.
  Ann, 78.
  Bartholomew, 36 *bis*.
  Elizabeth, 66, 118.
  Emote, 92.
  Godfrey, 12.
  Henry, 25, 133.
  Joan, 2.
  Johanna, 101.
  John, 1, 4, 21, 23, 73, 77 *bis*, 99, 101, 103 N., 136.
  Margaret, 27, 30.
  Mary, 71, 73.
  Nicholas, 48.
  Robert, 33, 59, 66, 71.
  Thomas, 28, 48, 118.
  William, 43, 59, 78.
WHARAM,
  Ann, 25 N.
WHARNCLIFFE,
  Earl of, 25 N.
  Lord, 25 N.
WHEATNALL,
  Agnes, 92.
WHETE,
  Agnes, 6 N.
  Johanna, 149 N.
  Katherine, 149 N.
  Robert, 149 N.
  Thomas, 6 N.
  William, 85 N., 149, 149 N., *bis*, 151.
WHISTEN,
  Joan, 3.
WHITEHEAD,
  Richard, 155 N., 156 N.
WHITELEY, or WHITLEY,
  Elizabeth, 3, 10.
  Ellen, 42.
  Jane, 40.
  Thomas, 22.
WHITMORE,
  Cecily, 1 N.
  William, 1, 1 N., 161 N.
WHITTAKER, or WHITTACRESS, &c.,
  Ann, 146.
  Elizabeth, 72.
  John, 65.
  Nicholas, 72.
  Thomas, 82, 92.
  Widow, 82.
  William, 33, 60 *bis*, 65, 146.
WHITWELL,
  Lawrence, 30.
WIGFALL,
  Ann, 61.
  Dorothy, 127.
  Elizabeth, 71.
  John, 28, 61, 71.
  Michael, 138.
  Richard, 29, 49.
  Thomas, 49.
WILD,
  Francis, 58.
  George, 63.
  Helen, 25.
  Jane, 21, 29.
  John, 33, 58, 63, 77.
  Mary, 77.
  Thomas, 43.

WILD (*continued*),
  William, 110 N.
WILDSMITH,
  Elizabeth, 5.
  Robert, 26.
  Thomas, 7, 106.
  Widow, 80, 133 N.
WILKINSON,
  Alice, 2, 121.
  Ann, 11, 15, 29, 68, **75, 113** N., 114 N., 134 N., 145.
  Catherine, 51, 114 N., 134 N.
  Edmond, 115.
  Elizabeth, 12, 22, 60, 63, 102 N., 121 N.
  Ellis, 62.
  Francis, 77, 100.
  George, 58, 114 N.
  Hannah, 41 N.
  Helen, 14, 121 N.
  Henry, 40, 50, 75, 77 *bis*, 114 N., 117, 125, 134, 134 N.
  Hugh, 19, 50, 54.
  Humphrey, 57.
  Isabel, 35, 47, 69, 77, 121 N.
  James, 53, 114 N.
  Jane, 121 N.
  Joan, 5, 10, 23, 108, 109, 121 N.
  Johanna, 20, 85, 93.
  John, 21, 58 *bis*, 61, 65, 69, 114 N., 125, 134 N., 140 N., 145 N., 149 *bis*, 150 N., 151, 155.
  Julian, 29, 114 N.
  Margaret, 18, 19, 39, 95, 114 N.
  Mary, 35, 77, 126 N.
  Michael, 49.
  Nathaniel, 126 N.
  Nicholas, 42, 108, 114 N.
  Ralph, 84, 84 N., 139, 156.
  Richard, 102 N., 114, 157 N.
  Robert, 22, 26, 30, 33, 33 N., 44, 47, 51, 53, 54, 58, 59, 61, 62, 63, 68 *bis*, 77, 84 N., 102 N. *bis*, 113, 113 N., 114 N., 121 N., 125, 128, 129 N., 134 N., 139, 145, 152.
  Simon, 50.
  Susan, 74.
  Thomas, 12 N., 13, 84 N., 102 *bis*, 102 N., 114 N., 121 N., 134 N., 146, 153, 156, 156 N., 158, 162.
  William, 4, 9, 24, 33 N., 41 N., 49, 57, 61, 85, 102 N., 114 N., 121, 121 N., 123 N., 127 N., 128, 134 N., 136, 142 N.
WILKINSON, *alias* DEY,
  Jennet, 102 N.
WILLECARS, See WHITTAKER.
WILLIAMSON,
  John, 130 N.
WILLY,
  Agnes, 13.
  Alexander, 92.
  Dionis, 116.
  Elizabeth, 67, 156.
  George, 134.
  Helen, 3, 25.
  Isabel, 6.
  Jane, 133.
  Johanna, 156.
  John, 67.
  Richard, 34.
  Robert, 4, 4 N., 23, 94, 133, 156, 157 *bis*, 159.
  Uxor., 124.
WILSON,
  Agnes, 89, 89 N.
  Ann, 25, 41, 46.
  Christopher, 19 N., 90 N.
  Elizabeth, 89 M.
  Emote, 26 N.

WILSON (*continued*),
  Jane, 22, 89 N.
  Joan, 15.
  John, 140 N.
  Margaret, 25.
  Mary, 26 N.
  Mr., 132.
  Richard, 26, 26 N., 46, 89 N., 90 N., 125 N., 136 N.
  Thomas, 26 N., 89 N., 90 N., 125 N.
  William, 13.
WINGERWORTH,
  Joan, 43.
WINGFIELD,
  Ann, 78.
  Edward, 42, **78**.
  John, 42 N.
WINTER,
  Edmund, 157.
WINTERBOTHAM,
  Rc: 43.
  Uxor, 124.
  William, 132 N.
WOAKLEY,
  Richard, 41.
WOBKINS, or WOBKINS,
  John, 116 N.
WOLLEY,
  Helen, 122.
  Hugh, 26, 49.
  Thomas, 99.
  William, 49.
WOMBWELL,
  Ann, 92.
  Barbara, 14, 14 N.
  Elizabeth, 12 N.
  Henry, 100 N., 150.
  Hugh, 100 N.
  Isabel, 20, 20 N., 100 N., 129 N., 131, 131 N.
  John, 98, 100 N., 131 N.
  Margaret, 19, 19 N.
  Mr., 158, 159 *bis*.
  Nicholas, 12, 12 N., 100 N., 130 N., 131 N.
  Thomas, 12 N., 14 N., 19 N., 20 N., 98 N., 99, 99 N., 100 N., 129, 129 N.
  William, 100 N.
WOOD, or WODDE, &c.,
  Alexander, 10.
  Ann, 38, 43, 48, 77.
  Barbara, 145.
  Dionis, 18.
  Dorothy, 138.
  Elizabeth, 14, 42, 44, 58, 72.
  George, 43, 51, 53.
  Gilbert, 42.
  Gregory, 145.
  Isabel, 29.
  Jennet, 22.
  Joan, 109.
  Johanna, 20.
  John, 13, 106, **116, 133**.
  Lawrence, 11.
  Margaret, 53.
  Maria, 51.
  Mary, 62, 78, 145.
  Nicholas, 17, 72, 77, 128.
  Richard, 23, 24, 48, 62, 65, 67, 69, 145.
  Robert, 25, 62.
  Rose, 92.
  Sarah, 65.
  Susan, 67.
  Thomas, 140 N., 149 N.
  William, 31, 42, 58, 62, 69, 78.
WOODHEAD,
  Alice, 17.
  Grace, 14.
  Jennet, 30.

INDEX.

WOODHEWER,
    Robertus, 10 N.
WOODHOUSE,
    Francis, 35, **61,**
    Henry, 61.
    Isabel, 42.
    Joan, 4.
    John, 21.
    Mary, 72.
    Robert, 39, **72.**
WOODKIRKE,
    Alice, 102 N.
    Elizabeth, 156.
    John, 102 N., 140 N., **148** N.
WOODROVE,
    Ann, 51, 145.
    William, 51, **145.**
WORDSWORTH,
    Christopher, **3.**
    John, 3 N.
    Nicholas, 19, **19** N., **130** N.
    Thomas, 19 N.
    William, 2.
WORMALL,
    Elizabeth, 18.

WORMALL (*continued*),
    ———, **146.**
WORRALL,
    Alice, 129.
    Thomas, **129.**
WORSLEY,
    Edmund, 7.
    Mary, 22.
WORTLEY,
    Ann, 152 N.
    Isabel, 152 N.
    Right Honble. **James Stuart-**Wortley, 25 N.
    Mr., 129 N.
    Nicholas, 152 N.
    Richard, 121 N.
    Thomas, 140 N.
    Sir Thomas, 90 N.
WRIGHT,
    Elizabeth, 35.
    Francis, 117.
    Helen, 13.
    Henry, 32, 54.
    Isabel, 59.
    Margaret, **85.**

WRIGHT (*continued*),
    Richard, 54, 81.
    Robert, 16, 43, 117.
    Susan, 54.
    Thomas, 34, 36, 59.
    William, 44, 54.
WROE, see also ROE,
    Elizabeth, 20.
    Margaret, 10.
YATES,
    Edward, 141 N.
    Elizabeth, 129.
    Francis, 58.
    Helen, 4.
    Henry, 20.
    Robert, 58.
YORK,
    Archbishop of, 90 N.
YOUNG,
    George, 78.
    Luke, 73, 78.
    Robert, 73.
    William, 40, 40 N., 81 N.

INDEX OF PLACES.

INSTRUCTIONS.

An asterisk [*] after a number means that the name occurs more than once on that page, and after a number with the letter N attached, that it occurs in two or more notes on that page.

ABBEYFIELD, 33 N.
ADWICK-ON-DEARNE, 138 N.
ALDERWASLEY, 6 N.
AMERICA, 26 N.
ANDREW CARR, 152 N.
ANSTON, 26 N., 47 N.
ARDSLEY, 152 N.
ASHOVER, 81 N.
ASTON, 112, 113 N., 149 N.
ATTERCLIFFE, 16 N., 118 N.

BALBY, 150 N., 161 N.
BARKER HOUSE, 145 N.
BARKHOUSE, 82 N.
BARLEY HOLE, 26 N., 35 N., 142.
BARNBOROUGH, 112 N., 152 N.
BARNBY HALL, 112 N.
BARNES HALL, 2 N., 3 N., 6 N., 16 N., 20 N., 21 N., 22 N., 47, 90 N., 116 N., 121 N., 125 N., 130 N., 144 N.
BAWTRY, 26 N.
BEIGHTON, 112 N., 161 N.
BELLHOUSE, 50, 53, 55, 121 N., 134 N., 145.
BIRKHOUSE, 55.
BIRLEY, 8 N., 9 N., 18 N., 81 N*, 84 N., 85 N., 92 N., 103 N., 127 N., 140 N.
BIRLEY CARR, 46*, 49*, 50, 132 N., 139, 140, 143.
BIRLEY EDGE, 15 N., 46, 47, 48*, 50, 52, 53, 126 N., 128, 128 N., 139, 141, 142, 144, 144 N., 146.
BIRLEY HOLLINS, 102 N., 152 N.
BIRLEY HOUSE, 26 N.
BIRTHWAITE, 24 N.
BLITH, 143 N.
BRADFIELD, 2 N*., 9 N., 18 N*., 26 N*., 31 N., 35 N., 37 N., 54, 61, 88 N., 89 N., 90 N., 103 N., 112, 112 N., 116 N., 120 N., 141 N.
BRAMLEY GRANGE, 3 N., 38 N.
BRAMLEY HALL, 41 N.
BRAMPTON BIERLOW, 150 N.
BRAMPTON-EN-LE-MORTHEN, 31 N.
BRANDCLIFFE, 2.
BREREFIELDS, 150 N.
BRIGHTSIDE, 118 N.
BROKE HOUSE, 149 N.
BROMELEY, 70.
BROOMHEAD, 26 N., 89 N.
BRUSH HOUSE, 126 N.
BURNCROSS, 46, 49, 50, 53, 54.
BURROWLEE, 11 N., 141, 141 N., 142.
BURTON, 112 N.
BURTON ABBEY, 151 N.
BUTTERTHWAITE, 7 N., 42 N., 53, 57, 57 N., 98 N., 136 N., 143, 143 N.

CAISTOR, 26 N.
CALDERTON, 85 N.
CAMBRIDGE, 26 N.
CAWCROFT, 113 N.
CAWTHORN, 31 N., 47 N., 112 N.

CHAPEL GREEN, 140 N.
CHAPELTOWN, 19 N., 91 N., 140 N.
CHAPELL, 47, 48, 51*, 55, 56*, 63*, 136, 137*, 138*, 140 N., 141, 143, 145*, 146*, 150 N.
CHARLTON BROOK, 139, 140.
CLIFFE FIELD, 128 N.
COAL ASTON, 142 N.
COLDWELL, 85 N.
COLLEGE OF ARMS, 152 N.
COLMES, 103 N.
COLTROUGHS, 149 N.
COLYNTON HAVEN, 109 N.
CONINGSBOROUGH, 81 N., 120 N.
COPPINGLAND, 149 N.
COVENTRY, CONVENT OF, 149 N.
COWLEY, 1 N., 37 N., 47, 52, 122, 148 N., 151 N.
COWLEY HALL, 47 N.
CRESWICK, 5 N., 11 N., 15 N., 16 N., 32 N., 51, 98 N., 102 N., 118 N., 122 N., 124 N., 127 N., 137*, 137 N*., 141, 148 N., 152 N., 154.
CROOKS, 37 N.
CROSS HOUSE, 20 N., 55, 137, 142, 142 N., 143, 146.
CROWDER HOUSE, 12 N., 33 N., 41 N., 113 N., 114 N., 126 N., 134 N., 146.

DALTON, 149 N.
DARFIELD, 150 N., 151 N.
DARLEY HALL, 41 N.
DARLEY, MANOR OF, 41 N.
DARRINGTON, 155 N.
DARTON, 2.
DARWENT, 16 N.
DENBY HALL, 32 N.
DENNARY, 149 N.
DERBY CO., 6 N., 7 N., 12 N., 26 N., 104 N., 142 N.
DERWENT ABBEY, 26 N.
DIPKAR, 113 N.
DOBFIELD, 85 N.
DOEFIELD, 49, 52, 53, 55, 57, 142.
DONCASTER, 26 N., 134 N., 155 N.
DUBLIN, 90 N.
DUNGWORTH, 16 N., 86 N.

ECCLESFIELD, 1, 2 N., 3 N., 4 N., 5 N., 6 N., 7 N., 9 N., 11 N., 13 N., 16 N., 19 N., 24 N., 26 N., 39 N., 46*, 47*, 48*, 49*, 50*, 51*, 52*, 53*, 54*, 55*, 56*, 57*, 58*, 63*, 80 N., 81 N., 82 N., 83 N*., 84 N., 85 N., 86 N., 88 N., 89 N., 90 N., 91 N., 94 N*., 97 N., 98 N., 99 N., 100 N., 101 N., 102 N*., 103 N*., 106 N., 109 N., 110 N*., 112, 112 N., 113 N., 114 N., 115 N., 116, 116 N., 118 N., 119 N., 120 N., 121 N*., 122 N., 123 N*., 125 N., 126 N., 127 N., 128 N., 129 N*., 130 N., 131 N., 132 N*., 133 N., 134 N., 135 N*.,

ECCLESFIELD (continued),
136 N*., 137*, 138*, 139*, 139 N*., 140*, 140 N., 141*, 141 N., 142*, 142 N*., 143*, 144*, 145*, 145 N., 146*, 148, 148 N., 149*, 150 N*., 151*, 152*, 153, 154, 155 N*., 156 N., 157 N., 161 N.
ECCLESFIELD HALL, 14 N., 31 N., 39 N., 148 N.
ECCLESALL, 2 N., 3 N.
ECKINGTON, 104 N.
EDGE, 56.
EDGEFIELD, 37 N.
ELAND, 166.
ELLERSLIE LODGE, 11 N.
ELLIOT FIELD, 161 N.
ELLIOT LANE, 52, 54, 57, 139, 140.
EWES, THE, 13 N., 103 N.

FELKIRK, 151 N.
FINKLE STREET, 138 N.
FIRBECK, 60 N.
FOXHILL, 1 N., 20 N., 94 N., 132 N., 138, 138 N., 141, 141 N., 144.
FULLWOOD, 115 N., 116 N.

GILTHWAITE, 143 N.
GLOSSOP, 112 N.
GRANGE BRIDGE, 55.
GREASBROOK, 100, 129 N.
GRENALGHESYDE, See GRENOSIDE.
GRENOFIRTH, 21 N.
GRENOSIDE, 6 N., 18 N., 37 N., 47, 48, 49*, 52*, 53, 127 N., 138*, 139, 142*, 146.
GRUBB HOUSE, 80 N.

HAGGE, 48, 53, 137, 142, 142 N., 144.
HALDWORTH, 2 N., 6 N., 11 N., 31 N., 116 N.
HALLAM, 10 N., 134 N.
HALLFIELD, 46, 47, 50.
HANDSWORTH, 112 N.
HARTLEY, 150 N.
HARTLEY BROOK, 47, 52, 58, 85 N.
HARTLEY NETHER, 6 N., 85 N., 90 N., 132 N., 149 N.
HASLECLOUGH, 126 N.
HASLEHOUGH, 62, 155 N.
HATFIELD, 80 N.
HATFIELD HOUSE, 1 N., 80 N.
HATTE BROOK, 55.
HAWLYNE, 107 N.
HEADON, 137 N.
HEMSWORTH, 12 N.
HERRINGTHORPE, 2.
HESLEY, 46, 138, 151 N.
HESLEY FARM, 31 N.
HIGH GREEN, 24 N., 45, 52, 56, 63.
HIGHGREEN HOUSE, 26 N.
HIGH HAZLES, 41 N.
HIRST, 53.

INDEX.

HOLLEN HOUSE, 50, 146.
HOLLY HOUSE, 46, 55.
HOLMES HOUSE, 50.
HOLMES NETHER, 3 N.
HORBERY, 41 N., 47, 123 N., 143, 149 N.
HORNCASTLE, 7 N., 150 N.
HOULTON, 103 N.
HOWSLEY, 90 N.
HOWSLEY HALL, 3 N.*, 19N., 25 N., 41 N., 47, 51, 80 N., 81 N., 82 N., 105 N., 137, 140, 140 N., 144, 144 N., 145.
HOYLAND, 126 N.
HOYLE HOUSE, 63.
HUDDY HOLLINS, 48, 50, 51.
HULLOCK, 3 N.
HUNSHELF, 47 N., 115 N.
HUNTER HOUSE, 139.

IRELAND, 8 N., 90 N.
IVEYARD, 148 N.

JENEPOOL, 136 N.
JENFIELD, 81 N.

KILLAMARSH, 16 N.
KIMBERWORTH, 139 N.
KIRKTHORPE, 151 N.

LANGTON, 112 N.
LAUGHTON-EN-LE-MORTHEN, 53 N., 80 N., 149 N.
LAWCOCK FIELD, 149 N.
LEE CHAPEL, 151 N.
LETWELL, 12 N.
LINCOLN COLLEGE, OXFORD, 9 N.
LINCOLN CO., 7 N., 26 N., 103 N., 150 N.
LONDON, 21 N., 126 N.
LONDON, TOWER OF, 21 N.
LONGLANDS, 149 N.
LONGLEY, 12 N., 36 N., 49, 52, 54, 55, 81 N., 103 N., 114 N., 134 N., 137, 143, 146*.
LOUNDSIDE, 126 N.
LOWER SHIRE, 55.
LYNTHWET, 100 N.

MACHON BANK, 2 N., 3 N.
MACHON HOUSE, 80 N.
MARSH HOUSE, 148 N.
MARSTON, 152 N.
MARYLAND, 26 N.
MASBOROUGH, 33 N.
MEADOW HALL, 150 N.
MEXBOROUGH, 130 N., 138 N., 150 N.
MIDDLETON, 46.
MIDDLETON GREEN, 49, 55, 139.
MIDDLEWOOD, 150 N.
MILNEFIELD, 142 N.
MORELAY, 100 N.
MORTOMLEY, 41 N., 46*, 47, 49*, 50*, 51*, 52*, 53, 54*, 55*, 56*, 60*, 99 N., 128 N., 129 N., 135 N., 136*, 137*, 138*, 142, 144*, 145*, 146*, 158, 159*, 161.
MORTOMLEY HALL, 47 N.
MORTOMLEY LANE-END, 54.
MUCKLETON, 21 N.

NETHER HARTLEY, 6 N., 85 N., 90 N., 132 N., 149 N.
NETHER SHIRE, 47, 49, 51*, 54, 55*, 137, 143.
NEWARK, 4.
NEWHALL GRANGE, 33 N., 151 N.
NEWLAND, 24 N.
NORMANTON, 151 N.
NORTH LEES, 122 N.
NORTON, 12 N, 110 N.

NORTON LEES, 7 N., 12 N.
NOTTINGHAM CO., 90 N., 137 N.

OAKES, 46, 49, 51, 53*, 57, 145*.
OAKES COLLIERY, 41 N.
ONESACRE, 18 N*., 19 N.
ORIEL COLLEGE, OXFORD, 41 N.
OUGHTHORPE LANE, 36 N.
OUGHTIBRIDGE, or UGHTIBRIDGE, 19 N., 26 N., 35, 35 N., 46, 154 N.
OUGHTIBRIDGE HALL, 26 N., 59 N., 125 N.
OVERSHIRE, 145.
OWLERTON, 53, 107 N.
OWLERTON BRIDGE, 152 N.
OWLERTON HALL, 107 N., 144 N.
OXFORD, 9 N., 41 N.
OXSHIRE, 55*, 56*.

PARKGATE, 48, 50, 140.
PENISTONE, 11 N., 19 N., 26 N., 47 N., 112 N.
PONDS, 26 N.
PONTEFRACT, 113 N.
POTTERHILL, 46, 49, 143*, 145, 146, 146 N.

QUEEN'S COLLEGE, CAMBRIDGE, 26 N.

RAVENFIELD, 37 N.
RAWMARSH, 112 N., 113 N., 131 N.
RENISHAW, 26 N., 31 N.
RETFORD, 4, 151 N.
RIVELIN LODGE, 2 N.
ROCHE, 159.
ROSSINGTON, 26 N.
ROTHERHAM, 1 N., 4, 5, 9, 12 N., 15 N., 19 N., 31 N., 50, 103 N., 112 N., 115, 129 N., 130 N., 132 N., 134 N., 140, 142 N., 143 N., 149 N., 151 N., 152 N., 155.
ROYSTON, 151 N.
RYFARECROFT, 149 N.

ST. MARTIN'S VINTRY, 21 N.
ST. MARY'S LANE, 3 N.
SALOP. CO., 21 N.
SANDALL, 151 N.
SCADSBY, 140 N.
SHEFFIELD, 1 N., 2*, 2 N., 4, 5*, 9*, 9 N., 11 N., 14 N., 19 N., 26 N., 31 N., 33 N., 34 N., 35, 37 N., 39, 42 N., 47 N., 51, 112 N., 120 N., 121, 121 N., 126 N., 134 N., 139, 139 N., 143 N., 145 N., 148 N., 152 N.
SHEPHERD'S CASTLE, 19 N.
SHETEHOUSE, 19 N.
SHIRE, 6 N.
SHIRECLIFFE, 14 N., 151 N., 161 N.
SHIRECLIFFE HALL, 81 N.
SHIRECLIFFE PARK, 152 N.
SHIREGREEN, 1 N., 8 N., 39 N., 46, 47*, 49*, 50, 51*, 52, 53*, 54*, 80 N., 90 N., 102 N., 113 N., 123 N., 132 N., 134 N., 135 N., 137, 138, 142, 143, 143 N., 145, 145 N., 146*.
SHIRE, NETHER, 47, 49, 51*, 54, 55*, 137, 143.
SHIRE, OVER, 145.
SILKSTONE, 155 N.
SINDERWELL, 56, 109 N.
SKINNERTHORPE, 145 N., 152 N.
SKIRE HALL, 130 N.
SKYERS, 38 N.
SMITHY CARR, 144, 145.
SODHOUSE, 50, 53, 137.
SOUTHALL, 36 N.

SOUTHEY, 1 N., 8 N*., 19 N., 37N., 46, 48, 50, 52*, 54, 56, 57, 81 N., 86 N., 118 N., 122 N., 126 N., 132 N., 133 N., 135, 135 N., 138, 144, 145, 158*, 159*, 161, 162.
SOUTHEY HALL, 36 N.
SOUTH OTTERINGTON, 11 N.
SOWDYKE, 142, 143*.
STAINFORTH, 123 N., 126, 135 N.
STANNINGTON, 95 N., 114 N., 136.
STEAD, 18 N.
STEELBANK, 134 N.
STENEBRIDGE, 152 N.
STERE HEAD, 112, N.
STONYCROFT, 85 N.
STUB WALDEN, 134 N.
STURCH HILL, 140 N.
SUGWORTH, 90 N.
SWAFFHAM, 41 N.
SWAITH, 3 N.

SYNOCLIFFE [or THUNDERCLIFFE] GRANGE, 54, 56, 124 N., 137.
SYNOCLIFFE GRANGE BRIDGE, 49.

TANKERSLEY, 3, 37 N., 50, 112 N., 128 N., 151 N.
THIRSK, 11 N.
THORLEY, 149 N.
THORNSEATS, 116 N., 141 N.
THORPE, 50, 90 N., 135 N., 138.
THOXLEE, 112 N., 113 N.
THRIBERG, 26 N., 80 N., 81 N.
THUNDERCLIFFE [or SYNOCLIFFE] GRANGE, 12 N., 14 N., 19 N., 20 N., 31 N., 56, 98 N., 99 N., 100 N., 126 N., 131 N.
THURCROFT, 143 N.
THURGOLAND, 25 N.
THURNSCOE, 112 N., 113 N.
TICKHILL, 12 N., 113 N., 140 N.
TOADHOLE, 4 N., 54*, 55.
TREETON, 112, 112 N., 113 N.
TREETON MILL, 161 N.
TREETON SMITHY, 161 N.

UGHILL, 103 N., 120 N.
UGHTIBRIDGE, see OUGHTIBRIDGE.
UPPER HOUSE, 47 N.

WADFIELD, 81 N.
WADSLEY, 42 N., 46*, 47*, 48*, 49, 50*, 51*, 53*, 54*, 55*, 56*, 57, 58*, 60*, 62, 63*, 64, 82 N., 98 N., 103 N., 107 N., 114 N., 115 N., 120 N., 121 N., 122 N., 136, 137, 138*, 139*, 140 N., 141, 142, 143*, 144, 144 N., 145, 146*, 155, 155 N., 159*.
WADSLEY-BRIDGE, 50, 80 N., 144, 161 N.
WADSLEY HALL, 115 N.
WADSLEY SMITHIES, 161 N.
WAKEFIELD, 25 N., 36 N., 151 N.
WALDERSHELF, 115 N., 116 N.
WARDSEND, 8 N., 15 N., 36 N., 46, 48, 49*, 158, 158.
WARLDSEND, see WARDSEND.
WATH-UPON-DEARNE, 2, 25 N., 100 N., 134 N., 140 N., 151 N.
WENTWORTH, 3, 18 N., 26 N., 38 N., 99 N., 112 N.
WENTWORTH-WOODHOUSE, 100N., 130 N., 131 N.
WESTHALL, 99 N.
WESTMONHALGH, 116 N., 155 N.
WESTNALL, 115 N., 116 N., 155 N.
WHALEY, 150 N.

INDEX.

WHARNCLIFFE CHASE, 19 N., 22 N.
WHEATCROFT, 113 N.
WHISTON, 20 N., 112 N.
WHITE HOUSE, 134 N.
WHITLEY, 15 N., 47, 48, 49*, 51*, 53*, 54, 55*, 63*, 80 N., 81 N., 102 N., 125 N., 132 N., 136*, 137 N., 139*, 140*, 141, 143*, 144*, 146*, 146, 149 N., 150 N., 154, 161 N.
WHITLEY HALL, 2 N.*, 7 N. 11 N., 16 N., 26 N., 30 N., 110 N., 125 N., 132 N.
WICKERSLEY, 2 N.,
WINCOBANK, 8 N., 47, 48*, 49*, 50*, 51, 52, 54*, 55, 114 N., 123 N., 126 N., 128 N., 135, 135 N., 136 N., 138, 141, 143.
WINDMILL HILL, 30 N., 32 N., 43 N., 136.

WINKLEY, 114 N.
WOLLEY, 151 N.
WOLLEY HALL, 148 N.
WOLVERHAMPTON, 41 N.
WOMBWELL, 100 N.
WOODALL, 152 N.
WOODALL HALL, 151 N.
WOODES HALL, 151 N.
WOODFIELD, 1 N., 133 N.
WOODHEAD, 55.
WOODHOUSE, 49, **50, 52, 54, 55.**
WOODLAND, 80 N.
WOODSEATS, 6 N., 31 N., 43, 50, 53, 81 N., 131 N., 136, 137, 139, 141, 143, 149 N., 150 N.
WOODSIDE, 37 N.
WORRALL, 13 N., 50, 51, 103 N.

WORTLEY, 21 N., 26 N., 126 N., 128 N., 145 N., 152 N.
WORTLEY HALL, 26 N.
WRAGBIE, 151 N.

YORK, 80 N., 81 N., 82 N.*, 83 N., 90 N.*, 94 N.*, 97 N.*, 98 N.*, 100 N.*, 101 N., 103 N.*, 106 N., 107 N., 109 N., 110 N.*, 113 N., 114 N., 115 N., 118 N., 119 N., 120 N., 121 N.*, 122 N., 123 N.*, 125 N.*, 126 N., 127 N., 128 N.*, 129 N.*, 130 N., 131 N., 132 N.*, 133 N.*, 134 N., 140 N., 142 N., 143 N.*, 148 N., 149 N., 150 N., 152 N., 161, 161 N., 162.
YORK CO., 24 N., 33 N., 131 N., 135 N.*, 151 N., 161 N.

Leader & Sons, Printers,
Sheffield.

www.ingramcontent.com/pod-product-compliance
Lightning Source LLC
Chambersburg PA
CBHW021732220426
43662CB00008B/817